CURRENT RESEARCH IN EGYPTOLOGY 2011

Proceedings of the Twelfth Annual Symposium

which took place at

Durham University, United Kingdom
March 2011

edited by

Heba Abd El Gawad, Nathalie Andrews, Maria Correas-Amador,
Veronica Tamorri and James Taylor

OXBOW BOOKS
Oxford and Oakville

Published by
Oxbow Books, Oxford, UK

© CRE and the individual authors, 2012

ISBN 978-1-84217-498-2

A CIP record for this book is available from the British Library

This book is available direct from

Oxbow Books, Oxford, UK
(Phone: 01865-241249; Fax: 01865-794449)

and

The David Brown Book Company
PO Box 511, Oakville, CT 06779, USA
(Phone: 860-945-9329; Fax: 860-945-9468)

or from our website

www.oxbowbooks.com

Front cover illustration: Ancient Egyptian statue of a servant girl © The Oriental Museum, Durham University

Printed in Great Britain by
Short Run Press
Exeter

Contents

Symposium papers not included in this volume v

Introduction vii

Tell me your name and I can tell you how your kingship was: The royal names
of the first three Ptolemies (323–222 BC) (*Heba Abd El-Gawad*) 1

The Old Kingdom tomb of Pehenuka and the attribution of fragments
from the offering scene (*Keith R. Amery*) 15

Figured ostraca from Deir el-Medina (*Joanne Backhouse*) 25

The Egyptian ascension mythology of the Old Kingdom and the phenomenon
of star phases (*Bernardette Brady*) 40

Goddesses Gone Wild: the Seven Hathors in the New Kingdom (*Asha Chauhan Field*) 48

The early precursors of tomb security (*Reg Clark*) 55

'Living in a material world': understanding and interpreting life in an
Egyptian mud house (*Maria Correas-Amador*) 75

Wood exploitation in ancient Egypt: where, who and how? (*Flavie Deglin*) 85

Antonio Bernal de O'Reilly and the discovery of ancient Egypt
in Spain (*Javier Fernández Negro*) 97

The influence of Christianity on burial practices in Middle Egypt
from the fourth to the sixth centuries (*Deanna Heikkinen*) 107

Legitimation and ontological changes in the royal figure of
Queen Hatshepsut (c. 1479–1458 BC) (*Virginia Laporta*) 117

The Phenomenon of "personal religion" in the Ramesside Period, from the "Poem"
of Ramses II through to the Prayers of Ramses III (*Diana Liesegang*) 127

The Encircling Protection of Horus (*David Ian Lightbody*) 133

Visual and written evidence for mourning in New Kingdom Egypt (*Emily Millward*) 141

The Welshpool Mummy (*Pauline Norris*) 147

More ways of analysis: the differences *faces* of a stela (*Stefania Pignattari*) 152

Classifying dreams, classifying the world: ancient Egyptian oneiromancy
and demotic dream books (*Luigi Prada*) 167

Aspects of trading with New Kingdom Egypt (*Birgit Schiller*) 178

On defining myth: comparisons of myth theory from an egyptological
viewpoint (*David Stewart*) 189

Manipulated corpses in Predynastic Egyptian tombs: deviant or normative practices? (*Veronica Tamorri*) 200

Hippo goddesses of the Egyptian pantheon (*Aroa Velasco Pírez*) 210

Papers presented at Current Research in Egyptology XII and not included in this volume (in alphabetical order)

ANDREWS, Nathalie (Durham University) *Threats, identity and personhood in the Papyrus of Ani.*

ATHERTON, Stephanie (University of Manchester) *Rearing sacred birds in Ancient Egypt.*

BORTOLANI, Ljuba Merlina (University College London) *The snake, the lion and the scarab: Egyptian images of the primordial/creator god in a Greek magical hymn.*

BRYAN, Cathie (The British Egyptian Society) *A new slant on Egyptianising architecture in England 1837–1935.*

COOPER, Julien (Macquarie University) *The cosmographic expression "god's-land:" a textual study in Egyptian geographic phraseology.*

FIGUEIREDO, Alvaro (National Museum of Lisbon/IMI) *The Lisbon mummy project: preliminary results of the radiographic study (CT multi-Detector / 64) of the human mummies in the collection of Egyptian antiquities in the National Museum of Archaeology, Lisbon.*

FIRST, Grzegorz (Jagiellonian University) *The icon of Pantheos: research on the phenomenon of polymorphic deities in late Egyptian religion and iconography.*

FRANZMEIER, Henning (Freie Universität Berlin) *News from the Vizier (Pa-)Rahotep: Sedment tomb 201 revisited.*

GAUTSCHY, Rita (University of Basel) *Chronology of the second millennium BC.*

GREGORY, Stephen (University of Birmingham) *Roman Egypt or Egyptian Rome: the significance of Egyptian obelisks in the diffusion of ideology.*

HUANG, Tzu-Hsuan Maxime (Chinese University of Hong Kong) *Memory album of life course: a tentative study on elite tomb decorations of Old Kingdom Egypt and Han China.*

KESHK, Fatma (Leiden University) *Origins and development of early urbanism in Egypt: research questions.*

LANKESTER, Francis (Durham University) *Egypt's central eastern desert rock art: distribution, dating and interpretation.*

MCGARRITY, Luke (University of Birmingham) *The Tale of Woe: problems and reception.*

MONTGOMERIE, Roger (University of Manchester) *The characterisation of ancient lung particles.*

RIDEALGH, Kim (Swansea University) *Talking to God: the Role of Amun in the Late Ramesside letters.*

Symposium papers not included in this volume

PRICE, Campbell (University of Liverpool) *Archaism and filial piety: an unusual Ptolemaic pair statue from the Karnak cachette.*

ROWLAND, Megan (University of Cambridge) *Hoarding Heritage?: searching for the philosophy behind Egypt's 'retentionist' antiquity regulations and legislation.*

SOLIMAN, Daniel (Leiden University) *Reconsidering statues: the three-dimensional sculpture of Amenemhat IV and Neferusobek.*

STARING, Nico (Leiden University) *Memory sites: on the use and re-use of the New Kingdom necropolis at Saqqara.*

TAYLOR, James (Durham University) *Describing religious landscapes: pilgrimage accounts and monastic landscapes in Egypt.*

WEBER, Anke (Freie Universität, Berlin) *Dinner for one: the food of the deceased in New Kingdom offering table scenes at Deir el-Medina*

Introduction

After a successful eleventh conference being held in Leiden University (The Netherlands), the twelfth Current Research in Egyptology conference returned to the United Kingdom to be hosted by Durham University in March 2011. The conference gathered both speakers and attendees from all corners of the world. The aim of the 2011 conference was to highlight the multidisciplinary nature of the field of Egyptology. Papers in these proceedings reflect this multidisciplinarity, with research based on Archaeology, Linguistics, Cultural Astronomy, Historiography, Botany, Religion and Law, amongst others. By means of one or several of these disciplines, contributors to this volume approach a broad range of subjects spanning from Prehistory to modern Egypt, including: self-presentation, identity, provenance and museum studies, funerary art and practices, domestic architecture, material culture, mythology, religion, commerce, economy, dream interpretation and the birth of Egyptology as a discipline.

ABD EL GAWAD is approaching the royal names of the first three Ptolemies as one of the various modes of presentation used by the royal figures. The paper offers an insight on the issue of royal image management and the actual audience of the archaeological evidence.

AMERY reflects on how the current means of assessing antiquities at the point of export is not sufficient for determining the value of archaeological artefacts. This is done through an analysis of fragments of offering scenes attributed to the Old Kingdom tomb of Pehenuka.

BACKHOUSE is examining the images of women on beds and in pavilions at the tombs of Deir El Medina. These scenes are created by the workmen for their own purposes and do not normally appear in the formal repertoire of Egyptian art.

BRADY offers an approach towards the study of the divine myths from the perspective of cultural astronomy. The paper focuses on a particular star phase type showing the sequence of its observed movements and how it bears a strong parallel to the narrative of the ascension of the king in the Pyramid Text.

CHAUHAN FIELD investigates the role of the Seven Hathors during the New Kingdom, whom seem to have a more particular role and function within the Egyptian pantheon than the many other deities who exist in groups of seven or hebdomads.

CLARK is tracing the early development of tomb security in Ancient Egypt from the Late Palaeolithic (c. 21000–12000 BC) until the end of the Naqada IIIA period (c. 3300–3150 BC). The main aim of Clark's paper is to examine, by tracing the development of tomb architecture from the Predynastic Period onwards, whether many of the architectural elements that were incorporated in Egyptian tombs were a consequence of the need to protect the burial, rather than the result of monumental or religious considerations.

CORREAS-AMADOR explains the manner in which an ethnoarchaeological study of modern mudbrick houses can help re-establish the link between material and context, an essential connection to achieve a holistic understanding of ancient Egyptian domestic architecture.

DEGLIN presents a status report on the possibility of the existence of wood exploitation in ancient Egypt through our current botanical knowledge and a re-examination of particular textual and iconographic sources.

FERNÁNDEZ NEGRO is following the steps of Antonio Bernal de O'Reilly in Egypt in order to highlight the legacy he left in his book *In Egypt* where he provided his own outlook on the history of ancient Egypt, a historical contribution that silenced the echoes of European influences in Spain.

HEIKKINEN is exploring the influence of Christianity on burial practices in Middle Egypt through archaeological evidence. The paper discusses in detail the various shifts in burial practices during the period from 400 to 640 AD.

LAPORTA is discussing why Hatshepsut was crowned as king, providing a re-examination of the usurpation of Tuthmosis III and attempting to find some answers to the confusing question of why Tuthmosis III retained Hatshepsut's courtiers and followed her building programme.

LIESEGANG is exploring the phenomenon of personal religion in the Ramesside Period, from the "Poem" of Ramses II through to the Prayers of Ramses III. This is done through examining the related literary evidence in an attempt to shed some light on the relationship between the king and the god.

LIGHTBODY is looking into the use of Egyptian royal encircling symbolism, represented by the shen ring. The paper describes how and why this symbolism was incorporated into royal artworks, architecture, decoration and rituals.

MILLWARD is addressing the mechanism of mourning in New Kingdom Egypt. The paper focuses on the New Kingdom tombs of the Theban elite, more specifically, on the wall decoration contained within these superstructures.

NORRIS is giving an account of a project to trace the provenance of one cartonnage and how it came to be found at the Welshpool Museum in Wales.

PIGNATTARI is reporting on her current research on an organic group of Middle Kingdom stelae (1987–1759 BC), forming the main part of a corpus of documents belonging to a functionary called Djaf-Horemsaf, chief of at least three expeditions to the turquoise mines of Serabit el-Khadim, in Sinai, in the years 6, 8 and 9 of Amenemhat IV(1772–1763 BC).

PRADA is providing an insight on ancient Egyptian oneiromancy and demotic dream books. The paper reveals the wealth of unpublished sources on this topic which clearly show strong links between the demotic and the earlier *oneirocritica*.

SCHILLER is following the activities of the merchants and their trade in an Egyptian harbour as well outlining possible problems encountered in the trade connections of New Kingdom Egypt with the Eastern Mediterranean area.

STEWART is seeking to frame the problem of myth in Ancient Egypt by surveying the definitions and approaches of more general myth studies, attempting to provide mediation between the divergent opinions in Egyptology concerning myth.

TAMORRI suggests that deviant burials in Predynastic Egypt do not necessarily reflect social exclusion or rejection, but are likely to be merely another burial type in a wide repertoire of burial practices.

VELASCO PÍREZ is looking into female hippos, whose form was adopted by several goddesses in the Egyptian pantheon. Some of these gods have two names while others remain anonymous; the paper attempts to resolve the question of how many hippo goddesses the Egyptian pantheon had.

Introduction

The twelfth meeting of the Current Research in Egyptology conference not only witnessed the gathering of the future names of Egyptology but also a reunion of Durham University's Egyptologists. This was reflected in the conference's keynote speakers Dr Toby Wilkinson, Dr Penny Wilson and Dr Karen Exell who presented the past, the present and the future of Egyptology tradition at Durham University. Dr Wilkinson's arrival at a complex time within the Department of Archaeology helped ensure the successful continuation of Egyptology at Durham. As well as a renowned Egyptologist in her own right, Dr Penny Wilson has supervised a number of students that have gone on to become curators and lecturers at United Kingdom and overseas universities such as Dr Karen Exell, who was at the time of the conference the curator of Egypt and the Sudan at the Manchester Museum, University of Manchester. Through their work, it has been possible for many postgraduate students to undertake research on a wide range of Egyptological subjects.

The editors would like to thank the following institutions who kindly supported the Current Research in Egyptology XII conference: The Department of Archaeology at Durham University, Durham University's Graduate School, the Durham Centre for the Study of the Ancient Mediterranean and Near East, The Egypt Exploration Society, the North East Ancient Egypt Society, Oxbow Books, Durham Tourist Information Office and Durham Oriental Museum.

The editors would also like to thank Dr Penny Wilson, Dr Toby Wilkinson, Dr Kathryn Piquette, Dr Karen Exell, Ms Lyn Gatland, Mr Nico Staring, Dr Gillian Scott, Dr Stuart Weeks, Ms Rachel Grocke, Dr Campbell Price and Dr Angus Graham for chairing the conference sessions and stimulating vibrant discussions which will certainly boost current and future research in Egyptology.

The Editors
Heba Abd El Gawad, Nathalie Andrews, Maria Correas-Amador,
Veronica Tamorri and James Taylor

October 2011

Tell me your name and I can tell you how your kingship was: The royal names of the first three Ptolemies (323–222 BC)

Heba Abd El Gawad

Introduction

If it were not for Ptolemy V's cartouches inscribed on the Rosetta stone and the bilingual approach adopted by the Ptolemaic kings, Champollion attempt to decipher the code of the ancient Egyptian language would have failed. Therefore, our present knowledge of ancient Egypt could be mainly attributed to Ptolemaic royal names.

The kings' names written in hieroglyphs on the various monuments represent the most fundamental precondition of assuming the office of a Pharaoh. Due to the iconographic potential of the hieroglyphs such names held more than the linguistic significance (Baines 1998, 121; Quirke 1990, 9–11). The names were an indication of historical, religious and cultural events. Hence, modern scholarship has regarded the royal protocol as one of the major 'propaganda' techniques adopted by the royal organisation to promote desired political and religious beliefs among the peoples of the kingdom (Leprohon 2010, 2; Blöbaum 2006, 3–4; Quirke 1990, 4–6; Bonhême and Forgeau 1987, 3).

Despite this general agreement on the potential of the names to promote political and religious ideologies, the royal protocol has never been treated as a means of communication through which the king's self was presented. This act of communication could be analyzed according to the information theory formulated by Shannon (1948). The theory provides a mathematical and philosophical view of the transmission of information. Although its practical applications are concerned mainly with engineering, it embeds human activities in an essentially social context, and therefore is applicable to linguistic and artistic expressions. In an act of communication we have to distinguish the source (author, sender) of the message, the channel through which the message is transmitted (medium) and the receiver (audience, reader).

In this paper we will attempt to analyze the royal names of the first three Ptolemies as a means of communication used by the kings to present themselves to their various audiences. Various factors led to the choice of the first three Ptolemies as a case study. First, the first three Ptolemies have deservingly gained the reputation of being the "propaganda machines" of the Hellenistic period (Lund 1992, 23). The argument was primarily based on their efficient adoption of local Egyptian traditions. They have always been praised for being the foreign rulers who "accommodated" the most to Egyptian culture and perfectly justified their claims of being Pharaohs of Egypt (Hölbl 2001, 23–24; Manning 2010, 91–92). The royal names were one of the means through which the Ptolemies, like any other ruler of Egypt, native or foreign, presented themselves to their audiences. Thus a closer investigation to the royal names of the early Ptolemies will provide us with a better understanding of the role the royal names played in the self-presentation of ancient Egyptian rulers. Second, they were the inaugurators of the Ptolemaic dynasty and rulers who began dynasties have always set a noteworthy pattern of Egyptian royal names in terms of legitimisation (Leprohon 2010, 2–3; Bonhême 1988, 4; Aufrère 1982, 19). An insightful approach towards the early Ptolemies' royal names will help us to establish the role the royal names played in providing foreign kings with the legitimacy needed to rule Egypt.

The aim of this paper is to identify the various messages portrayed in the royal names, their origins and nature. In addition to the actual authors of such names, their audiences and the impact it had in presenting the early Ptolemies and consolidating their rulership will be considered.

The messages

Each of the five royal names served a specific purpose within the process of creating the political and religious identity of the king. The Horus name reflected the identification of the king with Horus and the theological position of the king as Horus on earth to other deities. The *Nbty* name signified the king's close association with both regions of Egypt and the duality of the geographical balance of the "Two Lands" in the person of the king (Baines 1995, 127; Bonhême 1988, 4). While the golden Horus name still inspires some debate, the traditional explanation for it is that it reflected the strength and power of the king as the avenger Horus, the victor over Seth (Beckerath 2000, 6; Blöbaum 2006, 4). As with the *Nbty* name the coronation name was meant to reflect the king's ability to keep both lands united. The birth name was the name given to the king at birth and provided a dynastic name for the royal house (Quirke 1990, 3–4).

Thus the epithets used for each name were meant to reflect such aspects and bore the political and religious messages personal to the dynasty or the king in question. The epithets mirrored how each king should be perceived by his audiences and served as the main headlines of the king's career defining his royal identity. The following is a discussion of the various messages portrayed in the royal names of the first three Ptolemies (for the transliteration and the translation of the royal names discussed see Table 1).

The legitimate ruler

From an Egyptian viewpoint, the gods were the actual rulers of the world who preserved the political unity of Egypt and accepted the king as their legitimate representative on earth only after performance of the coronation rituals (Bonhême and Forgeau 1988, 16). Whether or not the early Ptolemies had been actually crowned in an Egyptian manner has been heavily debated; the first evidence of a Ptolemaic king who underwent an official coronation is Ptolemy V as recorded on the Memphis decree (Koenen 1993, 41–8; Stephens 2003, 14). Yet, granting the king his complete royal protocol theoretically implies that he had undergone the formal coronation process. The titulary in this particular case served as evidence of the acceptance of his rule by the priests, not of his coronation (Bonhême and Forgeau 1988, 116–117).

For the Ptolemies, being accepted by the Egyptian priesthood was crucial in assuming the office of a pharaoh. Alexander the Great and his Macedonian predecessors observed Persian rule in Egypt firsthand and realized how the power of the local priests should not be underestimated.

The royal names of the first three Ptolemies (323–222 BC)

King	Horus Name	Golden Horus Name	Nbty Name	Coronation Name	Birth Name	Greek Cult Name
Ptolemy I	*wr phtj nsw qnj* The great of might, the strong king	NA	*jtj m sḫm ḥqȝ nṯr* who possess the Two Lands with power as ruler	*stp n Rꜥ mry Jmn* The chosen by Re the beloved of Amon	*Ptlmjs* Ptolemy	*nṯr.wj nḏtj.wj* The saviour gods
Ptolemy II	*ḥwnw qnj* The powerful Horus	*wr phtj* The great of might	*sḫꜥj.n sw jt=f* His father made him appear	*wsr kȝ Rꜥ mry Jmn* Powerful is the Ka of Re, the beloved of Amon	*Ptlmjs* Ptolemy	*nṯr.wy sn.wy* The sibling gods
Ptolemy III	1) *ḥkn nṯrw rmṯw ḥr=f m šsp.n=f nswy.t m ꜥ jt=f* Rejoicing the deities and the Egyptians with his face, his image is as royal as his father 2) *wr phtj jr ꜥd.t m bṯnw=f* The great of might who massacres his enemies	*qn nḏtj nṯr.w jnb mnḫ n Tȝ mrj* The powerful of protector gods, the protective of the wall of Egypt	*wr phty jrj ȝḫt nb ḥb.w sd mj Ptḥ Tȝ ṯnn jtj mj Rꜥ* The great of might, doing that which is useful, Lord of the years of the Jubliee like Ptah –Tatenen, the ruler like Re	*jwꜥw n nṯr.wy sn.wy stp (.n) Rꜥ sḫm ꜥnḫ (n) Jmn* The heir of the sibling loving gods, who is the chosen of Re, the living image of Amon	*ptwlmjs ꜥnḫ ḏ.t mry Ptḥ* Ptolemy, living forever, the beloved of Ptah	*nṯr.wy mnḫ.wy* The benefactor gods

Table 1. Royal names of the first three Ptolemies with translation.

Ptolemy I's efforts to form a coalition with the Egyptian priesthood began as early as his satrapy. The text in the Satrap decree, dating to regnal year seven of Alexander IV (311 BC), illustrates the early intentions of Ptolemy, the satrap at the time, to legitimise his rule and to be constrained by priestly expectations, within a traditional royal context (Schafer 2011, 7; Manning 2010, 93–94; Hölbl 2001, 84). The second and third Ptolemies followed the same tactics and acted piously toward the priestly institution and the Egyptian gods. Such measures must have surely contributed to the length of the Ptolemaic dynasty by establishing support from institutions representing the Egyptian audience.

The first three Ptolemies were granted a royal protocol as an indication of the tacit approval of their rule by the Egyptian priests, for this approval to be explicit; they had to seek the recognition of the gods as being legitimate and to prove being the sons, or the nominal sons, of their deceased but legitimate predecessors (Baines 1998, 128–129). The royal names were the primary means of introducing the new king to his kingdom as a legitimate ruler who has been granted the approval of the deities and is the heir of an equally legitimate predecessor. Fulfilling these two main conditions, in addition to performing the religious rituals and preserving world order, provide the new king with the legitimacy needed to rule Egypt. The following is a discussion of how these two main aspects were reflected in the royal names of the early Ptolemies to present them as legitimate rulers.

Divine approval

The divine approval of the early Ptolemies was portrayed in their royal protocol mainly through their coronation names, and only in the case of Ptolemy III did it extend to the birth name. Ptolemy I was identified as 'the one chosen by Re', and 'the beloved of Amon'. Similarly, Ptolemy II was the beloved of Amon in the second epithet of his coronation name while the first epithet, praised 'the ka of god Re'. Ptolemy III's divine recognition was expressed by borrowing the first epithet of Ptolemy I's coronation name 'the one chosen by Re' in his own coronation name and the addition of the epithet 'beloved of Ptah' to his birth name.

The coronation names traditionally evoked the essential character and activities of the king in relation to the god of creation, Re. Ever since the Eleventh Dynasty it was a custom to have the name of the sun god Re in the name: this reinforced his position as king of the gods, and underlines the importance of solar theology to kingship, as in the coronation name of king Montuhotep II Nebheptra (Leprohon 2010, 3; Quirke 1990, 24–25; Bonhême 1987, 222). This tradition was maintained by the first three Ptolemies, as we have seen, in their coronation names in which their relation to Re was stressed.

Ptolemy III's divine approval was not restricted to his coronation name as was the case with his predecessors yet it extended to his birth name which could be seen as an attempt to identify Ptolemy III as being approved by the gods not only from the instance of his accession to the throne but from as early as his birth. Amon, who has been only mentioned in the passing in the Ptolemaic royal names so far, was in Ptolemy III's royal protocol replaced by Ptah: the god of Egyptian kings who was at the head of the dynasty of the gods and, at the end of the third century, became the patron god of the insurgent Theban kings (Hölbl 2001, 80). The god Ptah was a primordial god and a god of creation who had a strong emphasis on the ideology of kingship as he was the 'Lord of Maat', 'Father of the gods' and 'King of the Two Lands'. Being favoured by Ptah links the king to the facets of Egyptian kingship which were specific to god Ptah (Baines 1998; Hölbl 2001, 80). The direct link to Ptah in the Ptolemaic titulary was inaugurated by the names of Ptolemy III and continued to exist till the reign of Ptolemy

XII in a direct link of the Ptolemies to the local institution of kingship. The addition of epithets expressing divine approval to the birth names existed from the eighteenth dynasty up till the Roman period (Beckerath 2000, 282–386).

Legitimate heirs

As the inaugurator and founder of a new dynasty it would be difficult to identify Ptolemy I in his royal names as being the direct physical heir of a legitimate ruler. This dilemma was solved by labelling the first Ptolemy as the founder of a new era instead. The Horus and *Nbty* names of Ptolemy I marked the beginning of a new dynasty; the former satrap appeared now in the guise of Horus 'great in strength, strong king (*nswt*)'. The direct reference to the king as ruler is extremely rare and the concise version in the name of Ptolemy I is quite unique. The assumption of the office of the pharaoh by Ptolemy I in the royal names is shown as a legally important step; the *Nbty* name which was created for Ptolemy I gave the reason for this process 'the one who conquers with power, a virtuous ruler', a direct reference to the special circumstances of his legitimation.

Being the heir of Ptolemy I and his co-regent during his final years of reign made Ptolemy II's presentation as a legitimate ruler by succession seem natural enough. The golden Horus name of the second Ptolemy made direct reference to the special circumstances by which Ptolemy II ruled 'he whom his father crowned': a direct reference to Ptolemy I's deliberate choice of Ptolemy II to act as his co-regent and become the second Ptolemaic king, thus securing his claims to rule by succession. To refer to this aspect of Ptolemy II's legitimation in his golden Horus name, a name which probably presents the king as the representative of Horus who is the avenger of his father rather than his coronation name which has been normally the case, seems logical as the golden Horus name itself implies the relation between the king and his father.

The same measures were adopted for Ptolemy III. He primarily ruled as a co-regent as evident in the Mendes stela where he was referred to as the crowned prince, Ptolemy son of Ptolemy. The third Ptolemy's Horus name bore the message of the king being the heir of an equally legitimate successor 'he has received the kingship from his father'. The message in this instance is direct and distinctive especially in the choice of the word 'kingship'. As an already crowned prince during the reign of his father Ptolemy II, Ptolemy III's reference to his legitimacy through succession was in no need of hidden meanings or coded messages, it was an emphasis of an already existent political reality.

Ptolemy III was not only presented in his royal names as the successor of Ptolemy II's royal entity but as the heir of his divine identity as well. In his coronation name the third Ptolemy was expressly referred to as 'the heir of the sibling gods', a direct reference to Ptolemy II and Arsinoe II and their identification within the Ptolemaic dynastic cult. In this case Ptolemy III is not only succeeding the royal identity of Ptolemy II but his divine form as well. This approach did not only provide the third Ptolemy with a divine identity for himself but expressed the integration and acceptance of the dynastic cult of the Ptolemies within the Egyptian religious sphere. The coronation name of Ptolemy III marked the first reference of the sibling gods in Egyptian sources.

The manner of legitimising by succession was to be continued in future titularies of Ptolemaic kings and was a convenient vehicle for outlining the particular circumstances of family history. The passing on of power was visually represented on the scenes of ancestor worship in temple reliefs as well.

The powerful king

Alexander the Great created his own personal trademark, he did not assume typical grand royal titles such as Great King or King of Kings within his Greek subjects, yet he used the simple title of *basileus*, king. As such Alexander has exercised his own individual form of sovereignty over a land he had 'won by spear', ruling it at his own discretion (Ma 2003, 125; Gruen 1996, 116). By these measures, Alexander created a kind of 'super national' kingship whose legitimacy rested on military victory creating a new ideology of kingship among the Greeks. Thus the Ptolemaic style of kingship following the model set by Alexander was a blend of legitimacy secured through Egyptian religion and through military power (Manning 2010, 93).

The military nature of the early Ptolemies has been reflected in their royal names with epithets highlighting the strength and power of the first three Ptolemies. Ptolemy I in his Horus name appeared as: the 'great of might', 'the strong king' a clear reference to his successful attempts in securing the rule of Egypt to himself and protecting the Egyptian territories. A similar message was implied in Ptolemy I's *Nbty* name which describes the king as the preserver of Egypt's unity, here the king was presented as 'he who possess the two lands with power' another reference of the power qualities of the first Ptolemy through which he gained his legitimacy and managed to rule over both Upper and Lower Egypt.

Both the Horus name and the *Nbty* name of Ptolemy II portrayed him as the powerful ruler of Egypt despite the classical narrative claims of his poor health and the fact that he did not physically lead the army in any of the wars occurring during his reign (Fraser 1972, 68). Despite all of these claims the second Ptolemy was depicted in his royal names as the powerful strong king in a direct concise manner. In his Horus name he is referred to as the 'strong Horus', an epithet created only for the second Ptolemy, the direct reference to an Egyptian king as Horus in royal names is exceptional and existed only in this case. While in his *Nbty* name the presentation of the king's strength was borrowed from his father's Horus name 'great of might' reflecting not only the king's strength but the borrowing of naming elements from his predecessor.

Ptolemy III's royal names drew upon the traditional theme of the cultic role of the king as protector in his Horus name, *Nbty* name and golden Horus name. Compared to earlier Ptolemies, Ptolemy III's royal names put more emphasis on his presentation as a powerful king, not only in having three out of the five names to express this aspect but in the innovation in the wording as well.

In Ptolemy III's second Horus name he is depicted like his grandfather as the 'great of might' but the epithet was amended into a longer version to suit the personal case of Ptolemy III and the phrase 'who massacres his enemies' was added in reference to his victory in the Second Syrian war; a clear evidence of the timely manner of the names and their political relevance. The *Nbty* name 'strong is the protector of the gods, a mighty wall for Egypt' a clear reference to his successful policy of making Egypt into a great power and this is interwoven with the theme of the king being protector not only for the subjects but for the gods as well. What is more is the allusion to his role as protector of Egypt; a direct reference to Alexander the Great who was marked as the 'protector of Egypt' on account of his Horus name (Beckerath 2000, 282). The final presentation of Ptolemy III as the protector god existed in the first phrase of his golden Horus name which was amended from Ptolemy I's Horus name 'great of might'.

The divine king

Foreign rulers also had to assume the religious role of the pharaoh, if they were to secure their success. This holds true for the Persians and the Romans. Alexander the Great and the Ptolemies took particular care to act as cultically relevant kings and thus gain acceptance as the central figure of Egyptian religion (Stephens 2003, 25–26; Koenen 1993, 32). The divine aspect of the first three Ptolemies appeared in their royal names in two forms either within the epithets of the main five royal names or through the Egyptian translation of the Greek cult names.

The divine nature of the early Ptolemies was mirrored within the names of Ptolemy II and Ptolemy III. The second Ptolemy was directly referred to as the powerful Horus which strictly emphasised Ptolemy II being the incarnation of Horus on earth. The direct link between Ptolemy II and Horus has been reflected in various occasions during his reign both in Egyptian and Greek sources. For example, Callimachus referred to the second Ptolemy in his poems as the Horus king and visitors to the temple of Philae dedicated their visits to Ptolemy II, the Horus king in demotic (Stephens 2003, 36). It would be difficult to discern whether the reference to Ptolemy II as Horus in sources is reacting to certain political or religious events or if it was only initiated by his direct representation as the powerful Horus in his royal protocol.

With Ptolemy III divine aspects of the Ptolemaic kings began to appear more, as was reflected in both his golden Horus name and his coronation name. In epithets such as 'Lord of the jubilee-festivals as well as Ptah Tatenjenen', the pharaoh is here compared with the king Ptah who is at the head of the dynasty of the gods: this is a definite sign of the transfer of the king's ideology onto the Ptolemies and comes as a consequence of the increasing importance of god Ptah. Unlike Ptolemy II the third Ptolemy was not likened to Horus yet he was likened to Amon as being his living image, as marked in Ptolemy III's coronation name. The association of Ptolemy III with Ptah and Amon mirrors his presentation as the divine king of the North of Egypt, by linking him to god Ptah, and to the South through being the living image of Amon, thus he is the patron divine king of Upper and Lower Egypt.

The Greek cult names grew out of Greek thinking and identified the various qualities of a *basileus* and provided the identity of each royal couple in the Ptolemaic dynastic cult (Hazzard 2000, 12–13; Minas 2000, 3–4). The names were literally translated into ancient Egyptian and existed in Egyptian settings as well (on the Greek cult names and their translation in Egyptian ideologies see Abd El Gawad 2010, 1–14; Koenen 1993, 36). The title of 'saviour gods' was granted to Ptolemy I and his wife Berenike in reference to donations to cities and temples. Ptolemy II and Arsinoe II were portrayed as 'the sibling gods' in a clear association with their sibling marriage and the introduction of this new ideology to the Greek world, yet their presentation as sibling gods existed within the Egyptian sphere after their death as well. Finally, Ptolemy III and Berenike II were presented in their Greek cult name as 'the benefactors', clear reference to their various acts of piety towards the cults and the subjects.

Origins of epithets
The epithets used for the royal names of the first three Ptolemies ranged between epithets borrowed from predecessors and innovative epithets which were exclusively composed for each Ptolemaic king.

BORROWED EPITHETS

This adoption of predecessors' epithets was a common practice within the royal names. Reusing epithets of a legitimate forerunner provided a mythical link between the new king and his ancestors and supported his claim to rule.

Analysis of the epithets of the first three Ptolemies revealed that the epithets reused in the royal names of the early Ptolemies echoes the New Kingdom and Late period of ancient Egyptian history (Table 2). In general they comply with the general code of practice of the reuse of such epithets except for two cases: first the use of 'powerful is the Ka of Re' in the coronation name of Ptolemy II and the combining of both 'the chosen by Re', 'the beloved of Amon' in one name.

Wsr k3 R^c 'Powerful is the ka of Re'

While the coronation name of the first Ptolemy echoes the New Kingdom and the Macedonian rule, 'powerful is the ka of Re' which formulates the first part of Ptolemy II's coronation name would take us back to king Userkare of the sixth dynasty. After king Userkare the phrase only re-appeared in the royal protocol of the second Ptolemy. The surprising fact in this case lies not only in the re-using of an Old Kingdom royal name but in the specific choice of Userkare. Userkare is generally regarded by historians as the king who opposed his processors, Teti's royal line and was most likely an usurper to the throne whose reign lasted for only one year (Qanwati 2003, 158).

Classical historical narratives offer us a logical explanation for this unexpected link between Ptolemy II and Userkare. According to classical sources when Ptolemy I took Ptolemy II as a co-regent, he was bypassing his son from his first wife, Eurydice, the daughter of Antipater: Ptolemy Keraunos, Meleager and the third son whose name is unknown. Ptolemy II, one of at least three children born to Ptolemy I by his third wife, Berenice, was neither the obvious heir to the throne nor had he established an early reputation as a military leader capable of guiding and leading the country (Fraser 1972, 67). Hence, Ptolemy II and Userkare were both indirect heirs to the throne, an indirect heir to the throne would need a higher level of support by the deities and it seemed that being the one chosen by the gods was not sufficient in this case, because the king needed to be an incarnation of the god Re himself.

The similar historical circumstances surrounding the accession of Userkare and Ptolemy II might thus give some validity for the sudden appearance of 'powerful is the ka of Re' once again in the royal titulary. After Ptolemy II 'powerful is the Ka of Re' marked its final appearance in the coronation name of Ptolemy V. However, the fifth Ptolemy was the direct heir of the royal Ptolemaic house. In this case the link was not intended to refer to the fact of being an indirect heir to the throne but to link Ptolemy V, who was thirteen at his accession to throne, to Ptolemy II, who has been perceived as the actual founder of the dynasty, as evident in the temple relief presentations to remind the nation of the glorious days of the Ptolemaic period.

'The chosen by Re', the beloved of Amon'

The 'chosen by Re' and 'the beloved of Amon' in themselves were common additions to the royal names from the New Kingdom but they would never have constituted a complete throne name in and of themselves. The only instance in which such phrases formed solely a complete throne name was in the case of Alexander the Great (Beckerath 2000, 232) probably as a direct reference to the special circumstances of his legitimisation. Thus, these phrases state the essential elements of divine lineage in the context of concrete and historical circumstances by which the

Epithets	Horus Name	Nbty Name	Golden Horus Name	Coronation name	Birth Name
wr pḥtj	Amenhotep II, Amenemess, Ramesses II, Seti II, Siptah, Sethnakht, Ramesses III, Chechanq V			Ramesses XI, Osorkon II	
stp n Rꜥ mry Jmn				Alexander the Great	
stp n Rꜥ				Tuthmosis I/III/IV, Amenhotep I, Amenhotep III, Horemheb, Seti I, Ramesses II, Amenemes, Seti II, Siptah, Sethnakht, Ramesses IV/VII/IX/X, Smendes, Psusenes, Osochor, Siamon, Chechanq I/II/III/V/VI, Osorkon I/II, Takelot II, Pamaÿ	
jtj m sḫm		Sonbef	Amenhotep II, Psusenes I, Osorkon II		
wsr k3 Rꜥ				Userkare, Chendjer	Userkaf
mry Jmn	Pinedjem			Amenhotep III, Merenptah, Amenemes, Seti II, Siptah, Taousert, Sethnakht, Ramesses III/VI/VI/IX/ X, Psusenes I, Siamon, Chechanq III,/IV, Chabaka, Ptolemy I	Ramesses II, Sethnakht, Ramesses IV/V/ VIII, IX/X/XI, Pinedjem, Smendes, Neferkare, Psusenes I, Amenope, Siamon, Chechanq I/II/III/IV, V/VI/VIII, Osorkon I/II/III/IV, Takelot II, III
nb ḥb.w sd	Ramesses II, Merenptah, Amenemes, Ramesses III/IV/VII		Amenhotep III, Ramesses VI		
mry Ptḥ					Seti II, Chabataka

Table 2. The epithets borrowed by the early Ptolemies and the royal names of earlier kings in which they previously existed.

Macedonian rulers become pharaohs: Alexander the great, Philip Arrideus, Ptolemy I appeared as 'chosen' by god and the 'beloved' son, namely as the desired and the legitimate successors of the gods in their office. By these measures, divine support of the new rulers seems to be secured, as evident in their coronation names. Hence, in the case of Ptolemy I, the re-use of the coronation names of the Macedonian kings was meant to mark an ideological continuity between the Ptolemaic dynasty and their predecessors.

INNOVATIVE EPITHETS

Despite of being foreign rulers of Egypt, the royal names of the early Ptolemies witnessed various innovations in the epithets used. This could be perceived as announcement of the beginning of a new era which needs new forms by which to present the king. The names of the first three Ptolemies mainly revolved around the legitimation of the early Ptolemaic kings, thus most of the innovative epithets were created to serve this purpose. We find the dominant presence of the theme of the king being royal in the first names of Ptolemy I as an indication of the transition of his status from satrap to king as in *nsw qni ꜥnd ḥḳꜥ tnr*. While in the second Ptolemy's names the innovation lies in the direct link between the king and god Horus *ḥwnw qnj* and to the special circumstances of his succession *sḫꜥj(.n) sw jt=f*.

In Ptolemy III's names we have 'Rejoicing the deities and the Egyptians with his face, his image is as royal as his father', 'The powerful of protector gods, the protective of the wall of Egypt', 'Lord of the years of the Jubliee like Ptah – Tatenen, the ruler like Re', 'The heir of the sibling loving gods, who is the chosen of Re, the living image of Amon'. These are all epithets of praise to the deities and mainly refer to the special circumstances by which the third Ptolemy secured his succession in addition to introducing the dynastic signatures of the Ptolemies to the audience of the names.

RE-USE BY LATER PTOLEMIES

Ptolemy V and Ptolemy VIII both borrowed epithets from Ptolemy II and Ptolemy III, Ptolemy V re-used the chosen *wsr kꜣ Rꜥ* from Ptolemy II and the *nb ḥb.w sd mj Ptḥ Tꜣtnn* from Ptolemy III's golden Horus name (Beckerath 2000, 236) while Ptolemy VIII borrowed the epithet added to the birth name of Ptolemy III and the Greek cult name (Beckerath 2000, 240). During the reign of both Ptolemy V and Ptolemy VIII the Ptolemaic period had already lost its powers not only externally but internally as well and reviving the early Ptolemaic period as a reminder of past glories was echoed in various aspects including the royal names.

Authors

It was the task of the lector priests to compose the royal protocol of the Egyptian kings. This is evident from the inscription on the statue of Udjahorusnet in which he describing his role towards the integration of the Persian ruler Darius and the various responsibilities left upon him, among which was the composition of the Persian king's royal name (Lloyd 2007, 101). Alexander the Great was crowned in Memphis and chose Memphis to be his capital in Egypt which enabled him to revive the glory of the Old Kingdom and linked himself to god Ptah. The Ptolemies followed Alexander's example and chose to be crowned at Memphis (Hölbl 2001, 79; Thompson 1988, 118). Thus from the beginning a relationship of cooperation existed between the priesthood of Memphis and the Ptolemaic royal house.

The strong bond between the high priests of Memphis and the Ptolemaic kings and the choice of the king to be crowned in Memphis suggests that the Memphite priests must have been the actual authors of the Ptolemaic royal names; however, no direct evidence exists to support such a claim except the analysis of the political circumstances. For a royal protocol that is composed in Memphis one would expect the existence of the god Ptah within the epithets. Yet, there was no mention of god Ptah in the royal names of the first and second Ptolemies. This phenomenon should not be seen as accidental, wording of the royal names and the political and religious messages they normally bear suggest a careful choice on the part of the priests. A, perhaps, logical explanation could be a political manoeuvre of presenting the first and second Ptolemies as being neutral to the two major religious powers which had dominated the religious scene in ancient Egypt: the priesthood of Memphis and that of Thebes. Thus, the absence of the mention of god Ptah in the titulary could be to avoid being presented as being in favour of Memphis over Thebes at such a crucial period of the formation of the Ptolemaic dynasty in Egypt.

During the reign of Ptolemy III the favouring of god Ptah and the priesthood of Memphis became apparent in his royal names and this is reflective of the political and religious atmosphere at the time. Ptolemy III initiated the priestly synods (Hölbl 2001; Thompson 1988) and acted piously to the religious institution, as evident in his benefactor Greek cult name and the Canopus decree. The reign of Ptolemy III was the peak of the strong bond and direct engagement between the Ptolemaic kings and Memphite priests, as is evident in the complex royal names laden with elaborate religious components and epithets of praise. At the end of the third century BC Ptah went on to become the patron god of the insurgent Theban Kings (Hölbl 2001, 80).

Audience

Only one percent of the population in most periods were literate. If the population rose from one million during the Old Kingdom to seven million during the Greco-Roman period with the Greeks forming the majority of the literate, the numbers of the literate will have been 10,000–50,000. Central administration together with religious entities is privileged by literacy (Baines 2007, 49–51). Thus the royal names had limited accessibility within the Egyptian society due to the high illiteracy levels among the majority of the population.

Yet, as a means of communication the royal names must have been intended to an audience even if that audience was limited. In order to identify the limited audience the names were projected at we have to identify first the medium on which the names existed and then we would be able to assess who were the royal names messages intended to. In a survey of the royal names of the first three Ptolemies it was concluded that the medium used to portray the royal names were: the temple walls, stelae, statues, foundation deposits, rings.

Temple walls

The five royal names and the dynastic cult name were depicted on the walls of the temples. The percentage of the existence of each name varied. The coronation and the birth names were the ones portrayed most often followed by, in ascending order, the Horus name, the *Nbty* name, the golden Horus name, the complete royal protocol and the dynastic cult name. The audiences of temple reliefs were probably:

- Gods and Ancestors
- Members of the elite
- Descendants, for whom the present king became an Ancestor

These three groups of audiences are key in providing the king with the legitimacy and acceptance he was seeking in his royal names. An interesting phenomenon which appeared for the first time with the coronation name of Nectanebo II reappeared once again in the royal names of Ptolemy II in which the hieroglyphic signs were locally adapted to the audience. The depiction of the gods was interchangeable. In Upper Egypt, Amon, the patron god in the south, was mostly depicted first then followed by god Re, while the contrary occurred in Lower Egypt, Re was at the forefront. Thus the message is being tailored to the audience, in this case the gods, to ensure acceptance within the religious realm. The local adaptations of the god signs in the case of the coronation names of Ptolemy II was restricted to the medium of the temple walls and was not extended to the other medium.

Stelae

The complete royal protocol with the dating formula mainly inscribed the stela with the individual coronation and birth names. The stelae were set up within the temple precincts and shared the same audience as the temple walls (Simpson 1996, 252, 266; Bernard 1992 II, 47). However, the size and the position of the stelae inside the temple meant that the texts on the stelae would be less accessible than on the temple walls as the reader of the text would have to kneel before the stela and spend time in front of it, sometimes waiting for the light to highlight the inscription, which might have not always possible for the people making up the temple audience.

Statues

As with the stelae the Egyptian style statues of the Ptolemies existed within the temple precincts which limited their audience to the three groups identified above (Stanwick 2003, 6; Ashton 2001, 3–4). The names depicted on the statues were restricted to the coronation and birth names.

Foundation deposits

Foundation deposits most commonly occur inside or under the foundations of both secular and non-secular buildings. Deposits inserted in or beneath the structure after the dedication rites were finished do not qualify as foundation deposits (Baines 2007, 56). True foundation deposits are often found under doorways, under the corners of buildings, or beneath the corners of individual rooms or halls in "royal and private tombs, temples, palaces, forts, and town walls"; however, the exact location where the ancient Egyptians were required to place them has not yet been defined.

The names inscribed on the foundation deposits were the coronation names and the birth names. Given the setting of the deposits it seems that the audience would be restricted in this case to the gods.

Rings

Various golden Ptolemaic rings have been retrieved especially from Alexandria (Stanwick 2002, 44); naturally enough all the rings are inscribed with the birth name of the king, Ptolemy in hieroglyphs, given the personal nature of rings and how they represent a personal possession rather than a public property. It is interesting that the inscriptions on the rings are in hieroglyphs rather than Greek, however the rings are oval in shape which matches the design of the cartouche. Whether the ring was carved oval to match the cartouche or vice versa would be difficult to establish today.

Three main groups have been identified as the possible audience of the royal names: the Gods and ancestors, the elite and the descendants, but the existence of any of the groups as the audience depended on the medium used to present the royal name. It seems that the royal names were intended for only the small percentage of the literate population who could gain access to the medium. The selective nature of the audience of the royal names, unlike that of visual imagery, suggests that it was not intended for public dissemination, yet it was only intended for those who were involved in the legitimisation process and whose acceptance of the king was crucial for the Egyptian world order.

Conclusions

The royal names of the first three Ptolemies were used to mainly reflect the special circumstances by which each of the three kings legitimised his claim to rule. They were short, direct and concise for the first two Ptolemies and more elaborate and elongated for the last Ptolemy, by which time the relationship between the Egyptian priesthood and the royal house was strongly established. The names presented the kings as being legitimate, divine and powerful and played an important role in providing the Greek kings with an Egyptian royal identity in terms of establishing one of the most important criteria of assuming the office. The names succeeded in reflecting the careful choice of wording of the royal names and the somehow, limited vocabulary. Given the literacy level of society and the accessibility of the medium on which the names were inscribed, it became evident how the names were mainly intended for those who mattered in terms of providing the kings with the legitimacy they need to rule Egypt. The royal names of the early Ptolemies introduced them to their kingdom as the inaugurators of a new era in which power was a key factor, reviving the glory of the Old and New Kingdom which has been long lost.

Bibliography

Abd El Gawad, H. (2010). Out of bounds: Priests' property. The status of the Ptolemaic Kings at Memphis. In Maarten Horn, Joost Kramer, Daniel Soliman, Nico Staring, Carina vanb den Hoven and Lara Weiss (eds) *Current Research in Egyptology 2010. Proceedings of the eleventh Annual Symposium*. Oxford, Oxbow Books.

Ashton, S. (2001) *Ptolemaic Royal Sculpture from Egypt: The Interaction between Greek and Egyptian Traditions*. British archaeological reports, 923. Oxford, Archaeopress.

Aufrère, S. (1982) Contribution à l'étude de la morphologie du protocole "classique". Bulletin de l'Institut français d'archéologie orientale 82: 19–73.

Baines, J. (1998) "Ancient Egyptian Kingship: Officials Forms, Rhetoric, Context". In J. Day (ed.) *King and messiah in Israel and the Ancient Near East*: Proceedings of the Oxford Old Testement Seminar, Supplement Series 270: 136–160. Sheffield, Sheffield Academic Press.

Baines, J. (2007) *Visual and Written Culture in Ancient Egypt*. Oxford, Oxford University Press.

Beckerath, J. (2000) *Handbuch der Ägyptischen Königsnamen*. Münchner Ägyptologische Studien 49. Mainz, Philipp von Zabern.

Bernard, A. (1992) *La prose sur pierre dans l'Égypte hellénistique et romaine* I–II. Paris, Centre National de la Recherche Scientifique.

Blöbaum, A. I. (2006) *Denn ich bin ein König, der die Maat liebt: Herrscherlegitimation im spätzeitlichen Ägypten; eine vergleichende Untersuchung der Phraseologie in den offiziellen Königsinschriften vom Beginn der 25. Dynastie bis zum Ende der makedonischen Herrschaft*. Aegyptiaca Monasteriensia. Aachen, Shaker.

Bonhême, M. A. (1987) *Les noms royaux dans l'Égypte de la Troisième Période Intermédiaire*. Bibliothèque d'étude 98. Cairo, Institut français d'archéologie orientale.

Bonhême, M. A. and Forgeau, A. (1988) *Pharaon. Les secrets du pouvoir*. Paris, Colin.

Fraser, P. M. (1972) *Ptolemaic Alexandria*. 3 Volumes. Oxford, Clarendon Press.

Gruen, E. S. (1996) "Hellenistic Kingship: puzzles, problems, and possibilities". In P. Bilde *et al.* eds., *Aspects of Hellenistic Kingship*, 116–25.

Hazzard, R. A. (2000) *Imagination of a Monarchy. Studies in Ptolemaic Propaganda*. Phoenix Supplementary Volume 37. Toronto, Buffalo, London.

Hölbl, G. (2001) *A History of the Ptolemaic Empire. Translated from German to English by Tina Saavedra*. London, Routledge.

Koenen, L. (1993) The Ptolemaic King as a Religious Figure. In A. W. Bulloch (ed.) *Images and Ideologies. Self-definition in the Hellenistic World*, 25–113. Berkeley, University of California Press.

Leprohon, R. J. (2010) Patterns of Royal Name-Giving. In Elizabeth Frood, Willeke Wendrich (eds), *UCLA Encyclopedia of Egyptology*, Los Angeles. http://digital2.library.ucla.edu/viewItem.do?ark=21198/zz001nx697.

Lloyd, A. B. (2007) Darius I and Egypt: Suez and Hibis. In *Persian responses: Political and cultural interactions with(in) the Achaemenid empire*, ed. Christopher Tuplin: 99–115. Swansea, Classical Press of Wales.

Lund, H. S. (1992) *Lysimachus: A Study in Early Hellenistic Kingship*. London, Routledge.

Manning, J. G. (2010) *The Last Pharaohs. Egypt under the Ptolemies 305–30 BC*. Priceton and Oxford, Princeton University Press.

Minas, M. (2000) *Die hieroglyphischen Ahnenreihen der ptolemäischen Könige*. Aegyptiaca Treverensia 9. Mainz, Philipp von Zabern.

Qanawati, N. (2003) *Conspiracies in the Egyptian Palace, Unis to Pepy I*. London, Routledge.

Quirke, S. (1990) *Who were the Pharaohs? A History of their Names with a List of Cartouches*. London, British Museum Publications.

Schäfer, D. (2011) *Makedonische Pharaonen und hieroglyphische Stelen. Historische Untersuchungen zur Satrapenstele und verwandten Denkmälern*. Studia Hellenistica 50. Leuven; Paris; Walpole; MA, Peeters.

Shannon, C. E. (1948) "A Mathematical Theory of Communication", *Bell System Technical Journal*, Vol. 27, 379–423, 623–656.

Simpson, R. S. (1996) *Demotic Grammar in the Ptolemaic Sacerdotal Decrees*. Oxford, Griffth Institute.

Stanwick, P. E. (2002) *Portraits of the Ptolemies: Greek Kings as Egyptian Pharaohs*. Austin, University of Texas Press.

Stephens, S. (2003) *Seeing Double: Intercultural poetics in Ptolemaic Alexandria*. Berkeley, University of California Press.

Thompson, D. J. (1988) *Memphis under the Ptolemies*. Princeton, Princeton University Publications.

The Old Kingdom tomb of Pehenuka and the attribution of fragments from the offering scene

Keith R. Amery

The name Pehenuka or Pehen as it appears in its abbreviated form is largely absent from the history books. This is because, like the near contemporary tombs of Nyankhnesut and Seshemnefer and many other mastabas of Sakkara dating to the Old Kingdom, Pehenuka is a name known almost exclusively through fragmentary reliefs which have appeared on the ancient art market in recent years. I first became aware of the offering scene from the tomb of Pehenuka, which will form the focus of this study, when I was searching for an unprovenanced antiquity in the international art market which had the potential to be reattributed to an archaeological context. An Egyptian relief with a hieroglyphic inscription seemed the most likely candidate, both because of the nature of the inscription which may give clues to its original context and because of my own background in Egyptology. I was writing my Master's dissertation at the time and wanted to test the archaeologists' contention that context really is key to a whole universe of potential research questions which would validate an otherwise decorative but interesting antiquity which, in terms of the market would prove to be a 'sleeper', that is an unrecognised but important artwork. This research is in turn intended to show that the current means of assessing antiquities at the point of export is not a fit system for determining value of archaeological artefacts, not least because, as in this case, the 'value' may be in the historical importance of an object (*i.e.* attribution) and not in its value in the commercial sense of what a collector or museum is prepared to pay for it on the open market.

I found a suitable candidate in a small (12" × 13") roughly shaped limestone relief bearing two partial figures of female offering bearers which was broken across the diagonal leaving one figure largely intact and the second offering bearer cut off across the mid-section (Fig. 1). Both figures were headless, suggesting the tomb from whence this relief had come had suffered major destruction in the removal of its reliefs. This would later prove to be important in the tentative reattribution of a further Old Kingdom relief fragment depicting the head of a female offering bearer sold through Bonham's London salerooms in 2003 (Fig. 2).

At the time I began my research the relief fragment depicting two female offering bearers was in the possession of a well-known American antiquities dealer based out of Washington D.C. As with any investigation the first thing to determine was where the relief had come from and if there were any publications associated with its discovery. The dealer's website description of the relief suggested the previous owner had obtained the relief from Royal Athena Galleries, a prominent New York gallery specialising in ancient art, but perusal of their widely published catalogues suggested this was not the case. Engaging in an e-mail discussion with the dealer we determined it was possible that the relief had not come from Royal Athena at all but the owner may have purchased it through one of Sotheby's regular specialist antiquities auctions. Although

Figure 1. Scene of two female offering bearers from the tomb of Pehenuka © Sands of Time Antiquities, 2007.

Figure 2. Unidentified head of a female offering bearer © Bonhams, 2003.

Sotheby's were forced to withdraw from the UK antiquities market in the 1990's following the scandal focussed on the antiquities department of their Bond Street auction house; they continue to dominate the American market from their New York salerooms. Sure enough the relief was duly identified in the catalogue of the June 2002 antiquities auction held in New York, but what was surprising was this was not a star lot, catalogued in detail and promoted as one of the few fragments of an Old Kingdom tomb still surviving, but was pushed to the back of the catalogue with the common and low value antiquities where it was even more mysteriously catalogued as a Late Period Copy in the style of Old Kingdom reliefs. The catalogue entry is given below:

"206
A LIMESTONE RELIEF FRAGMENT, EARLY 26TH
DYNASTY, CIRCA 664–600 B.C."

Finely carved in shallow relief with two ladies bearing offer- Ings striding to left, one holding a cloth, the other a basket, each wearing a diaphanous haltered dress and striated tripar- tite wig, a column of inscription between them.

"11 5/16 by 10 ¾ in. 28.9 × 27.3cm
$4,000–$6,000". (Sotheby's, 2002, 134)

The first thing you notice about the above catalogue entry is the misattribution to the Late Period which would automatically mislead any investigation into the provenance of the relief. The second obvious point about Sotheby's catalogue entry is there is no provenance information (*i.e.* prior collection data) supplied. The next thing you may notice, and certainly caught my attention was that despite passing through Sotheby's antiquities department and being in a private collection for six years between the Sotheby's sale and its appearance in a Washington gallery, no one it appeared had simply bothered to translate the short hieroglyphic inscription consisting of a single column of hieroglyphs containing just six symbols. Sue McGovern, had correctly realised Sotheby's dating was incorrect and correctly determined this was in fact a genuine Old Kingdom Relief and not a Late Period relief in the Old Kingdom style, but had made no further progress with an attribution at the time she offered the relief for sale some- time in late 2007 (McGoven, 2008a). The hieroglyphs are finely carved and easy to read. The inscription says "grgt Pehen" or "the estate of Pehen" (Jacquet-Gordon, 1962, 369).

Fortuitously, as this investigation was proceeding, Glenn Howard, another American antiquities dealer specialising in Egyptian antiquities offered for sale a substantial section of an Old Kingdom offering scene depicting seven female offering bearers (Fig. 3). This relief was also quite damaged and significantly the female figures were all headless, the relief being cut from the walls of a tomb at virtually the same height as the two figures which started this investigation. More importantly all the figures bore similar inscriptions referring to the estates of Pehen and this time the dealer had fully researched and catalogued the relief, or it would be fair to say the auction house from whence the dealer had obtained this significant fragment of the offering scene had done so. Howard's description of the relief contains the same errors as the auction catalogue so it is fair to say the dealer had done little more than copy the auction catalogue description

"An Egyptian Relief from the Tomb of Pehunuka – 110cm
Very Important Egyptian Frieze of A Shallow Door Relief of Pehunuka's Estate
Egyptian Fifth Dynasty (2494–2345 BC) Limestone 43.4 inches high × 12 inches wide"

Figure 3. Scene of seven female offering bearers from the tomb of Pehenuka © Christie's Images/The Bridgeman Art Library, 2005.

This shallow frieze relief frieze from the Fifth Dynasty (2494–2345 BC) depicts seven female offering bearers from the estates of Pehenuka, or 'Pehan', an inspector of Wa'ab priests at the pyramid Userkaf at Saqqara. Measuring almost four feet in length, the frieze features Pehenuka wearing a tightly-fitting sheath and walking to the left with the offering bearers carrying the gifts from Pehenuka's holdings (Fig. 3). A series of hieroglyphs between each figure notes the contents that are carried:

Wine of Pehen, figs of Pehen, bread of Pehen, two caskets of Pehen, two sycamore- fig trees of Pehen, the roasted grain of Pehen in a woven satchel.

"THIS IS A VERY RARE CHANCE TO OW N SUCH A LARGE AND IMPORTANT PIECE OF EGYPTIAN HISTORY FROM THE TIME OF THE PYRAMIDS! POR" (Howard, 2008)

The relief was identified as having come from an English private collection conveniently dated to 1970, coincidentally the year of the UNESCO Convention on the Means of Prohibiting and Preventing the Illicit Import, Export and Transfer of Ownership of Cultural Objects (hereafter referred to as the UNESCO Convention), and had subsequently, we are told, been in an American private collection, both descriptions which are unverifiable and therefore meaningless. The Glenn Howard relief now positively confirmed the identification of the Washington relief as part of the same offering scene, but the question I wanted answered was where had these reliefs been since the discovery of the tomb of Pehenuka in the 1840's and 2002 when the unprovenanced relief first appeared on the international antiquities market. As it turns out the unprovenanced fragment of two female offering bearers was the first of four confirmed or suspected fragments of the offering scene from the tomb of Pehenuka now identified by the author and its appearance as a 'sleeper' to be later identified by scholarship is troublesome to say the least.

The Glenn Howard relief gave us the positive identification to attribute the relief to a known tomb, and therefore start the virtual reconstruction of the offering scene and hopefully identify other fragments of the tombs decorative scheme. Howard himself had obtained the relief not from a major specialist antiquities sale at one of the major auction houses, Sotheby's or Christie's, but from a local auction house in Dallas, Texas amongst a small collection of Egyptian antiquities sold as part of a general antiques and decorative arts auction (Heritage Auction Galleries, 2007, 297) The Crow Art Partnership had arranged a sale with the Heritage Auction Galleries and the fragment of seven offering bearers was included amongst a small collection of about a dozen antiquities from sources other than the Crow Art Partnership. It is believed from the timing that Glenn Howard obtained the relief at this sale. Research determined the relief of seven female offering bearers had first appeared on the market suddenly in April 2005 when it was offered for sale by Christie's in their London specialist antiquities sale as lot 147 (Christie's, 2005, 38). Like our relief of two fragmentary female offering bearers, the larger relief was offered with no provenance information and despite a relatively modest estimate of £9,000–£12,000 remained unsold at this time, suggesting wary dealers and informed collectors were already concerned by a lack of provable provenance. Howard would later establish an antiquities consultancy 'Consign Ancient Art' and re-offer the relief in 2010 when he informed the author the relief was in the possession of a collector from the United Arab Emirates (Howard, 2010). Like all the relief fragments discussed in this essay, the current whereabouts of this relief is at present unknown.

In analysing inscribed reliefs from ancient Egypt the first research tool to turn to is the Topographical Bibliography of Ancient Egyptian Hieroglyphic Texts, Reliefs, and Paintings by Bertha Porter and Rosalind Moss. Sure enough the second part of Volume 2 covering the private cemeteries of Memphis, including Saqqara tell us all that was known of Pehenuka up until 1978 when the Griffith Institute of Oxford published this reference work (Porter and Moss 1978, 491–2). The majority of reliefs known from the tomb of Pehenuka up to this point were in the Egyptian Museum in Berlin except for one hunting scene, also acquired from the American antiquities market which is now in the Brooklyn Museum, New York (Bothmer, 1978, 67–69).

In 2008, the same year as the two reliefs so far discussed appeared in the international antiquities market, a third adjoining relief fragment from the offering scene of Pehenuka appeared in the April 2008 antiquities auction of Christie's London saleroom (Christie's, 2008, 157–159). This time the relief was better preserved, cleanly cut with seven figures virtually intact including heads and feet. The provenance was given simply as "English private collection, 1970's". Again the provenance as given is suitably vague to fall within the agreed cut-off point for illicit antiquities set by the UNESCO Convention, 1970 but vague enough to remain hard to prove (Fig. 4).

This third relief had been previously offered for sale by Christie's at their New York auction rooms in June of 2004 when it had remained unsold against a healthy estimate of $100,000–$150,000 (Christie's, 2004, 81). For all three reliefs, the dealers and auction houses had relied on the fact that the tomb had been discovered originally by Richard Lepsius in the 1840's (Lepsius,

Figure 4. Eight female offering bearers representing the estates of Pehen © Christie's Images/The Bridgeman Art Library, 2004.

1849) and assumed that as the tomb was not currently known the provenance must be sound, despite the fact no reliefs (excepting the Brooklyn hunting scene, sold to the museum in 1964) had been recorded prior to the anonymous Sotheby's sale of 2002.

A fortuitous rediscovery of another Old Kingdom tomb, which holds the ignominious record as the most widely dispersed in terms of museums and private collections containing relief fragments is too close in geography and time to continue believing the Pehenuka reliefs have been languishing in undocumented private collections for one hundred and sixty years or more. In 2001 Iain Mathieson of the Royal Scottish Museum in Edinburgh was called to investigate the looting of a tomb in the Old Kingdom cemetery of Saqqara. In his report for the Journal of Egyptian Archaeology, published by the British Egypt Exploration Society "The Tomb of Nyankhnesut (re)discovered" (Leahy and Mathieson, 2001, 33–42), Mathieson describes the extent of looting and the historical removal of the reliefs from this and neighbouring tombs, such as the tomb of Pehenuka, to protect the nearby tomb of Ti. At the time of discovery in the 1860's it was decided by the Egyptian authorities to sacrifice what were then considered 'less important' tombs in order to stop museum agents and private collectors damaging the tomb of Ti for portable reliefs to display in their own collections (Brovarski, 1996, 34). Auguste Mariette published a plan of the tomb of Pehenuka in "Les Mastabas de L'Ancien Empire" in 1889 so the location of the tomb was still officially known at this date (Mariette, 1889, 370–372).

The difficulty of determining whether or not the reliefs currently circulating in the ancient art market are licit, relies on establishing a timeline for when the tomb could have been entered and the reliefs removed. We know from Lepsius monumental work the 'Denkmaler Aus Agypten und Aethiopen' (published 1849–1859) he was the discoverer of the tomb some-time in 1842 when the Prussian expedition uncovered over one hundred and thirty tombs in the area of Saqqara, Giza, Abusir and Dahshur. We know many of the reliefs he removed at this time were taken to the Berlin Museum which houses the biggest single public collection of Pehenuka reliefs including a significant scene of a sea-born military expedition, a fragmentary butchery scene, a desert hunting scene which adjoins the Brooklyn relief, the door jambs from a false door of Pehenuka, the inscriptions of which were published by Nigel Strudwick in a collection of Old Kingdom texts (Strudwick, 1995, 232) and a relief panel depicting a pair of male offering bearers which was subsequently loaned to the Gotha Museum and destroyed during bombing raids in the Second World War (Bothmer, 1978, 67). We know Mariette was able to publish a plan of the tomb in 1889 and like the neighbouring tombs of Nyankhnesut and Seshemnefer, both largely known from relief fragments circulating in the ancient art market, it disappears from view soon after that. Despite the offering scene being discussed by Helen Jacquet-Gordon in her 1962 work 'Les Noms des Domaines Funeraires sous L'Ancien Empire Egyptien', we know the reliefs from the offering scene did not start reappearing on the international antiquities market until 2002, when someone anonymously introduced a 'sleeper' to Sotheby's June auction to be rediscovered. We also know this is suspiciously close to the (re)discovery of the tomb of Nyankhnesut in 2001 when this tomb was reported to have been recently looted.

Helen Jacquet-Gordon's work allows us to start to reconstruct the order of the offering scene although the surviving fragments of the offering scene as identified do not correspond exactly to the numbering of the offering bearers as suggested by Jacquet-Gordon in 1962. The "grgt phn" which forms the main focus of this study is numbered 22 in Jacquet-Gordon's reconstruction of the estates of Pehen and is identified as coming from the Eastern wall of the main chamber of Pehenuka's mastaba, identified simply as 'room 1' by Porter and Moss (1978, 491). The two larger surviving fragments are identified as coming from the opposite (western) wall of the same chamber. The relief of eight offering bearers corresponding to estates numbered as 29–36, although in her reconstruction Jacquet-Gordon identifies estates 34–47 as destroyed. The more damaged relief of seven female offering bearers correspond to Jaquet-Gordon's estates 50–56 (Jacquet-Gordon, 1962, 366–370).

A final interesting point concerns the attribution of small antiquities and the fact that due to the violence with which the offering scene was apparently subjected to, many of the female offering bearers are today headless. It is important to note from the figures that do survive the position of the hieroglyphic inscriptions identifying the estates of Pehen(uka). Each figure faces left and as she walks forward raises the forward arm to balance a basket of offerings on her head. The identifying inscription for each estate appears before the female figure and just below the raised arm, in the void left by the action. In 2003 Bonhams of London offered a small (5" × 5.5") limestone fragment depicting the head of a female offering bearer in their October antiquities auction (Bonhams, 2003, 3). Not surprisingly, given what we have learned so far, the provenance is given simply as "Ex Private North American collection formed in the early half of the last Century". Despite extensive damage to the surface, the top of a raised relief looped hieroglyph can just be made out beneath the raised arm. Now if we compare the hieroglyphs from the names of Nyankhnesut and Seshemnefer-Heba, two other tombs known to have been destroyed for their reliefs, we will see that such a hieroglyph does not appear in these names in such a way as to appear in this position. Given the extent of the damage to the offering scene of Pehenuka, added to the fact that most of the known surviving figures are headless and the fact that the writing of the name of Pehenuka would place the flax rope hieroglyph with the looped top in just the right position, the tantalising possibility remains this small fragment of relief also belongs to the offering scene of the tomb of Pehenuka, as comparison with the similar scenes known to have been broken up for museums and the ancient art market (*e.g.* Nyankhnesut and Seshemnefer-Heba) suggest the figures from these tombs were removed largely intact and with great care by comparison with the wanton destruction wrought on Pehenuka's offering scene.

In 1989 the antiquities dealer Charles Ede wrote in his introductory Guide to Collecting antiquities:

> "Statues and even fragments of statues from the Old Kingdom are now hard to come by, but reliefs are still a fruitful field for the collector. Fortunately many fragments are either self-explanatory or still have readable 'captions' – a detail from a procession of female figures representing estates whose revenues were to be used for the upkeep of the tomb of an important priest of the 5th Dynasty" (Ede, 1989, 85).

Fortunately academic study of Old Kingdom reliefs has moved on since then and the decoration of Old Kingdom tombs has been extensively studied (*e.g.* Harpur, 1987) and yet published parts of the tomb of Pehenuka are few and far between. In 2005 Nigel Strudwick published the inscriptions from the jambs of a false door of Pehenuka and that's pretty much all we have of the once powerful 'inspector of Wa'ab priests of Userkaf'. Today we cannot even be certain when in the Late Fifth/Early Sixth Dynasty Pehenuka lived and worked, only that he must have lived after the burial of king Userkaf in whose mortuary temple he served. However, we do know that offering scenes such as 'the estates of Pehen' are particularly important during the Late Fifth and early Sixth Dynasties because they reflect a major reorganisation of the state administration at this time.

With the reappearance, albeit briefly of four fragments of the offering, scene giving a total of seventeen partial offerands and one head plus the reliefs known in the museums of Brooklyn and Berlin it is hoped that it will be possible to publish an account of the tomb in the near future. Needless to say the reliefs have disappeared back into the antiquities market and the current whereabouts of all four fragments herein discussed is currently unknown.

Despite the clear difference between archaeological value and commercial value, antiquities of foreign origin are subjected to the same standard test as Old Master paintings and Renaissance sculpture as they pass through the UK based ancient art market. That is to say they are assessed against the Waverley Criteria and financial value still takes precedent over importance to scientific recovery of information (DCMS, n.d.). Antiquities of UK origin are zero-rated for export. This means that every antiquity of UK origin, no matter how small or cheap must be subjected to export control and placed on an export licence if bought by a buyer from overseas. However if an antiquity is not of UK origin and has been in the country for a predetermined significant period (currently fifty years) it need not be submitted for licensing unless its commercial value reaches a significant value (currently £39,500) in which case it will then be compared against the 'Waverley Criteria' against which artworks are judged to determine their importance to the cultural heritage of this country. The Waverley Criteria, simply stated are three points of assessment as follows:

"Waverley 1 – Is it so closely connected with our history and national life that its departure would be a misfortune?
Waverley 2 – Is it of outstanding aesthetic importance?
Waverley 3 – Is it of outstanding significance for the study of some particular branch of art, learning or history?"

The last sale of a relief from the offering scene from the tomb of Pehenuka occurred in the UK in April 2008 when the relief of eight estates made £54,500 with buyers premium against an estimate of £40,000–£60,000 so although it would appear to more than meet the requirement for an export licence, even if you take off the buyer's premium (20% on lots above £10,000 and up to £250,000 at the time), with what was known of the tomb of Pehenuka at the time of the sale it is unlikely an export licence would have been stopped on the grounds of the Waverley Criteria given above. It is not of 'outstanding importance' in comparison to the Crosby-Garrett Roman Parade helmet sold By Christie's, London in October 2010 for £2.2 million (Christie's, 2010, 116–121). It may be argued it is of 'outstanding aesthetic importance' when compared to other Old Kingdom reliefs. The importance of the three/four fragments of the offering scene from the tomb of Pehenuka is in the fact that it represents all that may be left of the offering scene of this important Old Kingdom official's tomb and a significant part of the entire decoration of the tomb currently known. Bernard Bothmer discussed the Brooklyn animal scene in the Festschrift for the 150th Anniversary of the Berlin Egyptian Museum and Nigel Strudwick's translation of the false door jamb texts, as I mentioned at the outset of this article, is practically all we know about Pehenuka at present. There is no definitive study of the Berlin reliefs from the tomb of Pehenuka that we are aware of.

Now, what we know of the circumstances surrounding the reliefs' entrance into the market, any future sale would be highly problematic unless more detailed provenance, and by this I mean ownership rather than archaeological context, information is forthcoming. Given that antiquities tend to circulate in the ancient art market on a ten to twenty year cycle, the repeated short term sales of the offering scene fragments of Pehenuka suggest that the market is well aware of their problematic origins but we must await their reappearance to determine whether or not the antiquities trade acknowledges this difficult history. My current research as a PhD student is an investigation of the Dealing in Cultural Objects (offences) Act 2003 and self-regulation in the UK based ancient art market. The aim of this study is to determine whether the act has achieved its intended purpose of removing illicit antiquities from the legal trade in antiquities. My investigation into the Pehenuka reliefs suggest that parts of the international trade at least, still has some way to go in order to demonstrate fully a commitment to highlighting suspect antiquities and should not simply rely on previously published provenance information, which we have shown can be misleading, inaccurate and still raise concerns if properly investigated. Having said that, I would like to see the academic publication of antiquities in private collections and in the market place as a means of expanding our knowledge and restoring individuals such as Pehenuka to their rightful place in the history books. I do not accept that publication serves to increase the value of antiquities as the current market shows that investor-collectors will buy antiquities no matter what the price and the question of publication/provenance almost never arises. Auction prices for all antiquities show year on year increases despite the majority of antiquities being unprovenanced and unpublished. Surely it is better to record what we can and learn from such artefacts as those presented here, rather than simply pretend the market does not exist.

Acknowledgements

My thanks to Sue McGovern of Sands of Time Antiquities (DC Ancient Art) and Glenn Howard of Glenn Howard Ancient Art Ltd/Consign Ancient Art for discussing the Pehenuka reliefs at the time they were in the dealers' possession. I am grateful to all three auction houses of Bonhams, Christie's and Sotheby's for images and publication rights to the four offering scene fragments herein discussed. I am particularly grateful to Klaus Finneiser of the Egyptian Museum, Berlin for his clarification of the holdings of this institution and for access to important archival photographs for the study of the Pehenuka reliefs in Berlin. My thanks also to the staff of the Institute of Archaeology library at University College London for their help in accessing Egyptology references not found at City University. My thanks to my supervisors and Department at City University for making my attendance at CRE XII possible. Finally I must thank the organizers of CRE XII at Durham University for their hospitality and continued support in the publication of this research as well as the attendees who enthusiastically welcomed the initial paper on which this study is based.

Bibliography

Bonhams (2003) *Antiquities 30th October 2003.* London, Bonhams.
Bothmer, B. (1978) *Festschrift zum 150 jährigen Bestehen des Berliner Ägyptischen Museums (Staatliche Museen zu Berlin. Mitteilungen aus der Ägyptischen Sammlung).* Berlin, Agyptisches Museum.
Brovarski, E. (1996) Epigraphic and Archaeological Documentation of Old Kingdom Tombs and Monuments at Giza and Saqqara. In N. Thomas (ed.) *The American Discovery of Ancient Egypt: Essays,* 24–43. Los Angeles, County Museum of Art.
Christie's (2004) *Christie's New York, Antiquities, Tuesday 8th June 2004.* New York, Christie's.
Christie's (2005) *Antiquities including Property from the Leo Mildenberg Collection, Wednesday 20th April 2005.* London, Christie's.
Christie's (2008) *Christie's South Kensington, Antiquities Including Property from the Collection of the Princely House of Liechtenstein, Wednesday 30th April 2008.* London, Christie's.

Christie's (2010) *Christie's Antiquities, Thursday 7th October 2010*. London, Christie's.

DCMS (n.d.) *The Waverley criteria* [online] Available at <http://www.culture.gov.uk/images/publications/waverley_criteria.pdf> [Accessed 21 July 2011].

Ede, C. (1989) *Collecting Antiquities an Introductory Guide*. London, Hollington Books.

Harpur, Y. (1987) *Decoration in Egyptian Tombs of the Old Kingdom: Studies in Orientation and Scene Content*. London, Kegan Paul International.

Heritage Auction Galleries (2007) *Fine and Decorative Arts Auction including property from the Crow Art Partnership Collection, October 13th 2007 Dallas, Texas*. Dallas, Heritage Auction Galleries.

Howard, G. (2008) *An Egyptian Relief from the Tomb of Pehenuka – 110cm* [online] Available at: <http://www.trocadero.com/EgyptianAntiquities/items/720987/item720987store.html> [Accessed 15 January 2008].

Howard, G. (2010) *Discussion on provenance of Pehenuka offering scene*. [email] (Personal communication, August 2010).

Jacquet-Gordon, H. (1962) *Les Noms des Domaines Funeraires sous L'Ancient Empire Egyptien*. Cairo, Institut Francais d'Archeologie Orientale.

Leahy, A. and Mathieson, I. (2001) The Tomb of Nyankhnesut (re)discovered. *Journal of Egyptian Archaeology*, 87, 33–42.

Lepsius, K. R. (1849) *Denkmaeler aus Agypten und Aethiopen Band I: Unteraegypten und Memphis* [online] Available at <http://edoc3.bibliothek.uni- halle.de/lepsius/textb.html> [Accessed 19 July 2011].

Mariette, A. (1889) *Les Mastabas de L'Ancien Empire Fragment du Dernier Ouvrage*. Paris, F. Vieweg, Libraire-Editeur.

McGovern, S. (2008a) *A Very Fine Egyptian Limestone Relief Fragment* [online] Available at <http://www.dcancientart.com/proddetail.asp?prod=ES703> [Accessed 14 January 2008].

Porter, B. and Moss, R. (1978) *Topographical Bibliography of Ancient Egyptian Hieroglyphic Texts, Reliefs and Paintings III2 Memphis part 2. Saqqara to Dahshur Fascicle I*. Oxford, Griffith Institute.

Sotheby's (2002) *Antiquities & Islamic Art, New York, June 13th 2002*. New York, Sotheby's.

Strudwick, N. (1995) *Texts from the Pyramid Age*. Atlanta, Society of Biblical Literature.

Figured ostraca from Deir el-Medina

Joanne Backhouse

Introduction

Deir el-Medina, on the west bank of Thebes, has been extensively excavated since the beginning of the twentieth century. In addition to the considerable archaeological remains, the site has yielded over five thousand limestone ostraca (Bruyère 1952, 60). As a readily available source material they were predominantly inscribed with hieratic text, for administrative purposes, prescribing lists of workers, materials, accounts and letters, with a small proportion containing hymns to the gods, cult rituals and love songs (Bruyère 1952, 61). However, a significant number contain an image, so called 'figured ostraca.' Generally they are inscribed in black and red with occasional additional colours used. Satirical images, depictions of animals and human figures are the most common subject matter. This paper will examine a particular genre of image, that of women on beds and in pavilions. These scenes, created by the workman for their own purposes, do not appear in the formal repertoire of Egyptian art and hence are worthy of detailed study. This paper represents research to date for my PhD at Liverpool University. As such, it is very much a work in progress.

Source Material

Ernesto Schiaparelli worked systematically at the site between 1905 and 1909, for the Egyptian Museum in Turin, but died before completing a full excavation report. Consequently, although the Turin Museum has a large collection of figured ostraca, these have not been published in a comprehensive manner. Schiaparelli did publish four pieces in his 1923–1927 publication but these were from Valley of the Queens and did not include any images of women on beds or in pavilions (Schiaparelli 1923–1927 Vol. 1 figs. 120, 121, 124). Georg Möller later worked at the site for the Berlin Museum. He recovered both hieratic and figured ostraca, a selection of the latter being published by Shäfer (1916) and Brunner-Traut (1956). Although no detailed report of the excavation was produced, Rudolf Anthes (1943, 1–68) published a brief report, thirty years later, based on Möller's notes. However, this does not contain any further information regarding the figured ostraca found by Möller.

The Institut Français d'Archéologie Orientale (IFAO) took over the concession for the site from 1917. From 1922 until 1951, Bernard Bruyère directed the excavation and regularly published reports of their work, the most important for this study being the 1939 publication, which documents the 1934–1935 season and focuses on the village itself (Bruyère 1939). Bruyère did not catalogue or publish the figured ostraca in any detail. This was done by Jean Vandier D'Abbadie whose work represents the most comprehensive publication of figured ostraca to date (Vandier D'Abbadie 1937, 1946, 1959) although, it must be noted, for the purposes of academic study this work has serious limitations. There are very few photographs; most representations are line drawings and therefore are subject to individual interpretation. In addition, as all were drawn by the author, they are similar in style, consequently hampering the identification of any individual artist based on idiosyncrasies of style or composition. The limitations of this method of representation for the purposes of academic study have been noted by previous scholars (Peck 1985, 14).

A significant number of museums also have examples of figured ostraca which are unprovenanced. The majority are assumed to have come from Deir el-Medina due to stylistic similarities (Demarée 2002, 9). The most significant collection of such material, for the purposes of this study, is found at the Medelhavsmuseet in Stockholm. These came from the Gayer-Anderson Collection and were published by Peterson (1974). There are clear similarities between these and the excavated pieces from Deir el-Medina; consequently they cannot be excluded from the dataset.

Context

No excavation report provides any detailed contextual information regarding the find spots of individual figured ostraca. Bruyère (1952, 60–61) informs us that most were found in two locations, firstly in a heap of rubble to the south of the village and secondly in a pit to the north. This pit was more than fifty metres deep and thirty-five metres wide, so this was a substantial undertaking. It is believed it was dug in the Ramesside period, in an abortive attempt to reach the water table (Bruyère 1953, 129). The abandoned pit subsequently became filled with debris. Bruyère believed heaps of rubbish built up in the north and south locations as these were the only spots accessible for the accumulation of rubbish during the life of the village (Bruyère 1952, 61). Vandier D'Abbadie (1946, 1), using the finds of Bruyère, provides a little more information, noting figured ostraca were also found in the debris of houses and amongst the ruins of votive chapels. Meskell (2000b, 259) makes the important point that the site must be considered as a whole, not merely the enclosed village. The extended site encompasses houses beyond the enclosure walls, four hundred tombs in the necropolis, the chapel complexes and the Hathor temple. Indeed, Bruyère's successors identified between forty and fifty dwellings situated amongst tombs and chapels (Valbelle 1985, 120). This highlights the juxtaposition of the realms of the living and the dead in the community, in stark contrast to modern industrial society, which has much clearer demarcations. Those boundaries are more blurred at Deir el-Medina and we must be aware of this when attempting to contextualize the ostraca.

Dating

Despite the limitations of the contextual information it is possible to date the figured ostraca with a degree of certainty. This is based on the work of Černý (1935), as noted by Vandier D'Abbadie (1946, 5). Working for IFAO, Černý examined non-figurative ostraca, *i.e.* textual. From 1935 until 1951 he produced five volumes of work. Based on the epigraphy and royal cartouches on a number of pieces, he was able to date the non-figurative ostraca to the reigns of Seti I and Rameses II (Černý 1935). However, the figurative and non-figurative pieces can be dated as a group, as they were found together in the same locations and no figurative pieces have been found in the Eighteenth Dynasty remains of the site. Therefore, the ostraca can clearly be dated to the Nineteenth Dynasty, although it is also possible to attribute them to the Twentieth Dynasty as objects dating to the reigns of Ramesses III and Ramesses IV have been found in the same contexts.

Methodology

The present study focuses on images of women on beds and in pavilions. They were identified as a coherent group and classified as 'scènes de gynécées' by Vandier D'Abbadie (1946, 80). He suggested these scenes, taking place in what he identified as the female part of the house, depicted elite women in Egyptian society (Vandier D'Abbadie 1946, 81). I initially began examining these images as a secondary source of data. I was primarily interested in New Kingdom figurines and the objectification of the female form in New Kingdom material culture, *e.g.* mirror handles, cosmetic spoons and kohl pots. However, the images on the ostraca brought together, in a unique way, many separate elements that had been the object of my study, clearly identifying them as worthy of independent analysis.

In order to carry out the aforementioned study, a database has been constructed and each image entered, recording its component parts and details, for example if the main figure is facing right, if a servant is present or if the scene contains a child. In this way repeat motifs and correlations can be identified. It is hoped that, by deconstructing the iconography, the pertinent features of the scenes will become apparent and in doing so, will shed light on the purpose and intent of these depictions.

Preliminary Analysis of the Data

Two datasets have been identified, 'women on beds' (Fig. 1) and the smaller group 'women in pavilions or outdoor locations' (Fig. 2). As work progressed, it became apparent that these were clearly linked. The former group consists of images which depict any part of a woman on a bed; to date, this group contains twenty-nine ostraca; twenty-one are from Deir el-Medina, of which eighteen were found by Bruyère and three by Möller. An additional piece is known to have come from the Theban necropolis and is now in the Louvre (Keimer 1940–45, 4). Seven pieces with no provenance have been included in the dataset due to stylistic similarities; five are from the Gayer-Anderson Collection, now in Stockholm, and the remaining two pieces can be found in Munich.

Of those twenty-nine pieces, only twelve contain an image of a child, while seventeen do not. However, twelve of those seventeen are incomplete images (Fig. 3). Complete images are considered to be those in which both the foot and head ends of the bed are visible. Therefore, incomplete images could have contained a child, as part of the scene is missing. There are in fact only five complete images without a child. Two of these are very unclear (MM14070 and Berlin 21773) and it has been noted a child could be present in at least one (Peterson 1974, 103). It appears to be the norm for a child to be included in the scene. With regards to orientation, in twenty-four of the images the women on the bed turn to the viewer's right (Fig. 1). In only five instances does the woman face the viewer's left and only one of these includes a child, which is lying on the bed behind the women. Of the twelve images which include a child, in eight

Figure 1. Drawing of a figured ostraca, Deir el-Medina, example of 'women on beds' dataset. 2337, Present location – IFAO, based on Vandier D'Abbadie (1937 Pl. L).

Figure 2. Figured ostraca, provenance unknown, example of 'women in pavilions or outdoor locations' dataset. BM 8506, Present location – British Museum © Trustees of the British Museum.

examples the child is in front of the woman who is facing the viewer's right. Apparent there was a preference to orientation, with the main figure facing the viewer's right.

There are clear areas of significance within the scenes. The bed itself appears as an important and highly decorated item. Indeed, the most frequent motif across the dataset is the depiction of the god Bes on the feet of the bed as seen in Figure 1. This occurs in sixteen images, more than half of the dataset. Serpent imagery also appears on eleven of the bed frames (see in Fig. 1 and Fig. 3). This was possibly a reference to Mertseger, the serpent goddess who we know was worshipped at Deir el-Medina (Bruyère 1929). A stylized depiction of convolvulus leaves (a perennial weed) appears in fourteen of the images, often as prominent features of the scene, intertwined between figures. This gives a sense of nature and abundance, suggesting the outdoors. This links the scenes to the 'women in pavilions and outdoor locations' dataset which will be discussed later. Scenes of offering and presentation are also a common theme. The images have a clear emphasis on depicting a specific set of objects, with items under the bed (Fig. 1), in the background (Fig. 4) and being presented (Fig. 3). Mirrors appear in eleven scenes, most commonly under the bed but also in the background and as items of presentation. Kohl pots appear in seven scenes, always in conjunction with a mirror. Broad collars appear five times either in the background or as items of presentation, never under the bed. Perfume cones are depicted five times, either as items of presentation or under the bed. Patterns are clearly emerging, suggesting the scenes were constructed using a visual code, a symbolic language that held meaning to their creators and viewers. The objects depicted – mirrors, jewellery, make up and perfume cones – relate to adornment and beautification. Were these gifts presented at marriage ceremonies or births, with the

Figure 3. Figured ostraca from Deir el-Medina, example of an incomplete image. E14337, Present location – Louvre, Paris. Courtesy of the Louvre Museum, Paris.

bed symbolizing the place of procreation and the joining together of a couple? However, it is worth noting that the only males depicted in these scenes are servants; the emphasis is clearly on the female figures.

Within the dataset a small but distinctive sub-group has been identified, so called 'elaborate beds.' This comprises only two pieces, one in the Medelhavsmuseet, Stockholm (Fig. 4) and another one now in Berlin (21451) (Shäfer 1916, fig. 10). However, distinctive iconography defines them as a coherent group. In both scenes the bed has Bes feet, with scalloped edges and a thick mattress. In addition, in both scenes the main figure is facing the viewer's right, breast

Figure 4. Figured ostraca, provenance unknown, example of 'elaborate beds' subgroup.

feeding and appears naked except for a broad collar. Mirror and kohl pots are present either in the background or as items of presentation. These images have much in common with the 'women in pavilions or outdoor locations' dataset and serve as a link between the two groups.

The 'women in pavilions or outdoor locations' dataset comprises just three pieces, two excavated by Bruyère (Figs 5 and 6). The other piece (Fig. 2) has no provenance but has been attributed to Deir el-Medina due to similarities in style (Demarée 2002, 9). Again, highly distinctive imagery defines these pieces as a coherent group. A kiosk is clearly visible on two of the pieces (Figs 2 and 5), but all three have an abundance of convolvulus leaves, suggesting an outdoor location. As in the elaborate bed scenes, the women appear naked but are in fact intricately and elaborately adorned, with wigs and jewellery. They all wear a tripartite wig, broad collar necklace and have an unusual veil or a cape around their shoulders. They all sit on stools, facing right and are breast feeding. Mirror and kohl pot are presented clearly in two of the three scenes (Figs 2 and 5). In Figure 6 flowers may be presented, which would fit in with the rare and almost erased inscription which states 'to give beautiful plants and fruits, offerings of the gardens and fields alike' (Vander D'Abbadie 1957, 28). However, the interpretation of these designs as a mirror and kohl would be more consistent with the dataset. It has been suggested that the presentation of mirrors maybe part of purification rituals after birth (Kemp 1979, 52–53).

The hairstyles of the servants in these outdoor scenes are equally distinctive. In Figures 2 and 6 we see male servants with shaved heads and long locks, what Vandier D'Abbadie (1957, 23) called 'la meche de la temple'. This distinctive hairstyle is also seen on two fragments of ostraca now in Brussels (Werbrouck 1932, fig. 4; Werbrouck 1953, fig. 11). The female attendants

Figured ostraca from Deir el-Medina 31

Figure 5. Figured ostraca, Deir el-Medina, example of 'women in pavilions or outdoor locations' dataset. E2533, Present location – Louvre, Paris. Courtesy of the Louvre Museum, Paris.

Figure 6. Line drawing of a figured ostraca, Deir el-Medina, example of 'women in pavilions or outdoor locations' dataset. 2858, Present location – IFAO; based on Vandier D'Abbadie (1959 Pl. CXX).

also have idiosyncratic hairstyles (see Figures 5 and 6). Vandier D'Abbadie (1957, 23), called them 'meche ondulée.' The high pony-tail style, gives the head an elongated, conical shape. The servant in one of the 'elaborate bed' scenes (Berlin 21451) also has this hairstyle and is likewise holding a mirror and kohl pot (Shäfer 1916, fig. 10). A similar hairstyle is also depicted in a scene of animal parody. Here a young girl, possibly a servant, dances naked, before a kiosk (Peterson 1974, 102). Lastly, the same hairstyle is seen on a fragment in Brussels. All that now remains is the upper body of a young girl, who is naked and also holding a mirror and kohl pot (Werbrouck 1954, 98, fig. 9). It would therefore seem that this hairstyle is strongly associated with servant girls and the presentation of mirror and kohl pots.

Purpose and Intent

The prevalence of repeat motifs and correlations within the imagery suggests the scenes were constructed using set formulae, a symbolic language which held meaning to their creators and viewers. This raises the question of what significance was attached to these images and why were they drawn. It was originally assumed they held little importance to their creators as they were found broken, stained and disregarded (Vandier D'Abbadie 1946, 1). While it is suggested that some were practice pieces for tomb scenes and wall paintings, it was also believed the majority were works of leisure, doodles to pass the time (Vandier D'Abbadie 19, 118–119). However, there are too many patterns forming coherent groups for these to be random scribbles. Some are of quite intricate design and it is clear care and attention has been put into them. Many look like finished pieces, with colour applied (Figs 3 and 5). Is it possible they were objects in their own right? It is useful here to consider Meskell's definition of 'materiality,' which is the making of a thing from a non-thing (Meskell 2004, 2). In these terms the ostraca have clearly undergone a process of transformation. They were probably selected from debris, an image drawn upon them and in many cases colour applied. After handling a number of pieces, it must be acknowledged that they have a presence, a sense of being, in comparison to purely a flat two-dimensional image. My research to date suggests Meskell is correct in her assertion that the ostraca are both representational and physical objects (Meskell 2004, 148). Several of the complete scenes are approximately the size of a hand, some even larger, therefore they are not insubstantial pieces. It is possible they were used like stelae, as free standing objects to display images of significance.

Vandier D'Abaddie suggested some ostraca depicting figures or religious themes may have been ex-voto, built into walls of domestic chapels and close to altars. In his publication he does in fact note one example, an image of Sobek, which had traces of plaster around the edges. This had been built into the walls of a house (Vandier D'Abbadie 1946, 119). Nevertheless, it must be acknowledged, that none of the ostraca so far handled for this study provides any indication of having been mounted. Unfortunately, Bruyère's reports do not give a breakdown of where all the individual ostraca were found, although one is noted to have come from a tomb (Bruyère 1928, 22). This belongs to the 'women on beds' dataset and the imagery is consistent with others in that group.

Although scant evidence survives, similar imagery is painted on the walls of the houses at Deir el-Medina. Published material is limited; the best example is a female dancer found in house S.E. VIII (Fig. 7) (Bruyère 1939, 273). It was published in more detail by Vandier D'Abbadie (1938, 27). We can see the woman is naked except for a veil or a cape, which is similar to the veils worn by the women in the pavilion and outdoor scenes, on the figured ostraca. She appears to be on her toes as if dancing and is playing the flute. Bes, the most prevalent motif on the figured ostraca, is depicted possibly tattooed on her thighs. There is also an abundance of convolvulus leaves, again a common motif on the figured ostraca. Ostraca 2399, now in IFAO, also depicts a young girl bending as though she were in a dancing pose, naked except for a cape or veil, playing a double flute.

More fragmentary evidence was found in house S.E. I (Fig. 8), consisting of the remnants of a group scene (Bruyère 1923, 122). All that remained was four pairs of feet, two papyriform columns and a stool. Although incomplete, the image does suggest a seated figure on a stool, attended by servants, surrounded by convolvulus leaves, and consequently similar to the pavilion

Figure 7. Drawing of a water colour of a wall painting, Deir el-Medina, House S.E. VIII. Based on Vandier D'Abbadie (1938, PL. III).

and outdoor scenes on the figured ostraca. Bruyère (1923, 132) attempted to reconstruct this scene in light of these images. However, he believed the seated figure to be Hathor breast feeding her son Horus and consequently reconstructed the design by adding cow horns and a sun disk. The surviving evidence does not, in my opinion, provide any justification for this. Brunner-Traut's reconstruction (1956, fig. 5) was more plausible, with the breast feeding woman wearing the tripartite wig as seen on the figured ostraca discussed (Figs 2, 5, 6). There are also a number of similarities between the two wall paintings. Both were painted on whitewashed backgrounds, both have a triple striped edge delineating the scene. This pattern is located on the vertical edge in the case of the image of the dancer and on the horizontal edge in the case of the group scene. Also, as previously noted, there is an abundance of convolvulus leaves. Bruyère (1939, 264) believed the two wall paintings were painted 'without a doubt' by the same artist, whom he believed was also responsible for two wall paintings of Amenhotep I and his mother Ahmose-Nefertari among the same convolvulus leaves, as recorded by Budge (1914, no. 37993–37994). It is worth noting that both the wall paintings in S.E. I and S.E. VIII are multi-coloured, unlike the next group of scenes, which are confined to grey and white. Perhaps these multi-coloured scenes were the most significant; indeed Bruyère (1939, 60) described S.E. I as the most lavishly constructed and decorated of all *lits clos* (these structures will be discussed in detail below). Alternatively, the residents of these houses may have simply been more affluent. Perhaps poorer households, who could not afford such lavish wall paintings, owned similar images but on ostraca.

Evidence of the depiction of the god Bes also remains on the walls of at least seven houses (Bruyère 1939, 57–58). All scenes are drawn in white over a grey background. Two types can be distinguished; Bes is either depicted in profile making music and dancing or depicted frontally with arms and wings outstretched. In some houses, the god is depicted more than once. For example, in house N.E. X the remains of three panels were collected from the debris. Two side panels show Bes in profile, dancing, playing the tambourine and double flute. A third panel, which would have stretched above the door, shows Bes frontally with outstretched arms and wings, holding in his hands bouquets of lotus flowers (Bruyère, 1939, 58). These profile depictions give a sense of movement and life to the music and dance scenes. Profile depictions were the norm in Egyptian representation, frontal depictions being a rarity. However, nearly all the depictions of Bes, on the figured ostraca under consideration are frontal, with the depiction of the god, generally incorporated into the legs of the bed. He is most often seen with his hands on his hips, in a squatting pose, wearing a kilt and feathered headdress. In only one occasion (Berlin 21451) is he depicted making music, in another example of frontal depiction (Shäfer

Figure 8. Drawing of wall painting, Deir el-Medina, House S.E. I. Based on Bruyère (1923, 133).

1916, fig. 10). It is clear that on both the figured ostraca and the wall paintings Bes was a key component, incorporating both profile and the more unusual use of frontal depictions.

Another image of interest to this study was found in house C.V. II; this shows the bottom half of a scene depicting a woman at her toilette. As in previous cases, the figures are drawn in white over a grey background (Bruyère 1939, 311). Although it is not clear from the illustration, Bruyère (1939, 59) suggested she was being assisted by a naked slave. The inclusion of a naked female attendant is consistent with several images on the figured ostraca, for example Fig. 5. Consequently, although the evidence is limited, there are undeniable similarities between the figured ostraca and the depictions on the walls of houses. A possible explanation for these similarities could be that the former were practice pieces for the latter. However, we are still left with the question of why these images, which do not appear in the formal repertoire of Egyptian art, appeared in prominent positions in domestic contexts.

The archaeological context of the images may provide some insight. All images discussed have been found on the exterior of brick structures, which Bruyère called '*lits clos*' because they reminded him of a type of Breton bed in Britanny of that name (Bruyère 1939, 57). Of the seventy houses excavated by Bruyère these structures/*lits clos* were found in twenty-eight homes, always in the first room of the house (Bruyère 1939, 61). He identified seven different types. They were constructed in the corner of the room, often incorporating the exterior walls of the house. On average, they were 1.70m long, 0.80m wide and 0.75m in height. They were fully or partially enclosed and had a small staircase of between three and five brick steps, situated on the exterior wall (Bruyère 1939, 56–57). They were commonly plastered and white-washed; some had evidence of decoration still surviving. Bruyère (1939, 137) initially believed these structures to be 'mit-autel, mit lit d'accouchment', that is, both a cultic installation used to worship ancestors and a utilitarian feature, used to give birth in. Since Bruyère published this material there has been much debate regarding the purpose of the *lits clos* (Cherpion 2006, Koltsida 2006). Romano (1990, 26–27) advocates a more practical use, as a piece of functional furniture, questioning if villagers would have given up ten per cent of the rooms floor space to a birthing bed, used perhaps once a year. While this is a valid point, given the dimensions of the feature, the suggested alternative does not seem very plausible, as a couple would not have slept comfortably together in this structure, nor would it have been an ideal place for sexual relations. In addition the enclosed and raised nature of the feature would have hampered rather than assisted child birth. The location of the structure, in the first accessible room of the house, is itself an unlikely delivery spot, being very public in what would have been a crammed and enclosed village. Overall, the evidence suggests the structures had a cultic, as opposed to secular, function.

A cultic function is also suggested by the presence of niches or alcoves cut into the inner walls of the *lits clos* (Bruyère 1939, 60). Bruyère suggested these could be for stelae or busts, but they could also have contained the items depicted on the figured ostraca under consideration, for example mirrors, perfume cones, offering dishes *etc.* However, this is only speculation as Bruyère did not find any items in situ. Recesses were also found at ground level which could accommodate a table of offerings. This combination of niche and recess was present, for example, in house S.E.VIII, where the image of the dancer was found (Bruyère 1939, 273). Houses C.V and C.VI also contained a niche opposite the lit clos; as previously discussed, remains of Bes decorations were found in both these houses. Interestingly, the *lit clos* was not included in the original layout of the Eighteenth Dynasty houses. There is evidence that houses built at that time were later altered to include this feature, for example house N.E. II (Bruyère 1939, 61). It would appear that the *lit clos* became a desirable element in the Ninetieth and Twentieth

Dynasty home, therefore being concurrent with the figured ostraca under consideration. It is possible that it became a vehicle for display of important images and the niche and recess acted as receptacles for items possibly of cultic significance. Given the prominent position in the first room of the house, both the structure of the lit clos and the decoration may have acted as markers of prestige and status. The images may have been expressions of personal piety or celebrations of births and marriages; however, without direct textual references we can only speculate.

In the general repertoire of New Kingdom figured ostraca there are a limited number of parallels with divine representations which may help us understand the meaning and significance of the images under consideration. Ostraca HO49 from the Ashmolean Museum (Oxford) shows Renenutet, a serpent goddess of the harvest and divine nurse, sitting on a throne-like chair, breastfeeding a child. A male servant stands in front of her with his arm outstretched holding possibly a piece of fruit, in an offering gesture. This ostraca was given to the museum by Sir Alan Gardiner and is said to be from Deir el-Medina but has no firm provenance, nor is it published. Piece MM14006 from the Medelhavsmuseet in Stockholm depicts Isis suckling Horus (Fig. 9). The inscription gives the title, 'Isis Lady of the Sky' and names private individuals of Deir el-Medina. Similar images of goddesses breast feeding kings have been found inscribed in stone in chapel 15E at Deir el-Medina. This includes a much damaged image on a stela (Bruyère 1929, pl. VI) and another one on a fragmentary block of limestone (Bruyère 1929, fig. 20). In light of these images it is possible that the depictions of breastfeeding women at Deir el-Medina, were seeking to emulate the goddesses and that these women were looking for their protection and blessings for their children. However, it is also possible that the images had another layer of meaning. In the tomb of Nefer-renpet at Deir el-Medina (TT336) we see Mertseger, the serpent goddess of the site, breast feeding the tomb owner who, we are told, becomes a child again in another time (Bruyère 1929, fig. 21). Perhaps the images of breast feeding women did not solely relate to protection of the child in this life but also to his rebirth.

There are no clear divine parallels for the images from the 'women on beds' dataset. The closest similar depiction is part of the divine birth scene at Deir el-Bahri (Naville 1898, pl. XLVIII), portraying queen Ahmose sat on a bed. The god Amon, who has taken the form of her husband Tuthmosis I, sits opposite her, handing to her the ankh sign. These images were used to legitimatize the rule of Hatshepsut as divine daughter of both a god and a king. The bed is clearly visualized as the place of sexual union and the joining together of the couple for procreation. The idea of the bed as the place of sexual activities is also seen in the *Turin Erotic Papyrus* which, although unprovenanced, may have originated from Deir el-Medina (Toivari-Viitala 2001, 147). Based on items depicted and epigraphy, it is certainly contemporaneous with the figured ostraca (Toivari-Viitala 2001, 147). The papyrus has been divided into twelve scenes by scholars, with scene six showing a naked girl lying on a bed, trying to entice a man lying under the bed (Omlin 1973, pl. X). Images of beds themselves, in Egyptian representation are rare, consequently their context is significant.

Future Research

Work to date clearly demonstrates that the images of women on beds and in pavilions, on the figured ostraca, form a coherent group. The inclusion of repeat motifs and themes suggest these scenes were created using set formulae which held meaning and significance to their creators and viewers. It is highly likely that similar imagery was depicted on the walls of houses at Deir

Figure 9. Figured ostraca showing Isis sucking Horus, with names of private individuals from Deir el-Medina. MM14006, Present location. Medelhavsmuseet Museum, Stockholm. Courtesy of the Medelhavsmuseet Museum, Stockholm.

el-Medina. These representations must be viewed within the context of the society in which they were created. Therefore, in order to broaden our understanding of these images, my future research will assess their relationship to contemporaneous material culture. I will initially focus on three dimensional female figurines, examples of which were found at the site of Deir el-Medina in their hundreds, both on beds and standing alone (Bruyère 1939, 109). Many have similar iconography to the figured ostraca under consideration, for example convolvulus leaves and the inclusion of a mirror and child. I also intend to explore the objectification of the female form, which blossoms in New Kingdom Egypt. This includes the use of female figurines on mirror handles which, as objects themselves, were depicted frequently on the scenes under consideration, often held by naked servant girls.

Bibliography

Andreu, G. (2002) *Les Artistes de Pharaon: Deir el-Médineh et la Vallée des Rois*. Paris, Réunion des Musées Nationaux.
Anthes, R. (1943) Die deutschen Grabungen auf der Westseite von Theban in den Jahren 1911 und 1913. *Mitteilungen des Deutschen Archäologischen Instituts, Abteilung Kairo*, 12, 1–68.
Brunner-Traut, E. (1955) Die Wochenlaube. *Mitteilungen des Instituts für Orientforschung*, 3, 11–30.
Brunner-Traut, E. (1956) *Die Altägyptischen Scherbenbilder (Bildostraka) der Deutschen Museen und Sammlungen*. Wiesbaden, Steiner.
Bruyère, B. (1923) Un Fragment de Fresque de Deir el Médineh, *Bulletin de L' Institut Français d'Archéologie Orientale*, 22, 121–133.
Bruyère, B. (1928) *Rapport sur les Fouilles de Deir el Médineh (1927)*. Cairo, Institut Français d'Archéologie Orientale.
Bruyère, B. (1929) *Mert Seger á Deir el Mèdineh*. Cairo, Institut Francais d'Archeologie Orientale.
Bruyère, B. (1939) Rapport sur les Fouilles de Deir el Médineh (1934–1935). Cairo, *Institut Français d'Archéologie Orientale*.
Bruyère, B. (1952) *Rapport sur les Fouilles de Deir el Médineh (1945–1946 et 1946–1947)*. Cairo, Institut Francais d'Archeologie Orientale.
Bruyère, B. (1953) *Rapport sur les Fouilles de Deir el Médineh (1948–1951)*. Cairo, Institut Français d'Archéologie Orientale.
Budge, E. A. W. and Wallis, T. (1914) *Wall Decoration of Egyptian Tombs: Illustrated Examples in the British Museum*. London, Bernard Quaritch.
Černý, J. (1935) *Catalogue des Ostraca Hieratiques et Non-Litteraires de Deir el- Médineh*. Cairo, Institut Français d'Archéologie Orientale.
Cherpion, N. (2006) La Danseuse de Deir el-Medina et les Prétendus << lits clos>> du Village. *Revue des Archéologues, Historiens d'art et Musicologues de l'UCL*, 4, 11–26.
Demarée, R. J. (2002) *Ramesside Ostraca*. London, The British Museum Press.
Friedman, F. D. (1994) Aspects of Domestic Life and Religion. In L. H. Lesko (ed.), *Pharaoh's Workers: The Villagers of Deir el Medina*, 95–117, London, Cornell Press.
Keimer, L. (1940–45) *Études d'Égyptologie*. Cairo, Imprimerie de l'Institut Francais d'Archéologie Orientale.
Kemp, B. (1979) Wall Paintings from the Workmen's Village at El'Amarna. *Journal of Egyptian Archaeology*, 65, 47–53.
Koltsida, A. (2006) Birth-bed, Sitting Place, Erotic Corner or Domestic Altar? A Study of the so-called elevated bed in Deir el-Medina houses. *Studien Zur Altägyptischen Kultur*, 35, 165–174.
Meskell, L. (1998) Archaeology of Social Relations in an Egyptian Village. *Journal of Archaeological Method and Theory*, 5/3, 209–243.
Meskell, L. (2000a) Cycle of Life and Death: Narrative Homology and Archaeological Realities. *World Archaeology*, 31/3, 423–441.
Meskell, L. (2000b) Spatial Analysis of the Deir el-Medina Settlement and Necropoleis. In R. J. Demarée and A. Egberts (eds), *Deir el-Medina in the Third Millennium AD: A Tribute to Jac. J. Janssen*, 259–273, Leiden, Netherlands Instituut Voor Het Nabije Oosten.
Meskell, L. (2004) *Object Worlds in Ancient Egypt: Material Biographies Past and Present*. Oxford, Berg.
Naville, E. H. (1898) *The Temple of Deir el-Bahari*: Part II. London, Egypt Exploration Society.
Omlin, J. A. (1973) *Der Papyrus 55001 und seine Satirisch-erotischen Zeichnungen und Inschriften*. Torino, Edizioni d'Arte Fratelli Pozzo.
Peck, W. H. (1985) Review of 'Ancient Egyptian Figured Ostraca in the Petrie Collection, by Anthea Page, *Journal of Egyptian Archaeology*, 71. Reviews Supplement, 14–16.

Peterson, B. E. J. (1974) *Zeichnungen aus einer Totenstadt: Bildostraka aus Theben-West, ihre Fundplätze, Themata und Zweckbereiche mitsamt einem Katalog der Gayer-Anderson- Sammlung in Stockholm*, Vols. 1 and 2. Stockholm, Medelhavsmuseet.

Romano, J. F. (1990) Daily *Life of the Ancient Egyptians,* University of Pennsylvania, USA.

Schiaparelli, E. (1923–1927) *Relazione sui lavori della Missione Archeologica Italiana in Egitto*, 1903–1920, Vol. 1. Torino, R. Ministero Della Publica Instruzione.

Shäfer, H. (1916) Ägyptische Zeichnungen Auf Scherben. *Jahrbuch der Königlich Preussischen Kunstsammlungen*, 37, 23–51.

Toivari-Viitala, J. (2001) *Women at Deir el-Medina: A Study of the Status and Roles of the Female Inhabitants in the Workmen's Community during the Ramesside Period*. Leiden, Nederland Instituut Voor Het Nabije Oosten.

Valbelle, D. (1985) *Les Ouvriers de la Tombe: Deir el-Médineh à l'époque Ramesside*. Cairo, Institut Francais d'Archeologie Orientale du Caire.

Vandier D'Abbadie, J. (1937) *Catalogue des Ostraca Figurés de Deir el Médineh*, Vol. 1 and 2. Cairo, Institut Francais d'Archeologie Orientale du Caire.

Vandier D'Abbadie, J. (1938) Une Fresque Civile de Deir el Médineh. *Revue D'Égyptologie*, 3, 27–35.

Vandier D'Abbadie, J. (1957) Deux ostraca figurés. *Bulletin de l'Institut Français d'Archéologie Orientale*, 56, 21–34.

Vandier D'Abbadie, J. (1946) *Catalogue des Ostraca Figurés de Deir el Médineh*, Vol. 3. Cairo, Institut Français d'Archéologie Orientale du Caire.

Vandier D'Abbadie, J. (1959) *Catalogue des Ostraca Figurés de Deir el Médineh*, Vol. 4. Cairo, Institut Français d'Archéologie Orientale du Caire.

Werbrouck, M. (1932) Ostraca á Figures. *Bulletin des Musées Royaux d'Art et Histoire*, 5, 106–109.

Werbrouck, M. (1953) Ostraca á Figures. *Bulletin des Musées Royaux d'Art et Histoire*, 25, 93–111.

The Egyptian ascension mythology of the Old Kingdom and the phenomenon of star phases

Bernadette Brady

From as earlier as the period of the ascension mythology of the Old Kingdom of Egypt humanity has created stories of divine beings. These beings are those who upon their deaths ascend to the gods or they are beings that act as intermediates between the gods and humanity. Generally an analysis of these stories takes the path of biblical studies, theological debate, or in the case of the Egyptian texts, a consideration of grammar and the acceptance of a lack of understanding of intention (Faulkner, 1969 [2004], viii). However, this paper offers an approach to these stories from the perspective of cultural astronomy and it examines the nature of one of these narratives with an understanding of naked eye astronomy and an awareness of the potential for astronomy to be mythopoeic.

The pyramid texts of the Old Kingdom are a body of work which are the oldest known collection of religious writings. James Allen (2005, 1) list ten known engraved tombs which contain pyramid text. These texts are described by Samuel Mercer (1956, 1) as being, 'remnants of much earlier literature than that of the historical period in Egyptian history.' As complete as these text are Raymond Faulkner (1969 [2004], v) points out that they pose problems for any translator as the mythological intent is obscure.

The actual subject matter of the pyramid texts is that of the journey of the deceased king to his after life, and is described by Mercer (1956, 9–10) as:

> "... they [the texts] deal with the moral fitness of the deceased king, with his purification and embalming, with his divine parentage, his transformation into an eternal spirit, that is, his freedom from death, his declining in the West and rising in the East, his life as an imperishable star... they deal with his journey to the sky, by means of the boat of Rēʻ, or on a ladder, or on the wings of Toth, ..."

The Kings of the Old Kingdom period held a cosmic position within their nation. They were living gods, born of divine parentage, and upon their death they had the right to re join the eternal circumpolar stars. This dual and cyclic role of the divine king in both the heavens and the earth is seen in Davis (1977, 165–6) comments when he describes the role and power of the King in the following manner, 'In the ascent, the King re-enters the realms of celestial divinity and is given royal authority, just as he entered the world of men and was invested with similar authority.' The King's resurrection after death was considered essential for the continued well-being not only for the kingdom but for the entire cosmos. His actual divinity was defined by his unique procession of an immortal soul and his duality of existence was the subject of many utterances from the pyramid texts one example being, 'The spirit is bound for the sky, the corpse is bound for the earth', (§ 474) – Faulkner's translations are used throughout the text unless otherwise stated.

The narrative of the ascension myth follows a particular pattern. It begins with statements around the King's divine birth, and generally his own proclamation announcing that he cannot be lost to death, 'because I am a great one, the son of a great one, whom Nūt bore.'(§1145). From his divine birth he has the right to rule the mortal world as he will, after his resurrection, rule the cosmos.

The texts then speak of the King's death and his journey through the western horizon into the earthly Netherworld. However when in the Netherworld his sister Isis, also the star Sophis (Sirius) blocks the path of Osiris in claiming the dead king for the death, 'I am Isis; go behind me, O Osiris the King.' (§44). In some utterances Isis became pregnant by the dead King so she could give birth to the next divine figure, the next heir to the throne, 'Your sister Isis comes to you rejoicing for love of you. You have placed her on your phallus and your seed issues into her, she being ready as Sothis, and Har-Sopd has come forth from you as Horus who is in Sothis.' (§632).

The King begins his journey to the eastern horizon where he is destined to resurrect as a god. This is the birth place of the gods, and as the King himself states, 'I am ferried over thereon to yonder eastern side of the sky, to the place where the gods fashioned me, wherein I was born, new and young.' (§344) and, 'The King stands on the eastern side of the celestial vault, there is brought to him a way of ascent to the sky…' (§326).

From this point in the mythology we are repeated told that the king is a star, that the king is destined for the imperishable stars, and that he rises using a celestial ladder, step by step or that he has, 'soared to the sky as a heron, I have kissed the sky as a falcon' (§891–892). Or other texts have the King proclaiming, 'My head is a vulture; I will ascend and rise up to the sky. The sides of my head are the starry sky of the god;' (§1303). His ascent is described either by bird or ladder or the hand of Nūt, his mother. Whatever is his method of ascent his journey is always towards the celestial north, 'I ferry across in order that I may stand on the east side of the sky in its northern region among the Imperishable Stars, who stand at their staffs and sit at their East; I will stand among them…' (§1000–1001).

The timing of the King's ascension is less clear. There are many lines of text that talk of the dawn light, rising in the dawn and being like the morning star however there are other texts that appear to make contradictory statements, 'I am born in the night; come, for I am born'. (§714), and also, 'I was conceived in the night, I was born in the night, I belong to those who are in the suite of Rēʽ, who are before the Morning Star'. (§132), and, 'May you traverse the sky, being united in the darkness; may you rise in the horizon, in the place where it is well with you.' (§152).

A longer passage reads:

> 'O King, free course is given to you by Horus,
> you flash as the Lone Star in the midst of the sky,
> you have grown wings as a great-breasted falcon,
> as a hawk seen in the evening traversing the sky.'
> (§1048–49).

Or the same passage in Allen's (2005, 134) translation for found in the tomb of Pepi I:

> 'Ho Pepi! You will be given passage by Horus. You will wear the headband as the sole star in Nut's midst, your winds will grow as those of a big-breasted falcon, as a facon seen in the evening.'

Also other utterances have the king announce, ' I am a star which illumines the sky, I mount up to the god that I may be protected, for the sky will not be devoid of me and this earth will not be devoid of me for ever. I live beside you, you gods of the Lower Sky, the Imperishable Stars.' (§1454–1455). Utterances such as this describe the king becoming a star which rises in the evening light. This star is located in the lower sky (the northern part of the sky) and he is destined to join the circumpolar stars.

Faulkner who in 1969 published a translation of the Pyramid Texts accepted the ascent of the king occurred in the evening sky. However, he tentatively suggested that the Lone Star described as the king in his ascent was that of Venus as the evening star. He pointed out that the morning star of some texts, which seem to suggest the ascent occurring in the morning light would be referring to Phosphorus, Venus at dawn and the Lone Star (in Mercer's translation this is named the 'unique star' while in Allen's it is the 'sole star') belonged to a second set of texts, separate to the first, in which the Lone Star was Venus as Hesperus, setting in the west in the evening. He argued that the passage which likens the ascent of the King as a star which is like 'a hawk seen in the evening traversing the sky' (§ 1048) supported a western horizon setting Venus and that reference to the east and the star rising were scribal errors. Faulkner (1966, 160–1) implies however that this suggestion is simply because he cannot see any other potential candidate for the King's bright star.

However the sheer repetition of the words, 'eastern horizon', and 'rising' in the text does tend to suggest that this is the intended meaning; at least the translators leave us in little doubt. The King having died goes to the west. With the help of others, amongst who is his sister the star Sophis (Sirius), he moves to the eastern horizon where he rises as a bright star. This bright star then joins the circumpolar stars representing the eternal or imperishable gods.

The simple fact is that this is exactly what some stars do, they set in the west and after a period of time they will rise just after sunset and then for a length of time varying from days to months depending on the star, they will act in the manner of a circumpolar star, thereby being seen to join the imperishable stars.

The Forgotten Star Phase-Types

Star phases are clouded with a great deal of misinformation and most people, including many scholars, assume that there are only two ways that the stars move; that being a star is either circumpolar, or a star will rise and set and sometimes disappear from view from the night sky. There are in fact three ways that a star can move for a given location, but before discussing this forgotten phase it is worth noting the possible reasons for this confusion. The source of this omission can, most likely, be traced back to the emergence of Greek astronomy.

Goldstein and Bowen (1983, 331) argue that from the period of Hesiod (active around 700 BC) to the time of Eudoxus (*c.* 408–*c.* 347 BC) Greek astronomy was focused on the construction of star calendars. These calendars, or later the parapegmata, were unconcerned with the nuances of star phase types. If a star was selected as a date marker it was done so for its ability to be, for example, the morning rising star at a key time of the year. It was of little interest if later in the year, when another star became the morning rising star that that star behaved very differently. Practicality was the motivation of these calendars, not accuracy of the understanding of naked-eye astronomy. This can be seen in Hesiod *Works and Days* where he used the stars as an instrument of common cultural knowledge in order to blend seasons, calendar and labours. Hesiod (2006, 19) linked grape picking to the rising of Arcturus before the dawn light 'But when Orion and Sirius come into mid-heaven, and rosy-fingered Dawn sees Arcturus, then cut off all the grape clusters...' While harvesting and ploughing were linked to the Pleiades (Hesiod 2006, 13), 'When the Pleiades, daughters of Atlas, are rising, begin your harvest, and your ploughing when they are going to set. Forty nights and days they are hidden and appear again as the years moves round, when first you sharpen your sickle.' Hesiod thus referred to one of type of star phase – the disappearance for a period of time from the night sky – but for him its use of timing was important not the need to acknowledge it as just one type of star phase. Indeed Hesiod's work reveals a sky put to work: a freely available, non-location specific and a consistent perpetual calendar. Hesiod's star calendar actually freed the individual from tracking the date by observing the location of the rising or setting sun. Such solar observations were depended on a location specific view of the horizon and thus could not be transported to another location. A star calendar however would work over the entire area of the Greek world enabling merchant and sailor to move around the different kingdoms and still be able to observe the sky to ascertain the date. In this way the constellations may have had their mythology but Hesiod's use of the sky was a pragmatic focus on the farmer's, merchant's or sailor's view of the horizon. Users of a Greek star calendar were not required to know the difference between a morning rising star belonging to one type of phase and a morning rising star belonging to another, they only needed to note that the star *was* the morning rising star.

This stripped-down style of naked-eye astronomy evident in the Greek star calendars continued into the Roman era. When Ovid (43 BC–17/18 AD) produced his *Fasti*, the actual terms he employed for describing the different sun/star/horizon events show his unconcern or unawareness of the star phases (Keightley 1839, 206–7). Each one of Ovid's star rising or setting terms are ambiguous when applied to the actual star phase types themselves. Ovid used six terms for his calendar stars but in fact 16 terms are required if one is to clearly describe the star phases. Claudius Ptolemy (90–168 AD) however was aware of the different phases and wrote of them in his work *Phases of the Fixed Stars*; however did not name the different stages he only described them (Ptolemy 1993, 6). Ptolemy's work however was the exception and his astrological and astronomical texts were far more widely used then his calendar text. Thus when scholars sought to understand the star phases they appear to have turned to the traditional calendar text of Hesiod and Ovid with their striped down star phasing descriptions.

Thus in 1969 when Faulkner was struggling to place the contents of the pyramid texts into naked eye astronomy he, like most other scholars, seemed to be unaware of the different star phases and, not understanding that a set of stars can rise in the early evening light and take on the motion of circumpolar stars, preferred the idea of a bright setting Venus rather than a rising star.

Thus in describing the star phases and in order to avoid confusion this paper employs the following terms. The term *heliacal* is used exclusively for the transitional star/sun/ horizon events happening at sunrise, while the term *acronychal* is used exclusively for the transitional star/sun/horizon events that are happening at sunset. A transitional event is defined as an event in a star phase when a star's observed behaviour is moving to the next part of its phase. For the non-transitional events the terms morning rising or evening setting are used. The terms 'true' and 'apparent' are used as defined by Ptolemy, to distinguish from a sun/star/horizon event where the star is exactly aligned with the sun (true) and that of a sun/star/horizon event where the star can still be seen (apparent).

Star Phase Types in brief

For any sub-polar latitude, there are three distinct groups of star movement visible in the night sky.

Group 1 – Always visible, never rising or setting

The first group are those stars that will be visible every night, for the whole night. These stars are never seen to touch the horizon and appear in the sky at sunset and will still be visible in the sky at sunrise. These stars are called Circumpolar Stars.

Group 3 – Sometimes visible, sometimes rising or setting

This third group is generally assumed to be the only other group of visible stars. These stars have a pattern of returning to visibility in the night sky on a set date after a set period of invisibility (failing to rise during the night). Consequently at certain times of the year the star is not seen over the course of the entire night. This period of invisible begins when the star is seen to set at sunset and it ends when the star is seen to rise at dawn. These stars can never act in a circumpolar-like manner and belong to the group or phase type named by Ptolemy as Arising and Laying Hidden (ALH). A star will belong to this ALH phase if in its position on the celestial sphere it is located on the opposite side of the ecliptic to that of the observer. These stars were referred to in the Pyramid texts as the Unwearying stars (Faulkner 1966, 157). Unwearying because they followed a perpetual pattern of entering the Netherworld and 'dying' to be born again some weeks or months later, and this pattern to be repeated every year. These stars were tied to the mortal world of eternal repetition of life and death probably because they, when visible, were always seen to touch the horizon, the mortal world, at some time in the night.

Group 2 – Always visible, sometimes rising or setting

This group consist of stars which may rise or set at some time in the night, yet will be visible for every night thought-out the year. At a set date a star from this group will appear to act like a circumpolar star. It will be visible in the night sky at sunset and will fail to set by the time of the following dawn. This circumpolar-like behaviour begins when the star is seen to rising at sunset and ends when the star is seen to set at dawn. This group or phase type contains the stars that Ptolemy defined as undergoing a period of Curtailed Passage, (CP). A star will belong to the CP phase if in its position on the celestial sphere it is located on the same side of the ecliptic to that of the observer but was still low enough in declination that it was not a circumpolar star.

Both star phase types of ALH or CP appear to be mythologized within the Egyptian Pyramid Texts but it is stars that belong to the CP phase, that embrace all of the components of the ascension mythology of the king.

The star's observed behaviour for the CP phase is as follows:

Stage 1: The star is seen to be setting during the night, eventually at a set date in the year the star will be just seen to set at sunset. (Apparent evening settings for CP phase type). However unlike other stars that are seen to set at sunset and thus enter the Netherworld, and begin a period of invisibility for a series of night, these stars of the CP phase will instead appear to 'die' on the western horizon but will then appear to deny death by rising again later on that *very same* evening.

Potentially from the Egyptian mythological perspective, such a star has overcome death.

Stage 2: The star will then continue to set and then rising again later in the same night but each rising will be at an earlier time each successive night until finally it is seen to be rising at sunset. (Apparent acronychal rising for CP phase-type).

Stage 3: At the next sunset the star appears in the eastern night sky having *already* risen and stays above the horizon for the whole night – acting like one of the circumpolar stars.

Stage 4: Successive nights reveal the star becoming visible at sunset in a position higher in the sky, appearing to move upwards into the sky in a series of steps.

Thus the star that has already defied death by not disappearing into the Netherworld, has now rose in the north east, like a great bird, or on a ladder. It proceeds to ascend to the heavens, step by step and is observed to behave like a circumpolar star.

Stage 5: The star is then seen to rise at an earlier time every night until eventually one evening it is seen rise in the dawn light. However it will be visible later that night and seen to set in the early evening. (Apparent morning rising for the CP phase-type).

As the year progresses the star moves into setting at sunset – the apparent evening setting as described in Stage 1.

Thus the movement of stars which belong to this phase produce a phenomenon which is identical to that described in the pyramid text of the king's ascension to the sky as a star. Thus if the argument of this paper is accepted and the ascension myth of the king is considered the mythologizing of the curtail passage (CP) star phase then the next question is; which star or stars would best fill Faulkner's quest for the Lone Star?

At the latitude of Egypt all stars that lie north of the ecliptic will undergo the CP phase describe above. However some stars will have curtailed passage and behave like a circumpolar star for only a few days, while others may maintain their curtailed passage for some weeks some even a few months. However there is one star that is very bright, and for the period of 2400 B.C.E. maintained it circumpolar-like behaviour for 80 days and was linked, through the horizon, with Sirius. This star is Vega, with a magnitude of 0.3, in the constellation the Lyra. It was also known to the Greeks as the Great Swooping Vulture who carried the souls of the dead to the other world.

At the time of the creation of the pyramid texts every year in early May, Vega and Sirius would have been seen together on the horizon (see Fig. 1). Sirius would have been setting and this marked the beginning of its journey into the Netherworld as it would not be seen again for around 45 days. However at the same time Vega would have been rising and beginning its ascent to the circumpolar stars.

There are other bright stars that could strongly compete for the title of Lone Star but none have such a mythic and naked-eye astronomy relationship to Sirius. Notwithstanding this tantalising star and mythology parallel, the aim of this paper is not however to suggest an identity of Faulkner's Lone Star but rather to illustrate the potential mythopoeic nature of the star phases themselves.

Additionally this style of myth, where a divine being descends or ascends from the heavens was not exclusive to the Egyptians. They appear in the Greek concept of the *theioi Andres,* men who are born as immortals of a divine parent and whose life was deemed virtuous or of great service to mankind. Upon their death they ascended to the heavens (Talbert 1975, 421–2).

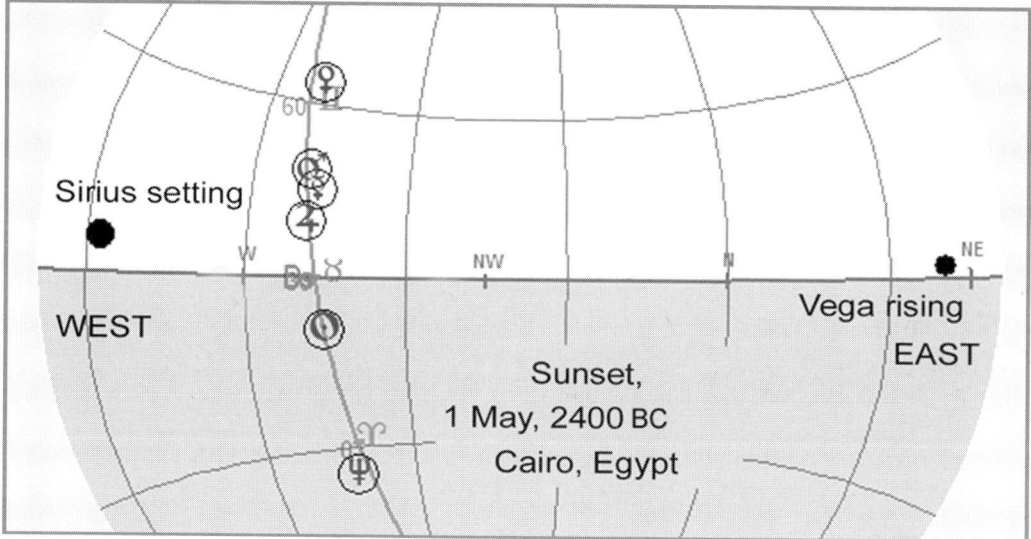

Figure 1. Sunset for 1st May 2400 B.C.E. for the latitude of Cairo, Vega and Sirius are both on the horizon. Sirius is entering the Netherworld on the western horizon beginning it period of 45 days of invisibility while Vega is rising on the eastern horizon and begins it period of acting like a circumpolar star.

Diodorus of Sicily ([1939]) summed this up when he spoke of Hercules,

> As regards the gods… men of ancient times have handed down to later generations two different conceptions: certain of the gods, they say, are eternal and imperishable… But the other gods, we are told, were terrestrial beings who attained to immortal honour and fame because of their benefactions to mankind, such as Heracles,… and the others who were like them.

Where the idea of men becoming gods was not acceptable within a given theology then as Nordell (1889, 342) states, emerging from the Babylonian and Jewish traditions we find angels. Special beings who may or may not have wings, who sit on the hand of God and carry his message to the world of mortals:

> 'Praise the Lord from the Heavens, …praise him, all his angels … Praise him Sun and Moon, praise him all you shinning stars… Ps 148:2 (1972).

Or from the New Testament:

> 'The poor man died and was carried by the angels to Abraham's bosom.' Luke 16:22.

This paper has focused on one particular star phase type showing that the sequence of its observed movements bears a strong parallel to the narrative of the ascension of the king in the Pyramid Text. Additionally, by reconstructing the night sky for the period of the Pyramid Text a sequence of rising and settings can be observed which involved the bright stars Sirius and Vega. Sirius, known to the Egyptian as the star Sophis was associated with Isis while later the Greeks saw Vega as a great vulture who carried souls to the heavens. Consequently based on the visual evidence of the movement of the stars as well as the mythological themes this paper has argued that the ascension myth of the king is in part a mythic description of this star sequences. Furthermore this stellar theology may also be the seed within the Greek notion of humans that become gods and later the idea of a star's movements contributing to the origins of the doctrine of angels or intermediate beings who move between the mortal world and the heavens. Allen (2005, 1) considers the religious themes within the Pyramid Text as having a strong link to the biblical world. By acknowledging a link between Ptolemy's star phase of CP (curtailed passage) and the mythology of the ascension of the king then the sky itself becomes one of the cultural vehicles for the transmission of these religious myths.

Bibliography

Allen, J. P. (2005) *The Ancient Egyptian Pyramid Texts.* Atlanta, Society of Biblical Literature.
Anthes, R. (1959) Egyptian Theology in the Third Millennium B.C. *Journal of Near Eastern Studies,* 18, 169–212.
Campion, N. (2000) Babylonian Astrology: Its Origin and Legacy in Europe. In Selin, H. (ed.) *Astronomy across Cultures, The History of Non-Western Astronomy.* Dordrecht/Boston/London, Kluwer Academic Publishers.
Conman, J. (2003) It's about Time: Ancient Egyptian Cosmology. *Studien zur Altägyptischen Kultur,* 31, 33–71.
Davis, W. M. (1977) The Ascension-Myth in the Pyramid Texts. *Journal of Near Eastern Studies,* 36, 161–179.
Diodorus, S. ([1939]) The Library of History of Diodorus Siculus. III. Available: http://penelope.uchicago.edu/Thayer/E/Roman/Texts/Diodorus_Siculus/6*.html [Accessed 9 October, 2010].
Donadoni, S. (ed.) (1997) *The Egyptians.* Chicago/London, The University of Chicago Press.
Dunand, F. and Zivie-Coche, C. (2004) *Gods and Men in Egypt, 3000 BCE to 395 CE.* London, Connell University Press.
Faulkner, R. O. (1966) The King and the Star-Religion in the Pyramid Texts. *Journal of Near Eastern Studies,* 25, 153–161.
Faulkner, R. O. (1969 [2004]) *The Ancient Egyptian Pyramid Texts.* Oxford, Clarendon Press.
Goldstein, B. R. and Bowen, A. C. (1983) A New View of Early Greek Astronomy. *Isis,* 74, 330–340.
Hesiod (2006) *Hesiod. Works and Days, Theogony and the Shield of Heracules,* New York, Dover Publications Inc.
Keightley, T. (1839) Fasti by Ovid, Introduction and Notes. Available: http://manybooks.net/support/o/ovid/ovidetext058fsti10.exp.html [Accessed 10 October 2005].
Lesko, L. H. (1991) Ancient Egyptian Cosmogonies and Cosmology. In Shafer, B. E. (ed.) *Religion in Ancient Egypt.* New York, Cornell University Press.
Mercer, S. A. B. (1956) *Literary Criticism of the Pyramid Texts,* London, Luzac & Company.
New King James (1972) The Holy Bible. Nashville/Camen/New York, Thomas Nelson.
Nordell, P. A. (1889) Old Testament Word-Studies: 9. Angels, Demons, *etc. The Old Testament Student,* 8, 341–345.
Ptolemy, C. (1993) *The Phases of the Fixed Stars.* Berkeley Springs, WV, The Golden Hind Press.
Talbert, C. H. (1975) The Concept of Immortals in Mediterranean Antiquity. *Journal of Biblical Literature,* 94, 419–436.
Wells, R. A. (1992) The Mythology of Nut and the Birth of Ra. *Studien zur Altägyptischen Kultur,* 19, 305–321.

Goddesses Gone Wild: the Seven Hathors in the New Kingdom

Asha Chauhan Field

The Seven Hathors are the sevenfold form of Hathor, a complex goddess, who has aspects ranging from maternal to vengeful, as well as numerous links to other goddesses. The aim of this paper is to investigate the role of the Seven Hathors within the New Kingdom. Many Deities exist in groups of seven as hebdomads, but the seven Hathors seem to have a more particular role and function within the Egyptian pantheon. I will first look at how this role is most often summarised before addressing the evidence this is based on. The idea that they determined the fate or destiny of children is most often put forward; they are seen as Fates and *"lesser spirit like fairy godmothers"* (Kitchen 1999, 445). This interpretation clearly stems from the appearances of the Seven Hathors in tales specifically; the "Doomed Prince" and the "Two Brothers." In this way, the Seven Hathors have often become defined by their most well-known occurrences. The nature of their appearance in tales shall be examined first.

Their appearance in "The Doomed Prince:" p. Harris 500, vs. 4, 3–4.4

> It is a coming the Hathors did
> In order to command for him fates
> And they said he will die by the crocodiles
> Or the snake or likewise the dog.
>
> (Translated from Gardiner (1932, 1) for English version of full tales see Lichtheim (1976, 200)

So here the Hathors appear and foretell of three possible 'fates' for the newly-born prince. The nature of the fates relates solely to the manner of his death, and they give no indication of the length of his life span or life's achievement. It is never discovered whether the prediction of the Hathors comes true as the end of the tale is lost. There is the possibility that the overall outcome may well be that none of the assigned fates come to pass.

Here is their equally brief appearance in "The Tale of the Two Brothers," where they appear to foretell the fate of the wife of Bata. Papyrus d'Orbiney 9. 8–9.9.

> The seven Hathors came to her and they said with one mouth she will die by the knife
>
> (Translated from Gardiner (1932, 19) for English version of full tales see Lichtheim (1976, 207))

Bata's wife is not born, but made directly by Khnum. So once again fate is pronounced soon after the individual is given life. Notice that no other aspect of her future is covered. The nature of fate (*s3y*), in these examples, seems to suggest that man disposes of his own free will and that "fate" is limited to the length of a person's life or merely the means of their death. In both cases death is caused by the hostility of others, be they animal or otherwise.

The roles the Seven Hathors play in these two tales seem to be consistent with each other, but is it accurate to interpret them as a foretelling of fate? In both cases they predict the means of a violent death. The goddesses predict the means of death (not any other aspect of 'fate'); in both cases the cause of death, is unnatural, violent and sudden; the final outcome of both tales is unclear. It is important to note that the Hathors here do not appear to act in a way similar to the Greek fates. The Greek fates were thought to govern all events in a person's life; the Seven Hathors have a much more limited power displayed here. There is no evidence that they knew a person's life span, could control death, or would even be able to enforce the method of death they assign.

The truth of the Seven Hathors' prediction is unverified in both tales. In the case of "The Doomed Prince," the ending is lost; he is shown escaping the snake, but the ultimate outcome is unknown. Death by the crocodile, the dog or even escaping his 'fate' entirely remains possibilities. In "The Two Brothers" it seems unlikely that Bata's wife has a happy ending. Having betrayed and plotted to kill her husband during the course of the tale, he is then able to "judge her". The specifics of this are never dealt with, but one still cannot be completely sure that she received the death penalty or that it involved knives.

The Seven Hathors are referred to outside of narratives in this period; most commonly, in magic spells. The spells that feature the Hathors mostly fall into two categories: against animals, (bites, stings and poison); and against pain: this, often animal-induced. These types of spells are either for healing or for warding off wild animals. There is also one Ramesside love charm that seems to inspire an animalistic desire. So magic spells also show the Hathors are associated with the causes of violent death, but does this support the idea that they assign or predict it?

The possibility of an association with Isis and Horus mythology is thrown up by this spell against poison. Here, they are acting against a cause of violent and unnatural death, suggesting that they may, after all, have some power over the agents of the fates that we have seen them foretell in the tales:

> Out Quickly [Come] out following my utterance, O poison
> the 7 wounds at the forehead of the 7 Hathors,
> for the beautiful Horus is (or was) with them......O poison ......every scorpion who is in the limbs of (born of (<it is> [I]sis who says it, it is she who repeats it (Massart 1957, 176)

Another spell for catching scorpions:

> The seven children of Pre stood lamenting they made seven knots in their seven bands and the hit the one who was bitten (with them). May he stand up healed for his mother Isis in the night when he was bitten the protection is a protection of Horus! (Borghouts 1978, 77–78)

Perhaps the deaths of supernatural beings like demons were perceived by the Hathors. The following spell to ward off a 'Samanna-demon' incorporates the image of the Seven Hathors (Rochholz 2002, 66). Here, a group of Hathors perceive the demon's violent demise at the hands of Horus as part of the spell's magical narrative.

P. Leiden I 343+ 345, rto 5.12; 10.3–4; vso 13

> Another conjuration
> See I have outfaced you samana-demon! See [i have out]faced the one who is submerged in the limbs of NN born of NN- like someone who flies up stops and settles on a high place...... don't you know me samma-demon(But) see, it is MaiA who knows me, namely that I belong to the Itrq[...]AnA- tribe, those who speak with the snakes
> I have lots of words against you ! From the big pitcher of Seth I have drunk them
> Then the gods will learn of your death and then the Hathor goddesses will learn
> that your heart (HAty) has left (Borghouts 1978, 21)

The Hathors are evoked during the fight between Horus and the samanna-demon. The Hathors here seem to be acting as goddesses who perceive death, though this seems to be after the fact, rather than as a premonition. It could instead be that they hold some sway over the action of the unruly, violent force that the demon itself represents.

An exception to this form of spell is p. Leiden I 349, which shows evidence of action being taken against the Seven Hathors, their mouths are sealed This has been interpreted as a way to prevent them from pronouncing the manner of death and thus avoiding the 'fate' (Buk and Stricker 1940, 55).

p. Leiden 349 verso III, 6: another spell against scorpions: (Buk and Striker 1940, 59 and 62)

> I shall tell you of seven reports words (???).......
> you're on. You for daughter for her mother.
> I shall make the mountain strike
> (damaged line)...
> the big -tree, that stands
> In the presence of Re when he rises, to seal the mouth of.......
> seal the mouth of the seven Hathors from the house of Ptah in..
> (damage)

Most of this text is much damaged. This makes contextualising this reference to the Seven Hathors difficult; the incantation seems to include a magician actively sealing the mouths of the Seven Hathors. The power of seven as a magical number is seen throughout the spell. So the use of the Seven Hathors could just be a continuation of this. Compared to the other examples, where the Seven Hathors are mentioned in spells against scorpions, this is the only time when they are bound or sealed; presumably, this prevents them from intervening, and can be contrasted with spells asking for them to act. It has often been interpreted from their role in tales that sealing their mouths prevents them from declaring the manner of someone's death, in this case caused by a scorpion sting. It is similar to their predictions for the doomed prince, a death caused by an animal (Luck 1985, 21).

The Seven Hathors, it seems, can also be mentioned in spells unrelated to animals or deadly injury such as: a spell to get rid of a headache:

p. Hier BM (Gardiner) V verso 61–2

> I shall cause to fly The Seven Hathors in smoke to the sky (Rochholz 2002, 68–69)

This spell contains several threats of displacing the world order, with other threats made against gods, such as the Cow of the Hathor, Sobek, Anubis, Horus, and also of course the Seven Hathors. Though there is also this parallel example in a text from Deir-el Medina where, once again, they are acting against scorpion stings.

> I shall cause to fly The Seven Hathors burned up to heaven (Raue 2005, 256)
> (Rochholz 2002, 69)

Raue (2005, 256) seems to believe these spells are evidence of the Hathors being directly or indirectly responsible for the pains the body endures after a scorpion sting, and that this is the reason they are threatened and also have their mouth sealed in p. Leiden 349 . This interpretation of the texts is not wholly convincing, as other deities are threatened with similar fates within both spells, and p. Leiden 349 also mentions other things (that are unknown due to the damage) being sealed. The action taken against the Hathors is not unique within any of these spells.

Turin 137.12, seems to support this idea more concretely; the spell is against poison, though parts are damaged and the exact role of the spell unknown.

Turin 137.12:

> one found The Seven Hathors, the mistresses of the fire, which comes out of the inside (Rochholz 2002, 67)

This seems to support the idea that the Hathors are responsible for or have control over the physical pain of a scorpion sting.

Finally, the Ramesside love charm: a magical use of the Hathors that does not involve death or poison, but does refer to animals and fire.

Ramesside love charm/a love charm for a man, Cat. des ostraca heratiques littares de Deir el Madineh, tome I, No. 1057 pls, 31 and 31a:

> Hail to thee, O Re-Harakhte, Father of the Gods!
> Hail to you, O ye Seven Hathors
> Who are adorned with strings of red thread! Hail
> to you, ye Gods lords of heaven and earth! Come
> (make) (make) NN (f.) born of NN come after me,
> Like an ox after grass
> Like a servant- after her children
> ,Like a drover after his herd!
> If you do not make her come after me,
> Then I will set (fire to) Busirisg and burn up (Osiris). (Rochholz 2002, 67) (Smither 1941, 131)

Notice the language used to describe the woman's desire; the Seven Hathors help to generate this pursuing force, illustrated with bovine imagery. The influences the Seven Hathors exert in love spells appear to be somewhat volatile. It does not say how long the effect will last; it is possible that this is more a of a lust spell than a love spell, intended to generate only a temporary and torrid desire.

So what role do the Seven Hathors play in the spells? It is open to a variety of interpretations: to drive out pain and poison; protect the body; act against animals and demons; inspire an animalistic desire. They are also associated with fire and the sky/heaven. There is a possibility that the Seven Hathors, rather than causing pain, are somehow perceived as being in charge of all the elements of chaos that could also somehow cause a violent death. These seem to mostly take the form of wild animals, such as those in the"Doomed Prince." The Seven Hathors are also prominent in healing spells and spells against the bites and stings of animals. Perhaps the Hathors' frequent association with predictions of violent manners of death, seen in the tales, arises from their control over or affiliation with the agents that cause death and not from their ability to predict the future; the ability to come out and remove pain may be due to their having control over the poison itself. The Seven Hathors seem to have power over the human body and its reaction to outside forces causing desire, pain and death.

The seven Hathors are also shown in some artistic depictions, though these are rare. There is a small, ivory pot Louvre E 2529, dating from somewhere between the 18th to 20th dynasties; it has been identified as an "ointment-jar" though there is no real indication of what it may have held. The Seven Hathors are shown here on one side of the box. It has not been widely published, and the main source is Desroches-Noblecourt (1953, 29) who concludes that *there is no doubt that (il ne fait aucundoubteque (aucun doubte que))* the Seven Hathors are here appearing before a woman in order to foretell the fate of a newborn, but this seems an over-ambitious assertion. Of course, Desroches-Noblecourt (1953) based this opinion on the appearance of the Seven Hathors in tales where they are shown determining the circumstances of death, but we should also look at this in the context of the image on the other side of the box. The four faces of the pot portraying images of the Seven Hathors, wild animals, a fish caught in a net between two people and birds also caught in a net by someone in a boat. Out of these four sides the Seven Hathors may seem not to fit in; all of the other images contain animals, so at first glance the Hathors would be 'the odd one out', but perhaps the best way to interpret the Hathors is to try to consider them as part of this group, linked by this one object. The other illustrations on the jar can be seen as possibly alluding to tomb scenes and Horus and Seth's battle in the marshes, so the Hathors' role in a narrative might be the connection here. The possibility of there being some sort of animal on the boat would perhaps best be explained by a narrative thread too. But if it is not a narrative, how can these images work together?

Chaos is represented by the animals of the marshes and deserts (Robins 2000, 69). If you think of these wild animals as symbolic of wild forces, then the fish and birds are in nets, and so show chaos controlled. The Hathors appear before someone who holds a staff of some kind, so perhaps they are controlled too. There is the possibility that the Hathors are another form of chaos, possibly connected with violent deaths and animals, as we have seen in other occurrences, and that now they are confined just as much as a bird in a net, held in the power of the magician. Maybe the odd one out, or rather the before-shot is the side where the animals are seen to run free, uncontrolled by nets or magic. There is also the possibility that perhaps the Hathors here were benevolent deities, the woman's interaction with them having allowed the other scene, where chaos is controlled, to be possible; they are somehow in control of or are a part of these forces; the animals are confined with their permission.

There is only one personal monument showing the Seven Hathors: the Hanover 1935.200.226 and London BM EA 473 Block. It is the once piece of evidence from the new kingdom that stands against the idea of associating the Hathors with wild animals. Hathor, as a singular goddess, is often seen as a nurturing patron deity, protecting individuals. This monument seems to show that this role could be taken on by her sevenfold form in this period. The Hathors do not fully emerge from the stone; the faces do not appear to be very detailed they may also be holding hands; they are certainly touching. All this is similar to details on the ivory pot and would seem to indicate the strength and unity of their identity as a group who act together as one, possibly *speaking with one mouth*. There is an inscription on the back, containing a section that may be referring to *The Seven Hathors*.

> (my) children descendants
> In the presences of them saying before them lets one that best had I... be spoken
> among people who are (with me) is everyday

Von Bissing and Blok (1926, 85) believed there was a possibility that a section of lines 4 and 5 could be referring back to the Seven Hathors: "in the presence of them." However, the connection is not entirely clear, and to whom it refers can be interpreted in a number of ways. It could also refer to the people around Amenemhat or you can relate this part of the sentence to the children; the speaker wishes that they might daily stay amongst people. If the opening of the inscription refers to the Seven Hathors, this suggests that being in the presence of the Seven Hathors could offer some protection or benefit. The idea that the Seven Hathors could help your descendants does not fit in with their role in tales; you would not really want them with your child if they can only appear in order to foretell a violent death. Perhaps having them with you every day has an entirely different connotation that would have offered some benefit; possibly protection from wild forces. However, it must also be pointed out that this is the only known monument of its kind. It may show that a monument to The Seven Hathors was able to function to protect your descendants, but if there was a strong belief in this there would perhaps be more examples. It does show that it was appropriate to use the Seven Hathors in this context, which suggests that they can appear in the context of formal religion and monuments rather than just spells, tales and household religion.

The role of the Seven Hathors developed in later periods when they became a part of formal religion. Surviving Greco-Roman temples show the Seven Hathors given individual titles. The depictions of the Seven Hathors, in temples especially, often show them as part of a hebdomad with individual titles linked to place names. They are often depicted with instruments denoting an association with music, and there is the song of the Seven Hathors from the temple at Dendra. Seven bovine Hathors also appear in the form of seven celestial cows who are portrayed with four rudders representing the four cardinal points. These ladies are accompanied by the "bull of the west, lord of eternity". Generally, the Seven Hathors, in this period, become much more of an extension of the singular Hathor, showing many of her attributes in a hebdomad form. I would argue that, in most temple depictions, they are no longer the Seven Hathors of the New Kingdom, but simply a hebdomad form of Hathor. The grouping of seven is used for many other gods such as Knum and the Seven Hathors are Hathor's form of that idea; and though people in the Greco roman period may have been aware of the special role the Seven Hathors could play, their connection to fate death or chaos is not represented within temple depictions. Also, their role in magic evolves. The Seven Hathors seem to be present in love spells throughout the Coptic Period, wherein they become the seven virgins (Schimidt 1 (Meyer and Smith 1999, 94)).

Concerning the interpretation of the role of The Seven Hathors in the New Kingdom, I think I have clearly shown that comparisons with fairy godmothers and the Greek fates are more misleading than helpful. They are somehow instead to be associated with wild animals and the forces of chaos. Their role in spells seems to show them acting over physical feelings within the body: pain and lust. As well as protecting the body, they have a very personal impact on humans and how the forces of chaos may act against an individual. In this period, they are always shown acting in unison. They are shown speaking with one mouth, and depictions of them in art and in the "Tale of Two Brothers" seem show them as joined and connected, holding or touching hands. The under-developed facial features on the Hanover/BM block and the way they are depicted on the ivory pot seem to further enforce this idea. The Seven Hathors seem to channel 'mob mentality' or herd behaviour. Their group identity suggests that they might also have diminished individual responsibility; the many-faced group somehow distances the Hathors from the idea of a singular Hathor as a personal or maternal goddess you could relate to as an individual. They have a wildness brought about by being part of a group. I by no means suggest that the nature of the Seven Hathors was static and fixed. To quote Hornung (1982, 98–99):

> Egyptian deities do not present themselves to us with as clear and well defined a nature of that of the gods of Greece. The condition of god we encounter here is fluid, unfinished, changeable…it is evidently unnatural for Egyptian gods to be strictly defined. Their beings remain a fluid state to which we are not accustomed.

However, I think a better understanding of the Seven Hathors than has previously been published has emerged through my research.

Bibliography

Borghouts, J. F. (1978) *Ancient Egyptian magical texts* translated by J. F. Borghouts. Leiden, Brill.

Buk, A. and Stricker B. H. (1940) Teksten tegen schorpioenen naar pap. I 349. Leiden, Rijksmuseum van

Desroches-Noblecourt, C. (1953) Un 'lac de turquoise': Godets à onguents et destinées d'outre-tombe dans l'Égypte ancienne. *Monuments et Mémoires publiés par l'Académie des Inscriptions et Belles-Lettres* 47, 1–34.

Gardiner, A. H. (1932) *Late Egyptian Stories Bibliotheca Aegyptiaca I.* Brussels, Fondation égyptologique reine Élisabeth.

Hornung, E. (translated by John Baines) (1982) *Conceptions of God in Ancient Egypt: The One and the Many*. Ithaca New York, Cornell University Press.

Kitchen, K. A. (1999) *Poetry of Ancient Egypt*. Paul Åströms Förlag Documenta Mundi Aegyptiaca 1. Jonsered, Sweden, Coronet Books Inc.

Luck, G. (1985) Arcana Munsi: Magic and the Occult in the Greeek and Roman Worlds. Baltmore and London.

Marvin, W. and Meyer, R. S. (1999) *Ancient Christian Magic: coptic texts of ritual power*. Princeton, Princeton University Press.

Massart, A. (1957) The Egyptian Geneva Papyrus MAH 15274. MDAIK 15: 172–85.

Raue, D. (*1999*) *Heliopolis* und das Haus des Re: eine Prosopographie und ein Toponym im Neuen Reich. *Abhandlungen des Deutschen Archäologischen Instituts Kairo, 16*. Berlin.

Raue, D. (2005) *Die Sieben Hathoren von Prt* in Studies in Honour of Ali Radwan SASAE 34 vol. 2: 247–61.

Robins, G. (2000) *The Art of Ancient Egypt*. London, British Museum Press.

Rochholz, M. (1996) Zu den paletten für die 7 salböle. *Wege öffnen: Festschrift für Rolf Gundlach zum 56 Geburtstag*, 223–231.

Rochholz, M. (2002) Schöpfung, Feindvernichtung, Regeneration: Untersuchung zum Symbolgehalt der machtgeladenen Zahl 7 im alten Ägypten. Wiesbaden, Harrassowitz in Kommission.

Von Bissing, F. W. and Blok, H. P. (1926) Eine Weihung an die sieben Hathoren. *Zeitschrift für Ägyptische Sprache und Altertumskunde*. 61, 83–90

Von Bissing, F. W. and Blok, H. P. (1926) in The Zeitschrift für Ägyptische Sprache und Altertumskunde. 61, 83–90 Abb.

The early precursors of tomb security

Reg Clark

This paper discusses the early development of tomb security in Ancient Egypt from the Late Palaeolithic (*c.* 21,000–12,000 BC) up until the end of the Naqada IIIA period (*c.* 3300–3150 BC). This forms part of my ongoing PhD thesis on tomb security that aims to examine, by tracing the development of tomb architecture from the Predynastic Period onwards, whether many of the architectural elements that were incorporated in Egyptian tombs were a consequence of the need to protect the burial, rather than the result of monumental or religious considerations.

The Late Palaeolithic, an early beginning

The earliest intentional burial discovered in the Nile Valley was that of a child found at Taramsa Hill near Qena, which dates to the mid Middle Palaeolithic period (*c.* 55,000 BC), and consisted of little more than a scrape in the ground hastily filled with gravel (Vermeersch, *et al.* 1998, 475–8.) Later graves from the Upper Palaeolithic Period have also been excavated at Nazlet Khater 4 (*c.* 31,000 BC), in Upper Egypt and Wadi Kubbaniya (*c.* 19,000 BC) near Aswan (Wendorf and Close 2005, 12–14).

However, it is not until the Late Palaeolithic Period (*c.* 21,000–12,000 BC) that we have perhaps the first evidence of humans in the Nile Valley taking any further steps to protect their dead other than providing a back-filled pit by way of burial. It occurs in some graves found in a cemetery in Lower Nubia. The area, known as Site 117, is situated three kilometres north of Wadi Halfa on the east bank of the Nile, and is just south of Jebel Sahaba (Midant-Reynes 2000, 63–4). Here, some 12,000 to 14,000 years ago (*c.* 12,000–10,000 BC) fifty-eight bodies were interred in shallow oval pits. In addition to their soil backfill, in the majority of the burials thin undressed flat sandstone slabs (Fig. 1), varying from 25 to 50cm in width, had been used to cover the graves (Wendorf 1968, 954–7).

Figure 1. Sectional sketch of the typical arrangement of stone slabs over the graves at Site 117 at Jebel Sahaba (Drawn by the author after Wendorf 1968, fig. 4).

As the first instance of a culture tending for its dead in the area of the Upper Nile (Geus 1991, 57), these burials are possibly evidence of a desire to protect the tomb beyond the level one might ordinarily expect at this early date, as most early graves usually consisted of no more than a shallow pit scooped out of the desert backfilled and perhaps covered with a mound (Dodson and Ikram 2008, 31).

As for the purpose of the slabs, one possibility is that they were placed there to protect the burials from the depredation of wild animals, hunting dogs or possibly wind erosion, as due to their shallow nature the graves would have been inherently vulnerable to disturbance. Alternatively, the slabs may have been placed to simply form a memorial, but if their purpose was only that, then there would be no need to cover the entire grave itself, as a simple grave marker would have sufficed.

The Neolithic and Predynastic Periods

The Faiyum Neolithic Culture

The appearance of this culture occurred in the north of Egypt shortly before 5000 BC, suggesting a complete change in the nature of habitation in the Nile Valley, from what was fundamentally an Epipaleolithic hunter-gatherer society, to an economy based mainly on the production or obtaining of food (Butzer 1976, 9). However, this society seems not to have established any permanent settlements and rather to have relied on transient cereal cropping and fishing (Wenke 1989, 136). As a result no evidence has been found of any cemeteries or burials from excavations of the lakeside settlements (Arkell and Ucko 1965, 146).

Merimde Beni Salema

Evidence of the very first burials associated with settlements (c. 5000 BC), was found at one of the earliest established communities in Egypt that was situated some thirty-seven miles to the northwest of Cairo at Merimde Beni Salema in Lower Egypt (Grajetzki 2003, 1). For about one thousand years the inhabitants interred their dead in graves, most probably within the abandoned remains of their settlements (Kemp 1968, 22–33). When excavated the graves were found to consist of shallow oval pits (Fig. 2) in which bodies were placed in a contracted position wrapped either in skins or mats, and sometimes covered with the vestiges of plant remains before backfilling (Midant-Reynes 2000, 116). No other attempt appears to have been made to offer additional protection or security to the burial.

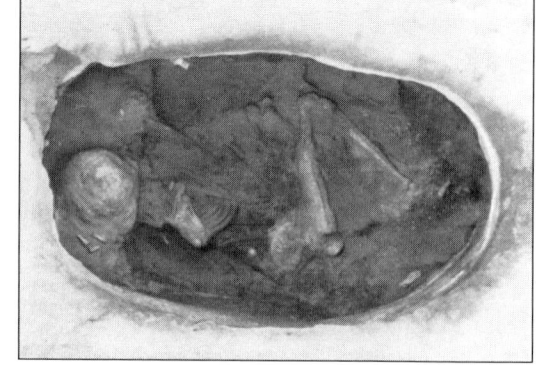

Figure 2. A shallow pit burial at Merimde with the body in a contracted position (Junker 1929, Taf. IIa).

The Badarian Culture

In Upper and Middle Egypt the earliest phase of the Predynastic era is the Badarian, *c.* 5000–4000 BC, named after the Middle Egyptian site at el-Badari (Lacovera 1988, 20; Wenke 1989, 137). The main sites were Deir Tasa, Hemamieh, Matmar and Mostagedda which, most likely, settled by *c.* 4000 BC (Wenke 1989, 137).

During the Badarian period, the typical burial was made in an oval or circular pit, with the contracted body within being swathed in a mat or goatskin (Fig. 3), and accompanied by an assortment of grave goods (Adams 1988, 17). After interment had taken place, the grave would be backfilled and it is generally thought, covered with a mound of gravel or sand (Reisner 1936, 1–3; Badawy 1954, 26; Dodson and Ikram 2008, 31).

From the viewpoint of tomb security, Reisner (1936, 245) has suggested that the function of a mound, during the Predynastic period, might have been both to provide further protection for the burial itself and to act as a focus for the provision of cult offerings for its occupant. Thus, Reisner (1936, 367) further argued, that the mound may have provided the prototype upon which the majority of later Egyptian grave superstructures were based.

Although, a mound of gravel would hinder a grave robber or foraging animal to a certain extent, the purposes behind this practice may have been utilitarian. Firstly, the excess soil from the pit would have been greater in volume than that necessary to backfill it, due to the addition of the body and grave goods, and thus was simply piled on top. Secondly, the mound may have been left there so that the extra soil compensated for the otherwise inevitable depression caused by the settling of the backfill over the grave's surface. Such depressions in graves are well known and caused by two factors. 'Primary depressions' that are caused by settling of the 'back-fill' in the pit and 'secondary depressions', which are caused by the decomposition and collapse of the abdominal cavity and the concomitant release of gases (Dupras, *et al.* 2006, 109).

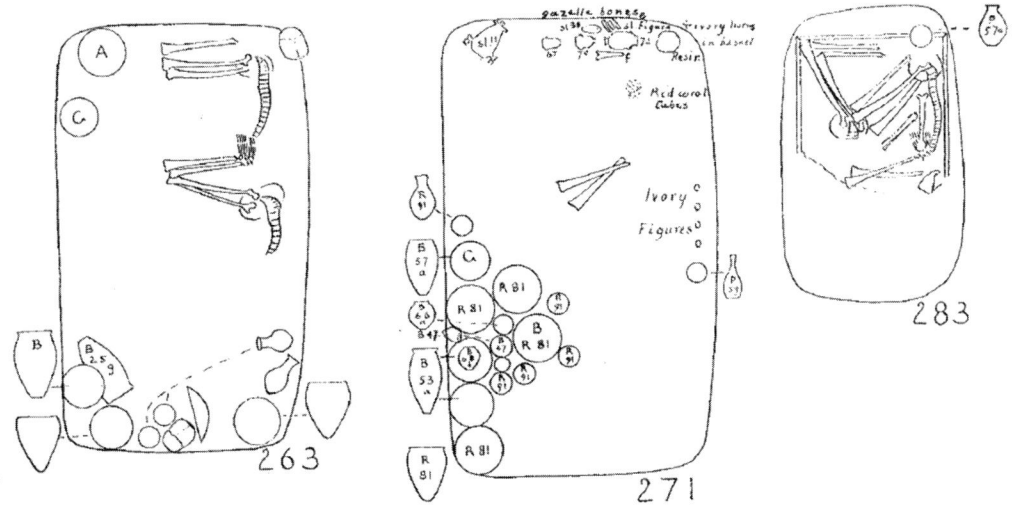

Figure 3. Courtesy of Österreichische Akademie der Wissenschaften. Assorted Badarian graves (Brunton and Caton-Thompson 1928, Pl. IX).

Figure 4. Graves with 'mounding' in 1918 at the Canadian military cemetery at Brookwood. (Courtesy of the Brian Parsons Collection).

This 'mounding' can be seen in the case of modern graves (Fig. 4), which once dug and subsequently closed, have the excess fill piled up over the burial to allow for settlement (Pers. comm. John Clarke of Brookwood Cemeteries Ltd. 17th March 2009). In addition, the mound also minimises the problem of cracking along the edge of the pit where the looser new fill breaks away from the compacted surround. (Connor 2007, 109). Concerning Predynastic burials, the presence of such a mound is still matter of debate (Reisner 1936, 1–3; Badawy 1954, 26; Dodson and Ikram 2008, 31), and whether this architectural feature was retained or levelled out is unknown and it is not easy to ascertain today whether it existed at all (O'Connor 2009, 153).

In either case, there is ample evidence that contemporary grave robbery was taking place, even at this early date, and was developing into one of the most unfortunate aspects of ancient Egyptian culture (Hoffman 1990, 143). At el-Badari Brunton reported that a grave at cemetery 5100 'contained a plundered female body, showing that the robbing of these graves began soon after the actual interments' (Brunton and Caton-Thompson 1928, 9). Indeed, Anderson (1992, 57–61) in her quantitative analysis of the Badarian burials excavated by Brunton, has demonstrated that grave robbers were regularly robbing the 'highly visible tombs' of high status individuals during this period. Her statistics show that larger graves possessing in excess of three grave goods were more frequently either robbed or 'disturbed' than those containing less, and that the looting was actually occurring during the Badarian period itself. Therefore, it is evident that tomb robbers were targeting the wealthier graves and becoming a problem even at this early date.

It is tempting to wonder therefore, whether from the point of view of the security of the tomb, such a 'tell-tale' mound was all that desirable in the long term, and to speculate that perhaps the grave was left to settle out level, as in the cemeteries of today.

Some of these burials excavated by Brunton at el-Badari were found to contain sticks and matting at the sides of the graves, which he concluded might have been the remains of some sort of collapsed 'roofing', intended to prevent sand and gravel from falling on the body. These, Brunton suggested, may have been made into a type of rigid 'tent' to keep the body free of sand, and would explain the apparent lack of any other roofing arrangements in the graves (Brunton and Caton-Thompson 1928, 18 and 20).

Another possibility is that this sort of 'tent' structure may have also been introduced to pre-empt other post-interment problems likely to arise with a burial. Firstly, it may have been intended to prevent any disruption by animals, which is a common cause of disturbance in burials, as scavenging carnivores, omnivores and rodents are all known to consume corpses (Connor 2007, 86). Secondly, perhaps it formed a secondary physical barrier in addition to the backfill to deter the intrusions of grave robbers. Thirdly, it could also have circumvented the need for a 'giveaway' mound over the pit, by obviating the inevitable 'depression' over the grave.

If we accept this latter scenario, the mound would then no longer be required to replace the settling and compacting fill of the grave pit and, as a result, offer additional security from the risk of being located by tomb robbers. Alternatively, if the mound *was* indeed considered to be a desirable feature of the grave and concealment was not an issue, the 'tent' may have possibly been installed as a support to prevent the mound's inevitable collapse from the effects of primary depression.

El-Omari

In Lower Egypt, just northeast of Saqqara and located at the base of Jebel Tura near Helwan, three settlement sites and two cemeteries dating to around 4000 BC mark the remains of the el-Omari culture (Hoffman 1990, 192). Contemporary with the late phase of Merimde Beni Salema, at el-Omari the dead were buried in shallow graves or into the remains of old storage pits (Mortenson 2005, 717), adjacent to the settlement or the individual habitation. In the graves, some of the bodies found were covered in reed mats and occasionally accompanied by a pot or a sporadic flint. The interments themselves were backfilled with sand or domestic debris. Noteworthy is that a number of the graves were covered by mounds of stones. The limestone blocks used in their construction were randomly placed and varied in size and number, some being quite large (Fig. 5) such as in graves F1–11 (Debono and Mortensen 1990, 72–5). Therefore, here too we possibly have an example of stones being used at an early date to protect a grave from disturbance by erosion, animals or robbers. A method that only appears again in the Early Dynastic period at cemeteries such as Abu Roash (See Klasens 1957, 64–5, Plates VIII.1–2 and IX.1).

Figure 5. Burial at el-Omari Cemetery F, showing heaps of stones covering grave F11 (Debono and Mortensen 1990: Fig. 42.2).

The Buto Maadi Culture

Also in Lower Egypt, at the start of the fourth millennium BC, evidence of another distinct, but slightly later culture appears with the Buto Maadi Culture, the sites of which are located to the east of the Nile, south of Cairo (Seeher 1999, 455). The major evidence comes from the three main cemeteries at Maadi, Heliopolis and Wadi Digla where, unlike at Merimde Beni Salama, cemeteries were distinctly separated from the settlement. The 600 burials recorded so far have shown no evidence of any sophisticated grave architecture (Fig. 6), as the majority of the interments were solitary burials in simple oval pits (Rizkana and Seeher 1990, 97; Seeher 1992, 226–8). It appears from vestiges of wood found in some of the graves, that a few of the bodies discovered may have been wrapped in mats and possibly covered in branches. (Rizkana and Seeher 1990, 98). However, unlike their contemporaries in Upper Egypt and Nubia, whose burials were now becoming progressively more elaborate, these graves are notable for the comparative paucity of grave goods or personal adornments (Wengrow 2006, 36).

In this case no attempt seems to have been made to improve the security of the grave, other than the branches, which may have been placed there to thwart scavenging animals.

Naqada I

The next phase of the Predynastic era is the Naqada I period, which dates to *c.* 3900–3650 BC (Hassan 1988, 138). The period was named after the largest site of Naqada and the majority

Figure 6. Burial with grave goods at Maadi, grave No. MA45 (Rizkana and Seeher 1990, Pl. III) Courtesy of J. Seeher.

of related sites can be found along the extent of the Nile from Hierakonpolis, in the south, to Abydos in the north. Although there are other sites at el-Badari and the Faiyum, the key centres are located at Abydos, Hierakonpolis and Naqada (Bard 2005, 31).

The majority of burials were simple oval or rectangular graves (Castillos 1982, 173–8) covered by rudimentary roofs of wood branches and twigs (Figs 7–8) supporting a covering of soil (Hoffmann 1990, 146). Petrie and Quibell describe the typical tombs in their original excavation report as 'vertical pits, with the body laid on the floor; and the pit in all wealthy tombs was roofed over with beams and brushwood' (Petrie and Quibell 1896, 18).

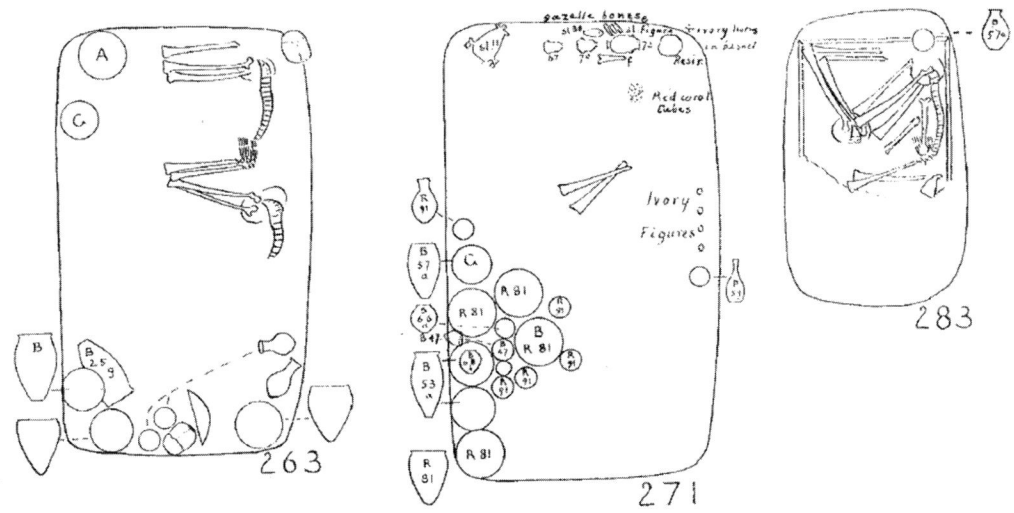

Figure 7. Rectangular shaped graves from Naqada (Petrie and Quibell 1896, Pl. LXXXIII).

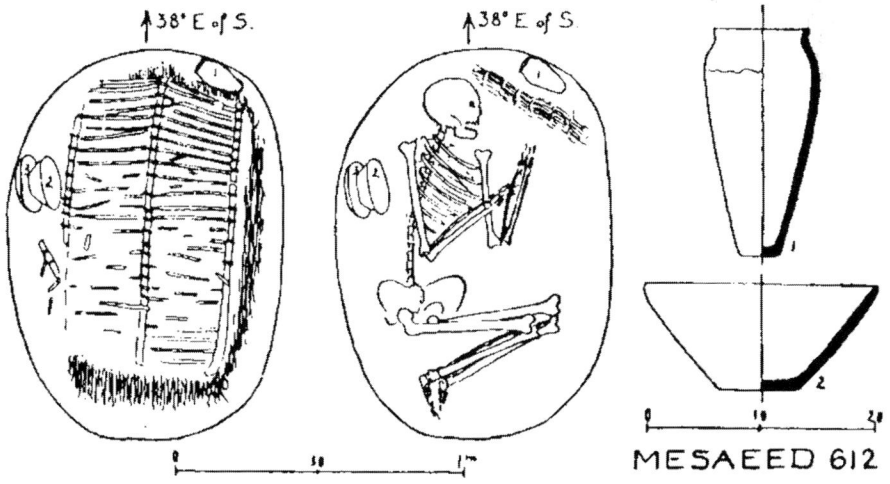

Figure 8. Wood and stick 'roofing', which Reisner describes as a 'tray', in tomb 612 at Mesaeed (Reisner 1936, fig. 182).

The inclusion of these roofs in the grave suggests that the previous discussion regarding the security aspects of the Badarian period applies here too. Possibly the roof was designed to thwart tomb robbers and scavenging animals as well as to prevent the previously mentioned 'primary' and 'secondary depressions'. Therefore, it could be regarded as another form of defensive measure to protect the tomb itself. In addition, the need to support a grave mound, if indeed there were one, should also not be excluded from the realm of possibilities.

Naqada II

In Naqada II (*c.* 3650 BC–3300 BC) (Hassan 1988, 138) the majority of burials take the form of the now ubiquitous grave pit, each containing a single body in a crouched position (Midant-Reynes 2000, 187).

That, during this period, a number of ordinary, non-elite, graves were also being systematically targeted by robbers is particularly evident from an excavation at Cemetery HK43 at Hierakonpolis (Friedman 1997, 2), which is dated to Naqada IIA–IIC (Friedman 1998, 5). Here the pattern of soil disturbance indicates that the robbers knew exactly where individuals were buried, and that what they were searching for (possibly a copper necklace) was situated around the deceased's neck. In some cases a cut in the fabric and matting surrounding the neck is the only indication that they were at work at all, such was the accuracy of their digging (Friedman 1997, 2). Interestingly, the likelihood that these graves at HK43 may have been marked with a mound of sand or stones, of which no trace remains today (Friedman 2008a, 20), may just have assisted the robbers in locating their booty.

However, it is during Naqada II that improvements in construction methods in tombs of the elite also become increasingly discernable. For example, grave walls in some of the more sophisticated tombs were now reinforced with liners. These, when present, were either made of a wattle of sticks and wicker, or wooden boards that kept the surrounding soil or sand away from the body. In both cases the tomb would have been roofed over with mats or sticks and possibly plastered with mud (Ayrton and Loat 1911, 8; Reisner 1936, 1; Baumgartel 1960, 125).

Whilst linen shrouds or mats were generally preferred to animal skins for wrapping the body during this period, the appearance of 'wealthier' burials also signals the first emergence of coffins. Initially these were made of basketwork, later also clay and eventually wood (Midant-Reynes 2000, 187). Additionally, for perhaps a selected few, the use of brick linings in graves was now becoming increasingly frequent (Wengrow 2006, 122), the function of which was undoubtedly to consolidate the sides of the grave, prevent the collapse of the surrounding soil or gravel matrix, and possibly support a roof (Podzorski 2008, 98). Although, in some cases, roofs were also constructed without a brick liner to support them, as in the unlined tomb B101 in Cemetery B at Abadiya (Petrie and Mace 1901, 33).

Possible purposes behind many of these developments, which permitted a larger grave to be constructed, may have been the further segregation of the body from contact with the surrounding ground itself (Spencer 1982, 33), and to provide additional storage space for grave goods, which were now more often placed further away from the body (Brewer 2005, 95). Although these innovations may have seemed desirable, as a consequence the hazard that resulted from this enlarged capacity for grave goods was inevitably that of attracting more tomb robbers.

Verification of these developments and their increased levels of sophistication can be seen for instance at Naqada, with the appearance of a differentiated elite burial ground known as

Cemetery T, dating to Naqada II (Kemp 1973, 42). The burials located there were generally larger than those of the adjacent non-elite cemeteries and were accompanied by numerous grave goods (Bard 1994, 112). Notably, tombs T10, T15, T20 and T23 in which brick linings were employed no doubt supported beams bearing wooden roofs (Kemp 1973, 41–2) (Fig. 9).

Whilst there is no evidence of a roof *per-se* over its burial pit, perhaps the earliest example of an elite or royal grave, and certainly the largest, is that of Tomb 23 found in the elite cemetery at Locality HK6 at Hierakonpolis, which dates to Naqada IIAB. It possesses one of the first examples of a superstructure and funerary enclosure (in wood and wicker) found to date (Adams 2004, 47–50; Friedman 2005, 40).

Although this superstructure is not definitely identified as a 'temple' for its associated tomb (Friedman 2008a, 26), evidence from its surroundings demonstrate that this tomb definitely belongs to a long established 'ritual precinct' (Friedman 2008a, 14–18). While these types of decorated lightweight superstructures may not have offered much physical protection to the burial itself, one might suggest that from the point of view of security the location of the tomb within a sacred space, such as the cemetery, would have no doubt offered a degree of protection from disturbance and robbery, at least in times of political stability. That HK6 probably remained the focus of ongoing ancestor veneration and cult for a considerable time is evident from beer jars found at the site and dating to at least the Third Dynasty (Friedman 2008c, 11)

A further example of this type of tomb complex, perhaps dating to Naqada IIB, can be seen from the excavations of the newly discovered Tomb 26 at the elite cemetery HK6 at Hierakonpolis. This has revealed remains of wooden boards preserved on a ledge running around the perimeter of the tomb (Fig. 10), suggesting that, like the tombs at Naqada Cemetery T, the burial chamber also in this case had a roof (Friedman 2008b, 1178–9).

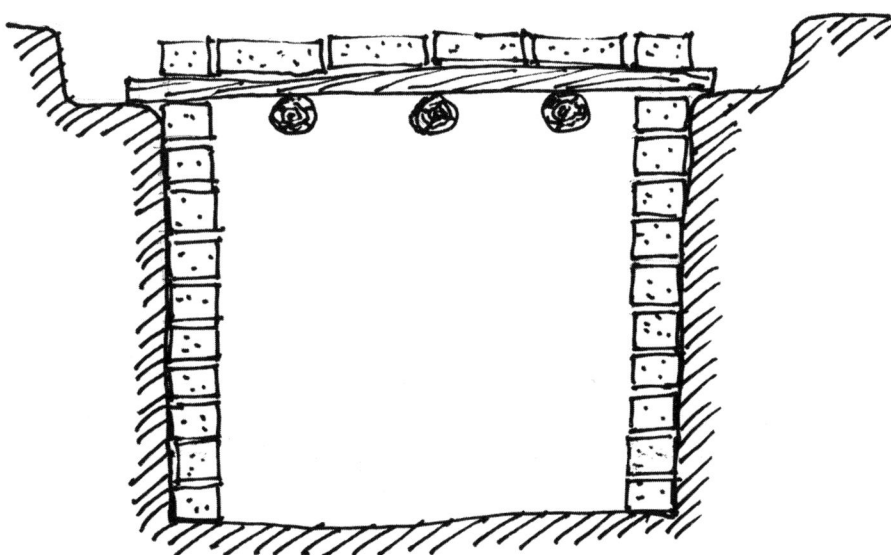

Figure 9. A typical section through a late Naqada II grave with a mud-brick lining and a wooden roof supported by beams (Drawn by the author after Spencer 1982, fig. 5).

Whether these roofs were topped with a mound, perhaps retained with a wooden or wicker wall as Reisner (1936, 5) speculated, or surmounted with a lightweight superstructure, as is suggested existed over the earlier Tomb 23 at Hierakonpolis, is unknown (Friedman 2008a, 18; *et al.* 2011, 187).

Slightly later in date, and contemporary with the other elite tombs from Cemetery T at Naqada (Kemp 1973, 42), is the famous decorated Tomb 100 at Hierakonpolis, dating to Naqada IIC (Figueiredeo 2004, 19). This tomb almost certainly had a wooden roof (Quibell and Green 1902, 20), as did many of its immediate neighbours, such as tomb 500, which still had the remains of wooden beams to support roof planking (Quibell and Green 1902, 22).

Interestingly, the location – some two kilometres from the elite cemetery HK6 – and architecture of Tomb 100 may demonstrate, in addition to its prototypical decorative scheme, a security response to an external threat. Evidence of burning from recent excavations of the complexes of Tombs 23 and D9 in Cemetery HK6, has led Friedman (2006, 11–12; 2008a, 22; 2008b, 1189 and n. 33) to suggest that the relocation of elite or royal burials from their traditional location at HK6 to the cemetery of the Painted Tomb, and the concurrent moving of the previously painted superstructure, decoration and 'chapel' underground, may have been a response to the deliberate burning and destruction of the lightweight superstructures and funerary artefacts. This damage was possibly caused by the destructive results of an unknown political upheaval or some other catastrophic event (Pers. comm. R. Friedman 7th May 2009). That instability and disorder existed during this period is evident from the investment in fortifications for 'royal' cities, such as Hierakonpolis, Naqada and Abydos, which seems to demonstrate the response of these communities to the stimulation of frequent threats (Williams 1994, 278).

Figure 10. Tomb 26 at Cemetery HK6 at Hierakonpolis, the ledge for supporting the roofing beams can be clearly seen (Friedman 2008b, fig. 11). Courtesy of the Hierakonpolis Expedition.

It is possible therefore that this change from the use of a superstructure to a subterranean complex could be regarded as one of the earliest tangible responses to a threat to the security of the elite or 'royal' tombs. Thus, it may represent a change in approach towards the design of high status and elite tomb architecture from this period onwards, as it would appear that security considerations had now necessarily become an important factor in the future development of tomb design.

Although, the incorporation of a roof in a tomb's design was undoubtedly successful in providing concealment and protection for the body and its grave goods, in the long term it would actually prove counterproductive. This was probably because a roof, however strong, made it actually easier to rob the contents, as it was now simply a case of tunnelling sideways into the void of the grave cyst, thus avoiding the roof itself, and then looting it in comfort, rather than having to excavate the whole pit of its backfill (Spencer 1982, 34).

Naqada IIIA to the start of Naqada IIIB

While undoubtedly the simple pit burial remained the norm for the non-elite as before (Lacovera 1998, 20; Dodson and Ikram 2008, 31), it is during this period, which begins *c*. 3300 BC (Hassan 1988, 138) that further developments in high status interments become evident. One example is that of Tomb 16B (dating to Naqada IIIA2) found in the elite cemetery at Locality HK6 at Hierakonpolis, which was fully lined with 'Flemish bonded' bricks, and it has been suggested, probably had a large central wooden beam running the length of its burial chamber to support a roof (Adams 2004, 41–2).

Corresponding to and, indeed, contemporary with Tomb 16B, is the famous Tomb U-j in Cemetery U at Umm el-Qaab at Abydos, which has been dated by its pottery to Naqada IIIA2 (Dreyer *et al.* 1998, 17). According to U-j's excavators, the layout of this rectangular, brick lined and multi-chambered tomb may have been modelled on a small palace of the period. Externally it measures approximately 10.1m × 8.2m × 1.5m, and still possesses the vestiges of its roof, made of layers of mat and plastered mud-bricks supported by acacia log beams of between 15–20cm in diameter (Dreyer 1992, 295–6; Dreyer *et al.* 1998, 4–6). The existence of these layers of roofing material and the location of the top of the mud-brick liner at 0.60m below the original desert surface (Dreyer *et al.* 1998, 4), suggests a roof and accompanying fill of substantial dimensions, which was intended to offer a considerable degree of security for its occupant and accompanying grave goods.

Therefore, it is possible that as in the case of Tomb 100 at Hierakonpolis, we may be seeing for security reasons a further development of the move underground of the earlier complex superstructure arrangements seen in 'high status' tombs. The return of such superstructures as a 'model palace' above ground does probably not occur again until the reign of Hor-Aha and his successors at Umm el-Qaab in the form of their associated funerary enclosures at nearby Abydos North (Dreyer *et al.* 1998, 19).

While these developments signal the appearance of larger and more complex elite or high status graves during this period, also of specific interest to this discussion are the contemporary graves just to the north of Hierakonpolis across the Nile on the east bank at el-Kab. Here the remains of a Naqada IIIA cemetery, containing nearly fifty tombs, has been discovered, together with a lesser number of Naqada IIIB–D graves (Wengrow 2006, 154), some of which incorporate security related features. Some of the most important graves (gauged by both tomb size and value of the funerary goods) are pit burials that incorporate undressed sandstone slabs (Hendrickx and Van Rossum 1994, 149). Rectangular in form, these tombs vary in their use of the stone. The slabs were either used to partially line the smaller graves, or as coverings for the graves themselves where, interestingly, the excavator notes that their placement preponderated over the funerary goods (Hendrickx and Van Rossum 1994, 151).

Of particular interest for the purpose of the paper from this site are two large graves dating to Naqada IIIA. Firstly number 69, which measured approximately 2.0m × 1.0m and, although disturbed, was found partially covered with two stone slabs. the largest one of which measured 1.40m long × 0.30m wide × 0.14m thick (Hendrickx and Van Rossum 1994, 186), and would have weighed approximately 155kgs (based on sandstone weighing 2.65kg/l (Arnold 1991, 28). Secondly, in much better condition, and undisturbed by tomb robbers, was the larger of the graves, number 85 (Fig. 11). It measured 3.10m long × 1.25m wide × 1.50m deep and had been roofed over entirely with four large slabs (exact dimensions not available) after the grave was backfilled (Hendrickx and Van Rossum 1994, 194). The associated pottery dates both the burials to Naqada IIIA2 (Hendrickx and Van Rossum 1994, 215).

Although, the use of stone like this is not generally characteristic for tombs of this period (Hendrickx and Van Rossum 1994, 151), it provides an interesting addition to the emerging battery of defensive measures in Egyptian tombs. The added benefits of using stone in this fashion to provide increased security are obvious. Whilst Hendrickx (1994, 151) has acknowledged that the function of the stones at this site may have been to also act as grave markers, the sheer weight and solidity of the slabs themselves would have provided a physical barrier to the depredations of tomb robbers. Indeed the effectiveness of their use in grave number 85 is attested by the undisturbed state of its contents, which were found intact (Hendrickx and Van Rossum 1994, 152).

Concurrently, in Lower Nubia security arrangements similar to those at el-Kab were utilised for the burials of the so called 'princes' of Seyala, at Cemetery 137, half a kilometre from Seyala at Naga Om Agag. Here three generations of nobles and their retainers belonging to the Late A-Group culture, which dates from Naqada IIIA1 to Naqada IIIA2 (Smith 1994, 372), had their tombs dug into the local clay and alluvium on the east bank of the Nile (Smith 1994, 361). Like some of the tombs at el-Kab, they were also roofed with 'sandstone slabs of considerable size and length' (Firth 1927, 201). The largest of these graves, tomb number 1, measured 2.85m long × 1.50m wide × 1.70m deep, and was originally roofed over with sandstone slabs (Smith 1994, 363) of which one had collapsed into the grave. When, during the excavation, the slab was finally removed, many artefacts in Egyptian style were revealed, including gold handled maces, copper items, stone vessels and Naqadan pottery (Firth 1927, 207–8). A nearby smaller tomb, number 6, measuring 1.40m long × 0.80m wide × 1.20m deep (Firth 1927, 211), provides an illustration of the typical roofing arrangement (Fig. 12).

Meanwhile, contemporary with the tombs at Seyala (Smith 1994, 376), several large high status tombs (Wilkinson 1999, 48), some of which have been dated to Naqada IIIA–B, were being prepared at a site known as Cemetery L at Qustul, also in Lower Nubia (Williams 1986, 1–2; 176–9). The graves took the form of large rectangular pits excavated into the alluvium, into the sides of which were dug burial chambers or *loculi,* whose entrances were blocked with layers of enormous stones (Seele 1974, 29).

Out of the 25 tombs found dating to this period, the most notable examples are L5, L9, L11, L19, L22, L23 and L24 (Williams 1986, 229–358). These are believed to be contemporary with the royal or elite tombs of Locality HK6 at Hierakonpolis, and it has been suggested that the largest examples

The early precursors of tomb security

Figure 11. Tomb No. 85 at el-Kab, showing the large sandstone slabs laid over the grave, the pottery dates the burial to Naqada IIIA2 (After Hendrickx and Van Vossum 1994, Plates LXIII and LXIV). Courtesy of S. Hendrickx.

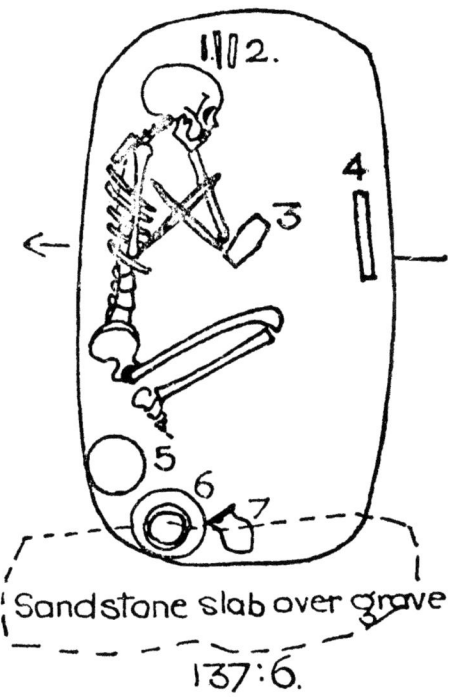

Figure 12. Tomb 6 in Cemetery 137 at Seyala, showing a sandstone slab in position over the grave (Firth 1927, 211).

(*e.g.* Tomb L23) are their direct forerunners (Williams 1986, 176). The biggest of all, Tomb L24, is regarded as broadly contemporaneous with tomb U-j at Umm el-Qaab (Wilkinson 1999, 48) and dates to Naqada IIIA2.

Tomb L23, to take as an example (Fig. 13), is a trench 9.25m long × 2.00m wide × 1.50m deep, with a side chamber or *loculus* cut in one end that stepped down and measured 4.80m long × 3.30m wide × 2.20m deep (Williams 1986, 344). Apart from the usual soil fill, it is not clear if any special arrangements had been made to close off access to the pit itself (Seele 1974, 35). The side chamber, which contained the burial and other items, had been deliberately sealed off with stone blocks, while the remainder of the tomb was used for the storage of large quantities of grave goods (Williams 1986, 14–20). Whilst this separation may have been intended to isolate the body from the grave goods, from the tomb security point of view the real benefit of the side chamber type of construction is that it took advantage of the geological characteristics of the surroundings of the tomb to form a strong natural roof over the burial itself, and thus offered more protection to the body in comparison to a simpler pit grave.

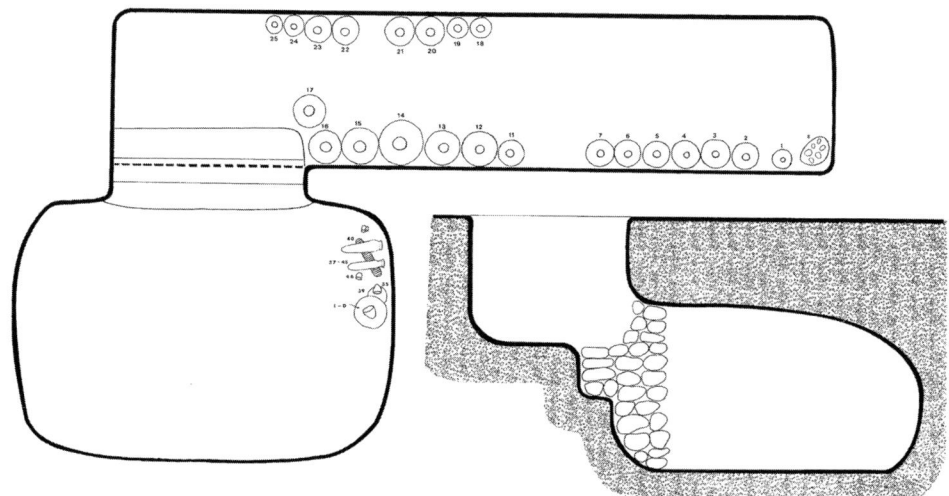

Figure 13. Tomb L23 at Qustul, showing the stone blocking to the burial chamber (Williams 1986, fig. 159). Courtesy of B. Williams and the Oriental Institute, Chicago.

Additionally, in order to rob the tomb, the pit would have to be first cleared of its backfill and grave goods and any intervening blocking removed before access could be made to the burial itself.

A comparable and contemporary design of grave, but located in Egypt, may similarly signal the adoption of the sealed side burial chamber or *loculus* as a means of security in Upper Egypt. Known as Burial 8 (Fig. 14), the grave was found intact by de Morgan at Kom el-Ahmar in Hierakonpolis opposite el-Kab (Needler and Churcher 1984, 111). It can be dated to Naqada IIIA from its finds, amongst which were wavy handled Naqada IIIA jars and an A-Group bowl (Williams 1987, 19, n. 38). The tomb measured 2.25m long × 1.05m wide × 1.53m deep and had a burial chamber cut into its base on one side. This measured 0.90m wide and a further 0.45m deep. Once the burial had been made and the grave goods installed, this was closed with stone slabs laid to form an angle and sealed with Nile mud. The whole was then concealed by filling the pit with a backfill to the surface (de Morgan 1909, 271–2).

Thus, it appears that at both Kom el-Ahmar and Qustul we have two of the earliest examples of a specific architectural attempt being made, to not only enhance the security of the body, but also concomitantly part the corpse from its accompanying funerary provisions by using a separate chamber with blocking. Interestingly, both contain a mixture of Naqada III and A-Group pottery

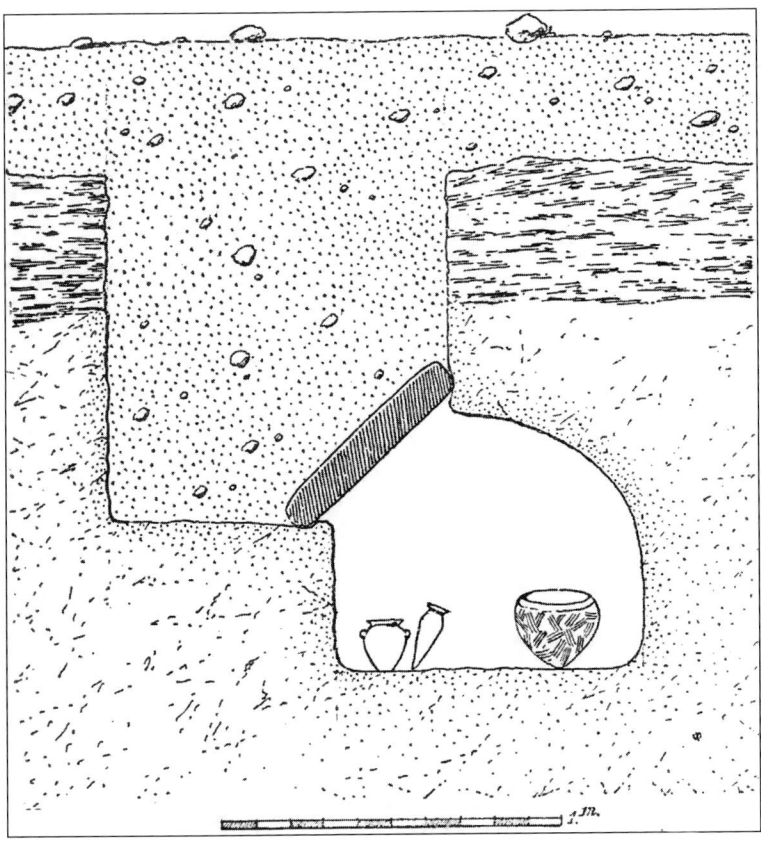

Figure 14. Tomb no. 8 at Kom el-Ahmar (Naqada III) showing large stone slabs blocking access to the burial niche (de Morgan 1909, fig. 130).

(Williams 1980, 15), which may indicate a high degree of interaction between the two cultures (Gatto 2003, 15).

Nearby, an example of possibly the earliest use of a stone 'portcullis' (Birrell 2000, 18) occurs in a higher status (in terms of both its size and location) tomb of similar design situated at Locality HK6 at Hierakonpolis (Friedman 2008a, 26).

Tomb 2 (Figs 15 and 16) possibly dates to Naqada IIIA–B by the similarity of its animal interments to those of tomb L23 at Qustul (Hendrickx *et al.* 2004, 117), this large elite tomb was entirely excavated into the surrounding sandstone and shale strata and had traces of mud plaster on the lower levels of its walls (Adams 2000, 23).

The tomb's pit descended through a 0.65m top layer of gravel and silt, into the rock to reach a total overall depth of 3.50m. It measured 6.25m long × 2.10m wide × 2.10m deep (Room A). Around its upper edge a 20cm deep step was cut to accommodate roofing beams. A hole cut into the base of Room A, at the south-eastern end (Room B) measured 3.00m long × 1.35m wide × 1.75m deep, and had a small tapering side chamber excavated on its eastern face (Room C) that measured 1.75m long × 1.50m wide × 1.70m high, and tapered down to 0.50m high (Hoffman 1982, 48). Two portcullises of cherty limestone were found propped up in the tomb. The excavators assumed that these were intended to close off Room C from B in a comparable manner to the stone walling of Tomb L23 at Qustul and presumably Room C would have then contained the deceased (Adams 2000, 23). One of the portcullises measured 1.40m long × 0.90m wide × 0.20m thick, and given that limestone weighs approximately 2.65kg/l (Arnold 1991, 28), would weigh about 667 kilos! It is also possible, given that the remains of mud plaster were found on the walls, that the portcullises might have been concealed by plastering, which could have undoubtedly increased the security of the burial chamber by concealing it from the view of potential plunderers.

Therefore, not only did this tomb benefit from the additional security provided by the natural stone roof created by its niche, but its use of shaped embryonic 'portcullis' slabs to prevent access to the burial also demonstrates a marked evolutionary progression, from the earlier use of dry stone as at Qustul, and the 'lean to' use of stone slabs at Kom el-Ahmar. A technological advance that would only be fully realised to its full potential many years later with the development of the sliding portcullis in the Early Dynastic period.

Figure 15. Tomb 2 at Locality 6 Hierakonpolis, showing the niche in the base and side and one of its associated 'portcullis' stones propped up at one end (Hoffmann 1982, Pl. 1.7). Courtesy of the Hierakonpolis Expedition.

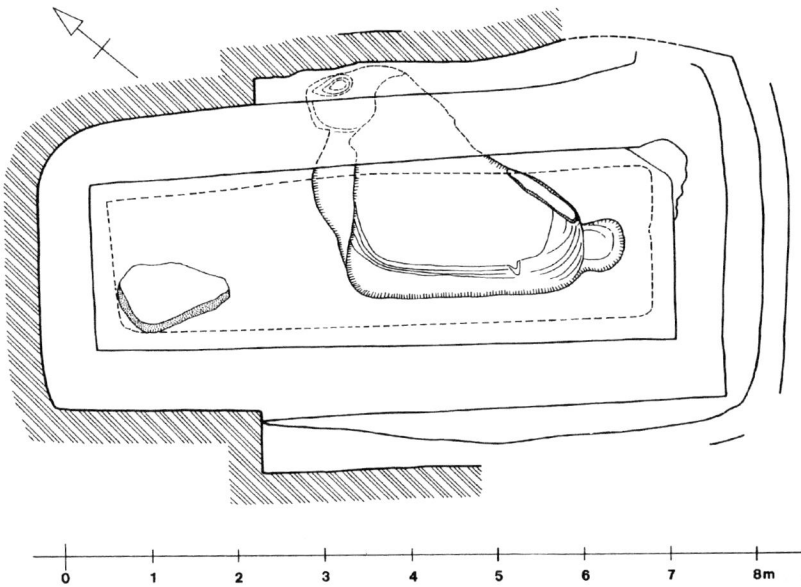

Figure 16. Plan of Tomb 2 at Locality 6 Hierakonpolis (Adams 1996, fig. 2). Courtesy of the Trustees of the British Museum.

Conclusion

The need for better security arrangements had been accelerated by the emergence of an elite class in a socially differentiated Egypt from Naqada I period onwards. In the larger tombs of the elite, increasing quantities of valuables were being included, leading to the concomitant problem of increased levels of tomb robbery (Hoffman, 1982, 146). With the ever-increasing amounts of grave goods being deposited in tombs, providing yet more opportunities for the unscrupulous, it is therefore reasonable to link the development of these early security measures with an urgent need to ward off the predatory attentions of the grave robber. Indeed, as Reisner (1908, 11) has suggested, it was probably this desire for richer burials, and the tomb robbers' concomitant determination to rob them, that drove the development of more complex tomb architecture in wealthier and more important graves, rather than religious motives or a yearning for increased monumentality. This rapid development of innovative architectural solutions to address the problem of tomb security would evolve in the Early Dynastic period (*c.* 3000–2686 BC) into what could be described as a virtual 'arms race', which would continue throughout most of Egyptian Pharaonic history.

Bibliography

Adams, B. (1988) *Predynastic Egypt.* Princess Risborough, Shire.
Adams, B. (1996) 'Elite graves at Hierakonpolis'. In J. Spencer (ed.) *Aspects of early Egypt.* London, British Museum Press.
Adams, B. (2000) *Excavations in the Locality 6 cemetery at Hierakonpolis, 1979–1985.* Oxford, Archaeopress.

Adams, B. (2004) Excavations in the elite Predynastic cemetery at Hierakonpolis Locality HK6: 1999–2000. *Annales du Service des antiquités de l'Egypte* 78, 35–51.

Anderson, W. (1992) Badarian burials: Evidence of social inequality in Middle Egypt during the Early Predynastic Era. *Journal of the American Research Center in Egypt* 29, 51–65.

Arkell, A. J. and Ucko, P. J. (1965) Review of Predynastic development in the Nile Valley. *Current Anthropology*, 6 No. 2, 145–66.

Arnold, D. (1991) *Building in Egypt: Pharaonic stone masonry*. New York, Oxford, Oxford University Press.

Ayrton, E. R. and Loat, W. L. S. (1911) *The Pre-dynastic cemetery at El Mahasna*. London, Egypt Exploration Fund.

Badawy, A. (1954) *A history of Egyptian architecture. Volume 1. From the earliest times to the end of the Old Kingdom,* [Cairo]. The Author.

Bard, K. A. (1994) *From farmers to pharaohs: mortuary evidence for the rise of complex society in Egypt.* Sheffield, Sheffield Academic Press

Bard, K. A. (2005) Predynastic Period, overview. In K. A. Bard (ed.) *The Encylopedia of the archaeology of ancient Egypt*, 31–5. London, New York, Taylor and Francis e-library.

Baumgartel, E. J. (1960) *The cultures of prehistoric Egypt Vol. II*. London, New York and Toronto, Published on behalf of the Griffith Institute Ashmolean Museum by Oxford University Press.

Birrel, M. (2000) Portcullis stones: tomb security during the Early Dynastic period. *Bulletin of the Australian Centre for Egyptology* 11, 17–28.

Brewer, D. J. (2005) *Ancient Egypt: foundations of a civilization*. Harlow, Pearson Education Limited.

Brunton, G. and Caton-Thompson, G. (1928) *The Badarian civilisation and Predynastic remains near Badari*. London, British school of archaeology in Egypt.

Butzer, K. W. (1976) *Early hydraulic civilization in Egypt: a study in cultural ecology*. Chicago, London, University of Chicago Press.

Castillos, J. J. (1982) *A reappraisal of the published evidence on Egyptian Predynastic and Early Dynastic Cemeteries*. Toronto, Benben Publications.

Connor, M. A. (2007) *Forensic methods: excavation for the archaeologist and investigator.* Lanham, Md.; Plymouth, AltaMira Press.

Debono, F. (1948) El-Omari (près d'Hélouan). Exposé sommaire sur les campagnes des fouilles 1943–1944 et 1948, *Annales du Service des antiquités de l'Egypte* 48, 561–569.

Debono, F. and Mortensen, B. (1990) *El Omari: a Neolithic settlement and other sites in the vicinity of Wadi Hof, Helwan*. Mainz am Rhein, Von Zabern.

Dodson, A. and Ikram, S. (2008) *The tomb in Ancient Egypt: royal and private sepulchres from the early dynastic period to the Romans*. London, Thames & Hudson.

Dreyer, G. (1992) Recent discoveries at Abydos Cemetery U. In E. C. M. v. d. Brink (ed.) 1992. *The Nile Delta in transition: 4th–3rd Millennium B.C.: Proceedings of the Seminar held in Cairo, 2–24 October 1990, at the Netherlands Institute of Archaeology and Arabic Studies*, 293–99. Tel Aviv & Jerusalem Brink. Distributed by the Israel Exploration Society.

Dreyer, G., Hartung, U. and Pumpenmeier, F. (1998) *Umm el-Qaab I: das prädynastische Königsgrab U-j und seine frühen Schriftzeugnisse*. Mainz, Verlag Philipp von Zabern.

Dupras, T. L., Schultz, J. J., Wheeler, S. M. and Williams, L. J. (2006) *Forensic recovery of human remains: archaeological approaches*. Boca Raton, Fla.; London, Taylor & Francis.

Figueiredeo, Á. (2004) Locality HK6 at Hierakonpolis. In S. Hendrickx, R. F. Friedman, K. M. Cialowiez, and M. Chlodnicki (eds) *Egypt at its origins: studies in memory of Barbara Adams: proceedings of the international conference "Origin of the State, Predynastic and Early Dynastic Egypt," Krakow, 28th August–1st September 2002*, 1–23. Leuven, Peeters.

Firth, C. M. (1927) *The Archaeological Survey of Nubia report for 1910–1911*. Cairo, Government Press.

Friedman, R. F. (1997) Excavations in the Predynastic cemetery at HK43. *Nekhen News* 9, 2–3.

Friedman, R. F. (1998) More Mummies: The 1998 Season at HK43. *Nekhen News* 10, 4–6.
Friedman, R. F. (2005) Excavating Egypt's early kings: Recent discoveries in the elite cemetery at Hierakonpolis. In B. Midant-Reynes and Y. Tristant (eds) *Origines Toulouse 2005: Predynastic and Early Dynastic Egypt. Origin of the state: Conference Abstracts,* 40–1. Toulouse.
Friedman, R. F. (2006) New tombs and new thoughts at HK6. *Nekhen News* 18, 11–12.
Friedman, R. F. (2008a) The cemeteries of Hierakonpolis. *Archéo-nil* 18, 9–29.
Friedman, R. F. (2008b) Excavating Egypt's early kings: Recent discoveries in the elite cemetery at Hierakonpolis. In B. Midant-Reynes and Y. Tristant (eds.) *Egypt at its origins 2*, 1157–94. Leuven, Peeters.
Friedman, R. F. (2008c) Remembering the ancestors: HK6 in 2008. *Nekhen News* 20, 10–11.
Friedman, R. F. (2011) The elite Predynastic cemetery at Hierakonpolis: 2009–10 update. In R. F. Friedman and P. N. Fiske (eds.) 2011. *Egypt at its origins 3*, 157–92. Leuven, Paris, Walpole MA, Peeters.
Gatto, M. C. (2003) Hunting the elusive Nubian A-Group. *Nekhen News* 15, 14–5.
Geus, F. (1991) Burial customs in the upper main Nile. In W. V. Davies (ed.) *Egypt and Africa: Nubia from prehistory to Islam,* 57–65. London, British Museum Press in association with the Egypt Exploration Society.
Grajetzki, W. (2003) *Burial customs in ancient Egypt: life in death for rich and poor.* London, Duckworth.
Hassan, F. A. (1988) The Predynastic of Egypt. *Journal of World Prehistory* 2, 135–85.
Hendrickx, S. and Van Rossum, V. (1994) *Elkab. V, the Naqada III cemetery.* Bruxelles, Musées royaux d'art et d'histoire.
Hendrickx, S., Linseele, W. V. and Friedman R. F. (2004) Animal burials and food offerings at the elite cemetery HK6 of Hierakonpolis. In S. Hendrickx, R. F. Friedman, K. M. Cialowicz and M. Chlodnicki (eds) *Egypt at its origins: Studies in memory of Barbara Adams,* 67–130. Leuven, Peeters.
Hoffman, M. A. (1982) *The Predynastic of Hierakonpolis: an interim report.* Giza, Egypt, Macomb, Ill, Cairo University Herbarium Faculty of Science; Dept. of Sociology and Anthropology Western Illinois University.
Hoffman, M. A. (1990) *Egypt before the pharaohs.* New York, Dorset Books.
Junker, H. (1929) *Vorläufiger Bericht über die Grabung der Akademie der Wissenschaften in Wien auf der neolithischen Siedelung von Merimde- Benisalâme (Westdelta),* [Wien], [Adolf Holzhausens Nachfolger].
Klasens, A. (1957) The Excavations of the Leiden Museum of Antiquities at Abu-Roash. Report of the First Season: 1957. Part I. *Oudheidkundige Mededelingen uit het Rijksmuseum van Oudheden* 38, 58–68.
Kemp, B. J. (1968) Merimde and the theory of house burial in Predynastic Egypt. *Chronique d'Égypte* 43, 22–33.
Kemp, B. J. (1973) Photographs of the Decorated Tomb at Hierakonpolis. *Journal of Egyptian Archaeology* 59, 36–43.
Lacovera, P. (1988) Funerary architecture. In S. D'Auria, P. Lacovara and C. H. Roehrig (eds) *Mummies and magic: the funerary arts of ancient Egypt.* Boston, Museum of Fine Arts.
Midant-Reynes, B. (2000) *The prehistory of Egypt from the first Egyptians to the first pharaohs.* Malden, MA, Blackwell Publishers.
Morgan, H. D. (1909) L'Egypte Primitive: Le Néolithique et l'énéolithique. *Revue de L'École D'Anthropologie* 19, 263–81.
Mortenson, B. (2005) El-Omari. In K. A. Bard (ed.) *The Encyclopedia of the archaeology of ancient Egypt,* 715–17. London and New York, Taylor and Francis e-Library.
Needler, W. and Churcher, C. S. (1984) *Predynastic and archaic Egypt in the Brooklyn Museum.* Brooklyn, N.Y, The Museum.
O'Connor, D. (2009) *Abydos: Egypt's first pharaohs and the cult of Osiris.* London, Thames & Hudson.
Petrie, W. M. F. and Mace, A. C. (1901) *Diospolis Parva: the cemeteries of Abadiyeh and Hu.* London, Egypt Exploration Fund.

Petrie, W. M. F. and Quibell J. E. (1896) *Naqada and Ballas*. London, B. Quaritch.
Podzorski, P. V. (2008) The Early Dynastic mastabas of Naga ed-Deir. *Archéo-nil* 18, 89–102.
Quibell, J. E. and Green F. W. (1902) *Hierakonpolis Part II*. London, B. Quaritch.
Reisner, G. A. (1908) *The early dynastic cemeteries of Naga-ed-Dêr: Part 1*. Leipzig, J. C. Hinrichs.
Reisner, G. A. (1936) *The development of the Egyptian tomb down to the accession of Cheops*. Cambridge, Mass, Harvard University Press.
Rizkana, I. and Seeher, J. (1990) *Maadi IV 4, The Predynastic cemeteries of Maadi and Wadi Digla*. Mainz, Zabern.
Seeher, J. (1992) Burial customs in Predynastic Egypt: A view from the Delta. In E. C. M. van den Brink (ed.) *The Nile Delta in Transition: 4th–3rd Millennium BC*, 225–33. Tel Aviv, van den Brink.
Seeher, J. (ed.) (1999) *Ma'adi and Wadi Digla*. London and New York, Routledge.
Seele, K. C. (1974) Excavations between Abu Simbel and the Sudan border. *Journal of Near Eastern Studies* 33, 1–43.
Smith, H. S. (1994) The princes of Seyala in Lower Nubia. In C. Berger, G. Clerc, J. Leclant and N. C. Grimal (eds) *Hommages à Jean Leclant*, 361–76. Cairo, Institut français d'archéologie orientale du Caire.
Spencer, A. J. (1982) *Death in ancient Egypt*. Harmondsworth, Penguin Books.
Spencer, A. J. (1993) *Early Egypt*. London, British Museum Press.
Vermeersch, P. M., Paulissen, E., Stokes, S., Charlier, C., Peer, P. V., Stringer, C. and Lindsay, W.(1998) A Middle Palaeolithic burial of a modern human at Taramsa Hill, Egypt. *Antiquity* 72, 475–84.
Wendorf, F. (1968) Site 117: A Nubian Final Paleolithic graveyard near Jebel Sahaba, Sudan. In F. Wendorf (ed.) *The Prehistory of Nubia*, 954–987. Southern Methodist University, Dallas.
Wendorf, F. and Close, A. E. (2005) Paleolithic cultures, overview in K. A. Bard (ed.) *The Encylopedia of the archaeology of ancient Egypt*, 6–15. London and New York, Taylor and Francis e-library.
Wengrow, D. (2006) *The archaeology of early Egypt: Social transformations in North-East Africa, 10,000 to 2,650 BC*. Cambridge, Cambridge University Press.
Wenke, R. J. (1989) Egypt: Origins of complex societies. *Annual Review of Anthropology* 18, 129–55.
Wilkinson, T. A. H. (1999) *Early Dynastic Egypt*. London, Routledge.
Williams, B. (1980) The lost pharaohs of Nubia. *Archaeology* 33, 14–21.
Williams, B. (1986) *The A-group royal cemetery at Qustul: cemetery L*. Chicago, Oriental Institute of the University of Chicago.
Williams, B. (1987) Forebears of Menes in Nubia: Myth or Reality? *Journal of Near Eastern Studies* 46, 15–26.
Williams, B. (1994) Security and the problem of the city in the Naqada Period. In D. P. Silverman (ed.) *For his ka: Essays offered in the memory of Klaus Baer*, 271–8. Chicago, The Oriental Institute of the University of Chicago.

'Living in a material world': understanding and interpreting life in an Egyptian mud house

Maria Correas-Amador

Introduction

The vast majority of ancient Egyptian houses uncovered thus far were built with mudbrick. In spite of this, archaeology has not focused enough on the implications of this building material for the interpretation of house remains. The physical properties of mud applied to construction and the way in which these affect the state of archaeological remains have been described by archaeologists (Kemp 2000; Spencer 1994), however, an investigation of the relationship between this building material and the temporal, geographical and sociocultural context in which the houses were embedded, is largely missing.

This could obey to the scarcity of integral studies concerning ancient Egyptian house remains, but also to the inherent difficulties of using archaeological remains to reconstruct the relationship between material and context. For this reason, an ethnoarchaeological study of mudbrick houses in Egypt not only can provide information about the particularities of the material, but can also provide a theoretical basis for the study of the contextual factors affecting domestic architecture.

The object of this research is, therefore, to investigate this relationship in modern mudbrick houses and to apply the conclusions to the understanding of the archaeological record. While a description of the materials in modern houses has been undertaken elsewhere (Correas-Amador 2011), this paper will focus on the study of the contextual factors influencing Egyptian mudbrick houses throughout the 20th century and their effect on material changes and developments. In addition, the selection criteria for the testing of those conclusions on domestic archaeological remains will be explained. However, the individual analysis of those remains is beyond the scope of this paper.

Evaluation of sources concerning ancient Egyptian houses

Sources of knowledge: the archaeological remains and the artistic evidence
Information regarding ancient Egyptian houses is drawn from three main sources: the analysis of archaeological remains, the examination of the artistic evidence – materialised in clay models of houses and representations on tomb walls – and ethnoarchaeological methods.

While the first two have dominated the research regarding ancient Egyptian domestic architecture, the latter has been thus far ignored, with the exception of Eigner's work (see Eigner 2006 and, indirectly, 1984).

The study of the archaeological remains was advanced by Ricke (1932), who undertook an extensive analysis of the floor plans of Amarna houses which would lay the foundations for the development of later approaches to the study of domestic architectural remains in Egypt.

In addition to providing individual analyses of a large number of floor plans previously excavated by Borchardt between 1907 and 1914 (Borchardt and Ricke 1980), Ricke also compared those floor plans with the purpose of finding design patterns which classify the various types of houses he found at Amarna. The most basic floor plan he identified consisted of a one-room house. Further complexity was shown in a tripartite room arrangement, with one of the three rooms also containing a staircase in certain instances. An elaborate version of this tripartite arrangement was given the name of Amarna *normalhause* (Ricke 1932, 3) – known in English as 'standard Amarna villa' (Lacovara 1997, 58) – which Ricke considered the archetypical house of this city.

On the basis of these findings, Ricke established a house typology according to the complexity of the floor plan patterns, with the one-room house being at the outset of a design development which culminated in the more elaborate Amarna *normalhause*. Far from being restricted to this site, Ricke saw this process as exemplary of the development that would have occurred across the whole of Egypt throughout ancient times. While the simplest types would have been widely spread in earlier history, they would have progressively been substituted by more elaborate options, eventually being reduced to lower class housing by the Amarna period (Baldwin Smith 1938, cited in Arnold 1989, 88).

This comprehensive interpretation regarding the development of houses throughout ancient Egyptian history has not only been challenged on the basis of the uncertainty regarding the representativeness of Amarna as a typical Egyptian city (Lacovara 1997, 60), but also on the grounds that the house remains excavated across Egypt prior to Ricke's publication were not numerous enough to give general validity to his conclusions (Arnold 1989, 75). Nevertheless, the terminology used by Ricke continues to permeate the analysis of ancient Egyptian houses (see, for example, Von Pilgrim 1996, 190 ff.; Hein and Jánosi 2004, 233).

Alternative attempts to establish an interpretative link between the remains of ancient houses found across Egypt have also focused mainly on a comparison and analysis of floor plans (Arnold 1989; Lacovara 1997), with varied conclusions. Individual evaluations of sites following from Ricke's work have also been undertaken, notably Tietze's exhaustive study of Amarna house sizes and the possible correlation between dimensions and social status (Tietze 1985).

Arnold (1989) attempted to explain the development of the Egyptian house from prehistory into ancient times. According to his interpretation, the first house type would have been the circular prehistoric house, which would have coexisted with the rectangular house from approximately 6000 BC, eventually replacing it completely by 3000 BC (Arnold 1989, 89). The rectangular house and the long house – developed from the former – were established as the standard house types and by the Middle Kingdom the 'Mediterranean court-centred house' – a rectangular house type in whose layout the courtyard played a central role – was present in houses such as those of Kahun. While this type of house remained unchanged into the New Kingdom, the courtyard would have been substituted by a roofed hall during this period, as shown in Amarna villas (Arnold 1989, 80).

In contrast to Arnold's interpretation, Lacovara (1997) presented a more flexible analysis based on the notion of the 'divided court', a basic layout on the basis of which infinite floor plans could be developed. One of these possibilities would have been realised in certain Kahun houses, which Lacovara described as tripartite houses with a front court or portico (Lacovara

1997, 66), rather than as 'Mediterranean court-centred house' prototypes (Arnold 1989, 90). In addition, he deemed the Amarna villas to be an exception based on an imitation of New Kingdom palace architecture, rejecting the role attributed to them by Ricke and Arnold as the culmination of the ancient Egyptian house development (Lacovara 1980, 60). This tripartite arrangement became linear in the New Kingdom with rooms following one another; however, after the Amarna period, the tripartite division would have been abandoned in favour of a return to more basic developments of the 'divided court' (Lacovara 1997, 67).

The analysis of artistic representations as a source of information to help understand the scarce archaeological remains of ancient Egyptian houses was undertaken most notably by Petrie (1907) and Davies (1929). Petrie found a series of clay models during his excavations in Rifeh, which he named 'soul-houses' (Petrie 1907, 14). While some of these appeared to represent offering tables, others depicted noticeably small houses which Petrie believed would have been representative of the homes of ordinary Egyptians (Petrie 1907, 20). On the other hand, Davies (1929) compared the representations of houses in Theban tombs and some clay and wooden models – amongst them, those found by Petrie in Rifeh – and concluded that they were depicting two distinct types of dwellings, 'town houses' and 'country houses', representing urban and rural areas respectively.

Clay and wooden models from the Middle and New Kingdom were also used to complement the interpretation of archaeological remains by later authors *e.g.* Arnold, who thought them to illustrate his theory of a transition from the open Kahun courtyard to the roofed Amarna hall (Arnold 1989, 77, 81).

A much less exploited source: Ethnoarchaeology. Re-establishing the link between material and context

Despite the fact that ethnoarchaeological studies can help re-establish the link between the material and contextual aspects of building in the archaeological record, their potential has hardly been exploited. Eigner (2006) was unique in his attempt to establish a broader connection between the features of modern and ancient Egyptian mudbrick houses. With the exception of certain authors, who included brief references to modern parallels to illustrate floor plan arrangement and house distribution in ancient Egyptian sites (see Lacovara 1997, 64 and Kemp 2006, 199, fig. 70), Eigner's work remains unparalleled.

The aim of Ethnoarchaeology is to understand and re-establish the relation between material culture and cultural context as a whole (David and Kramer 2001, 2).

Despite context being a central concept of modern archaeology (Cameron 2006, 22), its consideration has often been disregarded in the study of ancient Egyptian floor plans, even though such study has mainly relied on the comparison between sites of different areas and periods. The idea of context in archaeology can have various meanings, but these always refer to the connection of objects with their surroundings (Hodder and Hutson 2003, 171). That context in which the archaeological remains are embedded is in fact essential to recreate past human activity (Renfrew and Bahn 2000, 50).

This context is formed by a series of variables; Sanders (1990, 44) who based his research in the early Minoan settlement at Myrtos, identified seven variables that could affect the form and function of houses. These variables could be 'naturally fixed', (such as climate and topography) 'flexible' (available materials, economic resources and level of technology of the society) and 'culturally fixed' (function and cultural conventions). These variables would have integrated a code that would have been instantly understood by the population (Tsipopoulou 2006, 140). Context has in effect the ability to provide understanding (Barrett 2006, 194). However, the study of this context can often be difficult due to lacunae in the information regarding the environmental, cultural and social context surrounding these buildings. In certain cases, such information can be inferred from other media, such as artistic representation and literary sources, but the manner in which it relates to the architectural remains is unclear.

Sociocultural aspects are arguably one of the most important contextual factors involved in housing. Social interaction is construed, amongst others, by means of the built environment, and consequently, of houses (Rapoport 1976; Kamp, 1993; Last 2006, 120); therefore, archaeological remains can only be understood by taking into account the context which engendered them (Last 2006, 120). In spite of this, the consideration of the human factor and the reciprocate influence that this one and materials exert over each other has been largely neglected in the analysis and interpretation of ancient Egyptian houses.

Contextual analysis provides a useful tool for comparison (Barrett 2006, 195) and, in the case of mudbrick houses, ethnoarchaeology allows for a contextual analysis to which analogies, an essential tool for interpretation, can be applied (Cameron 2006, 22).

A contextual study of mud houses in the 20th century

The research identified four factors which appear to have had a direct influence in the original characteristics and successive changes in the building of Egyptian mudbrick houses across the 20th century. These are: the damming of the Nile and the introduction of cash crops, the Western influence and industrialization and the changes in land ownership. The identification of these processes is illustrative of the kind of contextual factors that may potentially influence house design and appearance, and which can lend themselves to the previously mentioned process of analogy which could help reconstruct part of the context of ancient Egyptian houses.

First of all, the damming of the Nile and the introduction of all-year-round crops changed agriculture and consequently had a deep impact on all spheres of rural life, including the structure and appearance of mudbrick houses, which were mainly present in the countryside.

The cultivation of all-year-round crops became necessary in the second half of the 19th century, due to the need to feed the fast-growing population, as well as to meet the external demand for products such as cotton, amongst other factors.

While cultivation in the Nile valley had relied on the annual flood for millennia (Ibrahim 2003, 73), these new crops required permanent irrigation. In order to make this feasible, it was necessary to raise the groundwater table. This would be achieved by damming the Nile; several attempts were made at this, the most important of which are: the Aswan dam (1902), the Asyut dam (1902), the Sifta dam (1902), the Isna Dam (1909) and the Nag'-Hammadi Dam (1930). These attempts culminated in the building of the Aswan dam at the end of the sixties (Ibrahim 1982, 63). The final building of the dam caused changes in landscape and land cultivation, and consequently affected the location, distribution, features, material and the number of existing mudbrick buildings.

Before the building of the dam, dense villages had to be built on high ground to escape the flood (Mahgoub 2000, 1), although in places where the flood was not a threat they also developed in low ground. This dense habitat was also encouraged by other reasons such as security (Mahgoub 2000, 1; Lozach and Hug 1930, 8) and the facilitation of tax collection and administration; to ensure this, the building of isolated houses was banned (Lozach 1930, 8).

Disperse patterns were also discouraged by the fact that proximity to crops was not necessary all year round, only during sowing and harvesting periods (Demangeon 1926, 172).

Due to a combination of these circumstances, houses in the centre and south of Lower Egypt were built close to each other, they were small and had thick walls; in addition, security and/or perhaps moral reasons, meant that these houses had none or few windows (Lozach and Hug 1930, 30).

However, the dam increased the possibility of building villages in low ground, given that no areas were now threatened by the flood (Demangeon 1926, 173; Mahgoub 2000, 5). While ordinary crops did not require permanent irrigation, all-year-round crops required constant attention, therefore encouraging a new type of habitat, the *ezbah* (Fig. 1), which developed close to irrigation canals in the form of hamlets or just rows of small houses (Demangeon 1926, 173). These ezbah usually had a rectangular form, built with a mixture of red and mud brick, with two or three rooms covered with a roof of mud bricks, and with a narrow courtyard used for animals. They normally hosted ten to thirty families (Lozach and Hug 1930, 39; Mahgoub 2000, 6).

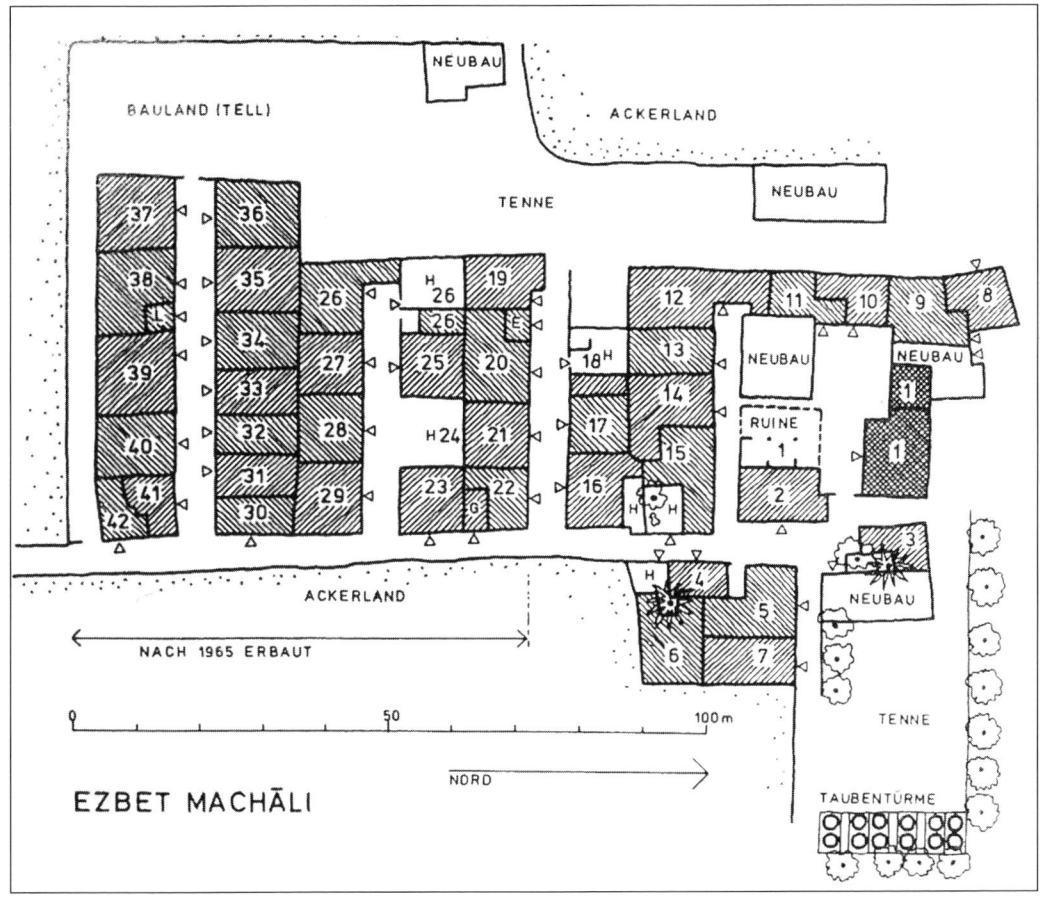

Figure 1. Ezbet Machali (Eastern Delta) Drawing by Dieter Eigner. Reproduced with permission from the author.

In addition to having an indirect effect on houses due to the described alterations to the rural environment, the building of the dam also affected individual buildings physically: with the rise of the ground water table, those buildings which existed prior to the changes collapsed (Ibrahim 1982, 66). Lastly, to build the dam itself 120,000 Nubians had to leave their homes and 70,000 abandoned their traditional mudbrick houses to be relocated by the government in Kom Ombo (Ibrahim 2003, 90).

Lastly, red brick and mud brick production relied on Nile silt. With the loss of Nile silt as a consequence of the building of the Aswan dam, it became necessary to obtain it from the banks of the Nile, or removing the topsoil, therefore affecting the river course and the soil productivity (Ibrahim 1982, 66). Finally, in 1985, Mubarak issued a decree banning these activities and closing red brick factories which relied on mud for their production (MacKenzie 1985, 10). While the real effect of this banning is arguable, it could have impacted the building of new mudbrick houses.

While the building of the dam was the main factor in the growth of dispersed habitational patterns in Lower Egypt, this type of housing was already widely spread in Upper Egypt before the dam, perhaps in response to differences in climate, rural economy and tradition (Lozach and Hug 1930, 113). To these considerations, economic factors must be added, since the development of either extended or dense houses could also have responded to the amount of land the individual had at his disposal (Gheith 1988).

For most of the 20th century, the lack of ownership probably discouraged the expansion of the habitat given that most fellahin had no or exceptionally little land of their own (Lozach and Hug 1930, 5). This meant that small, dense, taller buildings would have been needed. During the course of the first years of the 20th century and the First and Second World Wars, various initiatives to increase land ownership were launched; however these initiatives do not appear to have had a significant impact (Baer 1962, 84). In addition, the 'Law of Five Feddans' (1912) which remained in place until the 60s, protected small owners with less than five feddans of land (Baer 1962, 89). Whether the law actually had any effect on fellahin ownership is subject to debate, due to the number of other factors involved, such as the increase of prices, lack of available credits, *etc.* (Baer 1962, 90). One of Nasser's most important reforms was the land reform, which took 550,000 feddans from 1,758 landowners and redistributed to approximately 250,000 peasant families (Margold 1957, 9); although the actual impact of all these measures was relative (Marsot 2003, 94), they could have had an effect on the number of extended houses.

Sadat's 'open-door' policy, developed in the 70s, increased the dependence on Western countries by opening the Egyptian market to foreign imports, which included building materials (Marsot 2003, 143). Due to the economic difficulties at the time, many agricultural workers had to emigrate to oil-producing countries (Marsot 2003, 136); their return saw their struggle to re-adapt to their old village life, as well as a need to differentiate themselves from the people that had remained in their villages; in addition, they had the necessary money to build red brick houses, which became a symbol of high status in opposition to mud brick (Mahgoub 2000, 9).

In recent years, this trend in urbanization and Westernization, with the subsequent substitution of traditional rural architecture for western materials, such as red brick and concrete, has nothing but increased.

In summary, the characteristics and development of the traditional Egyptian house throughout the 20th century across different geographical locations, respond to a mixture of political, economic, sociocultural and environmental factors, all of which must be taken into account in order to fully understand the buildings.

This analysis has highlighted the complexity of factors involved in building choices, as well as theoretically informing the study of the contextual levels which affect the characteristics and development of mudbrick architecture. On the basis of the research undertaken, the following factors have been identified: the natural geographical conditions and human-made modifications to the environment, the particular economic and political situation, the cultural and social influences and the heavy weight of tradition in vernacular building, as well as the particular circumstances of each community and the ultimate private choice of the individual.

Archaeological applications

The information obtained through ethnoarchaeological methods is to be used, as explained, as the basis for a re-evaluation of domestic architectural remains. The material information obtained from fieldwork, together with the contextual factors identified, have determined the information to be selected from the publication of the archaeological sites.

With regards the natural geographical conditions, three areas with different environmental conditions were previously selected, namely the Delta (Lower Egypt), the Nile valley (Upper Egypt) and the Dakhleh Oasis (Correas-Amador, 2011). The research has identified that the varied environmental conditions can have an effect on house distribution and appearance, as exemplified by the differences described between Lower and Upper Egypt prior to the dam.

In addition, an examination of the effects of the building of the Aswan dam has highlighted the importance of assessing man-made alterations to the environment; in ancient Egypt, the building of canals is well documented, particularly through commemorative inscriptions (Breasted 1906), consequently, the effect of irrigation works should also be taken into account.

Thirdly, the economic circumstances must be considered, both at an institutional and at an individual level (*e.g.* including available resources, importance of trade, possibilities of the individual, *etc.*), as well as the political and administrative situation, in particular the balance of the estate/provincial dichotomy in each particular period. The role of involvement of authority in the planning of the development is also a key factor, as exemplified by the differences between organically-developed and planned settlements, such as the ezbah. In ancient Egypt, not only are there multiple examples of both types of settlements for different periods, but both models of settlement can be present within the same site, which highlights even further the importance of analysing the full context of each settlement individually.

In addition, the cultural and social characteristics attached not only to the period, but also to the area in particular, including the particular status – perhaps even ethnic background of the individuals, as has been suggested for Tell el-D'aba (Bietak 2000, 10) – plays a role in the building's distribution, construction and materials. In this sense, an investigation of the degree of influence of social class considerations in comparison to the other factors highlighted, will tie in with and put into perspective previous research regarding the classification of houses according to wealth, particularly the association between wealth and house size.

A number of diverse sites have been purposely selected in order to explore the impact of all the contextual factors described (Fig. 2). The criteria for the selection of these sites was intentionally based on sites in which different responses to the various contextual levels were available: the sites span from the Old Kingdom to the Late Period, but settlements have been selected regardless of the importance of the site in that specific period; the particular characteristics of the settlement studied, including whether this developed organically or as a result of state

Site	Period	Area	Phase/level	Dynasty	Houses
Giza	Old Kingdom	Kenthkawes Town (KKT)		4th	Houses A-K
Abusir	OK	South of temple Neferirkare		5th	all
Kahun	Middle Kingdom	Western town – workmen's houses		12th-13th	All (general descriptions)
		N wall: 5 large properties			All (general descriptions)
Elephantine	MK	South city of Chnum temple	XVb	Late 11th	H25b
		South city of Chnum temple	XVa	Early 12th	H25a
		North City	XIV	12th	H86
		South city of Chnum temple	XIII	12th	H10, H12
Lisht	MK/Second Intermediate Period	North - Cemetery	IIa	13th	A.13, A.33
Tell el-Daba	MK	F/I	stratum e	Early 12th Late 13th	I/20: 5, 6, 7, 8
Tell el Daba	SIP	A/V	stratum E/1, D/3, D/2	15th	032-33,056-59,056-60,081-083,092-093,173-176
Deir el Ballas	Late SIP	Houses by North Palace		Late SIP	House E
Memphis	New Kingdom	Kom Rabia:RAT	level IV	Early NK	rooms 7/23, 8/9/22, 15/16, 2/17/14, 19/20/5/26/27, 24/6
			level III	18th	
			level II	19th	
Amarna	NK	Workmen's village		18th	Gate Street 8, 9 (walled village)
		Main city		18th	grid 12, N 51.4, P 47.6, Q 46.2, O 48.11, P 47.19, O 47.8, M 50.10, N 48.12, N 49.6, Q 47.23, O 49.14, N 50.19, P46.33
El-Ashmunein	Third Intermediate Period	Site W	level 1b,2a,2b,3	22th-25th	j.10 and k.10
El-Ashmunein	TIP	Site W	levels 1c, 3	22nd, 24th, 25th	j.11 and k.11
Karnak	TIP	East of Amon's temple sacred lake	phase 1	21st	Houses I to VI
Karnak	Late Period	East of Amon's temple sacred lake	phase 2	26th	Houses A to H
Elephantine	LP	West	4a	27th	House M

Figure 2. Summary table of archaeological sites to be analysed.

planning are also related to the function of the site and of the particular area of settlement; therefore, this must also be taken into account.

In order to re-establish the associations between material and contextual factors, selected house features are being studied comparatively, bearing in mind the various site contexts. These features are divided into: external finishes (roofs, walls, doors, windows and other features – such as granaries) and internal finishes (ceilings, walls, doors, windows and others – such as columns and floors).

This analysis is yielding some interesting results with regards the reasons behind the recurrence of certain features, the distribution of space and the appearance of houses. It is expected that, upon completion of the research, a better knowledge of the factors involved in building choices will lead to a more holistic understanding of ancient Egyptian domestic architecture.

Bibliography

Arnold, F. (1989) A study of Egyptian domestic buildings. *Varia Aegyptiaca,* 5, 75–93.
Baer, G. (1962) *A history of land ownership in modern Egypt. 1800–1950.* London, Oxford University Press.
Barrett, J. (2006) Archaeology as the investigation of the contexts of humanity. In D. Papaconstantinou (ed.) *Deconstructive context. A critical approach to archaeological practice*, 194–211. Oxford, Oxbow Books.
Bietak, M. (2000) *Avaris. The capital of the Hyksos. Recent excavations at Tell el-D'aba.* London, British Museum Press.
Borchardt, L. and Ricke, H. (1980) *Die Wohnhäuser in Tell El-Amarna.* Berlin, Gebr. Mann Verlag.
Breasted, H. (1906) *Ancient records of Egypt. Volumes I to V.* Illinois, University of Illinois Press.
Cameron, C. M. (2006) Ethnoarchaeology and contextual studies. In D. Papaconstantinou (ed.) *Deconstructive context. A critical approach to archaeological practice*, 22–33. Oxford, Oxbow Books.
Correas-Amador, M. (2011) Egyptian mud houses: an ethnoarchaeological perspective. In M. Horne, J. Kramer, D. Soliman, C. van de Hoven, L. Weiss and N. Staring (eds) *Current Research in Egyptology 2010: Proceedings of the Eleventh Annual Symposium. Leiden University 2010*, 22–32. Oxford, Oxbow Books.
David, N. and Kramer, C. (2001) *Ethnoarchaeology in action.* Cambridge, Cambridge University Press.
Davies, N. (1929) The town house in Ancient Egypt. *Metropolitan Museum Studies,* vol. 1, n.2, 233–255.
Demangeon, A. (1926) Problèmes actuels et aspects nouveaux de la vie rurale en Égypte. *Annales de Géographie,* v. 35, no. 194, 155–173.
Eigner, D. (1984) *Ländliche Architektur und Siedlungsformen im Ägypten der Gegenwart.* Viena, Afro-Pub.
Eigner, D. (2006) *Wohnen in Ägypten.* In E. Czerny, I. Hein, H. Hunger, D. Melman and A. Schawb (eds.) Timelines: studies in honour of Manfred Bietak, Orientalia Lovaniensia Analecta 149, vol. 3, 331–338. Peeters Publishers/Department of Oriental Studies.
Kemp, B. (2000) Soil (including mud brick architecture). In P. Nicholson and I. Shaw (eds) *Ancient Egyptian materials and technology*, 78–104. Cambridge, Cambridge University Press.
Kemp B. (2006) *Ancient Egypt: anatomy of a civilization.* London, Routledge.
Gheith, M. and Ahmad, K. (1988) *Rural Society.* Dar Al Maarif Al Gamiaa, Alexandria.
Hein, I. and Jánosi, P. (2004) *Tell el-Dab'a. XI, Areal A/V: Siedlungsrelikte der späten 2. Zwischenzeit.* Wien, Verlag der Österreichischen Akademie der Wissenschaften.
Hodder, I. and Hutson, S. (2003) *Reading the past: current approaches to interpretation in archaeology.* Cambridge University Press, Cambridge.

Ibrahim, F. N. (1982) The ecological problems of irrigated cultivation in Egypt. In G. H. Mensching (ed), *Problems of the management of irrigated lands in areas of traditional and modern cultivation, report of an inter-congress meeting of the International Geographical Union Working Group on Resource Management in Drylands, 22–31 March, 1982, El Minia, Egypt,* 61–77. Hamburg, International Geographical Union.

Ibrahim, F. N. (2003) *Egypt. An economic geography.* London, I.B. Tauris.

Lacovara, P. (1997) *The New Kingdom royal city.* London, Kegan Paul International.

Last (2006) Potted histories: towards an understanding of potsherds and their contexts. In D. Papaconstantinou (ed.) *Deconstructive context. A critical approach to archaeological practice,* 120–137. Oxford, Oxbow Books.

Lozach, J. and Hug, G. (1930) *L'habitat rural en Égypte.* Cairo, Société Royale de Géographie d'Égypte.

MacKenzie, D. (1985) 'Egypt's great brick crisis'. *New Scientist* 30th May, p. 10.

Mahgoub, Y. (2000) The transformation of traditional rural settlements in Egypt. *IAPS Conference: Cultural and Space in the Built Environment Network. Second International Symposium of IAPS-CSBE network.* Amasya, Turkey, June. Available at http://www.slideshare.net/ymahgoub/egyptian-village-transformation (Accessed 9th May).

Margold, S. (1957) Agrarian land reform in Egypt. *American journal of economy and sociology,* vol. 17, 9–19.

Marsot, A. (1985) *A short history of modern Egypt.* Cambridge, Cambridge University Press.

Petrie, W. M. F. (1907) *Gizeh and Rifeh.* London, British School of Archaeology in Egypt.

Rapoport, A. (1976) *The mutual interaction of people and their built environment.* The Hague, Mouton.

Renfrew, C. and Bahn, P. (2000) *Archaeology: theories, methods and practice.* London, Thames and Hudson.

Ricke, H. (1932) *Grundriss des Amarna Wohnhauses.* Leipzig, J. C. Hinrichs'sche buchhandlung.

Sanders, D. (1990) Behavioral conventions and archaeology: methods for the analysis of ancient architecture. In S. Kent (ed.) *Domestic architecture and the use of space. An interdisciplinary cross-cultural study,* 7–60. Cambridge, Cambridge University Press.

Spencer, A. J. (1994) Mud brick: its decay and detection in Upper and Lower Egypt. In C. Eyre, A. Leahy and L. Montagno (eds) *The unbroken reed: studies in the culture and heritage of Ancient Egypt in honour of A. F. Shore,* 315–320. London, Egypt Exploration Society.

Tsipopoulou, M. (2006) Counting sherds at Neopalatial Petras, Siteia, east Crete: integrating ceramic analysis with architectural data. In D. Papaconstantinou (ed.) *Deconstructive context. A critical approach to archaeological practice,* 138–158. Oxford, Oxbow Books.

Tietze, C. (1985) Amarna: Analyse der Wohnhauser und soziale Struktur der Stadtbewohner. *Zeitschrift für Ägyptische Sprache und Altertumskunde,* 112, 48–84.

Von Pilgrim, C. (1996) *Elephantine, XVIII. Untersuchungen in der Stadt des Mittleren Reiches und der Zweiten Zwischenzeit.* Mainz am Rhein, P. von Zabern.

Wood exploitation in ancient Egypt: where, who and how?

Flavie Deglin

Introduction

Mainly because of lack of evidence, the technical sides of woodworking and the identification of plants from ancient Egypt have often been investigated by scholars, as opposed to the social and economic aspects of wood exploitation.

In the collective imagination, the landscape of ancient Egypt is very similar to today's landscape: a river lined with fields, some palm-trees and, all around, a vast desert.

It is true that Egypt is nowadays one of the world's driest countries where desert takes up 96% of the land. The country is planted with plenty of non-native plants such as Eucalyptus, Australian pine or Bougainvillea. Also, in order to feed the population, which has considerably increased recently, agriculture was developed on a large scale, leading to the disappearance of some plant species. Nevertheless, the present landscape of Egypt affects our vision of it in Antiquity. While Egypt was probably poorly provided with large trees capable of producing timber or wood in sufficient quantities – as the importation of timber which is well attested for in ancient Egypt seems to suggest – this does not mean that the country did not have trees as such or produce timber at all. Evidence for wooded areas is scarce, but there are, for instance, tomb-paintings and reliefs showing men cutting wood in what seems if not a forest, at least a large grove.

Therefore this paper, which is part of my doctoral research, aims to present a status report on this question, starting from our botanical knowledge and re-examining some textual and iconographic documents.

Local species: a botanical aspect

Thus, as already mentioned, the question of wood in ancient Egypt was often investigated by scholars through the technical sides of woodworking and the identification of plants. Botanists have been able to identify many indigenous species thanks to wall-paintings, texts and archaeological remains. The so-called "cabinet de curiosités" of Thuthmose III's (Beaux 1990) or the Theban tomb n° 81 of Ineni (Baum 1988) are good examples.

In Egypt, trees grew mainly in the Nile valley and in the oases of the western desert but, so far it has not been possible to determine specific areas. We note a large variety of trees and shrub species which were fit for hostile surroundings: some are salt-tolerant and drought-resistant (like the *acacia* subsp. *raddiana*), consuming little water; others, on the contrary, can survive during long inundation periods (like *acacia nilotica* or *faiderbia albida*) (Springel 2006, 2–14, 18–24).

The main trees used for timber and woodworking were the acacia tree and its subspecies, named SnDt in the Egyptian texts. Nowadays, there are more than a thousand species of acacia. Each one grows in different areas and has particular properties. The main species are:

Acacia nilotica (L.) Willd ex Delile which grows in the Nile Valley and oases of the Western Desert (Gale *et al.* 2000, 340–341; Germer 1985, 25–27; Killen 1980, 6; Lucas 1964, 446–447) (Fig. 1). It is a hard wood, excellent for fuel and charcoal but it was mainly used for timber in boat building and for tools.

The *acacia tortilis* subsp. *tortilis* (Forssk.) Hayne grows in the southern part of Eastern Desert, wadis along the Red Sea and the southern part of Sinai (Germer 1985, 89–90) (Fig. 2). It is a solid wood used for small objects which also has a high calorific value.

Ehrenbergiana is the strongest acacia and the *raddiana* was good for timber, but actually more useful for firewood and charcoal.

The sycamore, *ficus sycomorus L.* called nht by the Egyptians, grows in the Nile Valley, Sinaï and oases of the Western Desert and was used as timber in all kinds of woodwork thanks to its resistance to decay and because it was easy to carve and light (Gale *et al.* 2000, 345; Germer 1985, 124–125; Killen 1980, 6; Lucas 1964, 447–448) (Fig. 3).

Tamarisk, *tamarix aphylla* (L.) H. Karst. (Gale *et al.* 2000, 345; Germer 1985, 124–125; Killen 1980, 6; Lucas 1964, 447–448) was extremely useful as it provides strong and long pieces of wood for construction and coffins. This species grows everywhere in Egypt and it is the only one to become a full tree and not stay as a shrub (Fig. 4).

Other indigenous trees were less employed by carpenters, such as persea (*mimusops laurifolia*; Gale *et al.* 2000, 342; Germer 1985, 148–149; Killen 1980, 7), known under the name šw3b and used in joinery, carpentry and construction. The sidder, called nbs (*ziziphus spina-christi* (L.) Desf., Gale *et al.* 2000, 347; Germer 1985, 114–115; Killen 1980, 6; Lucas 1964, 446), was used as timber for joinery and for small items.

Sometimes, the Egyptian plum, *balanites aegyptiaca* L. Delile (Germer, 1985, 98–99) was used for boat building. Even palms were used for furniture and for roofing timber, most often in the oases, such as the dom palm, *phoenix dactylifera* L. (Gale *et al.* 2000, 347; Germer 985, 232–233; Lucas 443–444), and the date palm, *hyphaene thebaica* (L.) Mart. (Gale *et al.* 2000, 347–348; Germer 1985, 234–235; Killen 1980, 3; Lucas 1964, 444).

In general, it seems that Egyptians developed techniques in joinery or laminating in order to lessen the impact of low grade and fibrous timber in an attempt to fabricate a large sheet of material which was dimensionally stable and equally strong in all directions, like the 'plywood' used in a sarcophagus in the Step Pyramid of Djoser, Saqqara (Killen 1980, 9; Gale *et al.* 2000, 356–357, fig. 15.19).

Ancient landscape through texts

We may also quote the excerpts from a few classical authors who describe the Egyptian landscape and give information about specific areas. For example, Herodotus (II, 138) describes the shrine of Artemis at Bubastis as 'shaded over with trees': 'within is a grove of very tall trees (ἄλσος δενδρέων μεγίστων) growing around a great shrine where the image of the goddess is'. And he

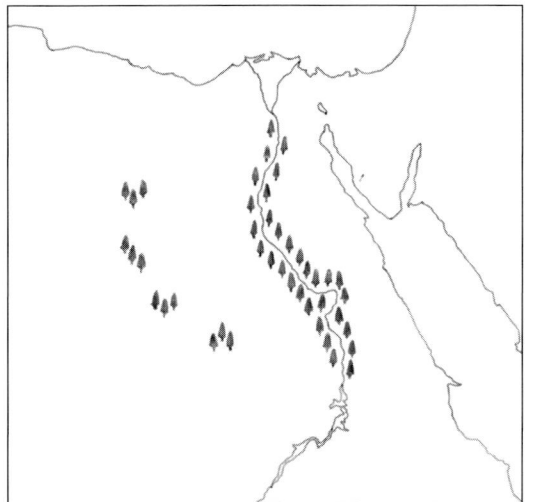

Figure 1. Map showing the current distribution of the acacia nilotica in Egypt.

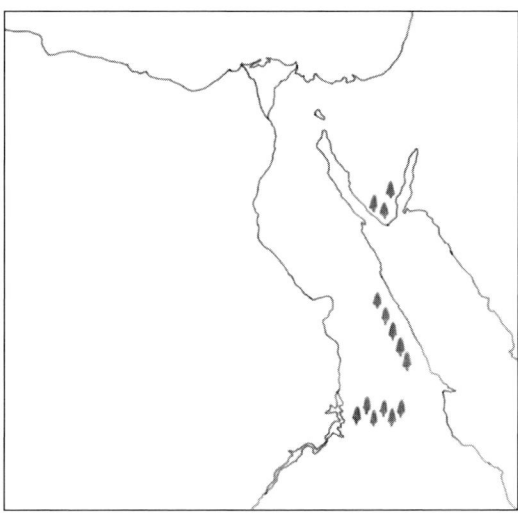

Figure 2. Map showing the current distribution of the acacia tortilis subsp. tortilis in Egypt.

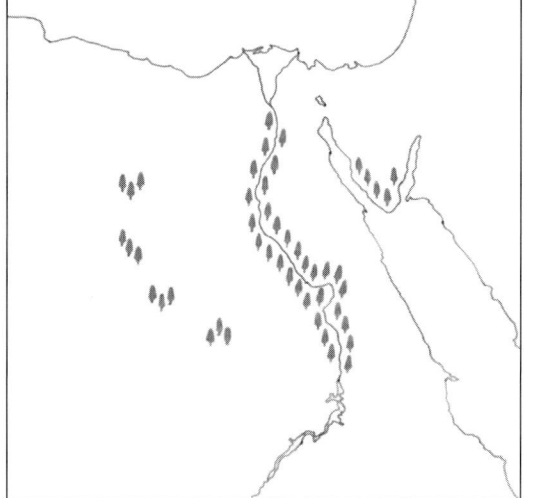

Figure 3. Map showing the current distribution of the ficus sycomorus in Egypt.

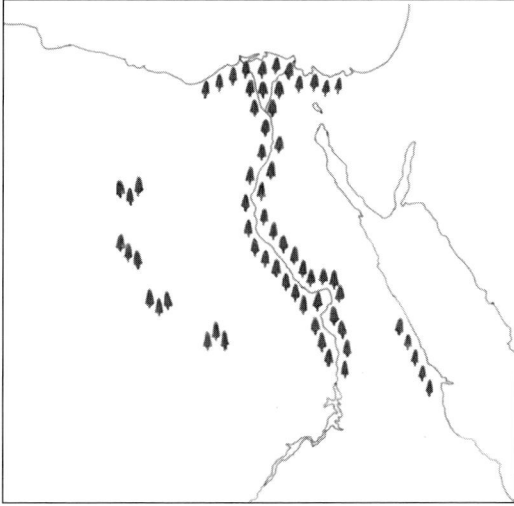

Figure 4. Map showing the current distribution of the tamarix aphylla in Egypt.

added 'here and there on the way trees are grown as high as the sky (δένδρεα οὐρανομήκεα)'. Gessler-Löhr (1983, 405, n.1337) and Rondot (1989, 261–262) referred to date-palms following texts from Dendera and Edfu. As for Strabo (XVII, I, 35), he mentions a city south of Memphis named Acanthos, corresponding to Acanthônpolis in Diodorus (I, 97) and documentary texts, together with its temple dedicated to Osiris and its 'grove of the Thebaic acanthi (Ὀσίριδος ἱερὸν καὶ τὸ τῆς ἀκάνθης ἄλσος)', *i.e.* the acacia-tree from which the Greek name of the city derives. Yoyotte pointed out the fact that Acanthonpolis was the actual Kafr Ammar. He mentions groves seen by many travellers and archaeologists and adds that the city was also named Shenâ-khen 'the living trees' and linked acacias growing there to a cult of Osiris (Yoyotte, 1961, 78, 100). So we should note that these groves, situated next to temples or shrines, could have been considered as holy and therefore not used for secular purpose or for exploitation.

Egyptian temples seem to have owned groves in the country. We find the basis of this statement in earlier documents as confirmed by the so-called great papyrus Harris (pHarris I) now in the British Museum (Grandet, 1994).

King Ramses III made a list of all the belongings and endowments of the major divinities of Egypt. This list states that Amon, Mout, Khonsu and all the lords of Thebes owned 433 gardens and groves (11,6; Grandet 1994a, 236; Grandet 1994b, 57, n. 224, pl. 10). For Ra in Heliopolis, it was 64 (32a,2; Grandet 1994a, 260–261, 266; Grandet 1994b, 118–119, n. 489, 495, 536, pl. 27, 32) and he gave to Ptah lord of Memphis 5 gardens and copses (Grandet, 1994a, 292; Grandet, 1994b, 180, n. 723)

If the terms *k3mw* (Garden, *Wb V*, 106(4–9)) and *šnyw* (Trees, *Wb IV*, 498(6)–499(5)) refer to vineyards, orchards and olive-trees, an estate with trees and two gardens of sycamores (65c14; 65c15; Grandet 1994a, 318; Grandet 1994b, 210, n. 877) was also offered to the minor divinities of the land.

> 65c14 *k3mw n nh3w* 2
> Garden of sycamores 2
>
> 65c15 *pr ʿpr(w) m ḫtw* 1
> Estate filled with trees 1

But, it seems that the king concluded that he would create a beautiful landscape filled with trees in order to please the deities and the Egyptians. That was the case in Medinet Habu (4,3; Grandet 1994a, 227; Grandet 1994b, 15–16, n. 69, pl. 4) and for the whole country in general (78,8; Grandet 1994a, 339; Grandet 1994b, 265, n. 953).

> 4,3 *šd=i mr m-b3ḥ=s bʿḥ(w) m nww dg3(w) m mnww ḥr 3ḥ3ḥw mi t3-mḥw*
> I have dug a canal in front of it filled with water, planted with trees and plants like in Lower Egypt
>
> 78,8 *Iry=I srwd t3 (r-)dr=f m mnww ḥr 3ḥ3ḥw di=i ḥms rḥyt m n3y=w šwbw*
> I've made the country flourishing with trees and plants, I've made that in order that the Rekhyt could rest under their shade.

The purpose of the different groves is still unknown. Were they ornamental, for fruit cultivation, or the exploitation of the wooden resources? Whichever the case, these few excerpts prove that Egypt was not the desert we imagined it to be.

Exploitation: studies through felling tree scenes

As already mentioned, Egyptian tomb representations provide us with several depictions of men cutting wood, which can be of some help for a better understanding of wood exploitation. So far, I have collected 18 scenes, from the Old Kingdom to the New Kingdom, some of them are unfortunately very fragmentary (Fig. 5).

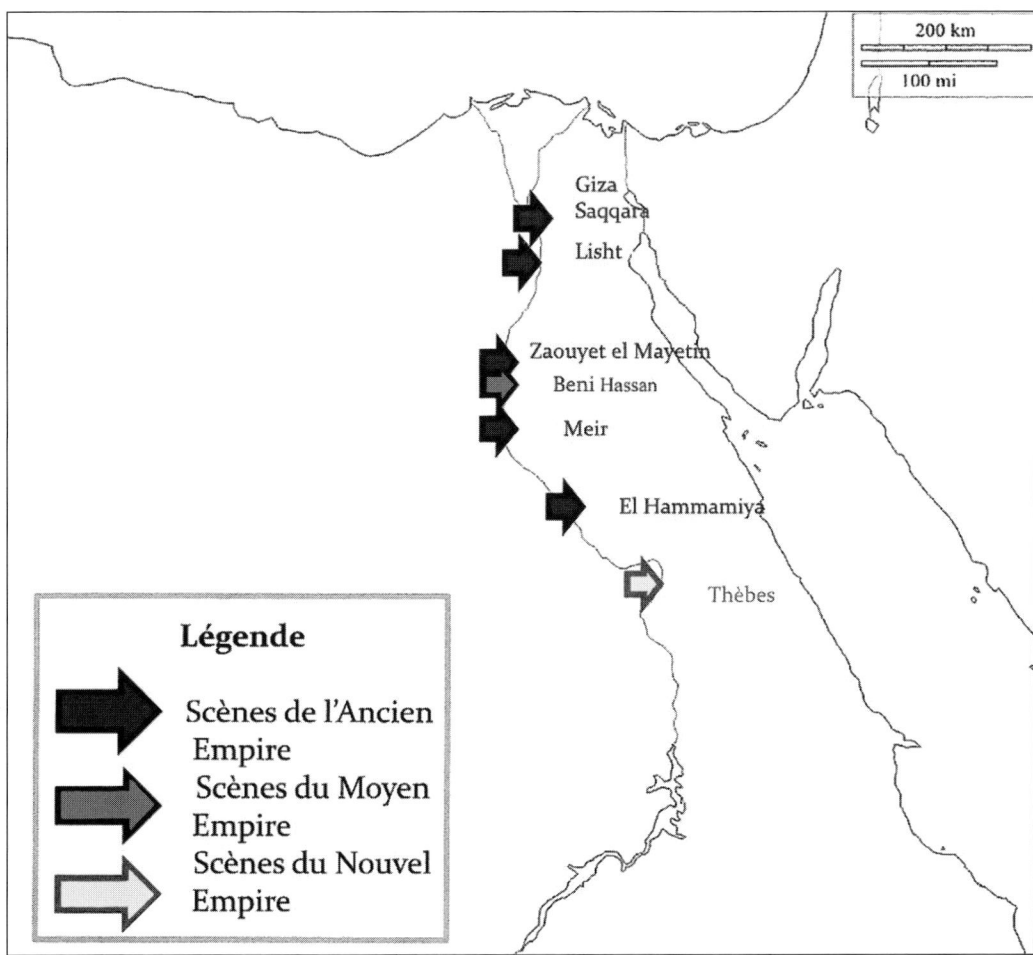

Figure 5. Map showing the location of the felling tree scenes found on tomb paintings.

For the Old Kingdom, there are 10 scenes dated to the 5th and 6th dynasties, found not only in Giza and Sakkara, but also in more 'provincial' necropolis such as Lisht, El-Hammamiya or Meir.

The pattern is always similar to the one in stela BS 994 of the British Museum (British Museum 1922, 6, pl. 17) (Fig. 6). This part of a tomb relief from Giza depicts in the top register a scene of boat building. Even though only the lower part of the workmen's body is visible, we can clearly see a man on the left felling a tree with his axe. Then, a gang of four men carry the trunk to a dockyard. On the right, there are carpenters squaring a log while another one at their back is chiseling the prow or poop of a boat.

For the Middle Kingdom, I have collected only one scene. It is found in the tomb of Khnoumhotep at Beni Hassan (Newberry 1893, pl. 29) (Fig. 7).

On the upper register of the west wall, we can see on the left, carpenters (*mdḥ*) working on a boat. Some are working with an axe, others with a chisel or an adze. Khnoumhotep, holding

Figure 6. Drawing of the stela BM 994 (after BM 994, British Museum, 1922, pl. 17).

Figure 7. Drawing of the scene from the tomb of Khnumhotep in Beni Hassan (after Newberry, 1893, pl. 29).

the title of prince ($rp^{c}t$), is in his sedan chair and a foreman is watching the carpenters. In the middle part of the register, two men with axes are cutting down a tree, from whose branches goats are feeding.

The scene looks like the one from the Old Kingdom, but it is one of the few which quotes the actions carried out by the characters.

Finally all examples from the New Kingdom come from the Theban necropolis. In TT52 (Davies 1927a, 60–65, pl. 18–19, 21) belonging to Nakht (18th dynasty, perhaps under the reign of Thutmose IV) (Fig. 8), on the lower register of the east wall, we can see a sowing scene. The register is divided in two parts by a thick and winding line, which draws a lake in the middle part. In the upper part, a man is kneeling to cut down a tree. The repetitive pattern of the tree and the attempt of achieving perspective by putting a certain kind of bush in the background strive to prove that it was a real grove.

Although they might hint to wood exploitation in the vicinity, we should keep in mind the fact that these scenes might also be part of decorum, *i.e.* they could be artistic conventions used to depict an ideal landscape and daily life: in fact, the same scene is found in TT 38 belonging to Djeserkareseneb (Davies 1963, 3–5, pl. 2) (Fig. 9), TT 52 belonging to Nakht (Davies 1927a, 60–65, pl. 18, 19, 21) and TT 57 of Khaemhat (Loret 1884, 113–132) (Fig. 10).

In these tombs, the pattern is the same: we have a woodcutter, men ploughing and the same winding line which draws a lake. This eventuality is even more accurate when we know that the tombs belonged to the reigns of Thutmose IV or Amenhotep III.

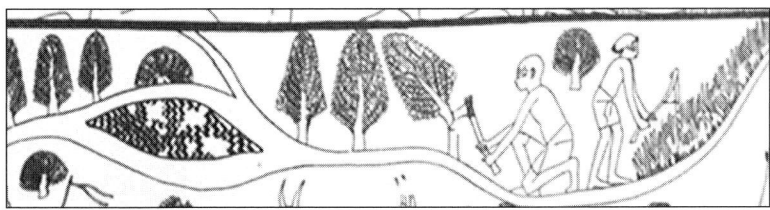

Figure 8. Drawing of the scene from the TT52 belonging to Nakht (after Davies, 1927, pl. 18).

Figure 9. Drawing of the scene from TT38 belonging to Djeserkareseneb (after Davies, 1963, pl. 2).

Figure 10. Drawing of the scene from TT 57 belonging to Kaemhat (after Wreszinski, 1923, pl. 189).

We may note that in the Old and Middle Kingdoms the wood scenes are mainly concerned with felling trees in the vicinity of dockyards. In the New Kingdom however, they occur within harvest and field works. There are only two scenes of a carpenter in a workshop. The first one is in the 5th dynasty mastaba of Nefer and Kaha in Saqqara (Moussa and Altenmüller 1971, 27–28, pl. 20–22), and the other one is in TT217, belonging to Ipouy, who lived under the reign of Ramses II (Davies 1927b, 70–72, pl. 36). In all cases, we have no depiction of storerooms.

Dockyards are in fact a place where wood exploitation plays an important part and, fortunately enough, the documentation is sufficient. For example, in the Reisner II papyrus, we find accounts of the dockyard workshop in the reign of Sesostris I (Simpson 1965), the BM 10056 papyrus refers to the administration of the dockyard of Perunefer (Glanville 1931, 105–121; Glanville 1932, 7–41) and in the Anastasi IV there is a letter regarding the repair of a bark (R°7, 9/8, 7, Caminos 1954, 159–164; Gardiner 1937, 42–43). In all of these, a high ranking official is at the head of the administration and an army of carpenters who fell wood in the vicinity, brought it to the dockyard and stored it there. The resource seemed to belong to the king and the royal administration. But sources show that private people also stored wood in their houses.

Supply and use of timber

We hold numerous accounts, in particular the specific case of an ostraca from Deir el-Medineh (Janssen *et al.* 2003, 1–28; Akiyama 1992, 70–82), mentioning wood quantities, but their destination and their place of storage are rarely specified. And, needless to say, we never get any information about the provenance of this material.

Accounts of Seti I, edited by W. Spiegelberg and now in the Bibliothèque Nationale of Paris under the inventory number 209 to 213 (Spiegelberg 1896), mention a requisition of timber by authorities. There we learn that an officer (*w'rtw*) visited the house of each inhabitant of a district in the southern part of Memphis.

The houses that are visited belong to high and middle ranking officers, religious entities (chapel of Qasarti, chapel of Amun) and royal institutions (estate of kings and queens); even the deceased must remove their timber.

Most of the pieces of wood mentioned in these accounts are ship's parts or pieces of wood suitable for this use: *wg3* (rib of the boat), *smkt* (support beam), *iswt* (plank).

A second source is the group of letters from the 12th dynasty, the so-called Hekanakhte letters found in Deir el-Bahari and today in the Metropolitan Museum under the number 22.3.520. One account on its verso contains records of pieces of wood.

```
1 sš n ḥt.w
2 trt ḥt 5 m pr-ḥ3
3 ḥt 3w ḥt m wb3
4 ḥt n b3k 1
5 ḥt nht 3 ʿ3 1
6 rwryt 1
7 3rt nt trt m š3w m ʿ3ʿ 60
8 im3 4
9 šnd(t) 5
10 šnd(t) s3w 1 ʿ3
```

> 1 Account of wood:
> 2 Willows 5 in the rear part of the house
> 3 Mast in the forecourt
> 4 Moringa woods 1
> 5 Sycamore woods 3, big
> 6 Ruryt-wood 1
> 7 Cabin of willow, equivalent to 60 planks
> 8 Ima-trees 4
> 9 Acacias 5
> 10 Acacia beam 1, big

This remarkable list, despite the accounts of timber being scarce, was not studied by Allen (Allen 2002, 19, 57–58, pl. 42–43), neither by James (James 1962, 54, 61–62), further from a statement concerning the vocabulary. Goedicke was the only one to write a short note saying that ship pieces could not be in an agricultural estate (Goedicke 1984, 96–97).

If we take a close look, most of the species are known; acacia, willow sycamore and moringa are indigenous species, and so must be *i3m* and *rwryt* wood. Therefore, for shipbuilding, not only could Egyptians use indigenous species that did not require the inevitable imports, but they also kept the resource in the form of ship pieces. A question remains: were pieces used for repairing barks or were they used as material?

The example of the use of wood in causeways

We can read in the satirical literary text of the Anastasi I papyrus (BM 10247), col 14, an excerpt relating to the building of a ramp (Gardiner 1911, 16–17, pl. 24–26).

> ¹⁴,¹ *wpi=i n=k shnt n nb ʿ.w.s. mi ntk p3y=f sš nsw sbi=k ḥry mnww wrw n Ḥr*
> ¹⁴,² *nb t3wy . mk ntk sš šs3 nty r ḥʿt mnf3t irw sṯw n mḥ 730 wsḫt mḥ 55 n 120 n*
> ¹⁴,³ *r gt mḥ m gš ḥr s3y*

> ¹⁴,¹ I will explain to you the command of your Lord, l.p.h., since you are his royal scribe; you are dispatched conveying great monuments for Horus
> ¹⁴,² the Lord of the Two Lands. See, you are the clever scribe who is at the head of the troops! There is to be constructed a ramp of 730 cubits in length with a width of 55 cubits, consisting of/containing 120
> ¹⁴,³ compartments filled with reeds and beams.

It seems that ramps required wooden beams, however we do not have information regarding the specific type of logs (*s3w Wb III*, 419(14)).

Iconography could help clarify this issue. In the famous scene of the colossus in the tomb of Djehoutyhetep in El Bersheh (Newberry 1894, 17–26, pl. 15), in the inner part, below the colossus, a gang of three men can be seen carrying a badly cut plank. It is written:

> *f3t ḫtw n sṯ in ṯt.w*
> Carry wood by the gang.

They follow a gang of men supplying water. At first, we could think that the workers drank the water but, on the upper register, on the sledge of the colossus we see a man pouring the liquid from a jar onto the soil.

However, there is no trace of wood in this scene. In fact, logs were not displayed under the sledge but, instead, planks were buried for a better distribution of weight. Mortar, stone chips and slipstones, sprinkled with water, made the way slippery.

Next, if we compare sources with archaeological finds, it appears that old pieces of boat were often re-used. This can be seen in Lahoun (Petrie *et al.* 1923, 11–12, pl. 7, 15), Lisht (Arnold 1992, 92, 93, 104, 107), Deir el-Bahari (Arnold 1979, 28, pl. 21b, 48) and Mirgissa (Vercoutter 1970, 178–180, 204–214, figs 3–5, 11–20). The pieces were identified thanks to the split for a leather fastening, and sometimes (from analysis by specialist from Kew gardens), acacia was used for the ribs or hulls of boats.

The core of a building ramp consisted of brick or rubble in which old shipbuilding beams were inserted and covered with layers of mortar and stone chips.

Conclusions

In this paper, I showed that the question of wood exploitation needs to be reviewed anew in order to achieve a better understanding of some economical aspects of this natural resource.

First, we have to differentiate between current and ancient landscapes since these did not remain unchanged through time. We must also detect the areas with wood presence through texts and tomb-paintings.

Then, comparisons between iconography, texts and archaeological remains can show us that local species were used as timber in the dockyards. Even though wood importation is better known through sources, I intend to prove that dockyards played an important part in the distribution and exploitation of indigenous wood. It seems that the royal administration directly used the resource as carpenters stocked it, transformed the raw material in several workshops belonging to the dockyard, and supplied wood to other workshops and people. Thus, ship timbers could be found everywhere in accounts and the hypothesis can be made that these pieces seemed to be the standard pieces for exchange, trade, store, used and re-used following personal purposes and need. CNRS UMR 8164, Halma-Ipel, Université Charles-de-Gaulle – Lille 3.

Aknowledgements

I am very grateful to Prof. D. Devauchelle, the supervisor of my doctoral thesis and Dr G. Widmer for carefully reading this article and for their advice. I would also like to thank the organizers of the CRE 2011 and the people who encouraged me during the conference for their kindness.

References

Akiyama, S. (1992) *The supply of wood to Deir el-Medineh* (デル・エル・メディーナに対する「薪」の「支給」), *Bulletin of the Society for the Near Eastern Studies in Japan* (日本オリエント学会) 35(1). Tokyo, 71–82.

Allen, J. P. (2002) *The Heqanakht Papyri*. New York, Metropolitan Museum of Arts.

Arnold, D. (1979) *The Temple of Mentuhotep at Deir El-Bahari from the notes of Herbert Winlock*. New York, Metropolitan Museum of Arts.

Arnold, D. (1992) *The Pyramid Complex of Senwosret I, The South Cemeteries of Lisht III*. New York, Metropolitan Museum of Arts.
Baum, N. (1988) *Arbres et arbustes de l'Egypte ancienne: la liste de la tombe thébaine d'Ineni (no 81), Orientalia Lovaniensia analecta 31*. Leuven. Peteers.
Beaux, N. (1990) *Le cabinet de curiosités de Thoutmosis III: plantes et animaux du «Jardin botanique» de Karnak, Orientalia Lovaniensia analecta 36*. Leuven. Peteers.
British Museum (1922) *Hieroglyphic texts from Egyptian stelae, &c., in the British Museum. Part VI*, London.
Caminos, R. (1954) *Late-Egyptian Miscellanies*. London, Oxford University Press.
Davies, N. de G. (1927a) *The Tomb of Nakht at Thebes*. New York, Metropolitan Museum of Arts.
Davies, N. de G. (1927b) *Two Ramesside Tombs at Thebes*. New York, Metropolitan Museum of Arts.
Davies, N. de G. (1963) *Scenes from some Theban Tombs (Nos 38, 66, 162, with excerpts from 81), Private Tombs at Thebes IV*. Oxford, Griffith Institute University Press.
Diodorus of Sicily, Oldfather H. C. (transl.) (1960), *Books I and II 1–34*, Loeb Classical Library. London, William Heinemann, Cambridge, Harvard University Press.
Gale, R., Gasson P., Hepper N. and Killen G. (2000) Wood, in Nicholson, P. T. and Shaw, I. (eds), *Ancient Egyptian Materials and Technology*, 334–371. Cambridge. Cambridge University Press.
Gardiner, A. H. (1911) *Egyptian Hieratic Texts, Transcribed, Translated and Annotated I Literary Texts of the New Kingdom*. Leipzig, Hinrichs.
Gardiner, A. H. (1937) *Late-Egyptian Miscellanies*. Bruxelles, Fondation égyptologique reine Elisabeth.
Germer, R. (1985) *Flora des pharaonischen Ägypten, Deutsches Archäologisches Institut Abbteilung Kairo 14*. Philipp von Zabern, Mainz-am-Rhein.
Gessler-Löhr, B. (1983) *Die heiligen Seen ägyptischer Tempel, Ein Beitrag zur Deutung skraler Baukunst im alten Ägypten, Hildesheimer ägyptologische Beitrage 21*. Hildesheim, Gerstenberg.
Glanville, S. R. K. (1931) Records of a Royal Dockyard of the Time of Tuthmosis III, *Zeitschrift für ägyptische Sprache und Altertumskunde 66*. Leipzig, J. C. Hinrichs, 105–121.
Glanville, S. R. K. (1932) Records of a Royal Dockyard of the Time of Tuthmosis III (Part II), *Zeitschrift für ägyptische Sprache und Altertumskunde 68*. Leipzig, J. C. Hinrichs, 7–41.
Goedicke, H. (1984) *Studies in the Hekanakhte Papers*. Baltimore, Halgo Inc.
Grandet, P. (1994a) *Le papyrus Harris I (BM 9999) vol. I, Bibliothèque d'études 109/1*. Cairo, Institut Français d'Archéologie Orientale.
Grandet, P. (1994b) *Le papyrus Harris I (BM 9999) vol. II, Bibliothèque d'études 109/2*. Cairo, Institut Français d'Archéologie Orientale.
Herodotus, Godley, A. D. (transl.) (1966) *Herodotus 1, Books I and II*, Loeb Classical Library. London, William Heinemann, Cambridge, Harvard University Press.
James, T. G. H. (1962) *The Hekanakhte Papers and Other Early Middle Kingdom Documents*. New York.
Janssen, J. J. Frood E. and Goeck M. (2003) *Woodcutters, potters and doorkeepers, service personnel of the Deir el-Medina Workmen, Egyptologische Uitgaven 17*. Leiden, Nederlands Instituut voor het Nabije Oosten, 1–28.
Killen, G. (1980) *Ancient Egyptian Furniture vol. I (4000–1300)*. Warminster, Aris & Phillips.
Moussa, A. M. and Altenmüller, H. (1971) *Old Kingdom Tombs at the Causeway of King Unas at Saqqara, The Tomb of Nefer and Ka Hay, Archäologische Veröffentlichungen Deutsches Archäologisches Institut Abteilung Kairo 5*. Mainz-am-Rhein, Philipp von Zabern.
Newberry, P. E. (1893) *Beni Hassan I, Egypt Exploration Fund [1893–1900], Archaeological survey of Egypt. Memoir: 1*. London, K. Paul, Trench, Trübner and Co.
Newberry, P. E. (1894) *El-Bersheh I (The Tomb of Tehuti-Hetep), Archaeological survey of Egypt: 3*. Londres, K. Paul, Trench, Trübner & Co.
Loret, V. (1884) *la tombe de Khâ-m-Hâ, Mémoire de la mission archéologique française au Caire1 fasc. 1*. Paris.

Lucas, A. (1962) *Ancient Egyptian Materials and Industries*. London, Edward Arnold (Publishers) Ltd.
Petrie, W. M. F., Brunton G. and Murray M. A. (1923) *Lahun II, The Egyptian Research Account. Publication 33*. Londres.
Rondot, V. (1989) Une monographie bubastite, *Bulletin de l'Institut Français d'Archéologie Orientale 89*. Le Caire, 261–262.
Simpson, W. K. (1965) *Accounts of the Dockyard Workshop at This in the Reign of Sesostris I, Papyrus Reisner II, Transcription and Commentary*. Boston, Museum of Fine Arts.
Spiegelberg, W. (1896) *Rechnungen aus der Zeit Setis I circa 1350 v. Christ mit anderen Rechnungen des Neues Reiches*. Strasbourg, Trübner.
Springel, I. (2006) *The desert garden, a practical guide*. Cairo, the American University in Cairo Press.
Strabo, Jones, H. (transl.) (1959) *Geography of Strabo 8, Book XVII and General Index*, Loeb Classical Library. London, William Heinemann, Cambridge, Harvard University Press.
Vandier, J. (1943) Note sur le transport du colosse d'El Bersheh, *Chronique d'Egypte 36*. Bruxelles, Fondation égyptologique reine Elisabeth, 185–190.
Vercoutter, J. (1970) *Mirgissa I*. Paris.
Yoyotte, J. (1961) Etudes géographiques. I. La « cité des acacias » (Kafr Ammar), *Revue d'Egyptologie 13*. Paris, C Klincksieck. 72–105.

Antonio Bernal de O'Reilly and the discovery of ancient Egypt in Spain

Javier Fernández Negro

Introduction

In the course of the 19th century, the history of Ancient Egypt was beginning to be rewritten. With Napoleon's expedition began a series of works which would give way to the birth of a science: Egyptology.

The contribution of European travellers during the eighteenth and nineteenth centuries was fundamental to the laying of the foundations in the historical research of Egypt. The reasons for these travels, which I will outline, were manifold; I will also outline the form that many of them took. These travellers usually had a very wise understanding of the Bible and the classical fonts. Their motivation was the desire to further explore the biblical scriptures, in addition to their admiration for the Orient. Their legacy for Archaeology – in the form of annotations concerning ruins and native legends, drawings and object analyses – is invaluable.

In the nineteenth century, Spain was a country immersed in complete political decadence at both national and international level after the loss of the American colonies; however the African war (1859–1860) meant Spain's return to international politics and this in turn allowed the rebirth of the interest of Spanish society for the Near East (Córdoba 2005, 748). In this context, Antonio Bernal de O'Reilly (Fig. 1) was one of these observers that set his aims on Egypt. In 1863 he was named consul of Syria and Palestine, occupying the position for the three following years. The result of his journey to this area and his stay there was a book whose title was *En Tierra Santa* (In the Holy Land). Published in its first edition in 1870, the book was divided in two parts. This paper deals with the first part, named *En Egipto* (In Egypt: this book is in fact a compilation of the letters (Fig. 2) that A. Bernal de O'Reilly sent to his friend Mesonero Romanos, who was an intellectual from Madrid, during his stay in Egypt). In this book of travels, Antonio Bernal de O'Reilly described his journey through the country of the Nile, which was an unmissable stop before visiting Jerusalem.

My goal is to trace the steps of the consul in the land of the Nile, as well as to highlight the legacy he left in his book – especially the historical contribution – that silenced the echoes of European influences in Spain, by providing his own outlook on the history of ancient Egypt.

The Spanish outlook on Egypt since the early nineteenth century until the travels of Antonio Bernal de O'Reilly

In Spain, direct knowledge concerning Egypt came principally from the rest of Europe. Mesonero Romanos, who wrote the prologue of O'Reilly's book, regretted the little evidence he had for the occurrence of Spanish travellers in the land of the Nile. Therefore, newspapers and cultural magazines were the main channels of information for Spanish people. Three different sources can be identified:

Firstly, the newspapers. In their pages, certain pieces of news concerning the discoveries in Egypt were included. The newspaper *La España* offers an example in its issue dated 19th of July, 1850, where it announced the publication of a book entitled *Monuments of Egypt and Ethiopia* (Suarez, 1850). The authors of this book were Lepsius and his team, showcasing their work in Egypt with the help of many illustrations. The Spanish newspaper said about the book:

Figure 1. Portrait of Antonio Bernal de O'Reilly.

> "En 1842 envió S.M, el rey de Prusia a Egipto al professor R. Lepsius acompañado de varios pintores tanto prusianos como ingleses, con el fin de explotar bajo el punto de vista de la Historia, Cronología, Filosofía, Mitología, Arqueología, Geografía y Corografía los monumentos de la civilización egipcia y etiópica, que se encuentran en el valle del Nilo y los países colindantes"

> (In 1842 the King of Prussia sent Lepsius to Egypt accompanied by several Prussian and English artists, with the goal to explore the monuments of the Egyptian and Ethiopian civilization located in the Nile Valley and neighboring countries, with regards their History, Chronology, Philosophy, Mythology, Archaeology, Geography and Choreography) (La España: 19th July 1850).

Secondly, the magazines for the general public. An example of these are *Museo de los niños* (Children Museum) and *Museo de las familias* (Family Museum). Both magazines enjoyed much coverage. The History of Egypt was here

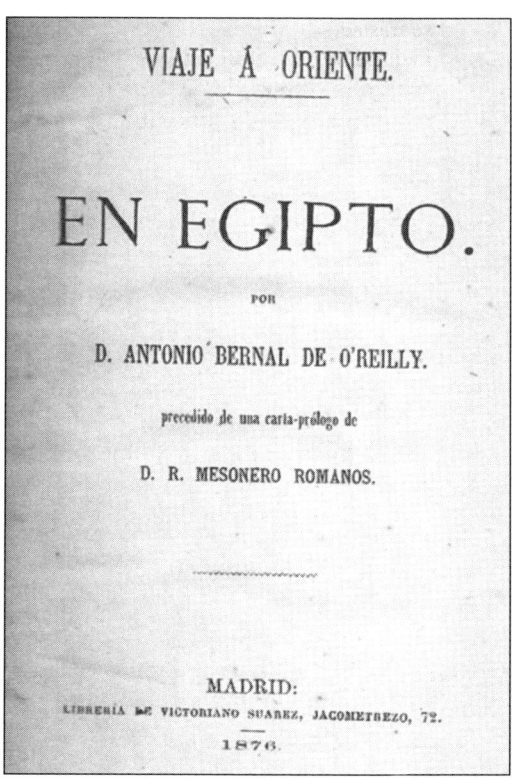

Figure 2. Antonio Bernal de O'Reilly's book front cover.

written with informative and cultural character, illustrated with many romantic pictures, a reflection of the fact that Orientalism was in fashion. In an issue of *Museo de las familias* (Sepulveda, 1850) the translation of a fragment of a work by Louis François Cassas entitled *Voyage Pittoresque de la Syrie, de la Phenicie, de la Palestine, et de la Basse Egypte* which he began publishing in 1799 was included. This issue also contained a short biography of the French artist, which stated:

> "Su deseo de viajar le condujo después a Asia menor, dibujando allí los restos de los monumentos antiguos que existen en la Tierra Santa, en Baalbek, en Palmira y en otros lugares célebres; habiéndose ocupado, apenas volvió a Francia, en publicar sus dibujos por medio del grabado".
>
> (His desire to travel led him then to Asia Minor, drawing here the remains of the ancient monuments that there are in Holy Land, in Baalbek, in Palmira and other notorious places: when he returned to France, he begun to publish his drawings in the form of engravings).

Finally, a series of cultural magazines are worth mentioning, such as *El instructor* (The Instructor) and *Mundo Pintoresco* (Picturesque world). Both of them published a scientific study of several monuments and ruins. In these publications we can see an analysis of the methodology employed by European Egyptologists in their first works. An example from Mundo Pintoresco (Mendoza, 1859), reads as follows:

> "En 1850 el gobierno francés envió a Egipto a M. Mariette para estudiar en los monasterios cristianos de las orillas del Nilo los manuscritos coptos y siriacos que en ellos se encuentran. Mr. Mariette se trasladó a su destino inmediatamente, y en una visita que hizo a las cercanías de Menfis halló indicios que le llevaron a descubrir la calle formada por esfinges y el Serapium o tumba del Dios Apis, de cuyo culto hablan Herodoto y otros escritores".
>
> (In 1850, the French government sent M. Mariette to Egypt to study the Coptic and Syrian manuscripts which can be found in the Christian monasteries of the Nile banks. Mr. Mariette visited the Memphis surroundings and found signs that led him to discover the sphinx street and the Serapeum or Tomb of the god Apis, of whose cult talked Herodotus and other writers) (Mendoza, 1859).

Bernal O'Reilly's analysis and reconstruction of ruins

Antonio Bernal de O'Reilly talks in his letters about places of archaeological interest, such as Alexandria, Heliopolis, Giza and Saqqara. O'Reilly's descriptions of the ruins are peppered with his knowledge of the Bible and classics authors (Herodoto, Diodoro and Strabo among others). He also describes the work undertaken there by European Egyptologists such as Lepsius, Bruhsch and particularly Mariette.

Giza

Great Pyramid

One of the places that O'Reilly visited was the Great Pyramid. In his description, he demonstrates his previous knowledge of the works undertaken there by Europeans Egyptologists. The consul referred to several aspects:

Firstly, O'Reilly wrote the dimensions of the Great Pyramid: 137 meters tall and 238 meters wide. On the other hand, O'Reilly knows that the Great Pyramid was more extensive in the past but in the fourteenth century, many rocks fell on to the ground due to an earthquake; then, those rocks were reused by the local people to build their houses. This is an example of the use of large archaeological pieces by locals, a phenomenon that has repeatedly occurred across history (Bernal de O'Reilly 1876, 217).

A largely common practice in 19th century was to compare the dimensions of the Great Pyramid with the dimensions of European monuments. This was done so that the readers could form an idea of the dimensions of these ancient constructions. On this occasion, O'Reilly compared the height of the Great Pyramid with the dome of the Basilica of St Peter's in Rome (132m), the dome of the Invalids in Paris (105m) and the Vendôme column, also in Paris (43m). (Bernal de O'Reilly 1876, 217).

In reference to who built the great pyramid, O'Reilly already knew that it was Cheops, not only from the accounts of Herodotus but also from those of Howard Vyse and John Shae Perring. The latter found the pharaoh's name in the pyramid and J. S. Perring published these works early in 1839 (Perring *et al.* 1839).The consul thought that the casing of the pyramid was built by Cheops' son and that the dimensions of the pyramid were connected to the duration of the pharaoh's reign. Although his theories were not correct he attempted a historical analysis of an Egyptian monument.

O'Reilly's novel theories about the archaeological remains also related to the methods of construction of the pyramids. The consul based his opinion on his *Readings and observations* (Bernal de O'Reilly 1976, 218). O'Reilly mainly described the process of rock extractions and their displacement. The workers firstly cut the stone down low and then they placed timbers into the holes; later, they cut the rest of the stone in order to drag them on rafts to the construction site using the Nile flow. A second method, which took place away from the Nile, was as follows: The workers built a road out of alluvium and achieved the desired inclination. After, the sun would harden the road. Thanks to this work, the rollers would have been driven with more facility. The stones would have been placed on the rollers and these would have been dragged by men and oxen. O'Reilly mentions that this system is similar to that which appears in the reliefs of Nineveh, which were discovered by Austen Henry Layard (Layard 1849, 79) and could be found in the British Museum already in O'Reilly's times (Bernal de O'Reilly 1976, 219). (In reality, the city that A. H. Layard thought to be Nineveh was in fact Nimrud).

Finally, O'Reilly also climbed to the top of the Great Pyramid and his feelings are worthy of mention. His exact words were:

> "Nuestra existencia crece y se desarrolla para dar espacio al alma que majestuosa tiende a elevarse hasta los cielos"
>
> (our existence grows and develops to give space to the soul that is elevated to the skies)
> (Bernal de O'Reilly 1976, 220).

The consul described the foremost function of the Pyramid: "being the door towards the sky" (Fig. 3). The consul also described everything else he saw and expressed his opinion that the monument in question reflected the greatness of the pharaoh.

In conclusion, this contribution shows that Antonio Bernal de O'Reilly was not a simple tourist. The consul wanted to give an answer to historiographical problems.

The Sphinx

O'Reilly described the Sphinx as being the Guard of the graves; he also knew that the monument was carved in the rock. The consul wrote about the dimensions (Fig. 4) and attributes of the monument based on the works of Mariette (1877). It is worth noting that the French diplomat removed the sand that was covering the sphinx and found a stele – the Dream Stele – object of comments by O'Reilly:

Figure 3. Two men on the Cheops pyramid by Edward, The second Giza Pyramid seen from the top of the Great Pyramid, Giza, c. 1826-1827. From Clayton, P. A. 1985, 67, fig. 10.

Figure 4. Photograph of the Sphinx by Roland Bonaparte (1887). Courtesy of the French National Library.

"Según las inscripciones jeroglíficas que han leído, representa la alegórica efigie de un dios solar (…). Cuando Mariette- bey la despejó del mar de arena que casi la enterraba (…). Se ha visto que tiene entre las garras una estela (…) en la cual está esculpido el retrato de Tutmosis IV, de la décima octava dinastía, ofreciendo al dios solar un sacrificio, por cuya razón se le atribuye a dicho monarca la construcción de este monumento".

(According to the hieroglyph inscriptions that have been read, it represents the allegorical effigy of a solar god (…). When Mariette-Bey cleared the large amount of sand that nearly buried it (…) it can be seen that it has a stele between his claws (…) in which a portrait of Tuthmosis IV of the 18th dynasty is carved, offering a sacrifice to the sun god by, for this reason the construction of this monument is attributed to this monarch) (Bernal de O'Reilly 1876, 228–229).

The consul thought that Tutmosis IV built this monument; however, we now know that this interpretation was incorrect. In fact, Tutmosis only rebuilt the Sphinx (Parra 2008, 221–226), to which he attributed the identity of a solar god named Harmaquis.

In addition, O'Reilly described the Sphinx temple and its preserved rooms: The nave, the sanctuary and the vestibule; this demonstrates the consul's ability to identify these rooms (Bernal de O'Reilly 1876, 228–229).

Mastabas of the high-ranking officials.

Other monuments of great interest are the Mastabas of Officials. O'Reilly entered one of them and described its parts. First, a quadrangular well was found, across which it was possible to descend via a ramp until reaching the sepulchral chamber, whose walls the consul described as containing, for example, cattle heads and other beasts heads, as well as a figure holding a crook, with a dog at his feet. Two aspects are worth (Fig. 5) highlighting:

Firstly, O'Reilly's count of the cattle heads. Although O'Reilly could not read hieroglyphs, he was not travelling alone; the consul explains in his letters that a travel companion deciphered the quantity of cattle heads: 834 oxen and 760 donkeys, amongst other beasts. (Bernal de O'Reilly 1876, 230). Secondly, O'Reilly made this remark concerning the official's depiction:

Figure 5. Tombs of the high-ranking officials by Luigi Mayer Cámara subterránea, cerca de las pirámides de Giza, in Views in Egypt, 1804. From Clayton, P. A. 1985, 70, fig. 14.

> "Me asaltó la idea de que si para colocarse de tal manera en efigie, le impulsaría la vanidad mundana ó su amor por la raza cuadrúpeda"
>
> (I thought whether this official's effigy featured due to his human vanity or to his love of animals) (Bernal de O'Reilly 1876, 230).

Here, O'Reilly's interpretation is influenced by his European mentality, since he thought that the official's effigy featured because he wished to overshadow the Pharaoh. This remark indicates that the consul was not familiar with Egyptian art conventions.

Anthropology

O'Reilly also analyzed the everyday life of people living in Egypt. This area of research is of great importance because Eastern societies have preserved many of their customs for centuries; therefore, it is possible to achieve knowledge regarding ancient societies by means of the study of some of the customs of contemporary societies.

When the consul walked along the streets of Alexandria he remarked on the snake charmers. O'Reilly described the games with these snakes (Fig. 6) and noted that:

> "la habilidad de estos hombres asciende a los siglos más remotos, pues se les ve en los grabados en monumentos y esculturas antiguas que representan las fiestas del paganismo"
>
> (these men's abilities existed prior to the last centuries, since they are depicted in ancient monuments and sculptures.) (Bernal de O'Reilly 1976, 121–122).

In addition, O'Reilly detailed the methods of snake capture practicedby the Arabs. These methods were already described by Herodotus, a fact acknowledged by O'Reilly.

On the other hand, the consul also contributed to the debate on the origins of the *fellahin*. O'Reilly put forward two theories; first, that the fellahin were direct descendants of the pharaohs;

Figure 6. A Snake Charmer (Medinet Habu, Thebes) by Karl Wilhelm Gentz (1872) Courtesy of the Dahesh Museum of Art.

second, that they were a result of a cross between Bedouins and peasants. O'Reilly supported this second theory. He compared the fellahin with the peasants in ancient times. He based this comparison on Herodotus and his explanation of the four classes in which Ancient Egyptian society was divided. The consul described several aspects of the everyday life of the *fellahin*: where and how they lived, their traditions, such as marriage, and the role of women in the family. Thanks to these analyses we can understand better the link of the *fellahin* with ancient societies (Bernal de O'Reilly 1976, 121–122).

In this, we can see a characteristic of the nineteenth century travellers: the analysis of the manners and traditions of Eastern societies. O'Reilly tried to see the ancient Egyptian society through these contemporary people, something which was of great interest but which had to be carried out with care, bearing in mind the centuries of differences between both periods.

Antonio Bernal de O'Reilly's heritage awareness

The issue of heritage was dealt with by O'Reilly on several occasions, one of them being during his visit to the Serapeum, in Memphis. The consul praised the task of those who brought to light the pieces and monuments that had remained buried under the sand, including the job of the museums that advocated the conservation of the objects. However, he had overcome the approach of the European collector and thought that the pieces were out of context in the

European museums. For him, the obvious thing to do to avoid spoliation was to close off the area and to work *in situ*.

In what concerned the restoration of the ruins and of particular objects, he advocated a few restorations faithful to ancient world history, fleeing from artistic restorations. In his own words:

> "¿Cómo, me pregunto, hoy que se hacen tratados para todo, no se hace uno (…) para sacar de la tierra los inmensos tesoros y conservar intactos tal cual fueron los templos y palacios, las plazas, los circos, termas y teatros"
>
> (I ask myself, if at present there are treaties for everything, why is there not a treaty (…).To preserve the immense treasures and ancient places such as temples, palaces, squares, circuses and theaters) (Bernal de O'Reilly 1876, 234).

In spite of his viewpoint, O'Reilly was aware of the period he was living in the collecting was in vogue and also he knew of the struggle between larger Europeans countries for political, economic and cultural supremacy. Therefore, antiques collecting was rather commercially motivated, something that he criticized with these words:

> "Se comercia en esto como en todo; y gracias que haya gobiernos que arranquen a la profanación, profanando ellos mismos las tumbas y los templos, las reliquias sagradas de las artes y el saber de otros tiempos"
>
> (Everything is traded. Thanks be given that there are governments which combat profanation, by profanating the tombs and temples themselves, the sacred art relics and the knowledge of other times) (Bernal de O'Reilly 1876, 235).

On the other hand the consul was grateful that governments were slowly intervening and attempting to regulate the problem of pillage.

Finally, I wish to include another one of O'Reilly's quotes concerning the importance of studying deposits in situ. While in the subterranean galleries of the Serapeum in Memphis, he stated:

> "Esta serie de tumbas contenía mil doscientas inscripciones, más o menos legibles, y las mejor conservadas están hoy en el Museo del Louvre"
>
> (This series of graves had contained one thousand two hundred inscriptions, more or less legible, and today the better preserved inscriptions are in the Museum of the Louvre) (Bernal de O'Reilly 1878, 236).

His legacy: The birth of the Spanish Egyptology: Eduardo Toda i Güell

In Spain, Antonio Bernal de O'Reilly was a transition figure between the antiques collectors and the Egyptological tradition that was born at the end of the 19th century with Eduardo Toda y Güell.

O'Reilly's knowledge prior to his trip came across in his book; when the consul travelled across Egypt, he already knew what area he was treading. His awareness concerning classical authors and European Egyptologists can be inferred from the pages of his book. In addition, he wished to propose solutions to certain archaeological problems. In summary, O'Reilly's purpose was definitely that of re-writing the history of ancient Egypt.

O'Reilly was also aware of the importance of the archaeology of that area and period and of the decontextualization that removing objects from their places of origin entailed. He knew about the importance of heritage and he advocated for a serious legislation to protect it.

Another aspect I would like to emphasize is the impact of his work in Spain. There were few accounts by Spanish travellers prior to O'Reilly's. The Spanish outlook would come from then on from a direct source, for O'Reilly's accounts broke with the idealization of the East and showed reality instead. Reality that appears in one of his quotes, when the consul was in Alexandria, and as part of his description of what he saw there, he said:

> "Tiene muy poco del fastuoso orientalismo que hemos soñado"
>
> (It has very little of the magnificent orientalism that we have dreamed of) (Bernal de O'Reilly 1876, 74).

After the death of the consul, the Royal Academy of History, with which he was collaborating, published a report in his memory. I have rescued from this report a paragraph that I consider to be excellent:

> "Y no son libros dedicados más que nada al recreo de sus lectores ,como el viaje de Lamartine, por ejemplo, y otros varios, llenos de fábulas ó buscando, con la popularidad, la satisfacción del amor propio de sus autores, sino trabajos formales en que resplandece la verdad, instructivos, por ende, y hasta con fines de edificación para con los que, sobre todo, quieren inspirarse en los sucesos que se narran y en el conocimiento exacto de los lugares de que fueron teatro"
>
> (The books of Antonio Bernal de O'Reilly were not dedicated to the leisure of the readership as the work of Lamartine for example, which was dominated by fables. Antonio Bernal de O'Reilly undertook serious, instructive work) (De Arteche 1897).

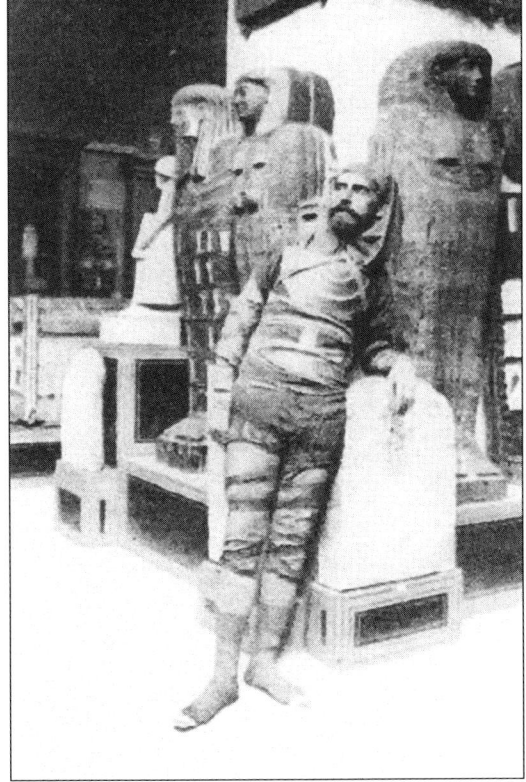

Figure 7. Eduardo Toda photographed in the Boulak Museum (Cairo, 1885). Courtesy of the SECC (State Society of Cultural Communication).

This paper was only an introduction to the works carried out by one of many forgotten figures. The contribution of Antonio Bernal de O'Reilly to historical science is enormously relevant.

In 1873 a new Spanish diplomatic travelled to Egypt and followed in the steps of the Antonio Bernal de O'Reilly. This diplomatic was Eduardo Toda i Güell (Fig. 7) who revolutionized the science devoted to the study of Ancient Egypt in Spain, hence becoming the first Spanish Egyptologist.

Bibliography

Bernal de O'Reilly, A. (1876) *En Tierra Santa. Viaje a Oriente. En Egipto*. Madrid, Librería de Victoriano Suarez. 2nd edition.

Clayton, P. A. (1985) *Redescubrimiento del Antiguo Egipto. Artistas y viajeros del siglo XIX*. Barcelona, Ediciones del Serbal.

Córdoba, J. Mª. (2005) Hasta los últimos confines. *Arbor* 711–712, vol. CLXXX, 747–755.

De Arreche, J. M. (1897) *Boletín de la Real Academia de la Historia*, vol. 5 XXX, IV.

Layard, A. H. (1849) *The monuments of Nineveh,* Vol. II. London, John Murray.

Mariette, A. (1877) *The monuments of Upper Egypt*. London, Trübner & Co.

Mendoza, R. (1859) *Mundo Pintoresco,* 28th August.

Parra, J. M. (2008) *Historia de las pirámides de Egipto*. Madrid, Editorial Complutense.

Perring, J. S., Andrews, E. J. and Birch, S. (1839) *The pyramids of Gizeh: from actual survey and admeasurement*. London, LTR-Verlag.

Sepulveda, F. (1850) *Museo de las Familias,* 25th October.

Suárez, C. (1850) *La España,* 19th July.

The influence of Christianity on burial practices in Middle Egypt from the fourth to the sixth centuries

Deanna Heikkinen

Due to its long history, ancient Egypt has been well studied; however, researchers traditionally have not given the period of Christian influence from 400 to 640 AD the same attention. During this period Christianity did affect the Egyptian culture, specifically burial practices. Christians in Egypt retained some Pharaonic burial traditions, yet Christianity's influence also led to numerous shifts in burial practices in this period. These shifts can be seen through archaeological evidence demonstrating several changes: in the direction of the corpse's head, in the manipulation of traditional face masks, in the use of Christian symbolism within the burial, in a reduction in the use of natron (a salt used to dry and preserve the body), in the type of fabric used, and in the absence of coffins. Burials from Middle Egypt, the area between Memphis and Luxor, specifically from the fourth to the sixth centuries, typically exhibit some, if not all of these conditions and provide compelling evidence for the influence of Christianity on Egyptian burial practices. Over a roughly 3,000-year period there was an evolution in Egyptian burial practices, but none of the changes were as dramatic as those that emerged with Christianity.

In the past, little scholarship existed regarding the Christian period in Egypt, and only in recent years have the Hellenistic, Roman, and Christian periods of Egyptian history been given much attention. However, several sites that include burials from this era are now being excavated throughout Egypt. These include the Middle Egyptian sites of Tell El-Hibeh (el-hiba); Karara; Fag al-Gamous and Hawara in the Fayoum Oasis; the Monastery of Epiphanius at Thebes; and Kellis and Dush (Douch) in the Western Desert Oases near Luxor. The work currently being conducted in these areas is helping close the gaps in the historical record.

These burials from late antique Middle Egyptian sites demonstrate a religious shift from traditional Pharaonic religion to Christianity. The most central feature of Egyptian burial practices was mummification, which became more complex over time (Grajetzki 2003, 48, 60, 68). Established burial practices were refined during the New Kingdom (1550–1069 BC) and into the Third Intermediate Period (1069–747 BC); these included the removal of organs, drying the body with natron, and filling the body cavity with resin before packing it with linen. Pharaonic burial treatments were completed by wrapping the body in flax linens and applying distinct wood, gold, or cartonnage facial masks before enclosure in elaborately carved or painted coffins. Mummies were buried on their side, facing east in a north-south axis during the Old Kingdom (2686–2181 BC) before being oriented on their backs in the head-east position during later periods (Ikram and Dodson, 24). Although condemned by the Emperor Theodosius (346–395), during whose reign Christianity became the official religion of the empire, and Anthony (*c.* 251–356), the first important model for monasticism in Egypt, a form of mummification nevertheless continued into the sixth century in Middle Egypt (Athanasius 1989, 246–249).

The embalming and preserving of the body declined during the Greek, Roman, and Christian periods. Yet some Pharaonic practices persisted, as is demonstrated by their continued use in Christian burials. These include the use of natron to preserve the body, the inclusion of masks on the deceased, and wrapping the body with linen shrouds and cordage. Although continued into the Greco-Roman and Christian periods, the practices involved in preserving the body were simplified.

Evidence from El-Hibeh shows that Christians continued to practice mummification in some form as exhibited through the use of natron to preserve the body of the deceased. From the excavations at El-Hibeh in 2005, two Christian mummies (mummy NGLP-7 and mummy NGLP-8) were discovered from a known Christian burial feature, the North Gate Looter Pit (NGLP) (Yohe et al. in press, 10–12). For the most part, NGLP-7 was intact upon excavation. NGLP-8 was not an intact burial; the body was missing the lower limbs (Yohe and Heikkinen, 2004–2007). The use of natron was an obvious feature found on both of these mummies. NGLP-7 had been treated with approximately twenty kilograms of natron, which was largely packed against the sides, abdomen, and thorax, and between the thighs. The legs, head, and arms were not packed with salt and, indeed, preservation in those areas was not as good. NGLP-8 was almost completely skeletonized due to the effects of exposure *in situ*. There was soft tissue preserved on the abdomen, buttocks, lower thorax, left shoulder, and right arm where natron was present, however the amount of natron used was significantly less than NGLP-7. The earlier Christian burials (mummies NGLP-1 through NGLP-7) from El-Hibeh were packed with a great deal of natron over the chest cavity, whereas the later burial (mummy NGLP-8) included only a sprinkling of natron over the chest cavity. (Yohe and Heikkinen, 2004–2007).

The use of natron has also been documented at other Christian burial sites. At a Christian cemetery near Dush in the Kharga Oasis, natron was used to preserve the bodies (Hauser 1932, 39). In these burials, the organs were not removed; rather small bags of natron were inserted next to them to preserve them. This is a continuation of Pharaonic practice. The body was then packed with natron to dry it out. Evidence from excavations at St. Mark's Monastery near Luxor also shows the use of natron in Christian burials (Prominska 1979, 113–117). All three burials from this report showed evidence that the body had been covered with natron before being wrapped in linen. Soft tissue preservation was evident on all three mummies as well. These burials serve as further evidence of the continuation of Pharaonic burial traditions during the Christian period in Egypt (Prominska 1979, 113–117).

Evidence from other sites reinforces the argument that there was a reduction in the amount of natron used over time in Christian burials; for example, at the Monastery of Epiphanius the use of small amounts of natron was also reported in the later burials (*c.* sixth century) (Winlock and Crum 1973, 48). The reduction of the use in natron in the burials from the late fifth through sixth centuries demonstrates a gradual decline in the use of the Pharaonic tradition of embalming in Christian Egypt.

Besides the use of natron, Christians continued Pharaonic traditions through the use of masks in their burials, a practice that had begun in the Old Kingdom (Winlock and Crum 1973, 29). The original purpose of the masks was to allow the soul of the deceased to recognize itself during its journey in the afterlife (Shaw and Nicholson 2003, 190). The reuniting of the soul with the body remained a key tenet of Egyptian funerary practices for over 3,000 years. Changes in the styles of masks occurred throughout the Pharaonic period. The first masks from the fourth to sixth Dynasties (2613–2181 BC) were created by using a thin coating of plaster directly over the face or linen wrapping (Shaw and Nicholson 2003, 172). During the First Intermediate Period, the

Middle Kingdom, the 18th and 26th Dynasties, and into the Greek periods cartonnage (painted linen) masks were common. It was during the Roman period (*c.* 30 BC–395 AD) that traditional masks were replaced by realistic mummy portraits. The appearance of mummy portraits occurred in the first century and continued into the second century AD (Grajetzki 2003, 127). These portraits were painted in the classical style and blended two traditions: the Egyptian funerary mask and the Greco-Roman classical portrait (Gschwantler 2000, 21).

While continuing to devote attention to the face, Christians make significant changes. Their use of masks reflects a very visible – even drastic – change in this tradition. The mask became more of a protrusion over the face that did not in any way resemble the face of the deceased (Fig. 1).

The projection over the face was comprised of matted grass covered by linen. The facial masks from mummies NGLP-1 through NGLP-7 at El-Hibeh varied in size, with the largest approximately ten centimeters long and thirty centimeters tall (Yohe *et al.* in press, 10). The inside of the structure was supported by palm fronds and filled with dried grasses. The linen cover was decorated with numerous bands of multi-colored cordage. Evidence from Christian burials at Tell El-Hibeh, Karara, and Fag al-Gamous cemeteries all exhibit this detail over the face of the corpse. Christians possibly continued the practice of protecting the face in order for the body to be resurrected; however, the appearance of the individual became less important than the spiritual union with God.

The mask was not the only aspect of the burial that contained linen and cordage; Christians also wrapped the entire body of the deceased in linen shrouds decorated with cordage. Both of these were a continuation from Pharaonic and Greco-Roman traditions.

Linen had been used since the Old Kingdom as a burial shroud and continued throughout the Greek and Roman periods. Traditional mummies were wrapped with strips of linen that were glued together to form a burial shroud around the corpse. The body would then be adorned with a mask, cartonnage, mummy board, or other accoutrements for the afterlife before being put into a coffin or coffins. The outer wrappings became more complex during the Roman period as geometric designs were created with different bands of multi-colored cordage, or ribbon (Ikram and Dodson 1998, 51).

In the earlier burials at El-Hibeh (*c.* third through fourth centuries), the use of linen with cordage on top of the body continued. Large pieces of linen were used to wrap the naked bodies of mummies NGLP-1 through NGLP-7. The material was coarse and primarily a natural flax color (Yohe *et al.* in press, 13). The earlier burials were naked underneath the shroud. Mummy NGLP-8 is unique at El-Hibeh in that he was wrapped with several tunics underneath a

Figure 1. Mummy NGLP-7. Facial protrusion wrapped in linen and cordage; photo D. Heikkinen.

very coarsely woven outer shroud. In addition, the earlier mummies were wrapped with different layers of cordage in a crisscross pattern; however, the later burial (NGLP-8) had only a few strands of cordage on it (Yohe et al. in press, 13). This decline in the appearance of the outer wrappings in mummy NGLP-8 may be attributed to the inclusion of more decorative inner burial shrouds found in later Christian mummies, and a de-emphasis on the outer shrouds.

Christian burials from other sites included the use of linen and cordage as well. Both intact burials and looted graves in the cemeteries of Kellis offer evidence of the deceased being wrapped in linen (Bowen 2004a, 17–26). Graves that had been looted still had remains of linen cloth in them, assumed to be part of the mummy wrappings from the Christian burials. Other intact graves had mummies wrapped in linen, while graves that had bodies not as well preserved had traces of linen, and thus there remained a consistency in the use of linen as a burial shroud. Burials at the Christian cemetery of Fag al-Gamous were interred in linen shrouds as well (Griggs 1992, 199–202). Monastic burials reveal the same use of linen to wrap the body. As with the lay burials, monks' bodies were fully encased in linen shrouds, reminiscent of traditional mummification practices from the Pharaonic period (Winlock and Crum 1973, 48). These monastic burials included four to six sheets of linen wrapped around the bodies, with finer linen closer to the body and coarser linen used as the outermost shroud. This pattern of using linen sheets as a burial shroud and then tying them with cordage is consistent among Christian burials in Middle Egypt and represents continuity in materials and stylization from burials from the Pharaonic and Roman periods.

Although there were several burial treatments that were carried over from the Pharaonic period into the Christian era, there are more pronounced differences in the Christian burial practices. These changes in burial treatments include the orientation of the body, the use of Christian symbolism, the inclusion of wool and purple dyes in the burial fabrics, the presence of clothing on the deceased, the absence of coffins, and evidence of mass burials.

The orientation of the buried body was associated with religious beliefs in ancient Egypt. During the later Pharaonic period, the bodies were placed on their back with heads to the east and the feet towards the west (Griggs 2005, 189). This alignment was to ensure that the west-facing bodies, if raised upon their feet, would be prepared to take the journey towards the west-setting sun. In contrast, Christian burials were placed in a head-west orientation among both the laity and monks (Davies 1999, 199). Griggs' (2005, 189) interpretation for this change is related to the resurrection. He asserts that Christ was to return from the East and thus the bodies would be in the correct position to see his return.

A great deal of archaeological evidence supports a distinct change in the orientation of the bodies. Griggs (2005, 189) notes that at the Fag al-Gamous cemetery that there is a drastic shift in the positioning of the heads that occurs early, near the end of the first century AD. The earlier mummies (pre-first century AD) at Fag al-Gamous are all buried with their heads towards the east along an east-west axis. Griggs also argues that although there were many differences in the economic statuses of the deceased, there was consistency in the position of the body. There is no evidence of admixing of head-east burials with the later head-west burial positions, leading Griggs to believe that this change was most likely due to a new population moving into the region or a shift in religious beliefs, that is, the influence of Christianity (Griggs 2005, 189).

Head-west burials are also found in all of the Christian burials at El-Hibeh, as well as other excavated Christian burial sites in Egypt (Yohe et al. in press, 7). During three different excavation seasons, 2004, 2005, and 2007, all of the Christian burials uncovered from the North Gate Looter Pit (NGLP) and surrounding cemetery were oriented with their heads to the west.

These burials included infants, children, women, and men from the third through sixth centuries (Yohe and Heikkinen 2004–2007). Christian burials from the Dahkleh Oasis and from the Bagawat cemetery in the Kharga Oasis were also buried with a head-west orientation (Bowen 2004b, 170). Head-west interments were also the normal pattern at numerous cemeteries in Kellis (Bowen 2004a, 22). Monastic burials also feature the head-west orientation of the body upon burial. At the cemetery associated with the Monastery of Epiphanius, eleven burials were all aligned on an east-west axis, with the heads to the west (Winlock and Crum 1973, 46). This practice reflects a total break from the traditional Egyptian belief system of ascending towards the western setting sun in the afterlife.

Whereas a head-west orientation of the body indicates an early connection between Christianity and burial practices in Egypt, Christians gradually developed other ways to incorporate their faith in this most ancient and meaningful practice. The use of Christian symbols on the body as well as within the grave itself became another means of expressing their devotion to Christ. Common Christian symbols found in burials from the third through sixth centuries include crosses, peacocks, and fish (Griggs, 2005, 191–192; Yohe *et al.* in press, 20). The El-Hibeh burials were relatively free of Christian symbols on the outer shrouds of the mummies; however, mummy NGLP-8 was buried with a tunic that featured peacocks on it (Fig. 2) (Yohe *et al.* in press, 20). The peacock was a symbol of the resurrection, and thus it was a very appropriate inclusion on Christian burial shrouds. Further evidence for Christian symbolism is found at a burial at the North Tomb at Kellis (Bowen 2004a, 22). This grave includes a *crux ansata* symbol (a Christianized adaptation of the Egyptian *ankh*, which was the symbol of life) on a seal. Christian symbols became prevalent in the later burials at Fag al-Gamous cemetery as well. One mummy had a burial shroud that featured a scene with animals, birds, and plant

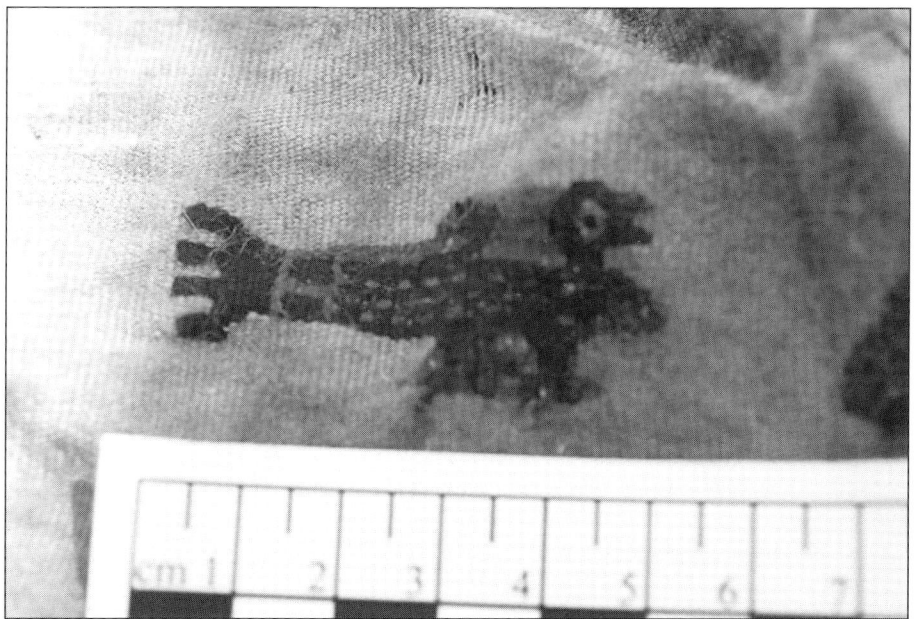

Figure 2. Detail of peacock from El-Hibeh mummy NGLP-8 burial shroud; Photo D. Heikkinen.

symbols (Griggs 2005, 191–192). Other burials at this cemetery have cross-shaped pendants interred with them. The Christian symbols found in burials sometimes come in the form of grave accoutrements; however, they are also commonly incorporated into the burial textiles, as uncovered at El-Hibeh.

The textiles used in Christian burials provide an even more obvious shift from Pharaonic funerary practices throughout Middle Egypt. Distinct changes from Pharaonic burial shrouds to Christian burial fabrics include the use of purple on the fabric, the inclusion of wool in the burial fabric, and changes in the types of linens and clothing that were used on the deceased. These changes are common throughout the graves found at El-Hibeh, Fag al-Gamous cemetery, Kellis and Dush, and other Middle Egypt sites discussed thus far.

Mummies NGLP-1 through NGLP-7 from El-Hibeh had similar textiles used for their burials (Yohe *et al.* in press, 5, 12). They were all buried with medium-coarse outer shrouds made of flax linen. Some Pharaonic burials from the Third Intermediate Period (1069–747 BC) and later included colored textiles that had been reused from household linens; however, it was predominantly plain or fringed linen that was used for wrapping the deceased during this period (Ikram and Dodson 1998, 162).

During the Roman Empire, the use of purple on textiles was restricted to the Emperor and his family (Pharr 1952, 288). Although it was outlawed by Theodosius and earlier emperors, Christians in Egypt used purple in their burial textiles. The two earlier mummies at El-Hibeh had burial shrouds that included purple (Yohe and Heikkinen, 2004–2007). In addition, mummy NGLP-8 also had purple woven into the burial shrouds. Griggs (2005, 195), who found purple on burial textiles at Fag al-Gamous cemetery, provides an alternative explanation regarding the inclusion of purple for burial fabrics: Christians believed that they could wear the "insignia of divinity or nobility without concern for Roman edicts." Purple is historically associated with nobility, and thus Christians may have included it in burial textiles because they saw the dead as being dignified by Christianity.

A significant difference in Christian burial shrouds from earlier Pharaonic cloth was the inclusion of wool. This innovation is a complete ideological break from the burial practices during the Pharaonic period. According to Pharaonic beliefs, wool was considered unclean and was never to be used in burial linen. According to the Greek historian Herodotus (1998, 126), "it was against religious law for them to take anything woolen into their sanctuaries or to be buried along with any woolen items." Christians did not have this belief, for the lamb was a symbol for Jesus and therefore wool was not considered to be unclean (Jensen 2004, 141). Wool was preferred for garments because dyes adhered better, making woolen textiles more vibrant and colorful than plain flax textiles (Lewis 1969, 10).

Wool was used at El-Hibeh and is most apparent in the burial shrouds of mummy NGLP-8. This mummy had wool inclusions on the four linen tunics in which he was wrapped. The wool elements were both embroidered onto and tapestry woven into the linen and included red, green, blue, purple, and orange threads. Woolen textiles were also present in the head-west burials from Fag al-Gamous cemetery (Griggs 2005, 190). One particular Christian burial from this cemetery was quite unusual (Griggs 1992, 200). A woman was buried with six woolen bath robes, described as such by Griggs since they span from the neck to the ankle and have long-sleeves. Each robe was placed on the body and included hand-sewn collars, cuffs, and hems. The robes were striped and were of different colors: green with red trim, purple with blue trim, and two each of red with blue trim and red with green trim. Along with these six woolen robes, the woman was buried with three woolen blankets and then wrapped in sixteen layers of coarse linen cloth (Griggs, 1992, 200). These robes indicate that the deceased was of high economic status. Other burials at the Fag al-Gamous cemetery also included woolen robes; however, they did not include more than one per individual. Griggs (1992) further notes that the earlier head-east burials were buried only with linen shrouds, thus demonstrating a clear innovation in Christian burial rituals.

In addition to the changes in the composition of burial shrouds, different types of clothing have been found on Christians in their burials. This is another development initiated by Christians. Pharaonic and even Greco-Roman mummies were buried naked, and only wrapped in linen strips or bandages as part of the mummification process. In contrast, Christians were buried wearing clothing. At El-Hibeh, mummy NGLP-8 was buried both wearing and wrapped in at least four tunics (Yohe *et al.* in press, 18). He was then wrapped in a very coarse burial shroud that served as the outer layer of his mummy wrappings. Tunics were also used in burials at other sites in Middle Egypt. In the North Tomb 16 at Kellis, a Christian juvenile was buried wearing a linen tunic (Bowen 2004a, 25). Monks were buried with the leather aprons and girdles that they had used in life (Winlock and Crum 1973, 49–50). This practice is documented at the Monastery of Epiphanius as well as other monasteries near Thebes (Deir el Medineh and Deir al Bahri) (Winlock and Crum, 1973, 76). The leather aprons were suspended from the shoulders and belted around the waists. The burial aprons of the monks showed evidence of wear, and Crum argues that the monks had taken their vows in these aprons.

Unlike the Pharaonic practice of burying the dead in flax shrouds before placing the body in a coffin, Christian mummies were buried in their textiles without coffins. During the Pharaonic period, coffins were made of stone or wood and were often carved and painted with scenes from the *Book of the Dead* that provided instructions for the afterlife. In elite burials, more than one coffin, set inside one another, was often used (Budge 1989, 426–429). In contrast, the Christian mummies at El-Hibeh were all placed directly in the sand (Yohe and Heikkinen, 2004–2007). NGLP was a large burial area within the cemetery that was dug in a Roman trash dump, identified as such by the assortment of broken pottery remains. After the bodies had been placed in the ground, these burials were sealed with limestone blocks scavenged from other areas of the site (one block had Pharaonic inscriptions believed to have been a temple block), grass bundles (which helped fill the pit, as sand most likely blew away), and mud bricks (Yohe and Heikkinen, 2004–2007). Included in this area were not only adults, as seen in NGLP, but children and infants as well. These sub-adult mummies were wrapped in linen with cordage around them and also placed directly in the sand.

Griggs (2005, 188) reported a similar absence of coffins at Fag al-Gamous cemetery. Some of the earlier head-east burials (Griggs argues that these are Greco-Roman pagan burials) had coffins in lower levels of the burial shafts; however, the later burials were all interred directly in the sand. This pattern is likewise found throughout monastic sites in Thebes, including the Monastery of Epiphanius (Winlock and Crum 1973, 46). There, the monks were buried without coffins right outside the boundary wall. An above-ground tomb was built to house the bodies; however, some of the graves had been dug outside the tomb's structure. The tomb was no longer standing when the site was excavated in 1912, but Winlock and Crum (1973, 46) were able to discern the architectural style from the remains of four corners that still stood. The tomb was built using a common, dome-styled architecture, primarily seen in chapels. Due to the placement of the burials though, the tomb was most likely built as a monument to the founder before any of the monks had died. They were then buried in the sand within or near the tomb as needed during the tenure of the monastery (Winlock and Crum 1973, 46).

Other burial sites in Middle Egypt demonstrate that Christians abandoned the use of coffins as well. Burials at the Kellis site were also placed directly into the ground, without coffins. Interments from the numerous necropoleis at Kellis all demonstrate the evidence of pit graves (graves dug into the sand) that do not include coffins. Some of the graves were sealed with mud bricks, like those at El-Hibeh. At Karara, coffins were not used in the Christian burials either (Ranke 1926, 4). Although, there is some evidence at Bagawat and Saqqara demonstrating that Christians did in fact reuse coffins from the Pharaonic, Greek and Roman periods; this practice was not widely distributed (Bowen 2004b, 170).

Christians further broke from Pharaonic practices by burying more than one person at a time in mass graves. This is a definite shift from the Pharaonic practice, in which burials predominantly featured single individuals interred in coffins or tombs (Griggs 2005, 190). Graves with two or more individuals buried at the same time is the pattern at El-Hibeh, Fag al-Gamous, and Kellis. The Christian cemetery at El-Hibeh has extensive evidence of mass burials. Excavations at NGLP unearthed several bodies from a single burial event. The original trench wall was discovered and, within it, mummies were stacked on top of one another, with varying amounts of sand between them (Yohe and Heikkinen, 2004–2007). The bottom-most individual was a male with a rattan ring around the facial protrusion. This is the only Christian mummy at El-Hibeh found with this treatment, and Yohe *et al.* believe it to be either an indicator of socio-economic status or a family marker (2004–2007). Above him, there were three more mummies stacked, two on top of each other without any fill between them. A 2007 excavation revealed more mass burials just east of NGLP within the same cemetery. This grave included several adults, children, and an infant. Within this burial area, just above the head of the deceased, a *gerid* (palm frond) was placed that stuck straight up for approximately fifty centimeters. These are believed to be grave markers to let the grave diggers know that there was a burial underneath. Further evidence of mass burials is documented by Griggs (2005, 190) at Fag al-Gamous cemetery. The head-west burials regularly have at least two bodies interred together, and in some cases as many as nine were buried together. The cemeteries at Kellis and Dush also show signs of mass burials, some bodies buried in tombs, and others interred in pit graves (Bowen 2004b, 170). In contrast, single graves are present at the Monastery of Epiphanius; however, this is because it was a cemetery for monks. Thus they would have been buried individually as they died, as opposed to being kept with the living, as was the practice of the laity.

The reason for the use of mass graves in the Christian period has yet to be determined; however scholars have put forth possible explanations for this practice. The Roman practice of keeping the body in the house or in chambers where people could visit the deceased may have continued and would explain the mass burials found in lay Christian cemeteries (Petrie 1889, 15). Christians may have possibly had mass burials due to a Christian practice of having one funeral for several individuals; or maybe several families pulled resources together to pay for one interment for several individuals. Griggs (2005, 192–193) and Yohe *et al.* (in press, 16) provide alternative theories relating to the mass burials: numerous Christians died around the same time, possibly from persecution, warfare, or illness. Warfare is rather unlikely due to the inclusion of so many infants, children, and women at El-Hibeh and Kellis; however, adults at El-Hibeh and Fag al-Gamous exhibit evidence of physical trauma. Mummy NGLP-7 from El-Hibeh, for example, died from a blunt blow to the back of the head, believed to have been caused by a sling bullet (a round stone put into a sling and flung towards its intended target). Griggs (2005, 192) notes that burials revealing major trauma to the crania and long bones represent only three percent of the burials in the third century AD, and rise in the fifth century AD to only five percent. Major trauma rose dramatically to fifty-eight percent of skeletons studied from the late third through mid-fourth centuries. Griggs' (2005, 192) explanation is that this period was a time of increased violence and persecution of the Christians. Disease as a cause for the mass burials is partially supported by the presence of the Justinian Plague in Egypt during the mid-sixth century (Rosen 2007, 210). This plague occurred later than some of the burials, yet disease or illness may explain the inclusion of women and children. These theories are not mutually exclusive, and it is most likely a combination of reasons that led lay Christians to bury their dead together.

Whereas most scholarship has focused on Pharaonic burial practices, this research has illustrated the evolution of burial practices during the Christian period of Egypt. During the first few centuries AD, Christianity greatly influenced Egyptian culture. From its onset in Alexandria in the first and second centuries AD, through the development of monasticism in the third and fourth centuries AD, and finally its spread into rural areas by the fifth century, Christianity was embraced by Egyptians. As is evident in their burial practices, Christians reconciled this new faith with with their traditional beliefs. In doing so, they retained some of the Pharaonic practices that had been used for thousands of years in the preparation of the deceased. Ancient Egyptians took great care in preparing their dead, and Christians continued this tradition. Even though burial practices evolved over time, Christians continued burial practices that had existed for thousands of years. Egyptian Christians blended their new religion with Pharaonic practices. Even though the process of preserving the body no longer involved the removal of the viscera, it did continue to focus on the preservation of the appearance of the deceased. The use of the mask, albeit greatly altered, may have served this same purpose. Both of these practices may also be associated with the resurrection, one of the most important Christian beliefs in relationship to death and dying. Christian burials demonstrate further continuities with the traditional Pharaonic and Greco-Roman burials through the use of linen shrouds and cordage to wrap the deceased. The use of linen dates back to the Old Kingdom and continued for over three thousand years, indicating the importance of burial traditions in Egyptian culture. In addition, the Roman innovation of decorating the body in geometric patterns with cordage continued beyond its association with pagan Roman burials.

Introduction of the new Christian religion also brought about a break in Pharaonic and Greco-Roman burial customs. Christians used new materials, such as wool and purple dyes, in their burial textiles; the dead were buried in newly woven tunics that displayed Christian symbolism. Peacocks, a symbol of the resurrection of Jesus, were included. Another innovative tradition was based on the belief that the dead were not polluting. In contrast to the Pharaonic period where cemeteries and towns were separated by the Nile, Christian cemeteries were no longer banned from towns and temples; people were buried next to churches and within the town. Christian innovations in burial practices, visible by the archaeological excavations, show a break in traditional Egyptian funerary rituals that had evolved over the course of 3,000 years.

This research has primarily focused on archaeological materials as evidence for Christian influence on burials in Egypt. Although limited, the archaeological excavations presented in this research provide the most useful information available to date on Christian burial practices. As more research teams, such as those at El-Hibeh, Kellis, and Fag al-Gamous, specialize in Christian burials, excavations will continue to increase our understanding of the continuities in and breaks from traditional Egyptian burial practices. There are other sources that could illuminate this topic further that are embedded in early Christian and secular papyrus documents that have yet to be translated, such as collections in the British Museum. Thus, further research is needed both archaeologically and in translating and publishing papyrus documents.

Bibliography

Athanasius, (1989) *Life of Anthony*. Translated by Tim Vivian and Apostolos Athanasskis. Kalamazoo, MI, Cistercian Publications.

Bowen, G. E. (2004a) Aspects of Christian Burial Practice. *Buried History* 40, 15–28.

Bowen, G. E. (2004b) Some Observations on Christian Burial Practices at Kellis. In G. E. Bowen and C. A. Hope (eds) *The Oasis Papers III: Proceedings of the Third Conference of the Dakhla Oasis Project*, 167–182. Oxford, Oxbow Books.

Budge, E. W. (1989) *The Mummy: A Handbook of Egyptian Funerary Archaeology*. New York, Dover.

Carrol, D. L. (1988) *Looms and Textiles of the Copts*. San Francisco, California Academy of Sciences.

Davies, J. (1999) *Death, Burial, and Rebirth in the Religions of Antiquity*. London, Routledge.

Grajetzki, W. (2003) *Burial Customs in Ancient Egypt*. London, Duckwork.

Griggs, C. W. (1992) General Archaeological and Historical Report of 1987 and 1988 Seasons at Fag al-Gamous, *Actes du IV ~ Congres Copte, Louvain-la-Neuve, Institut Orientaliste*, 195–202.

Griggs, C. W. (2005) Early Christian Burials in the Fayoum. In G. Gabra (ed.). *Christianity and Monasticism in the Fayoum Oasis: Essays from the 2004 International Symposium of the Saint Mark Foundation and the Saint Shenouda the Archimandrite Coptic Society in Honor of Martin Krause*, 185–195. Cairo and New York, The American University in Cairo Press.

Gschwantler, K. (2000) Graeco-Roman Portraiture. In S. Walker (ed.) *Ancient Faces: Mummy Portraits from Roman Egypt*. Routledge, NY, Metropolitan Museum of Art.

Hauser, W. (1932) The Christian Necropolis in Kharga Oasis. *The Metropolitan Museum of Art Bulletin* 27, 38–50.

Herodotus, (1998) *The Histories*. Translated by Robin Waterfield. Oxford, Oxford University Press.

Ikram, S. and Dodson, A. (1998) *The Mummy in Ancient Egypt: Equipping the Dead for Eternity*. London, Thames and Hudson.

Jensen, R. M. (2004) *Understanding Early Christian Art*. New York, Routledge

Lewis, S. (1969) *Early Coptic Textiles*. Palo Alto, Stanford University Press.

Petrie, W.M. F. (1889) *Hawara, Biahmu, and Arsinoe*. London, The Leadenhall Press.

Pharr, Clyde. (1952) *The Theodosian Code and Novels and the Sirmondian Constitutions*. Translated by Clyde Pharr. Princeton, Princeton University Press.

Prominska, E. (1979) Ancient Egyptian Traditions of Artificial Mummification in the Christian Period. In R. A. David (ed.) *Science of Egyptology*, 113–123. Manchester, Manchester University Press.

Ranke, H. (1926) *Koptische Friedhöfe bei Karâra under der Amontempel Scheschonks I bei El Hibe*. Translated by D. Baron and R. Yohe. Berlin, Verlag Von Walter de Gruyter & Co.

Rosen, W. (2007) *Justinian's Flea: The First Great Plague and the End of the Roman Empire*. New York, Penguin Books.

Shaw, I. and Nicholson, P. (2003) *The British Museum Dictionary of Ancient Egypt*. London, British Museum Press.

Taylor, J. (2000) Before the Portraits: Burial Practices in Pharaonic Egypt. In S. Walker (ed.) *Ancient Faces: Mummy Portraits from Roman Egypt*. New York, Routledge.

Winlock, H. E. and Crum, W. E. (1973) *The Monastery of Epiphanius at Thebes*. New York, Arno Press.

Yohe, R. M. (2003) Final Report on the El Hibeh Skeletal and Mummified Remains Studies, 2003 Season. Filed with Supreme Council of Antiquities, Egypt.

Yohe, R. M. (2004) Preliminary Report on the Results of the Salvage Excavations of Burial Chamber 1 and the North Gate Looter Pit at Tell El-Hibeh, Egypt, 2004 Field Season. Filed with Supreme Council of Antiquities, Egypt.

Yohe, R. M. and Heikkinen, D. (2004–2007) Field notes and personal experience. Archaeological excavations, Tell El-Hibeh, Egypt.

Yohe, R. M., Gardner, J. and Heikkinen, D. (ND) New Evidence of Coptic Mummification Techniques from Tell El-Hibeh, Egypt. In *Evolving Egypt: Innovation, Appropriation, and Reinterpretation* (British Archaeological Reports), forthcoming.

Legitimation and ontological changes in the royal figure of Queen Hatshepsut (*c.* 1479–1458 BC)

Virginia Laporta

Introduction

This work will focus on the reign of Hatshepsut and the changes to her royal figure. One special feature of the 18th Dynasty that must be considered is the enthronement of under-age kings, such as the first two Ahmoside kings and the following Thutmoside kings except for Thutmose I. This explains the leading role of the queens (as "Mother of King" – *mwt nswt* – and "Wife of King" – *ḥmt nswt*) who acted as regents for the underage kings. The immediate predecessors of Hatshepsut were Queen Ahmes and Queen Ahmes-Nefertari. They had a relevant position linked to political, religious and economic matters in the royal court of the first kings of the New Kingdom (Bryan 2003, 230; Roth 2005, 12; S. Roth 2009, 7). Even though there had been other queens from the Old Kingdom who became the king of Egypt, Hatshepsut's reign could be considered a turning point. One of the reasons for this is her decision to be recognized as "Son of Amun-Re" (*s3 jmn-rꜥ*) and enthroned as "Horus" (*ḥrw*). Taking these facts into account, the usurpation hypothesis and the revenge of Thutmose III are not enough to understand why she was crowned as king and why her memory was erased from the records. These hypotheses do not explain why Thutmose III retained most of her royal courtiers as well as following the same plan of monument restoration and expansion that began with Hatshepsut's co-regency. Neither do they properly justify why his successor erased her from the records almost two decades after her death.

Thus, it is the aim of this work to offer new conclusions on this matter, by considering the particular mode of thought of the ancient Egyptians. This was quite different from ours because it was expressed through an integrated discourse (Girard 1972; Eliade 1987; Otto-Harvey 1931, 1980; Ricoeur 1995). This kind of discourse can be considered the starting point for the interpretation of the surviving evidence – such as inscriptions, statues and constructions that show the ontological transformations of Hatshepsut – in order to understand the reasons that motivated these changes. From my point of view, the figure of Hatshepsut can be considered in the light of three ontological changes which are effected in her divine birth, her coronation as "Maat-ka-Re" and the posthumous erasure of her memory as a royal ancestor. These changes are visualized in the ritual scenes depicted in the temple of Amun at Medinet Habu, in the Chapelle Rouge from Karnak, as well as in other monuments erected during her reign (Dorman 2005, 267–268). They represent transitions where Hatshepsut is being linked in to the Egyptian king role, which is the limitation of primordial chaos and the imposition of cosmic order.

The Ancient Egyptian mode of thought

Evidence, like the inscription mentioned in the graffiti found in Aswan, which presumably belonged to Senenmut, make me wonder about the Ancient Egyptian's mode of thought. There, an official is depicted standing in front of the king, alongside a rather unusual reference to the royal figure of Hatshepsut. It can be read: 'The "king's daughter", great of praise, great of favor, and much beloved, the one to whom Re has given the real kingship among the Ennead' (Habachi 1957, 92). Moreover, in the next lines of the inscription the writer is even more direct and leaves no doubt of the subject to whom this whole matter is addressed. He reveals the subject through these references: '"king's daughter", "king's sister", "divine wife" and "great king's wife", "the king of Upper (and Lower Egypt)", "Hatshepsut"' (Habachi 1957, 92). Hence, the subject is clear. But is Hatshepsut related to the king or is she the king himself? How is it possible that she was two different persons – female and male – at the same time?

One important feature of the Ancient Egyptian mode of thought is the "multiplicity of approaches" (Frankfort 1978, 356, 362, 363, 379, 391, 432, 442; Evans-Pritchard 1956, 372; Bleeker 1973, 261–268; Iniesta 1992, 78; Cervelló Autuori 1996, 18–19; Flammini 2005, 12–13, 2008, 63) to the object expressed through an integrated discourse. By this quality, something could have more than one attribute without being nonsense or a contradiction. For instance, in the inscription mentioned above, Hatshepsut is described with different and opposing roles, such as daughter, sister and wife of the king, while she also was the king of Egypt. This multiplicity suggests that there was more than one plane of reality thus the natural world interacted with the supernatural or the sacred. This is the world of deities, which interacts with the natural world by allowing human existence under its constant tutelage, observance, regulation and promotion (Girard 1972, 268). Hence, every relevant aspect of human life is justified and given sense by being linked to the sacred.

In short, it can be said that the natural world was an emulation of the sacred one (Girard 1972; Eliade 1987; Otto and Harvey 1931, 1980; Ricoeur 1995). Material expressions of human interaction with the deities were symbols – *sacra* – used during rite celebrations. Of course, most of the aspects linked to deities could not be communicated or explained because they were mysterious. Nevertheless, someone who took part in a ritual celebration, as well as the rest of society, enjoyed the benefits resulting from rite performance (Deflem 1991, 14). One kind of rite I am particularly interested in is the rite of passage, analyzed by Arnold van Gennep. These "are ceremonies whose essential purpose is to enable the individual to pass from one defined position to another which is equally well defined". Therefore, change and transition are the most important features. This appreciation made me think of the ontological changes suffered by Hatshepsut. In her case, the transition was a substantial alteration of her original being as queen.

Divine Birth of Hatshepsut

One of the first steps of Hatshepsut's ontological changes was her identification as the heir to the throne, as is shown in Senenmut's cenotaph from Gebel Silsila, which bears an inscription that says: 'Live, the king's firstborn daughter, Hatshepsut, may she live, beloved of Amun, lord of the thrones of the two lands, king of the gods' (Urk. 4, 398; Dorman 1988, 114; 2001, 5). It is remarkable that during this phase of royal transformation she does not mention other Thutmoside kings, except for her father, Thutmose I. This was because, although the Thutmoside kings were enthroned and preceded her in the royal role, neither her husband nor her stepson had any bearing on her own designation as king. According to ritual convention, the dead king-father, identified with the god Osiris, passes the throne on to his son, who is alive and associated with Horus. However, Hatshepsut may have avoided mentioning those predecessor kings that related to her proper female court roles: such as being wife or regent.

The upper levels of her funerary temple in Deir el- Bahari specifically refer to her divine birth and her coronation. However, the entire architectural composition – taken as a whole – accentuates her legitimacy, focusing on the figure of the king, as the son of Amun (god of Thebes) and Re (god of Heliopolis) (Allen 2005, 83). From the 4th Dynasty onwards the King was recognized by the title, "Son of Re" (Roth 2005, 149) because it was associated with the sun in the ritual context of his coronation. Actually, 'the king was the Incarnation of Horus. He was not the sun itself' (Frankfort 1948, 170), owing his existence and royal condition to being the offspring of Re. In that sense, the divine birth of Hatshepsut actualized this legitimate antecedent, which dates back to the Old Kingdom and is connected to the cult of the Heliopolitan god, Re, together with the Theban god, Amun. It is illustrated by Hatshepsut's 'well-ordered juxtapositions of sequences of predicates of Amun and Re' (Assmann 2001, 191). Therefore, not only the divine birth scenes but all of the other instances of ontological mutation that Hatshepsut went through make sense from this perspective. In the case of Hatshepsut, her tie with Amun-Re was shown, on the one hand, in the theogamy myth and, on the other hand, in the oracle of the god (Urk. IV, 225, Breasted 1906, 81, IV, 201).

Thus, not only was she the offspring of the deities but also, as they had destined her for the throne of Egypt, the legitimate king. This legitimacy is evident in the references to primary elements (ontological), such as the seed or the 'pure egg' (Urk. IV, 359), appellations used by the Egyptians to link themselves to the cyclical creation of the world or with the origin of life and nourishment. In the inscription of the birth of Hatshepsut it is possible to see the role of the sacra, the sacred objects that act over the subject of a ritual. The inscription includes references to exotic fragrances and the smoke obtained from burning incense. Even though it is not known how or when these objects were used during the ritual, the incense as well as the fresh myrrh appear in the context of celebration (Urk. IV, 328). At that time the need for these kinds of resources can be taken as proof of the capacity of the Egyptian state, ruled by Hatshepsut, for exploiting natural resources from Punt, where Hatshepsut sent an expedition to search for luxury goods, such as fresh myrrh and incense plants (Urk. IV, 321, De Buck 1948, 48–53; Flammini 2007, 227–238; Gestoso Singer 2011, 146). The presence of these items shows the strong link that Hatshepsut had with the ancestor kings who were also capable of undertaking this kind of expedition, like the kings from the Middle Kingdom (Bard and Fattovich 2005; Fattovich 1993, 404; Fattovich 1996, 24; Michaux and Colombot 1998, 355–356; Phillips 1997, 423 and 426; Sayed 2000, 432).

According to the genealogy of Hatshepsut, she was the daughter of Thutmose I and his "Great Chief Wife," Ahmes. However, her status changed and she was reborn as a different person. Hence, once the divine birth ceremony was completed, Hatshepsut was identified as the offspring of the god, Amun-Re, and was no longer linked to the Thutmoside kings. During this ritual, the king-father of Hatshepsut, (Thutmose I), became – in ritual – the god, Amun-Re, himself, in order to conceive the future king, Hatshepsut. Thus it could be said that the god "actually incarnated" in the person of Thutmose I.

It is remarkable that, even though her image as a male king was fixed from her divine birth, Hatshepsut kept the female endings of her titles (Robins 1999, 111–112). A possible explanation could be that these gender parallels (depicted as a male king with female endings of her titles) were due to overlapping contexts: a ritual one, where Hatshepsut was a male king, and a natural context, in which she kept her female nature. In this way, the apparent "contradictions" of a literal reading are avoided. Whereas Hatshepsut was naturally a woman and, for that reason, daughter and wife of the king, during ritual celebrations, she was the enthroned king. Moreover, as the king she can be represented archetypically as a male person. This fact is even more evident in the depictions of the second ontological change to her figure, which occurs in her coronation as "King of Upper and Lower Egypt".

Coronation as "King of Upper and Lower Egypt"

One of the most important pieces of evidence that can be analyzed in relation to the second ontological change – identified with the coronation of Hatshepsut – is the geographical evidence. Her radical transformation into a king was accomplished in several different strategic territorial areas, from the Nile valley to the desert, where her transformation was carried out, from an ideological and symbolic perspective. Monumental display and the change of her status through written inscriptions were the methods through which Hatshepsut managed to portray her coronation in a way that made sense, given her exceptional situation. Thus, her inscriptions did not focus on the fact that she was a lady who became Horus or that she acquired her place due to the original heir being underage, but they concentrated on the gods' recognition of her as a legitimate king and on her belonging amongst the predecessor kings. For these reasons, although she shared the throne with young Thutmose III, it was quite clear that she had a leading role in the royal court. All in all, it is possible that Hatshepsut constructed this ideology for two specific purposes:

1) to link herself with her immediate predecessor kings, and
2) to re-initiate the cycle of time by re-establishing order through the cosmic creation of the natural world.

The testimony of the official, Djehuty, from Dra Abu el-Naga, in Middle Egypt (Bryan 2000, 230), confirms the testimony left from the Speos Artemidos Inscription of Hatshepsut (Allen 2002, 3). In this statement Hatshepsut makes it clear that she unified the State and expelled the Asiatics – Hyksos – from the Delta, just like her predecessor, King Ahmose I, effectively did at the beginning of the New Kingdom. It has been suggested that the Hyksos' links to Seth (Pritchard 1969, 268) can be understood as another reason why they were condemned as wicked. In this way, it is possible that the real intention of Hatshepsut in the inscription was to reinforce her kinship with Ahmoside kings; that is why it did not matter that the inscription referred to an episode that happened a century before Hatshepsut's reign. Besides, the Hyksos invasion and departure from the Delta can be understood as ritual symbols connected with the limitation of chaos (Allen 2002, 3).

The approval of the deities was also a crucial topic in the inscription. Gaining the approval of the solar deities was particularly important, and was shown by positioning the legitimate king, Hatshepsut in this case, with the god Horus. Other images depicting the Egyptian king's archetypal role are shown on the lower terrace of the funerary temple, where Hatshepsut is shown dealing with the "bearers of chaos" (Naville 1898, 160). Scenes of war, hunting and fishing depict the elimination of the bearers of chaos by the sacred person of the king, and the resulting order.

There are some exceptional issues from the reign of Hatshepsut relating to the role of her co-ruler, Thutmose III. The coronation of Hatshepsut did not cancel the one of young Thutmose, even though it was relegated to a secondary level and omitted from the inscriptions. Hence, it was not that Hatshepsut and Thutmose III were depicted always as coregents or as successive kings. Instead, she was depicted alone or together with the young Thutmoside king depending on the kind of context they wanted to establish for ritual. In modern chronologies, there are two different ways of dating their reigns: one based only on the years of reign of the Thutmoside king (*cf.* Roherig *et al.* 2005, 6) and another one, in which Thutmose III and Hatshepsut are mentioned as separate and successive kings, even though their reigns overlapped in chronological terms (*cf.* Barnes and Malek 2000, 36). Evidence from the co-regency of Hatshepsut and Thutmose III show that their depictions varied depending on context. For instance, where the aim was to show the royal power of Hatshepsut (in the obelisk inscriptions) she appeared alone as the only "King".

However, in a different kind of inscription, where the king worshipped a deity such as Hathor, for instance, both were depicted together. An example of such an inscription can be found in Serabit el-Khadim (Sinai). This could be because Hatshepsut was shown as the only king whenever she acted as the ritual subject. In this context, she was supposed to bear sacred power, and the presence of Thutmose III could be considered evidence of weakness in terms of human strength. Why? Because, being naturally a woman, Hatshepsut was weaker compared to a male king.

Moreover, considering the ideological conception of the Egyptians, where the king was identified with the state and its territory, the depiction of two contemporary kings – which was certainly an exception to the rule – could imply a weakness of the state itself. By contrast, in other contexts where gender differences did not have a relevant impact, both of them were represented. It has been suggested that this overlapping – simultaneous situations – was meant to show the transition of Hatshepsut as queen to King Maat-ka-Re (Dorman 2006, 52). However, this explanation is not convincing given that the Egyptians record transitional events and rites of passages, like the one that would turn Hatshepsut into a king (Conan 2002, VI y 12; Storch 2011, 60, 76, 168, 142). Hence, she was most probably mentioned with both titles because becoming a king did not mean she stopped being a queen. On the contrary, the queenly role was upheld while a new condition was added to the previous one.

To sum up, Hatshepsut used different resources to achieve the ontological change by which she became King. These were ritual celebrations, the erection of monuments and the adoption of fundamental royal attributes in order to revitalize ancient customs and consolidate her direct kinship relations with predecessor kings and gods. Nevertheless, the erasure of the memory of the queen/king from the records, a queen who was the only direct offspring from the Ahmoside Dynasty, is remarkable.

Posthumous Erasure as King

The last ontological change to Hatshepsut's figure can be seen in the erasure of her name and images. The cycle began with the first ontological change, her divine birth, followed by her coronation as Maat-ka-Re and it concludes with the "persecution of her memory" (Keller 2005, 294) started by Thutmose III. The posthumous elimination of the royal cartouches of Hatshepsut was crucial in shaping his reign as well as in justifying his dynastic legitimacy. There have been different suggestions as to the specific time of this profanation. Some elements were intentionally erased while others were left intact. It is possible to detect two different ways in which the royal figure of Hatshepsut was eliminated from the records: (Dorman 2005, 267) on the one hand, the replacement of her name by that of one of her Thutmoside predecessors, Thutmose I or Thutmose II, which occurred in the inscriptions located in Karnak; on the other hand, the intentional destruction of statues in her funerary temple. Not only was her name erased, but the references to her divine birth, such as the title, "son of Amun-Re," (*s3 jmn r^c*) were also hacked out.

However, in these cases, the name of the deity was not altered. In Karnak, the royal cartouches, which originally had the name of Hatshepsut together with the tutelary god of Thebes, Amun, were replaced by the names of previous and later kings. In this way, it is possible to find references to Thutmose I, Thutmose II and Thutmose III – in the Chapelle Rouge – as well as kings that ruled after the Amarna Period, such as Tutankhamon, Horemheb and Sethi I (19th Dynasty), which are shown on the VIII pylon. V. Davies argued that the replacement of one cartouche (Hatshepsut's) for another (Thutmose III's) was the result of a mistake, since 'occasionally, one finds errors in depictions from this era because either the scribes or the carvers mistakenly used male grammatical elements for Hatshepsut or female grammatical elements for Thutmose III' (Davies 2004, 61–62). However, the possibility of an "error" is not a plausible explanation when considered within the parameters of the Egyptian mode of thought, no matter how peculiar the situation – of the co-regency and the enthronement of a queen as king – was. For Egyptian society, an error meant disturbance of cosmic and natural order, the burst of chaos. Precisely, the most valuable thing to preserve, order, could not be damaged by an "innocent" distraction, from a scribe for instance. Hence, P. Brand's suggestion, that these kings were seeking to link themselves to the god, Amun-Re (Brand 1999, 134) by re-writing their names in the temple of Karnak, seems more reasonable.

Thus, the destruction of the epigraphic and material records of Hatshepsut's ontological changes as king of Egypt seems to have been a necessary step to consolidate the last ontological change, because of the strong kinship between Hatshepsut and Amun-Re. In fact, when Roth refers to her post-mortem legacy of reign, she argues that "oddly, her nomen (Hatshepsut, Beloved of Amun) was usually attacked more violently than her prenomen (Maat-ka-Re)" (Roth 2005, 277). Hence, the persecution avoided erasing her coronation name because it included the name of deities, Maat and Re. Taking this into account, it may be assumed that the erasure was specifically aimed at the divine birth records through which Hatshepsut became the "son" of Amun-Re. The hypothesis that the erasures are evidence of the posthumous revenge of Thutmose III loses its strength when we see that the elimination of the queen's name occurred almost twenty years after Hatshepsut's death. Moreover, the fact that records that identified her as royalty (king's daughter and king's wife) were not modified may further imply that the elimination did not include revanchist intentions by the Thutmoside king (Roth 2005, 281).

Hence, it was important to eliminate what had been said in Amun-Re's oracle when Hatshepsut became an heir to the throne. This explains why, for instance, in her funerary temple, only the reference to two newborns was erased. These represented Hatshepsut and her ka – (Silverman 1995, 70) who were presented by the god Thot before their father, Amun-Re, in the original scene that narrated the divine birth of Hatshepsut. Such episodes could be erased by the profanation and destruction of images that showed Hatshepsut as the "Son of Amun-Re" and then "King of Upper and Lower Egypt". The erasure could be considered "corrective" of the ritual celebrations performed previously – Hatshepsut's divine birth and coronation as king – and may have been carried out in order to erase her kinship link to Amun-Re and her identity as "Son of Amun-Re" and "King of Egypt".

The aggression levelled against her royal figure in the records of her funerary temple in Deir el-Bahari could be understood as a "re-actualization" of birth and coronation ceremonies. In this sense, this kind of action had a magical (Cervelló Autuori 2003, 84) purpose by which the Egyptians managed to re-define their natural world. Also, the underlying motive could have been the possibility that the memory of Hatshepsut as king proved Thutmose III's weakness. This was demonstrated by his inability to govern alone. Furthermore, he was a minor and also lacked kinship links to the Ahmoside kings. That is why both of these lines – Ahmoside and Thutmoside – were brought together by the enthronement of Thutmose III's son and successor, Ahmosis II, while the memory of Hatshepsut was completely eradicated. This fact explains the definitive erasure of the royal predecessor – Hatshepsut – through ritual celebration, which resulted in the elimination of her divine birth, her image and her coronation name. In the original images of Hatshepsut there is now an "empty" spot without any representation. Thus, the ritual context that was set up in the co-regency of Hatshepsut and Thutmose III was replaced by a new one, where Thutmose III was the only king.

Finally, the replacement or destruction of Hatshepsut's cartouches, which confirms the elimination of her role as a royal figure, could be thought of as an aggressive action. However, this was not connected to personal matters between Thutmose III and Hatshepsut. Instead, it was part of a larger ritual that the king had to perform in order to inaugurate an ordered cosmic cycle.

Final Conclusions

During the 18th Dynasty the enthronement of underage kings was common. As a result, queens gained an unusually prominent role in the royal court. In the exceptional situation in which a woman performed the traditional male role of Horus, as is the case of Hatshepsut, there was an extra ingredient: the relation of kinship between Hatshepsut and the Ahmoside kings on her mother's side. Because they did not have this link, the Thutmoside kings allowed her enthronement as king, and it was this too, which led to the posthumous elimination of her royal figure. This paper has focused on the reign of Hatshepsut and changes to her royal figure. Firstly, it has taken into account the mode of thought of the ancient Egyptians. From their point of view, it was possible to consider multiple approaches to the queenly and kingly roles performed by Hatshepsut. Furthermore, we have considered the celebration of rites of passage, as the expression of the sacred: the emulation of the supernatural world in the natural one. In this context, it is possible to understand the three ontological changes to Hatshepsut's royal figure:

1) the divine birth through which she became "son of Amun-Re" instead of Thutmose I's child;
2) her coronation as king "Maat-ka-Re," which was added to her previous queenly role;
3) finally, the "corrective" action performed in order to erase her kinship link to Amun-Re and her kingly entity.

Hence, the figure of Hatshepsut underwent several changes – reflected in her titles, clothing and other references in inscriptions where her name is mentioned – and not only did she become the king of Egypt but she was also the legitimate link between Ahmoside and Thutmoside dynastic lines. This kinship connected kings from the 18th Dynasty with predecessor kings dating from the origin of the Egyptian State. Thus, taking this into account it is possible to consider that

Thutmose III was displaced to a secondary role during the reign of Hatshepsut in order to legitimate the Thutmoside succession line. In conclusion, the re-invention of Hatshepsut in the different roles described above, together with the erasure of her royal figure, allowed her successors to inaugurate a new cycle where social stability and cosmic order were the common rule.

Acknowledgments

I would like to express my gratitude to the CRE organizing committee for this opportunity, and my advisors Roxana Flammini, Graciela Gestoso Singer and Deborah Sweeney for reading an earlier draft of this paper. I also want to thank Cecilia Lainz and Nathalie Andrews for improving my English. All errors are, however, my responsibility.

Bibliography

Allen, J. P. (2000) *Middle Egyptian. An Introduction to the Language and Culture of Hieroglyphs*. New York, Cambridge University Press.

Allen, J. P. (2002) "The Speos Artemidos Inscription of Hatshepsut", *Bulletin of the Egyptological Seminar* 16, 1–17, pls. 1y2.

Allen, J. P. (2005) The Role of Amun. In C. Roehrig, R. Dreyfus and C. Keller (eds). *Hatshepsut: From Queen to Pharaoh,* 83–86. New York, The Metropolitan Museum of New York & New Heaven and London, Yale University Press.

Assmann, J. (2001) [1984] *The Search for God in Ancient Egypt*, translated by D. Lorton. Cornell, Cornell University Press.

Baines, J. and Malek, J. (2000) *Cultural Atlas of Ancient Egypt*. New York, Checkmarck.

Bard, K. A. and Fattovich, R. (2005) Egyptian Sea Vessel Artifacts Discovered at Pharaonic Port of Mersa Gawasis along Red Sea Coast. Boston, Boston University, 1–2.

Bleeker, C. J. (1973) The Position of the Queen in Ancient Egypt, *La regalita sacra. The Sacral Kingship*. Leiden, Brill, 261–268.

Brand, P. J. (1999) Restorations in the Post-Amarna Period, *Journal of American Research Center in Egypt*, vol. 36, 113–134.

Breasted, J. H. (1906) *Ancient Records of Egypt* 2. Chicago, The University of Chicago Press.

Bryan, B. (2000) The 18th Dynasty before the Amarna Period (ca. 1550–1352 B.C.). In I. Shaw (ed.), *The Oxford History of Ancient Egypt*, 207–264. Oxford, Oxford University Press.

Bryan, B. (2003) Property and the God's Wives of Amun. In D. Lyons and R. Westbrook (eds) *Women and Property,* 1–15. Cambridge, Center of Hellenic Studies, Harvard University.

Burgos, F. (2008) *La chapelle Rouge. Le sanctuaire de la barque d'Hatshepsout*, CulturesFrance-ERC, vol. 2.

Cervelló Autuori, J. (2003) Aire. Las creencias religiosas en contexto. In E. Ardèvol Pierra and G. Munilla Cabrillana (eds) *Antropología de la religión. Una aproximación interdisciplinar a las religiones antiguas y contemporáneas,* 71–180. Barcelona, UOC.

Conan, M. (ed.) (2002) *Sacred Gardens and Landscapes: Ritual and Agency*. Washington, Harvard University Press.

Davies, V. (2004) Hatshepsut's Use of Tuthmosis III in Her Program of Legitimation. *Journal of American Research Center in Egypt* 41, 55–66.

De Buck, A. (1948) *Egyptian Readingbook*. Chicago, Illinois, Ares Publishers, 48–53.

De Morgan, J. (1894) *Catalogue des monuments et inscriptions de l'Egypte Antique: prem. serie, Haute Egypte.*

Deflem, Mathieu. (1991) Ritual, Anti-Structure, and Religion: A Discussion of Victor Turner's Processual Symbolic Analysis. *Journal for the Scientific Study of Religion* 30 No. 1, 1–25.

Dorman, P. (2001) Hatshepsut: Wicked Stepmother or Joan of Arch. In *The Oriental Institute News and Notes*, No. 168, 1–5.

Dorman, P. (2005) Hatshepsut: Princess to Queen to Co- Ruler. In C. Roehrig, R. Dreyfus and C. Keller (eds) *Hatshepsut: From Queen to Pharaoh,* 87–90. New York, The Metropolitan Museum of New York & New Heaven and London, Yale University Press.

Dorman, P. (2006) The Early Reign of Thutmose III: An Unorthodox Mantle of Coregency. In E. H. Cline and D. O'Connor (eds) *Thutmose III. A New Biography,* 39–68. Michigan, The University of Michigan Press.

Eaton-Krauss, M. (1998) Four Notes in the Early Eighteenth Dynasty. *Journal of Egyptian Archaeology*, vol. 84, pp. 205–210.

Eliade, M. (1987) *The Sacred and the Profane. The Nature of Religion.* Florida, Harcourt.

Evans- Pritchard, E. E. (1956) *La religión de los Nuer,* Madrid, Taurus.

Fattovich, R. (1993) Punt: the archaeological perspective in *Sesto Congresso Internazionale di Egittologia ATTI*, vol. 2, Torino, 399–405.

Fattovich, R. (1996) Punt: The Archaeological Perspective. *Beitrage zur Sudanforschung* 6: 15–29.

Faulkner, R. O. (1972) *A Concise Dictionary of Middle Egyptian.* Oxford, Griffith Institute.

Flammini, R. (2005) El antiguo Estado egipcio como alteridad: Cosmovisión, discurso y prácticas sociales (ca. 3000–1800 a.C.). *Iberia* 8, 9–26.

Flammini, R. (2007) El camino hacia el Punt. Evidencias textuales y materiales para una lectura de los contactos con Egipto en el Reino Medio. In *Actas de las II Jornadas Multidisciplinarias "Fuentes e Interdisciplina", del 25 al 27 de agosto de 2006, Instituto Multidisciplinario de Historia y Ciencias Humanas, Conicet*, 227–238.

Flammini, R. (2008) Ancient Core-Periphery Interactions: Lower Nubia During Middle Kingdom Egypt (ca. 2050–1640 B.C.). *Journal of World-Systems Research* 14, No. 1, 50–74.

Frankfort, H. (1978) [1948]. *Reyes y dioses. Estudio de la religión del Oriente Próximo en la Antigüedad en tanto que integración de la sociedad y la naturaleza.* Madrid, Alianza.

Frankfort, H. (1978) *Reyes y dioses. Estudio de la religión del Oriente Próximo en la Antigüedad en tanto que integración de la sociedad y la naturaleza.* Chicago, Chicago University Press.

Gardiner, A. H., Peet, T. E. and Černy, J. (1952–1953) *The Inscriptions of Sinai*, 2 vols. 2nd ed. 4–5th Memoir of the Egypt Exploration Society. Oxford, Oxford University Press.

Gestoso Singer, G. (2011) Trasplantando en el centro por Hatshepsut. *Cahiers Caribéens d'Égyptologie* 15, 139–162.

Gestoso Singer, G. (2005) The Obelisks of Hatshepsut: Legitimacy and Propaganda. *Göttinger Miszellen*, No. 207, 37–47.

Girard, R. (1972) *La violence et le sacre*, París, Editions Bernard Grasset.

Grimal, N. (ed.) (2006) *La chapelle Rouge. Le sanctuaire de la barque d'Hatshepsout*, CulturesFrance-ERC, vol. 1.

Habachi, L. (1957) Two Graffiti at Sehel from the Reign of Queen Hatshepsut. *Journal of Near Eastern Studies*, vol. 16, No. 2, 88–104.

Iniesta, F. (1992) *El Planeta Negro: Aproximación Histórica a las Culturas Africanas.* Madrid, Spain, Cyan.

Josep Cervelló Autuori, (1996) *Egipto y África. Origen de la civilización y la monarquía faraónicas en su contexto africano*. Barcelona, AUSA.

Keller, C. (2005) Hatshepsut's Reputation in History. In C. Roehrig, R. Dreyfus and C. Keller (eds) *Hatshepsut: From Queen to Pharaoh,* 294–298. New York, The Metropolitan Museum of New York & New Heaven and London, Yale University Press.

Laboury, D. (2006) Royal Portrait and Ideology: Evolution and Signification of the Statuary of Thutmose III. In E. H. Cline and D. O'Connor (eds) *Thutmose III. A New Biography*, 260–291. Michigan, The University of Michigan Press.

Laskowski, P. (2006) Monumental Architecture and the Royal Building Program of Thutmose III. In E. H. Cline and D. O'Connor *Thutmose III. A New Biography*, 183–237. Michigan, The University of Michigan Press.
Leser, K. (2009) *Maat-ka Ra Hatshepsut*. In http://www.maat-ka-ra.de/english/start_e.htm (VI/3/2009).
Lichtheim, M. (1976) *Ancient Egyptian Literature. A Book of Readings,* vol II: The New Kingdom. Los Angeles, London, University of California Press.
Michaux-Colombot, D. (1998) Geographical Enigmas Related to Nubia: Medja, Punt, Meluhha and Magan. In T. Kendall (ed.) *Ninth International Conference of the Society for Nubian Studies,* 353–363. Boston, Northeastern University.
Naville, E. (1898) *The Temple of Deir el- Bahari: Its Plan, its Founders and its First Explorers*. London, Egypt Exploration Fund.
Otto, R. and J. W. Harvey (1931) *The Idea of the Holy: An Inquiry Into the Non Rational Factor in the Idea of the Idea of the Divine*. Montana, Kessinger Publishing.
Phillips, J. (1997) Punt and Aksum: Egypt and the Horn of Africa. *The Journal of African History*, vol. 38, no. 3. Cambridge, Cambridge University Press, 423–457.
Pritchard, J. B. (1969) *Ancient Near Eastern Texts Relating to the Old Testament*, 3rd ed. with supplement, Priceton, Princeton University Press.
Robins, G. (1999) The Names of Hatshepsut as King. *The Journal of Egyptian Archaeology*, vol. 85, 103–112.
Roehrig, C. *et al.* (2005) Introduction. In C. Roehrig, R. Dreyfus and C. Keller (eds.). *Hatshepsut: From Queen to Pharaoh,* 2–8. New York, The Metropolitan Museum of New York and New Heaven and London, Yale University Press.
Roth, A. M. (2005) Models of Authority: Hatshepsut's Predecessors in Power. In C. Roehrig, R. Dreyfus, and C. Keller (eds) *Hatshepsut: From Queen to Pharaoh,* 9–14. New York, The Metropolitan Museum of New York & New Heaven and London, Yale University Press.
Roth, S. (2009) "Queen". In J. Dieleman and W. Wendrich (eds), *Encyclopedia of Egyptology*. Los Angeles, UCLA, 1–12.
Sayed, A. (2000) The land of Punt: Problems of Archaeology of the Red Sea and the Southeastern Delta. In Hawass, Z. (ed.) *Egyptology at the Dawn of the Twenty First Century. Proceedings of the Eighth International Congress at Egyptologist*, 432–439. El Cairo, American University in Cairo Press.
Sethe, K. (1904) *Das Hatschepsut Problem. Noch einmal untersucht*. Berlin, Verlag der Akademie der Wissenschaften.
Silverman, D. P. (1995) The Nature of Egyptian Kingship. In D. O' Connor and D. P. Silverman (eds) *Ancient Egyptian Kingship*. Leiden, New York and Köln, Brill.
Storch, A. (2011) *Manipulations. Language and Context in Africa*. Oxford and New York, Oxford University Press.
Troy, L. (1986) *Patterns of Queenship*, Series Boreas. Uppsala, Stockholm.
Tyldesley, J. (1996) *Hatshepsut. The Female Pharaoh*. London, Penguin Books.
Uphill, E. (1961) A Joint Sed- festival of Thutmose III and Queen Hatshepsut. *Journal of Near Eastern Studies*, vol. 20, No. 4, 248–251.
Urk. IV= Sethe, K. (1909) *Urkunden der 18. Dynastie*, vol. IV, Leipzig, J. C. Hinrichs´sche Buchhandlung.
Wb. I= Erman, A. and Grapow, H. (1971) *Wörterbuch der Aegyptischen Sprache im Auftrage der deutschen Akademien hrsg,* vol. 2, Berlin, Unveränderter Nachdruck.

The Phenomenon of "personal religion" in the Ramesside Period, from the "Poem" of Ramses II through to the Prayers of Ramses III

Diana Liesegang

Personal religion is one of the most interesting and influential historic – religious phenomena of Ancient Egypt. It is based on a long tradition with roots in the area of religious belief, cultic practice and the mental ideas of the right acting by the divine orders. Examples of this are the teachings of the Old and Middle Kingdom. This religious phenomenon presents an extraordinary concept of the personal relationship between the individual and the divinity, regardless of the status or power of a person. The evolution of personal religion, especially in the time of the New Kingdom, shows a highly interesting process from a specific religious – cultic aspect, to a concept of a new religious dimension, which had a big impact on the entirety of Egyptian society. This started with the Pharaoh and continued down to the common people.

The sources for the development of these new dimensions and their different spiritual appearances lie in the early 18th Dynasty, where a new imagination about the contact between the god and the people started to change the cultic life and the roles of the religious participants. The idea to do things in a good and right way, and to act at the will of the divine was connected with the picture of a generous father, who looked upon the people as his children or a shepherd caring for his herd (Assmann 1983, 183), an image depicted in the famous teaching of Merikare (Assmann 1987, 51). The god is presented as a generous creator of all things in the natural and cosmic world and cares about his people in a very positive and personal way. The picture of the good shepherd or herdsman is one of the most essential motifs in the conception of personal religion (Breasted 1912, 346), here emphasized by the famous words spoken by the god in the teaching of Merikare: "Well provided the people, the flock of God".

The Papyrus Boulaq 17 (P. Kairo CG 58038), which is dated to the time of the reign of Amenhotep II, is the earliest written testimony for the idea of a Creator-God, who is distinguished by his uniqueness as the 'One and Only' source of life (Luiselli 2004). The idea of a sole god, who creates all things and guides the fate of the world is an essential aspect of the phenomenon of personal religion and only presented in many written and artistic sources of this epoch. The god does not appear in only one special form, as one of his most important characteristics is his secret and hidden nature. He uses the media of light, air and the Nile to reveal a part of his nature to the populace. The relationship is characterized by the direct and open contact between the divinity and the worshippers without any third mediator constructing the spiritual exchange between the divine and the human world. The god, mostly Amun-Re, the most powerful god of the Egyptian pantheon in the beginning of the New Kingdom, possesses an open ear for the prayers of the common people and acts as an impartial judge, incorruptible and fair, an ethical example for the whole world (Assmann 1983, 264).

> "You are Amun, the Vizir of the poor!
> He never has to one who did not bribe said: "Go away from my Court!"
> "You are Amun, the ferry man, who runs over the poor!
> He never has to one who had not paid the fare thereof said:
> "Go away from my boat!" (ÄHG 1975, 388)

This special kind of personal contact, trust and nearness between the populace and their deities was independent of any religious support or control by the priests as cultic messengers and representatives of the pharaoh. The Egyptian king was the chief-priest and the mediator between the divine world and his people. A private person could now play the special role of spiritual messenger or mediator for the gods. A statue of Amenhotep, Son of Hapu, the famous official of Amenhotep III, bears an inscription where he invites the people to tell him his affairs for presentation to the gods.

> "You people of Karnak, who wanted to see Amun, come to me!
> I sign Your petitions. I am the reporter of this god!" (Urk.IV,1835)

This inscription is an excellent example for the loss of royal might and status of the Egyptian king as the most important contact between the gods and the populace. The king must share his function as a messenger with every private man. The hidden god is now approachable for every common man and the exclusive position of the sovereign as mediator between the divine and the human world is disappearing. There exist many archaeological traces for personal religion in the cultic and daily life of the common people, for example, the excellent model of the village of Deir el Medineh as a place of intensive cultic personal religious practice. Many written and artistic sources like papyri, ostraca, stelae or statues tell about the meeting between the worshippers and the gods. They tell about the wishes of the people in these days, about their calls for help in the case of illness, poorness or juristic sorrows, hoping on the divine mercy and justice.

The time of the early 18th Dynasty is significant for a lot of cultic practices, regulating the spiritual exchange between men and deities, and a very special form of manifestation of the divine element in the contact of the divinity with the Egyptian sovereign. The use of *omina*, dreams and almost oracles was a favourite method for the presentation of the divinity and his intentions concerning the relationship with the king and symbolized a new media of divine manifestation in the New Kingdom (Shirun-Grumach, 1993). The famous reports about the oracles of Amun-Re for Queen Hatshepsut and Thutmose III are excellent examples of the demonstration of the divine intention. The oracles were the divine tools for the election and legitimation of these two sovereigns as rulers of Egypt reflecting the divine will of Amun-Re (Assmann 1987, 51). This was an example of communication from the god explaining his divine intentions and commandments to the royal worshippers in the form of an oracle.

In the early 19th Dynasty there were a lot of new beginnings in politics, religion and culture, and the Ramesside period contains many testimonies for the impact of personal religion on the royal literature, demonstrating the change of the role of the Egyptian king in this period. A famous example is the so-called "Poem" of Ramses II about the Battle of Kadesh (1274 BC) against the Hittites. In a moment of greatest danger on the battlefield the Egyptian pharaoh offered a prayer to the god Amun-Re and called the god for salvation. The sudden arrival of his troops, which saved the life of the pharaoh in this military confrontation, was a sign for Ramses II that Amun-Re heard his call and sent him a positive response in the manifestation of quick military support. Ramses II calls the god his father, reminding him that a father does not ignore his son (Gardiner, 1960). This expresses one of the great themes of personal religion, namely that of the god as an ethical role model, a generous and merciful god that cares about his people.

"There is no god, who forget his creature."
"There is no god, who forgets him, who was active for him." (Assmann 1983, 160)

Ramses II shows with his insight into the power of Amun-Re another evident motif of personal religion, the immense worth of help from the divinity.

> "I found Amun more useful than millions of infantry, than hundreds of thousands of chariots and than a ten thousand of brothers and children united with one heart. There is no work of many men but Amun is more useful than they." (Gardiner 1960, 10)

The open and direct presentation of the Egyptian king in the moment of greatest danger, searching for help from the divinity in a situation of fear and loneliness, is a very special admission for an official royal text, and a great demonstration of numerous motifs of the phenomenon of personal religion. The "Poem" of Ramses II can be regarded as an extra-ordinary peace of Egyptian literature and furthermore as a unique example of personal religion in a royal inscription. The inscriptions of his successor Rameses III, the most important king of the 20th Dynasty and the last great sovereign in the New Kingdom, continue this model of presentation of the intensive relation and nearness between the pharaoh and the deities. This idea of contiguity is emphasized by a series of terms and sentences, which are typical for the language of personal religion, and can be found too in the prayers of the common people.

Ramses III is famous in history as the great warrior king and the victor over the Sea People. This image is immortalized in monumental battle reliefs in his temples. The pictures show the invincible king defeating his enemies and the inscriptions tell of the warlike power of Ramses III using a highly metaphorical language with aggressive images (Liesegang 2008, 78–80). It is interesting and really remarkable therefore, that another side of the personality and royal identity of Ramses III was overshadowed for a long time by history and science with the image of a great warrior. This other side symbolizes the full contrast to the picture of the warlike king and victor over the Sea people. Ramses III was a very religious sovereign, who made many precious gifts and donations to the temples; the great Papyrus Harris I presents the list of his enormous donations and monuments to the temple of Amun-Re and to the temples of other deities. It gives an impressive picture of the religious activities and generosity of Ramses III who expressed his loyal relation and gratitude to the gods through his piety.

More evident is the fact that the royal texts of Ramses III contain a great number of terms and motifs of personal religion, demonstrating the growing impact of the religious – historic evolution of the royal literature and ideology during the Ramesside period. The pharaoh speaks in a series of impressive prayers and hymns about his special contiguity to Amun-Re, his divine father. Amun-Re is also the ruler and divine judge of the life and the fate of the Egyptian king. Ramses III follows every commandment and wish of Amun-Re and he bows to the divine will of the god.

> "You set a lifespan, You fix Destiny,
> Fate and Fortune are governed by Your decree.
> There is no god who is your equal,
> but You alone are the Maker, of whatever exist." (ÄHK 1975, 415)

The king himself tries to fulfil all the wishes of the god who is again portrayed as the Creator-God possessing might over all things. The divinity handles and intervenes in the fate of the world and the lives of every single person, beginning with the pharaoh and ending with the common people. Ramses III obeys in every way the divine commandments and recognizes the positive results of acting in the name of Amun-Re. He realizes that accepting and following the divine orders is the best way for a contented life. Ramses III speaks by using the symbolic language of personal religion in a highly sensitive way, about the special position and the might of Amun-Re and shows himself as a humble and religious worshipper like his subjects.

> "I am aware of Your form, I know Your nature.
> I am versed in Your deity, more than any other god,
> and I have discovered the benefits of him who walks on Your way." (see ÄHK 1975, 410)

The king wants to give the best for Amun-Re and tries to create many gifts and great monuments, honouring the king of the gods who elected him as his son and as sovereign of Egypt. This model of "do ut des" underlines the intense affinity between the god and the king, and the system of performing benefactions in order to receive something positive back. Ramses III bows under the will of Amun-Re and gives him absolute might over his life and activities. The divine will now controls all acts. Every success of the king is coming through the might of Amun-Re, and every action in war and peace depends on the divine will of the divinity.

> "How much better is it, millions of times over him who relies on you, for him who trusts in you!"

Indeed, may you cause every land and every foreign land to know that you are the source of strength for Pharaoh, L.P.H., your son, over every land and foreign land. It is you who make the land of Egypt victorious – even your sole land without the hand of any army in it, but just your great strength which keeps it safe, because of the desire that you had made for Pharaoh, L.P.H., since you had beheld him."

The highly aggressive inscriptions about the wars of Ramses III against the Libyans and the Sea People present the picture of a dominating and powerful warrior king, who is invincible and victorious. The prayers and hymns of Ramses III show a serious, modest and very religious sovereign, wanting to do his best for his divine father, knowing at all times the privilege of being the son of Amun-Re and king of Egypt. The extraordinary relationship between Ramses III and Amun-Re obviously stands under the sign of the phenomenon of personal religion, and the texts show the might and the grace of the divine ruler and his royal son who depends on the attitude of the father for all his decisions and acts.

> "Everyone who hides himself in your presence.
> Never shall calamity befall him.
> And his throne is established in peace."

> "He who says " My father", concerning you,
> he is Lord of the Nine Bows." (see ÄHK 1975, 411)

Conclusion

The phenomenon of "personal religion", especially within the royal literature, has a mighty impact on the relationship between the king and the gods. The contact between the Egyptian sovereign and the divinity is supported by a spiritual exchange and cultic practice. The most remarkable aspect is the role of the king, whose image reflects a religious and modest sovereign, with the desire to make all things after the will of the god. He obeys all divine orders, shows himself in a humble habit and speaks words of the deepest religious devotion. This is an extraordinary aspect to find in comparison to the royal predecessors of Ramses III and Ramses II, who appeared in the cultic life undertaking the role of a priest, but the written sources of his reign show another priority contained within the royal inscriptions.

He also used the oracle of Amun-Re for his political decisions and inscribed the "Poem" on the walls of his temples, but he stood in another historic-political position, one century before Ramses III. The inscriptions of Ramses III are full of the motifs of personal religion and emphasise the absolute power of Amun-Re. The god orders the world and the fate of the people after his will. In the long tradition of the Egyptian royal self-presentation it was always an essential point that the pharaoh, as the living son and the representative of the god, appears in the cultic world in a very serious and religious manner. In these texts there is a dimension of intensive religious presence and imagination, which is extraordinary in the Egyptian royal literature.

Ramses III presents a new aspect when he speaks in the same way, and with the same words as his subjects. He acts like his people and stands now on the same grade with them, which means that he appears very human and personal. But this means also, that he loses something of his royal position and might. He cannot do or control something without the divine support of Amun-Re. In the early 18th Dynasty the support of the deities through an omina or an oracle was important for the legitimation of a king, but in the Ramesside period, and especially during the reign of Ramses III, it is a sign of total dependence on the gods and their divine will. The Ramesside period stood at the beginnings of a new start with the political desire to restore the imperial world of the 18th Dynasty. The adoption of the different political and religious ideas of their predecessors should have been a legitimisation and a motivation for the new Ramesside kings. Instead, it developed a change in the political system in the Egyptian empire and opened the way for a new form of political state in Egypt. Ramses II was the great role model for Ramses III, but he lived in different political time to his famous ancestor.

Ramses III shows himself in the royal literature as a very modest and deeply religious sovereign, obviously the royal propaganda presents him as a dangerous and invincible warrior king. His extraordinary prayers and his great donations and benefactions for the temples of the gods demonstrated his attitude and relation to the divine world. The cultural memory (Assmann and Hölscher 1984) of Ancient Egypt has Ramses III as one of the mightiest kings and last great ruler of the Pharaonic Empire. His reign is famous for his successful wars against the Sea People and the Libyans and for the dramatic fall of the Egyptian economy. However, the literary sources demonstrate the religious attitude of the king in the sense of a "gr m", a man who can be silent in the right moment as the teachings of Amenemope tell. The king appears as an individual with a very personal, emotional and intense relationship with the god, but also as a ruler who does not create history, or handle in a powerful way, as the "Lord of Acting". The inscriptions of Ramses III show his reign as a time of the zenith of deeply religious royal texts in the tradition of personal religion, and at the end of the mighty position as an active and influencing king. All might and decisions now come only from Amun-Re.

At this point it can be said that Ramses III was the most religious sovereign in the New Kingdom, and presents an extraordinary heritage of literature of the cultural world of Ancient Egypt. He appears as a humble worshipper in the same way as his people and this demonstrates the loss of the evident position of the Egyptian sovereign as the chief-priest and the mediator between the gods and the people; it also symbolizes the loss of political control. The king cannot approach his people anymore with the tool of religion. The changes in the position of the Egyptian king are a sign for the religious-political evolution in Egypt in this time, and a sign for a new distribution of the worldly might. Amun-Re and his priests gain more and more wealth and political influence, which increasingly grows in the late Ramesside period, preparing the way for the coming state of theocracy in the Third Intermediate Period.

Bibliography

Assmann, J. (1975) *Ägyptische Hymnen und Gebete*. Zürich und München, Artemis-Verlag.
Assmann, J. (1983) *Re und Amun*. Universitätsverlag Freiburg Schweiz.
Assmann, J. (1987) Die Zeit Hatschepsuts und Thutmosis III. in religionsgeschichtlicher Sicht. In *Ägyptens Aufstieg zur Weltmacht. Ausstellungskatalog, 47–55*. Mainz, Philipp von Zabern.
Assmann, J. und Hölscher, T. (1988) *Kultur und Gedächtnis*. Frankfurt am Main, Suhrkamp – Verlag.
Breasted, J. H. (1912) *Development of Religion and Thought in Ancient Egypt*. New York, Harper Torchbook.
Gardiner, A. (1960) *The Kadesh Inscriptions of Ramesses II*. Oxford, University Press.
Liesegang, D. (2008) "Visual Images" Ein königliches Ritual in versprachlichten Bildern. In *Mythos & Ritual*. Festschrift für Jan Assmann zum 70. Geburtstag, 77–81. Berlin, Lit Verlag.
Luiselli, M. (2004*) Der Amun-Re Hymnus des P.Boulaq 17 (P. Kairo CG 58038)*. Wiesbaden, Harrasowitz Verlag.
Shirun-Grumach, I. (1993) *Offenbarung, Orakel und Königsnovelle*. Ägypten und Altes Testament, Bd. 24. Wiesbaden, Harrasowitz Verlag.

The Encircling Protection of Horus

David Ian Lightbody

The aim of this paper is to present my current research into the use of Egyptian royal encircling symbolism, represented by the shen ring, and to describe how and why this symbolism was incorporated into royal artworks, architecture, decoration and rituals.

The phenomenon of circular symbolism was first identified in royal architecture by Flinders Petrie in the late 19th and early 20th centuries. Although his chronologies and his views on race have not stood the test of time, Petrie was right in almost every respect when it came to the architectural survey and analysis of Egyptian monuments. He first identified the circular symbolism as far back as 1883 when he carried out his meticulous triangulation of the pyramids and tomb chambers of the Giza plateau, and he wrote about this phenomenon at least five times, including in the journal Nature in 1925 (Petrie 1883; Petrie 1892; Petrie 1925; Petrie 1940; Petrie 1990). He concluded that "...these relations of areas and of circular ratio are so systematic that we should grant that they were in the builder's design" (Petrie, 1940). Other authorities on Egyptian pyramid and tomb architecture such as I. E. S. Edwards and Miroslav Verner have subsequently confirmed Petrie's conclusions (Clarke and Engelbach 1991, 118; Edwards 1979, 269; Jackson and Stamp 2002, 167; Verner 2003, 70), but none of them have provided a convincing explanation as to why this circular architectural symbolism was used.

In October of 2008 I published a report in which I set out a new archaeological analysis of Petrie's conclusions in full (Lightbody 2008), and in September of 2009 I presented the latest research results at the third British Egyptology Congress (BEC3). In that publication, and in the lecture, I postulated a direct link between the circular proportions in the architecture and the iconography of the shen ring and cartouche. Here, I do not intend to revisit the issue of the circular proportions in the architecture, which is now well covered. This presentation will elaborate on the association between the circular shen iconography and rituals of encircling protection for royal tombs, temples and sarcophagi, and the artefacts contained therein.

The protective symbolism was represented graphically, as a partially abstracted concept, by the shen ring. The shenu is also known in its elongated form as the cartouche, and was depicted as twin oval loops of rope, tied at the bottom. They encircle the pharaoh's *praenomen*, throne name, or *nomen*, birth name, in hieroglyphs. Other motifs and deities were closely associated with this ring and the cartouche, such as the royal falcon Horus, the royal uraeus snake and the vulture goddess Nekhbet. Together, they represented the ideas of royal protection and dominion over the encircled world, and scenes incorporating these icons were often depicted on the architectural elements of tombs and temples, particularly at entrances and on thresholds, such as under architraves, down door jambs or along the tops of enclosure walls. In this way they protected the royal building entrances and perimeters.

Regular Egyptology reference books normally state that shen means either 'eternity' (Wilkinson 2001, 208), or 'all the world encircled'. While it did carry these meanings in some contexts, the fuller meanings associated with the symbol are much more complex and far more extensive than first appearances would suggest. The Berlin hieroglyph dictionary of Erman and

Grapow, for example, provides no less than twenty four pages of definitions associated with the word shen, all different, but closely related, showing that the ideas associated with this symbolism were complex and extensive (Erman and Grapow 1971, 488–512). Falkner provides around sixty separate definitions in the form based word family of shen, all beginning with the glyphs V7 and N35 that make up the syllable of the word shen (Faulkner 2002, 267–270). Several in-depth analyses of the symbol have appeared in recent years (Barta, 1970; Bolshakov, 1997; Spieser, 2010; Sugi, 2003; Wilkinson 2003, 192–194), while other developed definitions are also available (Allen 2001, 65; Betro 1996, 195; Quirke 2001, 123; Shaw and Nicholson 1995, 267, 300, 301).

The basic meaning of the word shen in texts was 'encircle', but the wider definitions associated with the shen ring and cartouche ropes communicated the pharaoh's dominion over all that the sun encircles, and the concept of enduring protection. The Egyptian universe was his protectorate, and as a living manifestation of the sun god on earth, he was himself protected by the royal god Horus, whose name literally meant 'the one who is above'. The cartouche around his name therefore protected him for eternity, and expressed his dominion over Egypt and the protection of that territory.

The objective of this presentation, however, is not to review the full range of meanings carried by the shen symbol in Egyptian writing, literature or artwork, but to assemble a few demonstrative examples how the symbolism was extended to, and expressed through, the material culture of Egypt and in rituals. It can be identified in the decoration of the tombs and temples, and in the decoration of artefacts such as ceramic vessels, jewellery, sarcophagi and steles. The symbolism of pharaonic protection and dominion encompassed the architecture, to designate, delineate and protect enclosed royal spaces, and to the paraphernalia contained within those spaces. Just as the pyramids, temple and tombs were protected by encircling rituals and spells (*cf.* PT 534, Pepi I, §1277), this encirclement was depicted and embodied in the art and artefacts contained within these sacred places.

Although it is not the intention of this article to examine the textual meanings in depth, it is nevertheless useful to look at a selection of the relevant definitions from the form based word family of the word shen that directly relate to the circumferences of buildings and tombs and their protection. These definitions are listed in (Fig. 1), along with references to the sources in the relevant dictionaries through which the locations of the primary source texts and their dates of origin can be established. Significant meanings include the words protection, encircle, enclose, surround, circumference, perimeter and cartouche (Erman and Grapow, 1971; Faulkner, 2002), indicating the sort of contexts in which the word was used.

As was already noted, the shen and cartouche are usually drawn as a pair of rope loops, tied at the base. The shen and cartouche also display similarity with the oval symbols used to represent mud-brick enclosures of towns or estates in plan view, from the Early Dynastic period onwards (De Trafford 2007, 276; Kemp 2005, 96). Second Dynasty seals of Hotepsekhemwy containing the king's name are visually similar in form to the first cartouches used during the reign of the Third Dynasty kings Huni and Sneferu (Fig. 2). This is the first sign of a possible hybridisation of the shen ring symbol with the symbol for the perimeter of an estate or a temple building. This linking of the royal cartouche, royal enclosures and the king's name would have been similar to the way in which the palace facade serekh became linked to, and also contained, the king's name.

The ritual setting out of building plans through the stretching of the cord ceremony is attested from the Old Kingdom, and it seems plausible that the shen ropes are related to those used

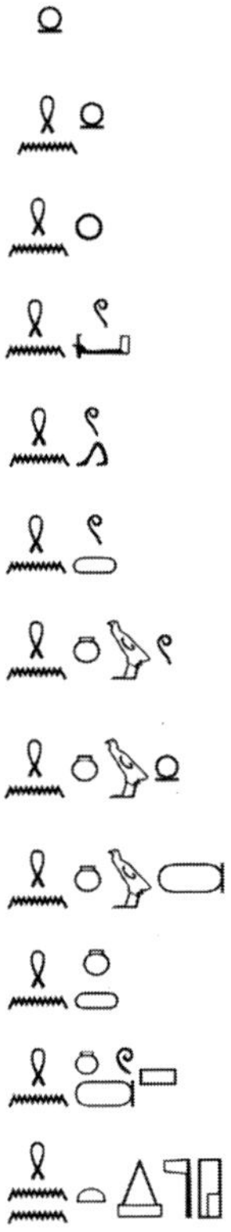

[Snw] protection sign, {V9}		E: pp488
[Snw] to encircle {V7 N35 V9}		E: pp489
[Snw] circuit, circumference, to be round, be oval {V7 N35 D12}		E: pp489
[Sni] (v.) encircle, enclose, surround, {V7 N35 V1 D40}		F: pp267
[Sni] (v.) encircle {V7 N35 V1 D54}		F: pp267
[Sni] (v.) encircle {V7 N35 V1 Z8}		F: pp268
[Snw] circuit, circumference, {V7 N35 W24 G43 V1}		F: pp268
[Snw] cartouche {V7 N35 W24 G43 V9}		F: pp268
[Snw] perimeter, enclosure wall {V7 N35 W24 G43 V10}		E: pp491
[Snw] enclosure {V7 N35 W24 Z8}		F: pp268
[Snw] cartouche - amulet {V7 N35 W24 Z7 V10 O39}		F: pp268
[Snwt mr Hwt nTr] The pyramid and temple are encircled {V7 N35 N35 X1 O24 R8 O6}		E: pp491

E = Erman, A. and H. Grapow (1971) Wörterbuch Der Aegyprischen Sprache, Vol IV.
F = Falkner, R.O. (2002) A Concise Dictionary of Middle Egyptian

Figure 1. Definitions from the form based word family of shenu.

in these foundation rituals (Greenwell, 2005). The establishment of temples and tombs seems to have included three separate rituals, one of which was the stretching of the cord ceremony which set the orientation, and another which involved an encircling of the building (Wilkinson 2001, 305), perhaps while setting out the boundary. Definitions of the word shen listed (Fig. 1) refer to enclosures and enclosure walls, and these support a close association between the pharaoh, the royal buildings (particularly the perimeters) and the iconography representing the king's name.

The examples that follow are intended to briefly illustrate some of the ways in which the symbolism was applied and expressed in the Early Dynastic, Old, Middle and New Kingdoms, with the intention of demonstrating the underlying meanings being communicated.

An analysis of the many ways in which the shen symbol was portrayed on material culture through the consecutive dynasties and kingdoms indicates that the symbolism maintained some of its original meanings right through from the earliest dynasties into the Old, Middle and New Kingdoms. While the iconography evolved in complexity, the meanings altered more subtly in ways associated with the changing applications and social contexts in which the symbolism was used.

The earliest known shen is Den's Shen from a Second Dynasty tag from the royal tombs at Abydos, found by Petrie (Petrie 1901; Pl VII Wilkinson 2001, 207). Already there we can see Horus and royal insignia including the palace façade motif in close proximity to the shen ring and the royal uraeus snake. The symbol for gold is also on this tag, and significant in this context. The king, particularly close to Naqada or Nubt, the golden city, was always associated with gold (Wilkinson 2001, 207). Protection of precious goods, control of the treasury, and more generally, control and redistribution of surplus were the fundamental functions of the kingship and the basis for its power. This tag could have labelled an item of the king's gold in the royal tomb.

Figure 2. Hotepsekhemwy seal, serekh and cartouche of Sneferu (author's illustration).

During this study I compiled a catalogue of occurrences of the shen symbol in Early Dynastic and Old Kingdom contexts. There are only around twenty surviving separate artworks and artefacts in which the shen was depicted from the First through Sixth Dynasties, but all of these were in high status royal contexts, such as on the reliefs of the subterranean chambers of the Step Pyramid, or as held in the hands of Hathor and a nome goddess in a royal triad statue of the pharaoh Menkaure (JE 46499, Cairo) from his Valley Temple at Giza.

Some of the applications are in imaginative and expressive works of art, and effectively communicate the meanings carried by the symbols.

A Fifth Dynasty alabaster vase of the pharaoh Unas, now in the Louvre (E 32372), is decorated with an encircling motif of Horus holding uraeus snakes and the shens (Fig. 3). The snakes in turn hold ankh symbols of life to the cartouche of Unas, around on the opposing side of the vase. This attractive application of the symbolism facilitates an understanding and appreciation of the meanings being expressed. By the Fifth Dynasty the artisans were already adept at finding new and imaginative ways in which to apply the same old royal symbols. These wings circle right around the vase so that the ankhs of life point at the cartouche from both sides, while the shens and snakes protect it from below. Horus protects the vase, and the cartouche of the pharaoh simultaneously.

Lines from the Pyramid Texts of the pyramid of Unas provide some textual proof of the relationship between these concepts during the Fifth Dynasty of the Old Kingdom. Although this line refers to the pharaoh's crown and not to the pharaoh himself, we can clearly verify that the idea of Horus, the kingship, encircling protection and the eye of Horus were already related in PT 221, Unas, §198d (Faulkner 2007, 49; Sethe 1908, 115) which reads "For you are Horus encircled by the protection of his eye".

Also from the Fifth Dynasty, although slightly earlier, a statue of the pharaoh Raneferef (Neferefre) has survived, with Horus protecting and encircling him with his wings behind his head, and with the shens held in his claws to either side. Two fabulous ceremonial vases, in the form of the 'hs' offering vase hieroglyph (W14) were also found in the excavations of his pyramid complex. They are decorated in the style of the falcon's wings, with blue and green faience feather-shaped tiles. This decoration is later echoed in the avian winged 'Rishi' coffins of the Middle and New Kingdoms, where the deceased was protected and encircled by the wings of Horus or Nekhbet. Encircling the Old Kingdom vases are the shen signs, and on the shoulder is a large protective eye of Horus. It would be interesting to establish what these contained, and in what specific ceremonies they were used, but their protecting symbolism is nevertheless clear.

Finally from the Old Kingdom, a red granite sarcophagus, probably of the pharaoh Baka was excavated from the remains of a little known pyramid complex in 1910, now simply known as "La Grande Excavation". These burial chambers were excavated at Zawyet el-Aryan, 5 kms south of Giza. The complex is often attributed to the pharaoh Baka, and although uncertain, it certainly dates to the Third or Fourth Dynasty. This complex is significant because of the red granite sarcophagus set into the granite floor of the subterranean burial chamber. This is cartouche shaped or at least oval shaped (Dodson and Ikram 1998, 246; Verner 2003, 241).

What we see in all of these different royal artefacts and complexes, and in the architecture, is the same traditional ideas of encircling royal protection being expressed in new and original ways, over and over again.

The symbolism did not die out at the end of the Old Kingdom, however, and examples of its application can be traced through into the Middle Kingdom, the New Kingdom and beyond.

The most direct examples of this symbolism being incorporated into architecture, decoration and design are, however, from the New Kingdom, and include the magnificent 18th Dynasty tomb chamber and sarcophagus of the pharaoh Tuthmosis III.

The fine red granite sarcophagus of this pharaoh in KV34 is clearly cartouche shaped and is decorated with a cartouche motif on the lid, perhaps echoing the Old Kingdom, red granite, oval sarcophagus of Baka. The goddesses Isis and Nephthys appear at alternate ends of the sarcophagus holding shen rings to encircle and protect the pharaoh.

Even more expressive of this protective symbolism is that the entire tomb is cartouche shaped. The oval shaped chamber encompasses the traditional symbols of protection in a most satisfactory way. As well as being an encircling cartouche shape and containing an exquisite cartouche shaped sarcophagus, the top of the tomb chamber wall is decorated with a band of the Kheker frieze,

Figure 3. Horus encircling the alabaster jar of Unas (author's illustration).

running in a continuous loop around the oval tomb like the top of a reed palisade (Dodson and Ikram 2008, 125; Kolodko-Dolinska 1990). This is protective symbolism reaching right back to the mythical origins of Egyptian royal enclosures and shrines, and signifies the protection of the sacred space within, just as the cartouche shape of the tomb does. The star studded roof shows that the space represented an open enclosure rather than a roof-covered temple or palace, and it is probably derived from earlier precursor structures that were above ground.

Perhaps for reasons of security, these traditional shrines or funerary enclosures were later 'moved' underground, but the symbolism remained.

These reed palisade enclosures designated a sacred perimeter around the pharaoh, from the earliest times. They were the precursors of the temples and palaces that were later built in mud brick and stone, and the precursors of the funerary chambers that were later cut out of stone in the Valley of the Kings. Remnants of just such palisade enclosures have been recovered above ground from tomb excavations near Hierakonpolis, such as Tomb 23 of the elite cemetery site HK6.

The purpose of the enclosures was to provide a ritually purified and protected space around the pharaoh, in life and in death, protected from the dangers outside such as snakes and other enemies and even from the intensity of the sun.

To fully understand this Egyptian symbolism and the meanings being expressed it is invaluable to understand the world in which the Egyptians lived, including their natural world, above and below. Archaeologists are used to studying landscapes as well as individual sites and excavations, but the investigation must be extended into the wider Egyptian world and into their natural world. Moving into this world lets us see how the ideas of the snakes and falcons became associated with the abstract concepts of encircling protection, and with the pharaoh himself.

The lowly snake is a defensive animal, but it stands its ground when threatened, and it can also strike out dangerously when provoked, like the pharaoh. Above, the vigilant falcon circles as it hunts its prey. Visitors to Egyptian temples in the late morning may often still see a snake or two on the ground, and occasionally a falcon circling above. These animals were also part of the Ancient Egyptian world, and they manifested the characteristics that the pharaohs wanted to invoke in themselves. Protection, territorial dominance, vigilance, and the ability to strike out when provoked.

Texts referring to the mythical origins of the Egyptian temple refer to these early palisade enclosures, and rituals of protection for warding off snakes and enemies (Reymond, 1969). Often the rituals included encircling processions where the pharaoh and his entourage would seem to have verified the integrity of the enclosure and bestowed sacred blessings to ensure its strength. I believe circumambulation ceremonies, such the Sokar festival, are descended from these early rituals of encircling protection and vigilance.

From the wider academic perspective, my research is not happening in isolation. Professor Richard H. Wilkinson of the University of Arizona has already published an article on these encircling ritual processions that took place upon the king's accession to the throne (Wilkinson, 1987) and at other significant times during his reign. I believe these rituals were performed around royal pyramids, tombs and tomb chambers (*cf.* PT 534 § 1277c) as well as the temples and palaces (De Trafford 2007, 279). Similarly, Barry Kemp, David O'Connor and Aloisia de Trafford have investigated the symbolic value of enclosures and the palace façade decorated walls in general (Kemp *et al.* 2004; O'Connor 2009, 178). They have not, however, associated these encircling walls with the shen ring and cartouche symbols, or the Khekher motif, and so this is the area my research is currently focussing on elaborating.

There is clearly ongoing research and development potential in this area and it is proving to be fruitful in terms of identifying corroborating evidence and arriving at positive conclusions. I will continue to carry out my own research into this matter and add my own analysis, conclusions and clarifications to the existing body of scholarship.

In conclusion then: Petrie was right to conclude that circular symbolism was used in the royal architecture of the Old Kingdom. The circular symbolism represented eternal royal protection encircling the pharaoh and his territorial dominion, and was represented by the shen, and/or cartouche symbols, often carried by Horus above. The cartouche and shen were not just decorative motifs. They were absolutely central to the ideology of kingship, and represented the importance of sacred protection for the pharaoh, his territorial domination and his unique status as Horus, the living son of Ra.

Perhaps because the symbols were so ubiquitous, early Egyptologists failed to appreciate their full significance. Based on a more comprehensive analysis we can now see that the Ancient Egyptians associated deeper concepts with these motifs, and expressed them in varied and imaginative ways. The meanings carried by these encircling symbols were much more complex and far more extensive than has been generally appreciated.

The author would like to thank Reg Clarke for help with the Kheker frieze source materials, and the organising committee of CREXII for hosting a memorable and enjoyable event. The author can be contacted at davelightbody@hotmail.com.

Bibliography

Allen, J. P. (2001) *Middle Egyptian, An Introduction to the Language and Culture of Hieroglyphs*. Cambridge, Cambridge University Press.
Barta, W. (1970) Der Konigsring als Symbol zyklischer Wiederkehr. *Zeitschrift fur Agyptische Sprache* 98, 5–16.
Betro, M. C. (1996) *Hieroglyphics. The Writings of Ancient Egypt*. New York, Abbeville Press.
Bolshakov, A. O. (1997) *Man and his Double in Egyptian Ideology of the Old Kingdom*. Wiesbaden, Harrassowitz Verlag.
Clarke, S. and Engelbach, R. (1991) *Ancient Egyptian Construction and Architecture*. Dover Publications.
De Trafford, A. (2007) The Palace Façade Motif and the Pyramid Texts as Cosmic Boundaries in Unis's Pyramid Chambers. *Cambridge Archaeological Journal* 17:3, 271–283.
Dodson, A. and Ikram, S. (1998) *The Mummy in Ancient Egypt. Equiping the Dead for Eternity*. London, Thames and Hudson.
Dodson, A. and Ikram, S. (2008) *The Tomb in Ancient Egypt: Royal and Private Sepulchres from the Early Dynastic Period to the Romans*. London, Thames and Hudson.
Edwards, I. E. S. (1979) *The Pyramids of Egypt*. Middlesex, Penguin.
Erman, A. and Grapow, H. (1971) *Wörterbuch Der Aegyprischen Sprache*. IV. Berlin, Akademie Verlag.
Faulkner, R. O. (2002) *A Concise Dictionary of Middle Egyptian*. Oxford, Griffith Institute.
Faulkner, R. O. (2007) *The Ancient Egyptian Pyramid Texts*. Stilwel, KS.
Greenwell, D. (2005) Ancient Egyptian Temples: The Foundation Ceremony and Foundation Deposits. *The Ostracon. The Journal of the Egyptian Study Society* 3–6.
Jackson, K. and Stamp, J. (2002) *Pyramid. Beyond Imagination: Inside the Great Pyramid of Giza*. London, BBC Worldwide Ltd.
Kemp, B. (2005) *Ancient Egypt. Anatomy of a Civilisation*. London, Routledge.
Kemp, B., Spence, K., Moeller, N. and Gascoigne, A. L. (2004) Egypt's Invisible Walls. *Cambridge Archaeological Journal* 14:2, 259–288.

Kolodko-Dolinska, M. (1990) Studies on the Kheker Frieze in the Temple of Tuthnosis III in Deir el Bahri. *Etudes et Travaux du Centre d'Archaeologie Medeterraneenne de l'Academie Polonaise des Sciences* XIV, 30–60.

Lightbody, D. (2008) *Egyptian Tomb Architecture. The Archaeological Facts of Pharaonic Circular Symbolism.* British Archaeological Reports International Series. S1852. Oxford, Archaeopress.

O'Connor, D. (2009) *Abydos. Egypt's First Pharaohs and the Cult of Osiris.* London, Thames and Hudson.

Petrie, W. M. F. (1883) *The Pyramids and Temples of Gizeh – 1st Edition.* London, Field & Tuer.

Petrie, W. M. F. (1892) *Medum.* London, David Nutt, 270, 271, Strand.

Petrie, W. M. F. (1901) *The Royal Tombs of the Earliest Dynasties. Part II.* London, Egypt Exploration Fund.

Petrie, W. M. F. (1925) Surveys of the Great Pyramids. *Nature* 942–943.

Petrie, W. M. F. (1940) *Wisdom of the Egyptians.* London, British School of Archaeology in Egypt and B. Quaritch Ltd.

Petrie, W. M. F. (1990) *The Pyramids and Temple of Gizeh – 2nd edition from 1885 republished in a new and revised edition with an update by Zahi Hawass.* London, Histories and Mysteries of Man Ltd.

Quirke, S. (2001) *The Cult of Ra. Sun Worship in Ancient Egypt from the Pyramids to Cleopatra.* London, Thames & Hudson.

Reymond, E. A. E. (1969) *The Mythical Origins of the Egyptian Temple.* Cambridge, University Printing House.

Sethe, K. (1908) *Die Altaegyptischen Pyramidentexte nach den Papierabdrucken und Photographien des Berliner Museums.* 1. Leipzig, J.C. Hinrichs'sche Buchhandlung.

Shaw, I. and Nicholson, P. (1995) *The British Museum Dictionary of Ancient Egypt.* London, British Museum Press.

Spieser, C. (2010) Cartouche. *UCLA Encyclopedia of Egyptology (electronic resource).* Frood, E. Wendrich, W. Ed. Los Angeles.

Sugi, A. (2003) The Iconographical Representations of the Sun God in New Kingdom Egypt. In Z. Hawass and L. P. Brock (eds) *Egyptology at the Dawn of the Twenty-first Century. Proceedings of the Eighth International Congress of Egyptologists, Cairo 2000. Vol 2. History, Religion.*

Verner, M. (2003) *The Pyramids: Their Archaeology and History.* London, Atlantic Books.

Wilkinson, R. H. (1987) The Coronational Circuit of the Walls, the Circuit of the *HNW* Barque and the Heb-Sed 'Race' in Egyptian Kingship Ideology. *Journal of the Society for the Study of Egyptian Antiquities* 15: 1, 46–51.

Wilkinson, R. H. (2003) *Reading Egyptian Art. A Hieroglyphic Guide to Ancient Egyptian Painting and Sculpture.* London, Thames and Hudson.

Wilkinson, T. A. H. (2001) *Early Dynastic Egypt.* London, Routledge.

Visual and written evidence for mourning in New Kingdom Egypt

Emily Millward

This paper aims to address an area of research that has scarcely been studied by previous scholars; the mechanisms of mourning in New Kingdom Egypt. As part of a wider study into this topic it has been found that many previous scholars have focused on the so-called 'Songs' and 'Lamentations' of the goddesses' Isis and Nephthys (Faulkner 1936, 121–140; Lichtheim 1980, 117–121; Bleeker 1958, 1–17). These are two texts from the Late Period that can provide an insight into the process of lamentation during temple rituals associated with the cult of Osiris.

Lamentation appears within a different context to mourning in ancient Egypt and therefore this paper will discuss mourning as it appears within a funerary context: an area that is in need of analysis. It is a topic that has a wide range of related sources, mainly visual but with some rare examples of accompanying text. These various sources will be assessed to uncover what they detail about the gestures and attitudes of mourning in New Kingdom Egypt. Here an idea, first introduced by Assmann will also be examined; this is a theory of a personal and authentic emotional attachment to the mechanisms of mourning presented alongside a theatrical purpose related to the funerary proceedings. Assmann (2001, 310), states that 'theatricality and authenticity were always closely connected in [funerary] representations', but he does not assess the extent to which one was more prominent than the other during funerary processions of the New Kingdom; this is an omission which will be covered in this paper.

The notion that the mechanisms of mourning during funerary processions had an amount of formulism will also be assessed in an attempt to ascertain the extent to which mourning was a necessary performance first and foremost rather than a genuine display of grief.

The evidence that will be discussed focuses on the tombs of the Theban elite dating to the New Kingdom and, more specifically, on the wall decoration contained within these superstructures. The variety of pictorial evidence, and the infrequent accompanying texts, can be analysed to give a comprehensive overview of mourning during New Kingdom funerary processions. According to a recent article by Hays ancient Egyptian funerals can be sub-divided into different stages which correspond 'to the practical steps taken following death' (Hays 2010, 1). These stages consist of first taking the deceased's body to the embalming workshop and then the embalming process itself, two actions that are not shown on New Kingdom Theban tomb walls. However, the subsequent stages of the funeral explained by Hays are commonly depicted, these are: taking the deceased to the tomb, consisting of the journey of the funerary entourage across the Nile on barges, followed by a procession along the west bank towards the tomb, then the final rites performed on the mummy of the deceased, culminating in the interment itself (Hays 2010, 1). This chronological sequence can be clearly seen depicted on a variety on New Kingdom tomb walls, some of which are discussed here, and it seems a sensible way to structure the study of the mechanisms of mourning described in this paper accordingly.

During the embalming ritual the process of mourning would occur via the recitation of ritual texts, the majority of evidence for these seen in Late Period examples (Smith 2007, 245–263). The first part of the funerary procession began as the embalmed body of the deceased was moved from the east bank of the Nile to the west bank. The deceased, housed inside the sarcophagus, would be accompanied on its final journey by a large group of people, including priests to perform the final rites outside the tomb, bearers to transport the many pieces of funerary equipment on foot to the tomb and, of course, the friends and family of the deceased who would be present in the capacity of mourners to grieve over the loss of their loved one. The journey across the Nile to the west bank, and indeed the funerary procession as a whole, does not appear to have been a decoration in every Theban tomb, however, those that do present these scenes offer a detailed insight into the mechanisms of mourning during the funerary procession.

A scene from TT50, the tomb of Neferhotep, (Hari 1985, 1; Davies 1973, IV–V) is of particular relevance to this area of study. In this wall decoration, two of the barges of the funerary entourage can be seen making their way across the Nile to the west bank – the beginning of the procession to the tomb. This scene continues from the east wall of the tomb and shows the mourners separated into two barges: nine women in the one on the left-hand side of the scene and six men and three women in the one of the right. Although they are physically segregated the gestures and attitudes that these two groups present are very similar.

All of the figures raise at least one of their hands to their heads in despair, whilst three of the female mourners and two of the male mourners appear to have their mouths open to create the wailing sounds that are often associated with mourning in ancient Egyptian society. Six, or possibly seven, of the women have their chests bared, although the exact number is difficult to ascertain due to some overlapping of the figures. One of the three female mourners present in the barge in the far right of the scene adopts the same gestures of mourning as her counterparts, however, it is notable that she is given the captain's position forward (Davies 1973, 40). It is unlikely that she is the widow of the deceased, who is shown in the barge carrying the sarcophagus at the back of the procession, but it is difficult to say for certain whether the prominent positioning of this particular figure is due to overcrowding on the funeral barges or whether it is used to display the important role played by mourners within the funeral procession.

On the other hand, it is clear from this scene alone that an initial idea of the types of gestures that were used during the journey across the Nile can be established.

Decorative imagery from other tomb walls also supports the indication from the tomb of Neferhotep that two of the more typical gestures of mourning are the raising the hands to the head and, most prominently in the case of the female mourners, the baring of the chest.

TT181, the tomb of Nebamun and Ipuky, displays a fragmented, but nonetheless insightful image of the funerary entourage during its journey across the Nile and the subsequent procession to the tomb (El-Shahawy 2005, 20–21).

The lower register of this particular wall shows the funerary barges making their way across the river and again the female mourners are noticeable in the vessel immediately preceding the sarcophagus of the deceased as their gestures mirror those seen in the tomb of Neferhotep. However, in contrast to the male mourners shown in the funeral barge in the tomb of Neferhotep, the men depicted here adopt a more sedate attitude of grief, merely sitting down with their heads upon their knees. Although this may appear to be an atypical mechanism compared to their female counterparts, one literary source does support the idea that this is a gesture is characteristic of people in mourning. The *Tale of Sinuhe* explains that after the death of King Amenemhat I 'the court was with head upon knee, and the nobles were mourning' (Simpson 2003, 55). Clearly this gesture was a position adopted by mourners in the Middle Kingdom and possibly earlier according to the dating of the *Tale of Sinuhe* (Simpson 2003, 54), and therefore may have been seen as a typical mechanism of mourning by the time of the burial of Nebamun and Ipuky, who were sculptors during the reign of Amenhotep III (El-Shahawy 2005, 21).

It seems sensible to conclude that overall the tomb of Nebamun and Ipuky presents mechanisms of grief that would have been common for mourners. Although there are fewer barges in the scene compared to the juxtaposing image from the tomb of Neferhotep, an understanding of what the scene is depicting and the gestures and attitudes of grief therein can be established and built upon by further study of the mechanisms during the successive stages of burial.

After completing the short voyage across the Nile the funerary procession would have reached the west bank and would immediately begin its final journey to the pre-prepared tomb on foot. Two images from TT409, the tomb of Samut (Negm 1997, 1), display the physical position of the mourners, and the gestures that they make, within the wider context of the funerary procession to the tomb.

The first chronological image is from the lower register of Wall F (Negm 1997, XXIII) and it depicts the funerary barges having just landed on the west bank. This immediately leads into the procession heading to the tomb on foot, depicted on the lower register of Wall G in the same chamber of the tomb (Negm 1997, XXV). A small group of female mourners can be seen in the upper half of a spilt register on Wall F looking towards the tomb while the bearers below them are carrying the funerary equipment, including the canopic chest housing the embalmed organs of the deceased, in a continuing procession.

The scene from Wall G shows that the funerary procession has physically moved on along the west bank of the Nile and then finally reaches its destination. A larger group of female mourners, again facing left but this time looking towards the final rites that are been performed outside the tomb, are in another split register with the final bearers of the entourage reaching the tomb. Looking at the closer detail of these particular images it is clear that these female mourners, probably the same women but at two different stages of the procession, show very similar gestures to those previously seen in the tomb of Neferhotep (Davies 1973, XXIV).

The scene on Wall F shows all of the figures save one in the first group with their hands raised to their heads, the exception being a female mourner on the far left who bends to the ground to pick up dust or dirt, presumably to throw over her face in another gesture of mourning. The latter is a gesture that would not have been possible during the earlier stage of the funeral and is here an addition to the typical gestures that have already been established.

As the scene continues onto Wall G this group of female mourners continues to adopt the same gestures and attitudes. Within the procession on Wall F, two small boys can also be seen walking alongside the bearers, carrying the canopic chest of the deceased; they both raise their arms upwards and the angle of their hands suggests that they too could be pouring dust or dirt onto their faces.

It is not only the visual evidence of this particular scene that alludes to the nature of mourning during New Kingdom funerary processions. Closer analysis of the hieroglyphic text on the immediate left of the group of female mourners on Wall F can be translated as 'Speech of the people who are in mourning' (Negm 1997, 25 and XXII). It is likely that this does not refer to an actual recitation spoken aloud by the group of mourners. Indeed, it may link to the loud wailings often associated with mourning in ancient Egypt, a mechanism that can be illustrated by the open mouths of the mourners in other tomb depictions (Davies 1973, IV–V).

For example, one of the best preserved scenes depicting a funerary procession on the west bank of the Nile comes from TT55, the tomb of the vizier Ramose (El-Shahawy 2005, 35). This illustrates female mourners carrying out the typical gestures of grief during the procession along the west bank, including raising their hands to their heads, exposing their breasts, and heaping dust or dirt onto their faces. Approximately six women in one group also appear to have their mouths open, most likely to wail or cry – the possible 'speech of the mourners' referred to in the tomb of Samut. The idea that a female mourner's 'speech' alludes to crying rather than the vocalisation of actual words is also the most probable reason why female mourners are often referred to as 'wailing women', a title which also relates to the cries of the goddesses Isis and Nephthys in their roles as the archetypal mourners of Osiris (Bleeker 1958).

Further to the emotion indicated by mouths shown open in wailing one younger female mourner at the front of the group, in the tomb of Ramose puts her arms around the waist of an adult female figure, most probably to offer or to receive comfort (El-Shahawy 2005, 34–35).

Although all of the females in this particular group of mourners have black dotted lines painted on their cheeks to represent tears (El-Shahawy 2005, 34–35) this is certainly not the case for every mourning figure in the tomb of Ramose.

It may be concluded that as not every female mourner in this particular tomb, or indeed in the other examples discussed here, are shown with tears on their faces that we are witness to representations of authentic grief in these specific examples.

If this is the case then a display of genuine emotion related to the mechanisms of mourning can be ascertained here. The previously discussed tombs of Neferhotep, Nebamun and Ipuky, Samut, and Ramose certainly display formulaic gestures and attitudes of grief and loss, possibly alluding to the theatrical aspect of the mechanisms of mourning, but it cannot be denied that it is human nature to grieve at the loss of a loved one and, along with the apparent physical gestures, authentic displays of mourning are clear in some instances.

Detail of the scene studied above from the tomb of Nebamun and Ipuky depicts two female mourners, possibly close relatives of the deceased, with tears running down their cheeks as they lovingly reach out to touch the sarcophagus as it is pulled towards the tomb (El-Shahawy 2005, 30). This appears to be a more spontaneous gesture of grief than those previously discussed. The accompanying hieroglyphic text names one of the females as Mutneferet, a daughter of one of the deceased, and it goes on to say 'Fare you well, fare you well, my father, fare you well' (El-Shahawy 2005, 30).

Although the majority of New Kingdom Theban tombs only depict mourners in the more typical, and perhaps theatrical, gestures of grief, it is clear that a certain amount of personal emotion was displayed by members of the deceased's family. Rather than the two female mourners in the tomb of Nebamun and Ipuky remaining anonymous, one of them is named.

Although texts alongside mourning figures are generally rare, a scene of the funerary procession from TT44, the tomb of Amenemhab, also names seven female mourners who are part of the entourage (El-Saady 1996, pl. 45). In the tomb of Nebamun and Ipuky, Mutneferet is not only named but she even has a few final words for the deceased, whom she specifically, and personally, states is her father.

On the other hand, due to the formulaic aspect of ancient Egyptian artwork this emotion from the mourners is not easy to assess in every case. This is clear when scenes showing the final rites outside the tomb of the deceased are studied. Once the funerary procession had reached its final destination on the west bank of the Nile the bearers would place the funerary equipment inside the tomb. Then, the final recitations and rituals, such as the Opening of the Mouth Ceremony, would be performed by priests who had accompanied the funerary entourage and who would place the mummy of the deceased in an upright position facing south (Hays 2010, 7).

Several tomb depictions display this final stage of the funerary process; firstly, the tombs of Amenemhab (El-Saady 1996, pl. 28) and TT277, the tomb of Amenemonet (El-Shahawy 2005, 77) display this late stage of the funerary procession with female mourners kneeling at the feet of the mummies, with hands raised to their heads. The female on the wall of Amenemonet's tomb has, her breasts exposed. The mechanisms of mourning depicted in these scenes are not only typical of the funerary procession as a whole, but the specific positioning of the female mourners is formulaic during the final stages of burial.

Therefore, the extent to which authentic, or more spontaneous, gestures of grief can be identified amongst the formulaic representations of mourning is subject to the style of ancient Egyptian artwork; a style that is not only apparent on tomb walls, but also in other mediums. For example, a 19th Dynasty vignette from the *Book of the Dead* of Hunnefer, created to accompany spell 23 'for opening the mouth of N' (Faulkner 1985, 54), likewise depicts two female mourners in similar positions and displaying identical gestures of grief to those in the sources studied above.

There do, however, appear to be cases in which typical gestures of mourning and authentic displays of grief are represented alongside each other during the final stages of the burial process. The tomb of Nebamun and Ipuky depicts an example of the mummies of the deceased being held in the usual upright position as they are purified by a stream of water flowing from a vessel, which is no longer visible, in the hands of a priest (Taylor 2001, 137). The female mourners are shown kneeling typically; one, with an exposed breast, raises her hand to her head in a formulaic gesture of mourning, but she also has her mouth open to let out a cry of grief, and both of the female figures have black lines representing tears painted onto their cheeks. This particular scene then is one of the best examples of Assmann's theory, as the authentic grief of the mourners is shown in direct connection to their more formulaic gestures and attitudes.

It can be concluded then, that the mechanisms of mourning in New Kingdom Egypt were formulaic. Although male mourners are sometimes shown in the same way, female mourners in particular, are shown with their hands raised to their heads, their breasts exposed, and are often bending to ground to throw dust or dirt upon their faces. Assmann (2001, 310) makes a clear distinction, seen particularly in the tomb of Nebamun and Ipuky (El-Shahawy 2005, 20–21), between the 'intense pain' displayed by female mourners and the calm grief of their male counterparts. Male mourners grieving in the more typical way adopted by women can however also be seen in the tomb of Neferhotep, (Davies 1973, V) and the earlier Memphite tomb of Ra'ia, (Martin 1991, 128). Although these gestures and attitudes are formulaic in many instances, the emotional motivation behind them is not. However, a certain amount of authentic grief would have driven the family and friends of the deceased to accompany the funerary procession and to act in such a way.

So, although some gestures may appear to be formulaic, and therefore not spontaneous, this does not mean that the emotional motivation behind these mechanisms is not authentic. It may then be that Assmann's theory of the close connection between genuine emotion and theatrical gestures in representations of mourning is plausible, as the tombs studied here certainly display both of these aspects in their decorative imagery. This paper is a only a part of continuing research to assess formulism within representations of mourning. It is an attempt to provide a thorough understanding of the mechanisms presented, whilst also offering an insight into the emotional motivation behind such gestures and attitudes.

Bibliography

Assmann, J. (2001) *Death and Salvation in Ancient Egypt*. New York, Cornell University Press.
Bleeker, C. J. (1958) Isis and Nephthys as Wailing Women, *Numen* 5, 1–17.
Davies, N. de G. (1973) *The Tomb of Neferhotep at Thebes*. New York, Arno Press.
Dodson, A. and Ikram, S. (2008) *The Tomb in Ancient Egypt*. London, Thames and Hudson.
El-Saady, H. (1996) *The Tomb of Amenemhab*. Warminster, Aris and Philips.
El-Shahawy, A. (2005) *The Funerary Art of Ancient Egypt: a Bridge to the Realm of the Hereafter*. Cairo, Farid Atiya Press.
Faulkner, R. O. (1936) The Bremner-Rhind Papyrus: the Songs of Isis and Nephthys, *Journal of Egyptian Archaeology* 22, 121–140.
Faulkner, R. O. (1985) *The Ancient Egyptian Book of the Dead*. London, British Museum Publications.
Hari, R. (1985) *La Tombe Thébaine du Père Divin Neferhotep*. Geneva, Éditions de Belles-Lettres.
Hartwig, M. (2004) *Tomb Painting and Idenitiy in Ancient Thebes, 1419–1372 BCE*. Turnhout, Fondation Egyptologique Reine Elisabeth.
Hays, H. M. (2010) 'Funerary Rituals (Pharonic Period)'. In J. Dieleman and W. Wendrich (eds) Los Angeles, *UCLA Encyclopedia of Egyptology*.
Herodotus, *The Histories*, trans. R. Waterfield [Oxford World Classics], (Oxford 2008).
Hodel-Hoenes, S. (2000) *Life and Death in Ancient Egypt*. New York, Cornell University Press.
Kampp-Seyfried, F. (2003) The Theban Necropolis. In N. Strudwick and J. H. Taylor (eds) *The Theban Necropolis*, 2–11. London, British Museum.
Lictheim, M. (1973) *Ancient Egyptian Literature: Volume I the Old and Middle Kingdoms*. Berkeley, University of California Press.
Lichtheim, M. (1980) *Ancient Egyptian Literature: Volume III the Late Period*. Berkeley, University of California Press.
Martin, G. T. (1985) *The Tomb Chapels of Paser and Ra'ia at Saqqara*. London, Egypt Exploration Society.
McDermott, B. (2006) *Death in Ancient Egypt*. London, Sutton Publishing Ltd.
Meskell, L. (2000) *Private Life in New Kingdom Egypt*. Oxford, Princeton University Press.
Negm, M. (1997) *The Tomb of Simut called Kyky: Theban Tomb 409 at Qurnah*. Warminster, Aris and Philips.
Parkinson, R. B. (1997) *The Tale of Sinuhe and Other Ancient Egyptian Poems, 1940–1640 BC*. Oxford, Clarendon Press.
Porter, B. and Moss, R. L. 2004. *Topographical Bibliography of Ancient Egyptian Hieroglyphics Texts, Reliefs and Paintings, Volume I Theban Necropolis: Private Tombs*. Oxford, Griffith Institute.
Simpson, W. K. (2003) The Story of Sinuhe. In W. K. Simpson (ed.) *The Literature of Ancient Egypt*, 54–66. New Haven, Yale University Press.
Smith, M. (2007) *Traversing Eternity: Texts for the Afterlife from Ptolemaic and Roman Egypt*. Oxford, Oxford University Press.
Stadler, M. (2008) 'Procession'. In J. Dieleman and W. Wendrich (eds) *UCLA Encyclopedia of Egyptology*. Los Angeles.
Taylor, J. H. (2001) *Death and the Afterlife in Ancient Egypt*. London, British Museum Press.
Werbrouck, M. (1938) *Les Pleureuses dans l'Egypte ancienne*. Bruxelles, Editions de la Fondation égyptologique reine Elisabeth.

The Welshpool Mummy

Pauline Norris

There is more to research than the odd 'Eureka!' moment in the laboratory or searching for references in a dusty library. Finding an original topic can be difficult but occasionally a subject will present itself in the most unusual circumstances. This is an account of a project to trace the provenance of one cartonnage and how it came to be found in a small country town in the middle of Wales, U.K.

Introduction

The cartonnage first came to my attention in 2009 when I was invited to join the Montgomeryshire Beekeepers Association on a visit to inspect the newly restored Bee House at Attingham Park, a stately home in Shropshire, England. There I met an ex-photo journalist from the *Powys County Times*: I mentioned my interest in Egyptology and he told me that, amongst his collection of two million negatives which he was trying to dispose of, there was a single negative depicting the 'Welshpool Mummy' and I could use it if I so wished. I asked for a copy, time passed and I eventually forgot all about the Mummy and the negative but many months later I received an email with the photo attached (Fig. 1). Further enquiries to the journalist revealed that the Mummy had been in the old Powysland Museum which was run by Welshpool Town Council, before being donated to the Ashmolean Museum, Oxford in 1960 and that was the last I heard from him.

By way of explanation: Powis and Powys

In true British fashion, all is not what it seems when it comes to names. The surname Powis is pronounced Po-wis (Kidd and Williamson 1985, 972) and Powys the geographical area is pronounced Pow-is but to add to the confusion, the two spellings appear to be interchangeable in current popular use. Powysland was an ancient kingdom covering the area around Welshpool in what is now the County of Powys in Wales and across parts of the West Midlands of England.

The Welshpool Museums

The original Powysland Museum was the first public museum in Wales. It was founded in 1874 by the Powysland Club, a group of local gentry and business men who, as was the custom in that period, appear to have been more interested in amassing 'things' in a Cabinet of Curiosities than creating a scientific collection.

Figure 1. The Welshpool Mummy in the old Powysland Museum. Reproduced by permission of D. Griffiths.

The museum building is a fine yellow brick Victorian edifice which has now been converted into apartments and it is no longer possible to access the basement to see where the Mummy had been housed. The Welshpool Town Council took over control of the Museum collection in 1930 and in 1974 moved it to its present location beside the Montgomery Canal.

The new Powysland Museum houses approximately ninety Egyptian artefacts, mostly pottery and shabtis from Beni Hasan, which were acquired from Garstang's collection which is now mostly held at the University of Liverpool. Garstang had realised that he had too many artefacts to cope with and had placed an advertisement with *The Times* of London, stating that anyone who would pay for the carriage could have some of the artefacts. Records at the Museum indicate that the cost of shipping Powysland's allocation of artefacts to Wales amounted to £1-14s-4d in old currency: today this would be roughly £1-72p! Such was the rather lax ethos in Egyptology and excavation at the time.

A search through Powysland Museum Catalogues (1922, 56) found only one entry relating to the Mummy where it is recorded that the Mummy was 'on centre of floor' ignominiously situated between a wooden model of a local church at nearby Guilsfield and the wild bird egg cabinet. The brief entry goes on to say that the Mummy was presented to the Countess of Powis by Tigravi

Pasha (an error which has been perpetuated – the correct name is Tigrane, see below) but it does not say when. A letter in the archives from the Town Clerk in May 1960 offered the cartonnage to the Ashmolean '…as a gift from this Council, permission for which has been granted by the Earl of Powis.' There is no record of how the cartonnage was transported to Oxford.

The Ashmolean records

The Welshpool Mummy is currently on display in the Ashmolean Museum (AN 1960.1288) with an information panel describing the donation of the Mummy by Welshpool Council. In the 1960s, Professor J. Černy and Dr. J. Harris read the title of the deceased as 'the songstress of the Harim of Amun, Meresamun' or, less likely, 'Merenamun' (Whitehouse 2009, pers. com.). I am grateful to Dr. H. Whitehouse, formerly of the Antiquities Department at the Ashmolean, for sending me photocopies of the records of the Mummy and related documents held at the Museum. The record card for AN 1960.1288 dates the coffin to *c*. Dynasty XXIII–XXIV and states that the provenance is 'Egypt (probably W. Thebes)'. The mummy is described as 'bound with linen, and enclosed in a cartonnage sleeve', which is laced down the back and does not appear to have been opened. The cartonnage has retained its brilliant colour and depictions of funerary and protective deities. The owner's name is inscribed vertically in hieroglyphs on the front of the anthropoid coffin. In December, 1967 the mummy was X-rayed in its case in a trial run by the Nuffield Institute for Medical Research but there does not appear to be a report available.

The Ashmolean Meresamun is often confused with a very similar cartonnage (OIM 10797) in the Oriental Museum, Chicago which belonged to 'a Singer in the Interior of the Temple of Amun', possibly from Karnak. The coffin is also laced down the back and is stylistically dated to the twenty second dynasty. This cartonnage became well known when it was the focus of an exhibition at the Oriental Museum in 2009 and has been well documented by Teeter and Johnson (2009).

A further note enclosed with the documents from the Ashmolean was a very brief undated report by an anonymous graduate volunteer researcher at the museum who had 'followed up all the leads in our archives, + reference books' (Whitehouse 2009, pers. com.). The second paragraph of this report concerns the connection of the Mummy with the Countess of Powis.

The Earls and Countesses of Powis

Unfortunately the researcher appears to have confused the several complicated title creations and the genealogy involved in the family records of the Earls of Powis and this has also been perpetuated in the records. The present creation of the title Earl of Powis is the third one: it was revived in 1804 when the successive numbering of the Earls re-commenced at one (Kidd and Williamson 1985, 973).

The researcher refers to the eighth Earl being the holder of the title when Tigrane Pasha visited the UK in 1885 and that this Earl died unmarried in 1891. There could not, therefore, have been a Countess of Powis to whom Tigrane could have presented the Mummy in 1885. This last statement is correct but in 1885 it was the third not the eighth Earl who held the title. According to the previous researcher, the ninth Earl then succeeded to the title when in fact it was the fourth Earl. At the time he inherited the title, the fourth Earl had been married six months previously in 1890 and this will be discussed below as it may be relevant to the current research. The volunteer researcher's error is rather unfortunate as the present Earl is the eighth and his son will not become the ninth Earl until his father dies (Kidd and Williamson, 1990).

Tigrane Pasha

It is known from the Powysland Museum Catalogue (1922, 56) that the cartonnage had been presented to the Countess of Powis by Tigrane Pasha, the Armenian son-in-law of the first Prime Minister of Egypt. He became the first Foreign Minister to the last Khedive of Egypt, His Highness Abbas II, and died in 1904. At the time, 'Pasha' was a title of high rank, the equivalent to a Governor, and was held by an official likely to have had contact with the British aristocracy abroad. Ironically, after his death one of his palaces in Cairo was turned into Le Palais des Amis de L'Art (www.egyptedantan.com, 2005).

'Who Was Who in Egyptology' (Bierbrier 1995, 415) records that Tigrane Pasha visited Britain in 1885 but there appears to be no record of him visiting Wales or having had any contact with the Earl and Countess of Powis. It is, therefore, possible that the cartonnage could have been brought to the UK between 1885 and Tigrane's death in 1904.

Tigrane was a member of the Committee for Archaeology in Cairo and had amassed a large collection of Egyptian artefacts in his palaces at Alexandria and Cairo. The catalogue of the collection (Collection, 1911) was published posthumously in French in 1911 by Abraham Albert Daninos Pasha, an Algerian/Egyptian Egyptologist. Daninos had been an assistant to Mariette and had excavated at a number of sites including Heliopolis and the Fayum. The catalogue records Tigrane's full name as Tigrane Pacha d'Abro. There is no record of the mummy ever being in the collection.

After Tigrane's death, the major part of his considerable collection of antiquities was bought by the Cairo dealer Michel Abemayor. The family Abemayor moved in 1950 to premises in Madison Avenue, New York where they continued to trade in antiquities, including Tigrane's collection which was sold off over the years to private collectors and museums world- wide (www.genovapress.com, no date).

Summary

Where did Tigrane obtain the Mummy? This question may never be answered. This is very much a report of work in progress and a number of hypotheses are being pursued.

The next pivotal question appears to be the date when the Mummy was presented to the Countess. Was it handed over by Tigrane before, during or after his visit to England? The fourth Earl's wife was Violet Ida Evelyn, a daughter of Lord Conyers and sixteenth Baroness Darcy de Knayth in her own right. If she had travelled to Egypt it is possible that she was presented with the Mummy by Tigrane Pasha before she was married and became Countess of Powis. The reference to a presentation to a Countess would then be correct etiquette for anyone writing about her after her marriage although the presentation occurred when she was still single. This will entail researching the Conyer family records to ascertain whether she did travel and if a gift of a mummy is mentioned.

It is known that the Mummy was in Powysland Museum in 1922 but where was it after Tigrane relinquished possession of it? The letter from the Town Clerk acknowledging the Earl's permission for the transfer of the Mummy needs to be traced to ascertain if any further evidence or leads can be obtained from it. The Powis estate and family archives may provide further information. The National Trust has also been approached for access to the archives at Powis Castle and the Estate Archives at the National Library of Wales are available for public perusal. These last consist of 12 cubic metres of records, 419 boxes, 24 files and 9 rolls – the examination of which is not a task for the faint hearted on a rainy afternoon.

If research can be compared with building a wall, then a few more bricks of knowledge have been added to this conundrum. Much still remains to be investigated but one conclusion has been reached: I will not be going on another Beekeeper's Outing!

Bibliography

Bierbrier, M. L. (1995) (Third revised edition) *Who was who in Egyptology*. London, Egypt Exploration Society.
Collection (1911) *Collection d'antiquités de Tigrane Pacha d'Abro*. Paris, Leroux.
Kidd, C. and Williamson, D. (eds) (1985) *Debrett's Peerage and Baronetage*. London, MacMillan.
Kidd, C. and Williamson, D. (eds) (1990) *Debrett's Peerage and Baronetage*. London, MacMillan.
Powysland (1922) Powysland Museum Catalogue.
Teeter, E. and Johnson, J. H. (2009) *Life of Meresamun: A Temple Singer in Ancient Egypt*. Chicago, Oriental Institute Museum Publications 29.
www.egyptedantan.com/le_caire/villages_et_agglomerations/tewfickieh (2005) (Accessed: 8 August 2011 (see page 1, 6, 8))
www.genovapress.com/index.php/content/view/2972/0 (no date). (Accessed: 8 August 2011

More ways of analysis: the different *faces* of a stela

Stefania Pignattari

This study is part of a still on-going research on an organic group of Middle Kingdom stelae (1987–1759 BC), forming the main part of a corpus of documents belonging to a functionary called Djaf-Horemsaf *(dȝf-ḥr.m.sȝ.f)*, chief of at least three expeditions to the turquoise mines of Serabit el-Khadim, in Sinai, in the years 6, 8 and 9 of Amenemhat IV(1772–1763 BC).

At Serabit el-Khadim, building activity has always been secondary to mining. However, in particular from the reign of Amenemhat III (1817–1772 BC), with the so called *Myth of Turquoise,* the exploitation of mines is transformed into a theological metaphor connected to the celebration of kinship. Thenceforth, Serabit el-Khadim became at the same time the place associated with one of the finest Egyptian minerals and the magic land where rituals essential for the monarchy took place (Bonnet and Valbelle 1996, 124–125).

The aim of this paper is to analyse Djaf-Horemsaf's documents beyond the usual prosopographical data, trying to obtain information about different aspects of the society of the time: religion, administration, socio-cultural composition and so on. The data set here described will be compared with the other material from Serabit el-Khadim highlighting both the similarities and distinctive features of the two corpuses.

Firstly, a short description of Djaf-Horemsaf's corpus is necessary. It comprises eight documents, all from Serabit el-Khadim; six stelae, two of which dating to year 6 (Figs 1 and 2; the numbers used in this paper for the documents are the same as Gardiner's *Inscriptions of Sinai (=IS);* Gardiner, Peet and Černý 1955), one to year 8 (Fig. 3), the fourth, joined to an offering table, to year 9 (Fig. 4), the fifth and the last undated (Figs 5 and 6). Other documents are a single offering table (Fig. 7) probably pertaining to stela 407 and finally a wall-inscription on the south wall of a chapel called the Shrine of the Kings (Figs 8 and 9); this last one has the aspect of a portico with four columns, with a part carved into the rocks (Fig. 10).

Figure 1. IS 119, year 6 (Adapted from Gardiner-Peet-Černý 1955, I, pl. XLII).

Stelae: classification and function

Djaf-Horemsaf, like his predecessor Ptahwer (*ptḥ-wr*, e.g. *IS* 108, 109, 110; 124 (b), 414; Bonnet and Valbelle 1996, 30), who worked during the reign of Amenemhat III, focussed his activity on the Shrine of the Kings. He enlarged the chapel and its porticus to the west as testified by inscription *IS* 123 on the wall of the shrine and by pillar-stela *IS* 130, probably accompanying a stela placed on the opposite side (Bonnet and Valbelle 1996, 93, fig. 117).

Djaf-Horemsaf was also responsible for the building of the porticus of Ptah's Shrine and for the conclusion of works at Hathor's shrine, just north of the previous one, as testified by three official stelae and an offering table presenting many references to these gods (Bonnet and Valbelle 1996, 95, fig. 120; *IS* 120; 122; 407).

Djaf-Horemsaf's stelae, as the other stelae from Serabit el-Khadim, are usually round-topped with their main faces oriented east-west and decorated according to their original location in the sanctuary: an offering scene on a side of a stela could be facing that deity honored in the chapel and built in front of that scene (Bonnet and Valbelle 1996, 76). Stelae can be classified into two different types: *official documents*, one for each expedition, and *private documents,* expression of personal pity of participants to expeditions.

Figure 2. IS 120, year 6 (Adapted from Gardiner-Peet-Černý 1955, I, pl. XLIII).

Furthermore, it is possible to differentiate the stelae according to what could be called, *structural stelae* and *free standing stelae.* Structural stelae, decorated on three of the four sides, were usually erected against a wall. They can provide elements to create the chronology of the works in the sanctuary. On the other hand, *free standing* stelae at Serabit el-Khadim can be considered as part of an organic system, an essential element of the site. Occupying the space year after year, the stelae illustrate the different activities of each king and the development of different rituals and mark processional ways.

The close relationship between temple and stelae is visible not only because stelae are used as structural elements but also conversely: for example stela 130 is actually a pillar of the Shrine of the Kings, but decorated in order to look like a stela (Bonnet and Valbelle 1996, 76).

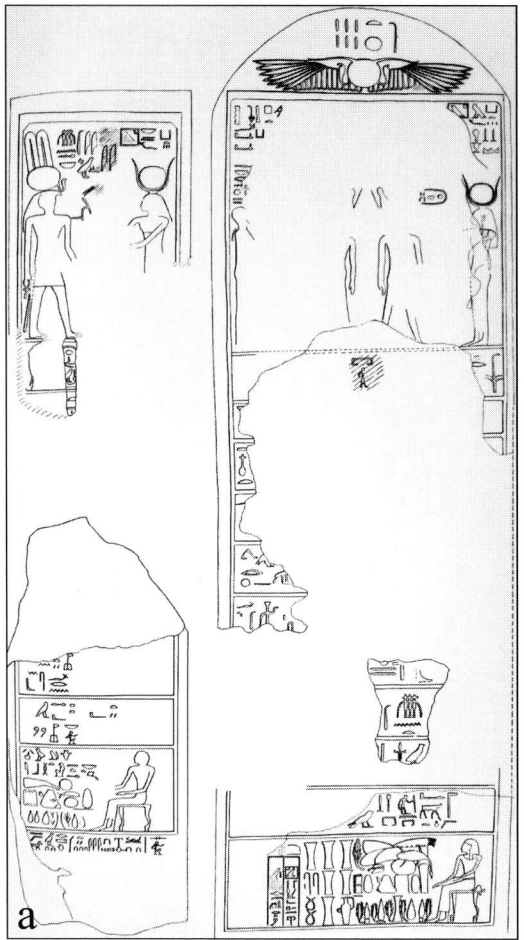
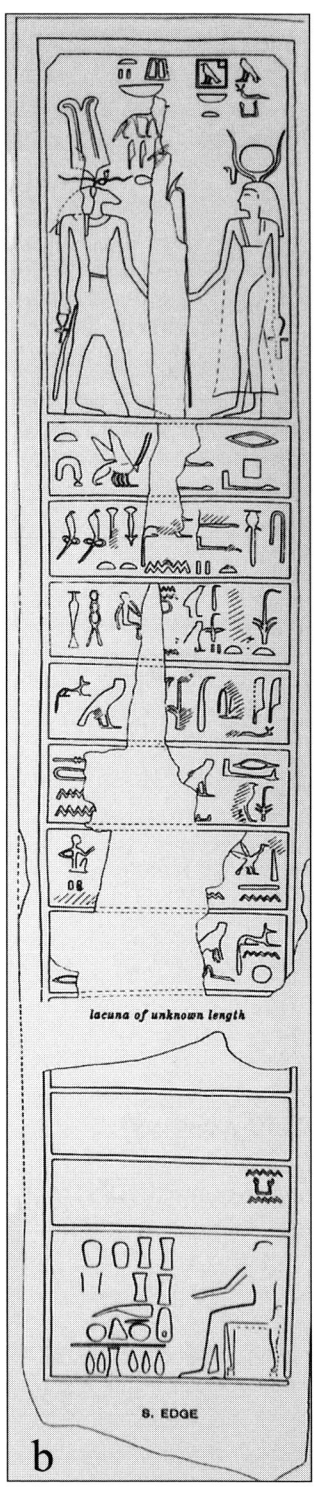

Figure 3: a and b. IS 121, year 8 (Adapted from Gardiner-Peet-Černý 1955, pl. XLVIII).

Participants

The *Royal acquaintance* (*rḫ nswt*) Djaf-Horemsaf, son of Renes-seneb, bears the title of *Sealbearer of the God* and of *Chief Interior-Overseer to the Treasury* (*ḫtmw-nṯr imy-rꜥ ḫnwty wr n pr ḥḏ*); both the most attested titles at Sinai brought by the chief of expedition in charge of the projects of Treasury abroad.

The importance attained by Djaf-Horemsaf is suggested by his representations as well as the dedicatory inscriptions in the Shrine of the Kings: that is in *IS* 123 (a), 123 (b) and the scene between them (Gardiner, Peet and Černý 1955, fig. 12, 127).

More ways of analysis: The different faces of a stela 155

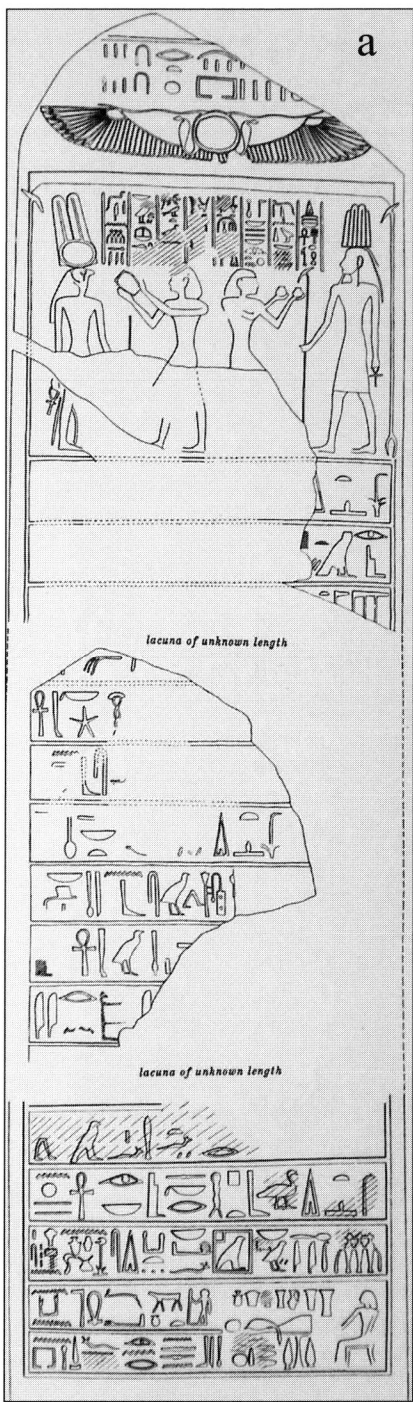
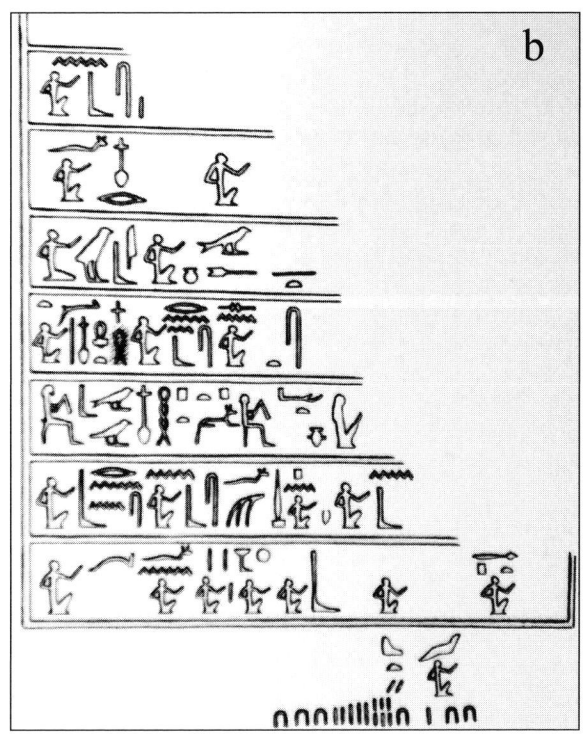
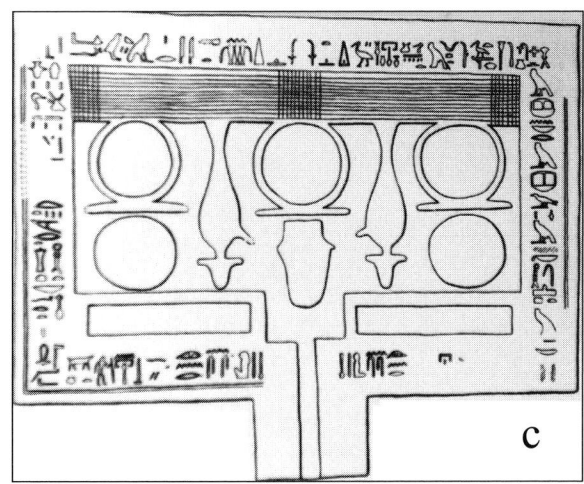

Figure 4: a, b and c. IS 122, year 9 (Adapted from Gardiner-Peet-Černý 1955, pl. XLV).

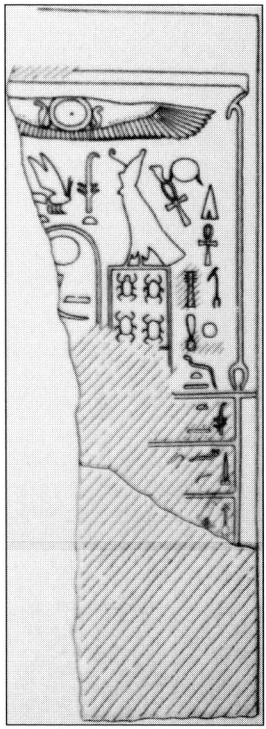

Figure 5. IS 130, year 9 (Adapted from Gardiner-Peet-Černý 1955, pl. XL).

Figure 6. IS 407, undated (Adapted from Gardiner-Peet-Černý 1955, pl. LXXXIV).

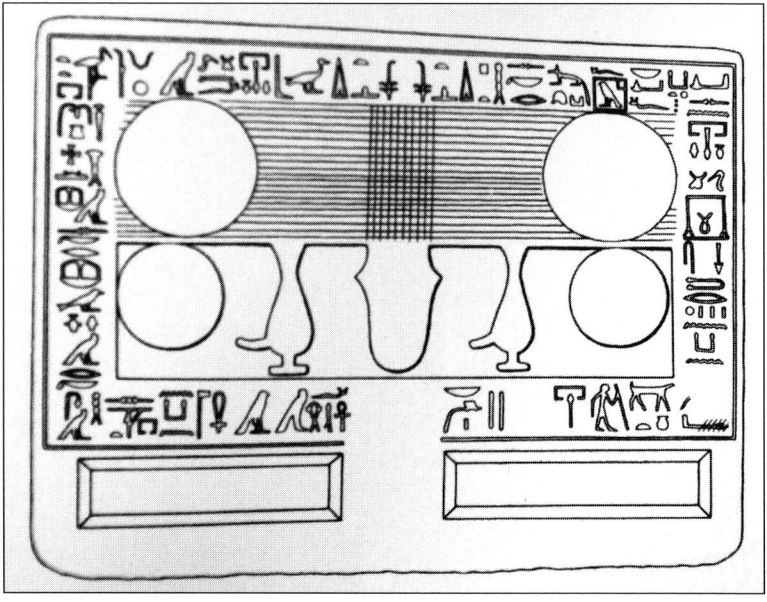

Figure 7. IS 408, undated (Adapted from Gardiner-Peet-Černý 1955, pl. LXXXVI).

For example, the words of Djaf: «[...] The beautiful present given to her [...]» (*IS* 123 (a), line 31) or «I have done this, by establishing her monuments [...]» (*IS* 123 (a), line 33) are really uncommon for a functionary, being more typical of regal phraseology. Moreover, in the very badly damaged scene between *IS* 123 (a) and 123 (b) a man is shown, probably Djaf-Horemsaf himself, before an offering-table; of the inscription above, only the name of the gods Khenty-khety and Ptah-Sokar remain.

The structure of the wall inscription is also significant: the whole *IS* 123 (a) inscription is in retrograde lines, while *IS* 123 (b) is not, and this creates a convergence towards the image of Djaf, whose presence in the context seems emphasized with the consequent isolation of the entire west side of the shrine, certainly datable to the reign of Amenemhat IV. The originality of this intent is proved by the dimensions of the hieroglyphs. The inscription was probably copied from a complete model by a sculptor without taking into account the direction of writing: in fact the signs become smaller as we proceed from left to right, probably as it was realized that the space available decreased.

As shown in many images from Serabit el-Kahdim (*e.g. IS* 116, 164, 72 *etc.*; Bonnet and Valbelle 1996, 137), the chief of expedition is involved in many ritual acts: he accompanies the king and is the priest represented in front of king and gods making the offerings of turquoise loaves, one of the most important rituals connected to kingship celebration (Bonnet and Valbelle 1996, 144; fig. 11).

He is the coordinator of the rituals and replaces the absent king in the adornment of the sanctuary with objects and architectural elements. This set of rituals was performed in order to grant the success of the expeditions. This is expressed by the offering scene from the Shrine of the kings, in which Amenemhat IV presents to Hathor the same goods usually given by the chief of expedition (*e.g.* vases, a sistrum *etc.* fig. 12; Bonnet and Valbelle 1996, 145).

Moreover, the sacral role of the chief of expeditions increases as the cult of the kingship becomes more meaningful probably because, from a simple functionary, albeit of high level, he progresses to become the king's delegate and to ensure him his cult. The importance of the role of the chief of the expeditions is particularly evident during the XII Dynasty, when both Ptahwer (*IS*, 108), *Sealbearer of the God* during the reign of Amenemhat III, and Djaf-Horemsaf are represented on the wall of the Shrine of the Kings, and probably reaches its apex with Djaf-Horemsaf himself (Bonnet and Valbelle 1996, 155).

In this regard, I would like to argue that the emphasis showed on the western side of the Shrine of the Kings could be regarded, together with other contemporary elements such as the almost complete disappearance of the god Sobek-Horus and of the centrality of the Fayyum region from the reign of Amenemhat IV (Zecchi 2010, 84), as a sort of declaration of stability and autonomy by the new king, recently ascended to the throne. Similarly to what his predecessor did in the temple of Medinet Madi at Fayyum, he elected a specific place to celebrate both the kingship and his own reign in which the identities of the two most important local gods were strongly marked and their roles vested with ceremony expressing themes connected with royal ideology on a local level (Zecchi 2010, 77; Zecchi 2001, 160; Bresciani, 2006).

Having described the iconographical aspects of the corpus of the documents under examination, I will now focus my attention on the *social* components therein represented. The official documents *IS* 120 and *IS* 122 present a long list of participants of expeditions, mentioning all categories of workers: the *Treasury chamber-keeper Ib* (*iry-ʿt n pr ḥḏ ib*), the *Sealer and assistant to the Treasury Nefermat* (*ḫtmw ḥryʿ n imy-r ḫtmt nfrm3ʿt*), the *Embalmer of Anubi* Ptah-Nefer (*wt Inpw ptḥ. Nfr*), the *Stone-cutter Renefseneb* (*ḥrty-nṯr rn.f-snb*), the *Priest of Hathor and Treasury chamber-*

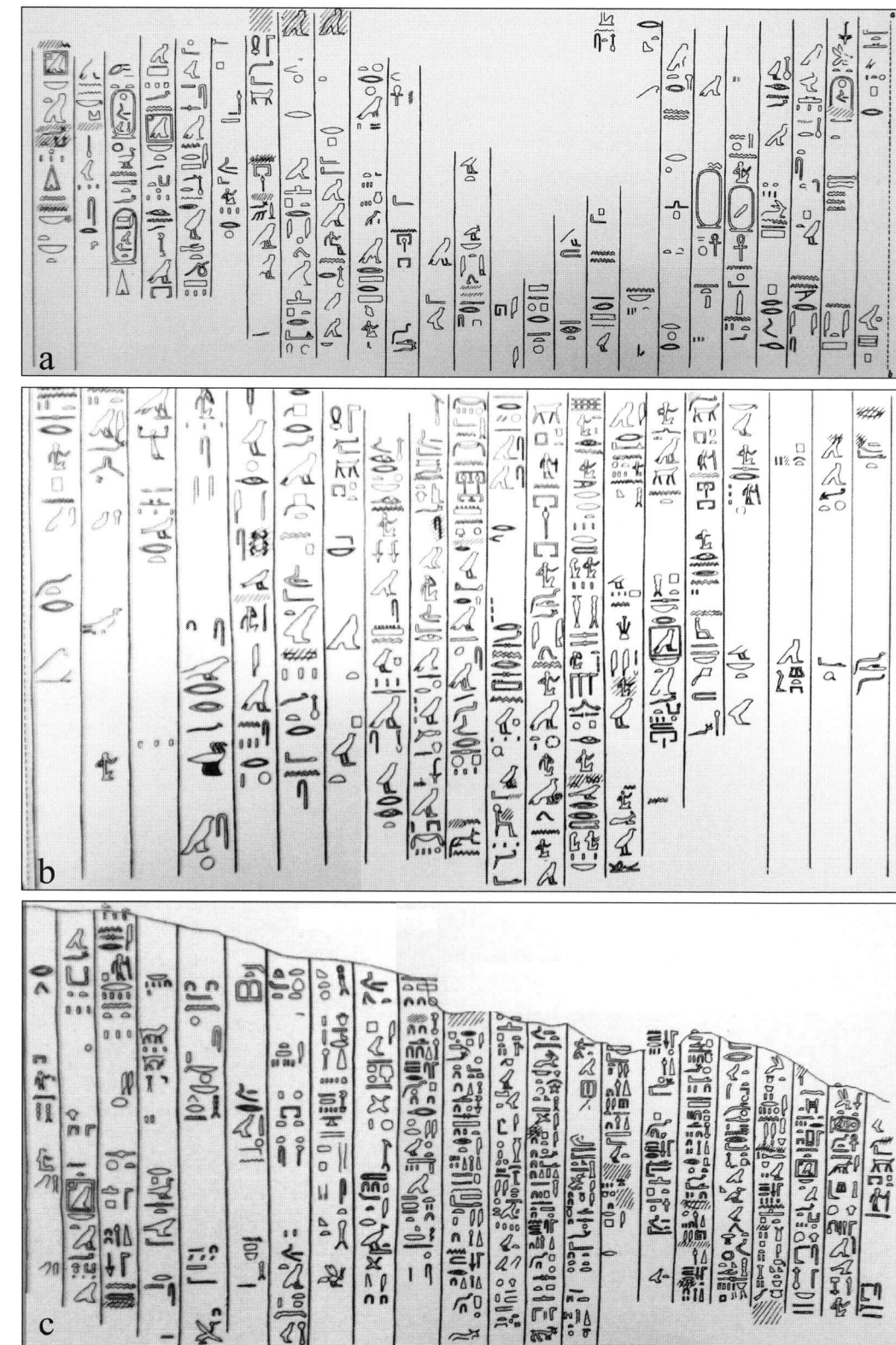

More ways of analysis: The different faces of a stela

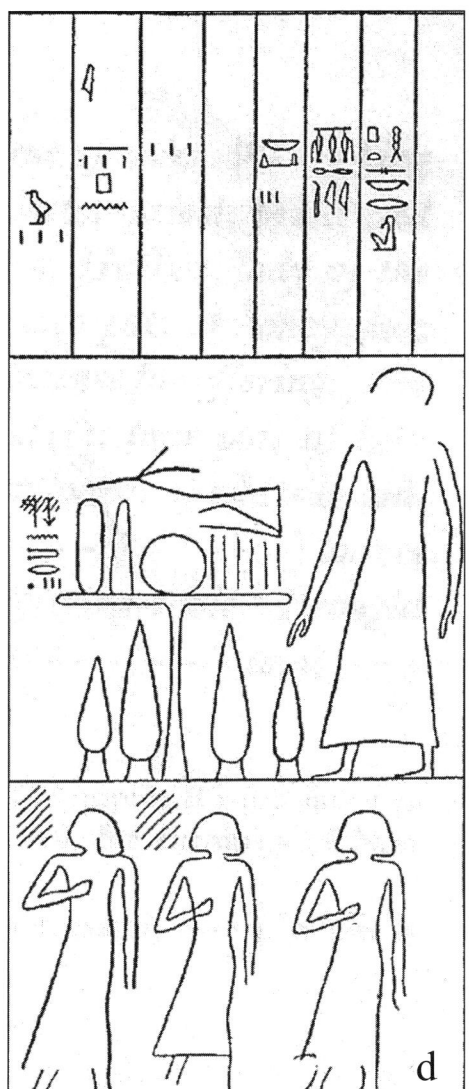

Figure 8: a, b, c and d. IS 123 (a), 123 (b), the image drawn between 123 (a) and (b), undated (Adapted from Gardiner, Peet and Černý 1955, pl. XLVI and figure 12, 127).

keeper Soped (*ḥm-nṯr n ḥwt-ḥr, iry-ʿt n pr-ḥḏ spdw*), ferrymen (*s n ḏʿtw*), peasants (*sḫtyw*), stone cutters (*ḥrtyw*), coppersmiths (*ḥntyw*), Asiatics (*ʿȝmw*), etc. (*IS* n. 120, 122; Bonnet and Valbelle 1996, 32). The precision shown in defining administrative roles seems to be a constant feature of Late Middle Kingdom stelae where the content is restricted to name and principal title of the owner. It has been observed (Quirke 2004, 9) that this *name + title* focus represents an act of selection prioritising one form of identity over others; arguably then, that cultural preference, specific to the late Middle Kingdom, produced the data set for the period. Therefore, one can suppose that the structure of administration, outlined in this period, witnessed a greater precision and demarcation of the official titles (Quirke 2004, 9; Berlev 1978, 45). Can this feature help to understand something more about the activity in Sinai?

First, from the cases of *The priest of Hathor and Treasury chamber-keeper* Sopedu and in a more interesting way, of the *Judge, lector-priest, scribe and prophet Ur-kherep-hemu, the Asiatic* (*sȝb, ḥry-tp ḥr(y)-ḥbt, šs, ḥm nṯr wr-ḥrp-ḥmw ʿȝm*) of *IS* 123 (b), it emerges that the union of religious and administrative roles is not a prerogative of the chief of expeditions. During their stay at Serabit el-Khadim, the members of expeditions were probably responsible for the local religious services, which were perhaps connected to some religious functions they already performed in the Nile valley (Bonnet and Valbelle 1996, 138).

Secondly, general data provided by the stelae inform of the presence of two or three craftsmen, competent for each sector of the work. On stela *IS* 122, the number of coppersmiths (*ḥntyw*) is increased to 16 and, as already noted, this increase in the number of blacksmiths could be related to the exploitation of copper, activity that probably took place in the surrounding valleys where there was enough space for at least part of the treatment (Bonnet and Valbelle 1996, 62).

The documents here analysed also provide some information about Asiatics. In stela *IS* 120 is the mention of 20 *ʿȝmw* from *rtnw*, that is, people from the Syro-Palestinian area, while one of the owners of stela *IS* 121 is the *interpreter from Asia Montuhotep* (*ʿw n stt mntw-ḥtp*, Gardiner 1950, S 25 and Ward 1982, n. 591). This title suggests that Montuhotep might have been a foreigner, probably from Asia.

Asiatic people are attested in many documents from the reign of Amenemhat III (*e.g. IS* 85, 87, 92,103,112, 115, 405); five of these describe the visit of "the brother of the prince of Retjenu, Khebded" (*IS* 85, 87, 92, 103 e 115; Bonnet and Valbelle 1996, 34; Cohen and Lake 2002, 43) and *IS* 112 depicts the arrival of this individual who comes riding on a donkey. On the basis of the quite marginal and stereotyped iconography, it has been argued that this people could have had a subordinate role, such as workmen or domestics. However, the presence of the already cited interpreter Mentuhotep and of two ꜥꜣmw, the *judge, lector-priest, scribe and prophet Ur-kherep-hemu* and the *Sealbearer of the god Ptahwer* (ḫtmw nṯr ptḥ-wr, IS 414), both represented in the Shrine of the Kings, suggests that Asiatics were also among the most important members of expeditions (for the discussions about the role of Asiatics in Sinai see *e.g.* Bonnet and Valbelle 1996, 34; Cohen and Lake 2002, 42–44).

The two last characters strongly connected to Djaf-Horemsaf being mentioned in his corpus, show a particularity in their name. The word *wr-ḫrp-ḥmw* is actually the title of the high-priest of Memphis used here as a first name (Gardiner, Peet and Černý 1955, 128, note N and Ranke 1938, 81, 18), while on stela *IS* 414 it is clearly said that *ptḥ-wr* is the *rn nfr*: namely not his real name, but the one acquired in the adulthood by which he was known in society. Probably, social progression required changes in personal identity, in the direction of, we could say, "Egyptianization".

Religion

The gods found at Serabit el-Khadim, represent an interesting field of analysis in general. Moreover Djaf's documentation is interesting because it both reveals unusual aspects of the traditional gods of the place and the presence of uncommon deities whose occurrence finds different explanations. The most important gods are Hathor and Ptah.

Figure 9. IS 124 (a), 124 (b), undated (Adapted from Gardiner, Peet and Černý 1955, pl. XLVII).

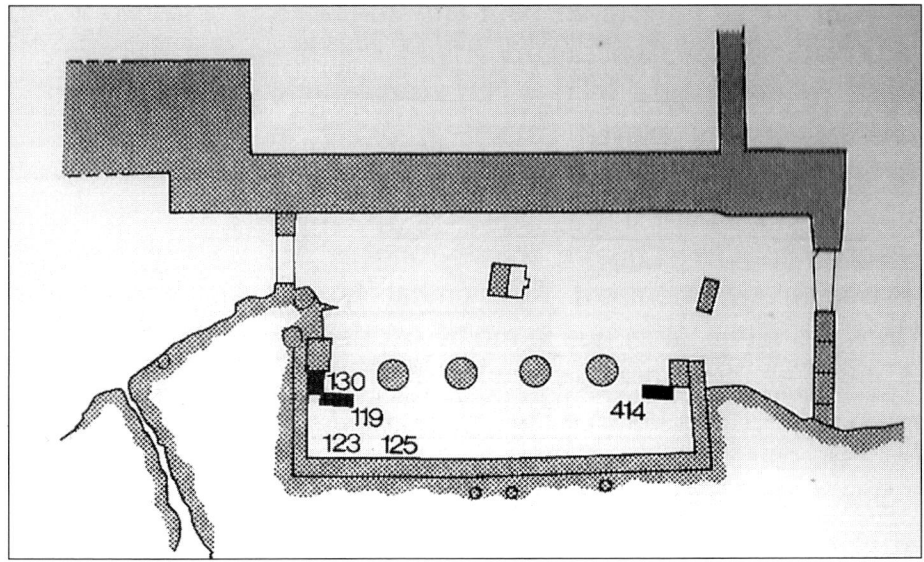

Figure 10. Shrine of the Kings (Adapted from Bonnet and Valbelle 1996, 93, fig. 117).

Figure 11. IS 116–164, undated (Adapted from Gardiner, Peet and Černý 1955, pl. XXXVI and LIV).

Hathor (ḥwt-ḥr)

Hathor, in Djaf-Horemsaf's corpus, bears the epithet of *Lady of turquoise* (*nbt mfk3t*, IS 120, 121, 123 (a), 124 (a), 125 (a–c)), of *Lady of the good colour* (*nbt inm nfr*, IS 124 (a)) and of *The One who resides in Djadja* (*ḥry.t ib ḏ3ḏ3*, IS 120). The third epithet, in particular, is very uncommon and is only attested in two other documents dating to the New Kingdom (*IS* 317 A and see Bonnet 1996, p. 38, fig. 189). *Djadja* seems to designate an unknown country with the determinative of the triple hills, and it is perhaps used here to indicate Serabit el-Khadim (Gardiner 1950, N

25). It is attested only in two other documents belonging to the New Kingdom (*IS* 317 A and see Bonnet and Valbelle 1996, 38, fig. 189). Both the other epithets refer to the specific role of the goddess as protector of the turquoise mines. Hathor *nbt mfk3t* appears during the reign of Amenemhat I, but the temple of Serabit el-Khadim is the first site in which Hathor has an epithet concerning precious material, the only epithet of this category influencing her protocol at other sites that had nothing to do with turquoise extraction and storage (Giveon 1978, 65).

During the Middle Kingdom, Hathor becomes the lady of foreign lands, of mines and quarries (Giveon 1978, 61–65) and many theories could be quoted to explain this. Possibly such theories may have their origin in the tradition of Hathor being the "goddess from afar", the eye of the sun sent out to the far south (Giveon 1978, 61; Bonnet and Valbelle 1996, 36–37; Aufrère 1991, 133–136). At Serabit el-Khadim, Hathor is almost everywhere, she is the owner of the temple in which she is worshipped in the shape of a woman only (Giveon 1978, 61–63) and she has a constant presence on stelae and inscriptions.

With reference to the parallels drawn between Medinet Madi and Serabit el-Kahdim, in the latter case Hathor becomes the equivalent of the goddess Renenutet of the Fayyum, who intercedes for the king, ensuring the monarchy (Bonnet and Valbelle 1996, 131).

Ptah (ptḥ)

Ptah is well attested in Djaf-Horemsaf's dossier: in the Shrine of the Kings he is *Lord of Ankhtawy* and Ptah *South of his wall* (*nb ꜥnḫ t3wy; rsy inb.f, IS* 124 (a); 125 a–c). Only in *IS* 124 is he called *Ptah who is under his moringa tree (ptḥ ḥry b3k.f)*. Finally in inscription *IS* 125 the god receives goods from king Amenemhat IV symmetrically to Hathor; this symmetry between the two deities is also found in stela 120. In the other four documents (*IS* 121, 122, 123, 408), Ptah receives goods also as *ptḥ-skr* and as *ptḥ-skr-wsir*.

Figure 12. IS 125, undated (Adapted from Gardiner, Peet and Černý 1955, pls. XLVII).

Together with Hathor, Ptah is the only god who has a personal place of cult, the so called Cave-south, and these documents might suggest that Dajf-Horemsaf concluded the building of the shrine which probably started at the end of the reign of Amenemhat III, when the documentation about this god starts to increase (Bonnet and Valbelle 1996, 40).

The presence of Ptah at Serabit el-Khadim can be explained by the fact that the god was the patron of craftsmen, and in particular the typical Memphite epithets, *South of his wall* and *Lord of Ankhtawy*, might derive from the role of the god as main protector of the expeditions for the eastern desert which came from the Memphite area (Tallet 2005, 151). He finally becomes one of the protagonists of the rituals connected with kingship, and in analogy to the symmetry with Hahor-Renenutet, he might correspond to Sobek of Shedet, the male counterpart of Renenutet at Medinet Madi (Tallet 2005, 154).

Djaf-Horemsaf's corpus is also interesting for the number of unusual gods, in particular Khenty-khety, Kherty, Neith and Nemty.

Khenty-Khety (ẖnty-ẖty)

Khenty-Khety on stelae *IS* 120, of year 6, and on *IS* 122, of year 9, is *Lord of Km-wr* (*nb Km-wr*) represented as an anthropomorphic falcon-headed god (Bonnet and Valbelle 1996, 42; Vernus 1978, 382), wearing the solar disk, ureus and two feathers on his head. In the first stela he grants the king many jubilees, while receiving an offering consisting of *nmst* vases. In the Shrine of the kings (*IS* 123 (a) and *IS* 123 (b) the name and the epithet *Lord of Km-wr* can be read, but the god was probably also represented. The presence of this god in that chapel as well as on the stelae dated between years 6 and 9 is significant: maybe it was between those two dates that the works in the Shrine of the Kings were finished.

Originally a crocodile god, in Serabit el-Khadim Khenty-Khety appears in his new form of falcon-deity directly connected with the city of Athribis in the Delta. From the end of the reign of Amenemhat III, Athribis perhaps becomes one of the most important starting points of expeditions, as suggested by the only other Middle Kingdom document known from Serabit el-Khadim referring to this god (Vernus 1978, 382 and *IS* 166) in which an *imy-rˁ ḫnwty wr n pr ḥḏ 'Imny*, Chief interior-overseer to the Treasury, Ameny is found, the same functionary mentioned in *IS* 28 from Wadi Maghara, dated to year 42 of Amenemhat III (only one other document mentions Khenty-Khety and it dates to New Kingdom: *IS* 423).

Like the other crocodile gods, such as Sobek from Fayyum, Khenty-Khety becomes a Horus, directly connected to royal rituals (Bonnet and Valbelle 1996, 42; Vernus 1978, 406; see also Zecchi 2010, 60–84).

Kherty (ḥrty)

Kherty is represented on the south edge of stela *IS* 120 with the epithet of *Lord of Sab* (*nb sAb*), an unknown place with the determinative of the triple hills (Gardiner 1950, N 25). It is worth noting that on the east face of the same stela we find the goddess Hathor bearing the other unusual epithet of *The One who resides in Djadja* (*ḥry.t ib ḏ3ḏ3*).

At Serabit el-Khadim, the god Kherty in the shape of a ram-headed god with horns, ureus and feathers, is attested with certainty just on this document. He wears a tunic and a short skirt with the bull tail; he is traditionally the god of Letopolis (*ḥm*), in the Delta (Bonnet and Valbelle 1996, 42–43).

Neith (nt)

On the private stela *IS* 121 of year 8, Neith appears as *Mistress of the green stone* (*nt nbt w3dw*). A hypothesis for this epithet can be that, once arrived in Sinai, Neith adopted a title linked to local characteristics (Aufrére 1991, 136). The problem is to understand *why* and *how* this goddess arrived in Sinai. A possible reason could be that Saïs, her main cult-centre in the Delta, was the place of origin of that expedition. Another reason could be her presence as an act of devotion made by one or both of the dedicators. However the role of Neith as protector of kingship (Te Velde 1977, 113; el-Sayed 1982, 92–93) and a possible identification between the goddess and Hathor in the role of Demiurge have also been noted, together with their affinity with minerals and stones (Aufrére 1991, 136 and note 267 in particular). Hathor and Neith were also identified in the city of Athribis, well attested in Sinai (*e.g. IS* 102, 122, 166, 423) where both goddesses bear the epithets of *Hathor the One who resides in Km-wr* and *Neith, Lady of the island of Km-wr* (*nt nbt iw n km-wr, ḥwt-ḥr ḥry.t ib km-wr*).

Nemty (nmty)

The private stela *IS* 119 of year 6 is quite interesting for different reasons: typology, position and god mentioned.

Stela *IS* 119 is a corniced stela. It is worth noting that, despite the fact that this kind of shape was generally used in rock inscriptions to announce the opening of a new mine gallery (Bonnet and Valbelle 1996, 60), in this case, it has instead been found in the Shrine of the Kings, with a walking god represented in the middle, holding a *wAs* sceptre in his left hand and an *anx* sign in his right hand. According to Gardiner's description (Gardiner, Peet and Černý 1955, volume II, 210, *IS* 414, pl. LXXXVI) its counterpart, stela n. 414 of Ptahwer, may have been very similar to this one.

Here god Nemty (Aufrère 1991, 132) is called *Lord of the East* (*nb i3btt*) and is represented in a sethian form. The only other source for the existence of this god as Seth comes from a New Kingdom round-topped stela in which the god is sitting in front of a rich offering table and is called *Lord of Tjebu* (*nb Tbw*, see Stele Chicago 10510 in van Siclen III 1990) in the X *nome* of Upper Egypt. As for Neith's unusual epithet, the sethian aspect of Nemty is quite easy to explain even if more articulated. The hieroglyphic for Nemty shows him as a falcon on a boat and he can be considered a double god represented both as falcon in connection with Horus, and as sethian-headed, connected with Seth. As explained by Te Velde (1977, 109–113), the world could be divided between Horus, lord of the home country who protects Egyptian people (*pꜥt*) and Seth, lord of foreign lands and desert, connected to foreigners and non-autochthonous inhabitants of Egypt (*rḫyt*) *par excellence* (Te Velde 1977, 112). So, in his sethian aspect, Nemty was lord of the foreign lands and desert as well as of foreign people; therefore it is not surprising that he chose this aspect when represented abroad (Te Velde 1977, 109–118).

In ancient Egypt a foreigner may sometimes be very hospitably received, but this position remains exceptional, considering the position of the stela inside the Shrine of the Kings, it could be seen as a sort of 'homage' to the foreigners working in Sinai. This hypothesis seems confirmed by the fact that this stela belongs to the same year of stela *IS* 120 which presents the explicit reference to *Retjenu* (Te Velde 1977, 112).

Many myths (Wilkinson 2003, 204–205; Aufrère 1991, 122) attempt to explain why a god from the south of Egypt would be present in Sinai. The practical reason is that probably his nome controlled the roads to the silver mines, a characteristic that makes him a god of border lands, naturally linked to the desert. However Nemty is cited also on a long list of theophoric names from a stela belonging to Amenemhat III, as the *Chamber-keepere Nemty* (*iry-ꜥt nmty*); *Nemtyiu (nmty-iw); Nemtyemat (nmty-m-ḥꜣt), Nemtyemsaf* (*nmty-m-sꜣf); Nemtymery (nmty-mry); Nemtyhotep (nmty-ḥtp) etc.* (*IS* 85). This could hint to the existence of a village in the Delta in which Nemty was worshipped and where the members of the expedition came from (Aufrère 1991, 386).

Many reasons may be found for the presence of numerous and varied deities: geographical, geopolitical, ideological and practical. We can find gods and goddesses associated with jobs, products and activities of the region; gods connected to the desert or foreign countries; deities connected to stones and minerals; and also gods at the starting point of the expeditions. In more complex cases all these reasons are present together. Moreover, the nature of these gods is influenced by local beliefs or by the fact that the gods chose to stress just particular aspects of their identity. This complexity gave birth to a proper local theology (Aufrère 1991, 118).

To conclude: Two offering tables

To show the complexity and variety of information conveyed by a stela, I would like to focus the attention on two offering tables *IS* 408 undated and *IS* 122 of year 9, certainly one, most likely both, part of two official stelae. By creating a parallel between them, some hypotheses could be formulated.

First, the insertion of a *ḥtp-di-nsw* formula or the addition of entire offering tables for personal utility in official stelae, cannot be overlooked, becoming a proof of the increasing importance of the chief of expedition (Bonnet and Valbelle 1996, 155). As pointed out by Vernus (1996, 835), on a monument mentioning at the same time both the king and a private man, two options are possible: it could be a private monument, but giving space to direct expression of royal ideology. Conversely, it could be a royal monument on which a private individual was admitted to inscribe his or her name, as a form of privilege (Vernus 1996, 835); the second option is that of Djaf.

Secondly, the affinity of the texts of the two offering tables cannot just be a coincidence. They both report a group of festivals which do not appear elsewhere in Serabit el-Khadim: *Festival of the Bread and Beer* (*ḥb wr t ḥnkt); Festival of Sokar (ḥb skr); Festival of Thot (ḥb ḏḥwty); Wag Feast (wꜣg); Festival of the Placing the Furnace (wꜣḥ ꜥḥ); Festival of the Opening of the Year (wpt rnpt); Festival of the Heat (rkḥ); Festival of the First of the Year (tp-rnpt)*. On the basis of bibliographical descriptions (Gardiner, Peet and Černý 1955, 207), the two offering tables should come from the area of the shrines of Hathor and Ptah, while, the stela of the offering table *IS* 122, found *in situ*, represents the final alignment of the stelae marking the space of the porticus of the goddess (Bonnet and Valbelle 1996, 31). Considering the structural function of this stela, and the important activity of Djaf-Horemsaf in this area, it could be conjectured that, the stela belonging to table 408, had the same role for the porticus of the god Ptah, marking here as well the conclusion of the works. The fact that in its *ḥtp-di-nsw* formula the offering is made explicitly to Ptah-Sokar instead of Khenty-khety seems to confirm the hypothesis.

From a chronological point of view, the two offering tables belong to stelae of the same year, but we know that there could only be one official stela for each expedition. According to the Turin Canon, Amenemhat IV reigned no more than ten years, so document *IS* 408 should be prior to *IS* 122, dated to year 9 and therefore the conclusion of the portico of Ptah should precede that of Hathor.

To conclude, a few words on the owner's name: on both offering tables, the dedicator does not appear with his complete name. On the first he is called dj'fy (dȝfy), on the second Horemsaf (ḥr-m-sȝ.f). The attribution to Djaf-Horemsaf is made certain for *IS* 122 by the presence of the stela, but there were doubts for *IS* 408. Considering the parallelism between the texts, I think that all doubts should vanish: it seems clear that the two parts of the name could be used independently and that it is Djaf-Horemsaf who chose to be remembered with both his names.

Bibliography

Aufrère, S. (1991) *L'Univers minéral dans la pensée ègyptienne.* Le Caire, Institut francais d'archeologie orientale.
Berlev, O. (1978), *Obščestvennye otnošenjia v Egypte epochi srednego carstva.* Moskva, Nauka.
Bonnet, C. and Valbelle, D. (1996) *Le sanctuaire d'Hathor maitresse de la turquoise.* Paris, Picard.
Bresciani, E. (2006), La decorazione delle pareti del tempio di Medio Regno. In *Medinet Madi, venti anni di esplorazione archeologica, 1984–2005,* 22– 41. Pisa, Università di Pisa.
Cohen, S. and Lake W. (2002), *Canaanites, chronologies and connections: the relationship of Middle Bronze IIA Canaan to Middle Kingdom Egypt.* Winona Lake, Ind. Eisenbrauns.
Gardiner, A. (1950) *Egyptian grammar: being an introduction to the study of hieroglyphs.* Oxford, Oxford University press.
Gardiner, A., Peet, T. E. and Černý, J. (1955) *The Inscriptions of Sinai,* Volumes I–II. London, Egypt Exploration Society.
Giveon, R. (1978) *The impact of Egypt on Canaan: iconographical and related studies.* Gottingen, Vandenhoeck and Ruprecht.
Quirke, S. (2004) *Titles and bureaus of Egypt 1850–1700 BC.* London, Golden house publications.
El-Sayed, R. (1982) *La déesse Neith de Sais.* Le Caire, Institut francais d'archeologie orientale.
Ranke, H. (1938) *Die Personennamen der Aegypter.* Madison (Wisc.), Universit.
Tallet, P. (2005) *Sesostris 3. et la fin de la 12.e dinastie.* Paris, Pygmalion.
Te Velde, H. (1977) *Seth, god of confusion: a study of his role in egyptian mythology and religion.* Leiden, E. J. Brill.
van Siclen III, C. (1990) New Kingdom Stelas. *Varia Aegyptiaca* 6, 51–52. San Antonio, Van Siclen Books.
Vernu, P. (1996) Refections et adaptations de l'ideologie monarchique a la Deuxieme Periode Intermediaire: La stele d'Antef-le victorieux. *Studies in Honor of William Kelly Simpson,* 829–842. Boston, Museum of Fine Arts.
Vernus, P. (1970) Sur une particularité de l'onomastique du Moyen Empire. *Revue d'Égyptologie 22*, 155–169. Paris, Editions Peteers.
Vernus, P. (1978) *Athribis. Textes et documents relatifs a la geographie, aux cultes et a l'histoire d'une ville du Delta egyptien a l'epoque pharanoique.* Le Caire, Institut francais d'archeologie orientale.
Ward, W. (1982) *Index of Egyptian administrative and religious titles of the Middle Kingdom: with a glossary of words and phrases used.* Beirut, American University of Beirut.
Wilkinson, R. (2003) *The Complete Gods and Goddesses of Ancient Egypt.* London, Thames and Hudson.
Zecchi, M. (2001) *Geografia Religiosa del Fayyum.* Imola, La Mandragora.
Zecchi, M. (2010) *Sobek of Shedet. The crocodile god in the Fayyum in the Dynastic Period.* Todi, Tau.

Classifying dreams, classifying the world: ancient Egyptian oneiromancy and demotic dream books

Luigi Prada

Introduction

Dreams in ancient Egypt are not a topic reserved only for specialists within the field of Egyptology, but have raised the interest of scholars in many different fields, including ancient Near Eastern studies, classics, social and religious studies, and have even been the object of comparative cultural and psychological analyses (see *e.g.* Quack 2010, 110 fn. 43; for a comparative cultural approach, see Shushan 2006).

A recent awakening of interest in the field has led to a new wave of research and to the publication of new studies on the topic (Szpakowska 2003 is the most complete available monograph), both on the phenomenon of dreams and dreaming in ancient Egypt and on the more specific issue of dream interpretation (most recently, see Szpakowska 2011). Nevertheless, despite substantial progress, particularly in the study of the textual evidence in its main manifestations (that is, papyrological and epigraphic), the topic is still not as well known and understood as it would seem to be. This is the case not only for the study of dreams in ancient Egypt as a whole, but also for ancient Egyptian oneiromancy, *i.e.* dream interpretation (bearing in mind that ancient dream interpretation looks at dreams as a means of divination to foretell the future, and is thus radically different from western modern dream interpretation, intended as a part of psychoanalysis: *cf.* Zauzich 1980, 92).

Dreams in the dynastic and in the Graeco-Roman Period: separation or continuity?

One of the chief issues is the stress that most studies have continuously placed on the evidence dating to the dynastic period, and in particular to the New Kingdom: consequently, attempts at a wider diachronic approach to the topic have been rare, and the view of the phenomenon given by most studies is heavily skewed, favouring the New Kingdom evidence over all that dating to later times. Such a situation would be somewhat understandable if we were faced with a scenario where most of the evidence dates to the New Kingdom and, more generally, to Pharaonic times, but this is not at all the case. As far as dreams are concerned, the Ptolemaic and the Roman Periods offer a body of evidence which is comparable and probably larger in size than the one available for the entire dynastic period, whilst the surviving evidence specifically for oneiromancy is undeniably much more abundant for the Graeco-Roman Period than for any other time of Egyptian history. Studies that propose to discuss ancient Egyptian dreams and oneiromancy therefore tend to arbitrarily omit from their analysis half, if not even more, of the evidence on the topic, and to focus on a relatively short, albeit crucial, period of time: it is worthwhile looking at the reasons why this happens (despite the apparently all-encompassing title of her monograph, even Szpakowska 2003, 2, points out that her study stops with the end of the New Kingdom, yet adds that the evidence from later times is by no means "unimportant, irrelevant, or any less Egyptian").

On the one hand, the New Kingdom and, within it, the Ramesside age star amidst all other dynasties because this is the time from which a large and important part of the Pharaonic evidence on dreams stems. Not only do we have several important biographical texts narrating dreams from both royal and non-royal individuals (for a handy overview, see the anthology in Szpakowska 2003, 185–201), but the only (until recently) known Pharaonic dream interpretation handbook, the hieratic pChester Beatty 3 r°, was also copied in the XIX dynasty (the reference edition remains Gardiner 1935, 9–23, pls. 5a–8a, 12a). Earlier periods offer much less material on the topic, while from the Third Intermediate and the Late Period more evidence is preserved, although this has perhaps not yet received as much attention as the New Kingdom one, in part on account of it being scattered over a longer time span. As non-royal specimens, there are for instance the so-called oracular amuletic decrees from the Third Intermediate Period and, from the very transition from the dynastic to the Ptolemaic Period, the biography of Somtutefnakht (on the former, from a dream perspective, see Renberg and Naether 2010, 62–63; on the latter, Perdu 1985, 108–109). Further, fragments of two other hieratic dream books also survive from the Late Period (see below), although these have received a full publication only very recently, and are therefore absent from earlier scholarly papers on the subject.

On the other hand, the relatively small attention paid by Egyptologists to the wealth of sources we have for the Graeco-Roman Period can be ascribed to many factors. One is certainly a problem in accessing the original textual evidence: whilst all the texts from earlier periods are in Middle or Late Egyptian, in hieroglyphic or hieratic scripts, Ptolemaic and Roman Period texts are instead mainly in demotic, whose study tends to be the prerogative of a smaller group within the Egyptological community. Moreover, since at least part of Egyptian society was by this time bilingual, one often also has to deal with texts written in Greek, which requires further scholarly specialisation, or the collaboration between Egyptologists and classical scholars: a phenomenon, that of the cooperation between Egyptologists/demotists and Greek papyrologists, which is still not very common. Sometimes, even the study of a single document requires such a level of collaboration, as in the case of a Ptolemaic letter, part in Greek and part in demotic, containing a dream account (edition in Renberg and Naether 2010, 50–59). Besides the language factor, another reason for the lesser degree of interest in dreams and oneiromancy in the later phases of ancient Egypt's history is undeniably connected to the long-lived bias that sees the Graeco-Roman Period, in the worst case scenario, as a time of decline and agony of the ancient Egyptian civilization, or, in the best case, as a completely new social and cultural reality where the indigenous Egyptian element plays a minor part, and which has no or very few features of continuity with earlier dynastic times. This skewed view, which sometimes seems to operate even at an unconscious level amongst Egyptologists, has been weakening in recent years through the publishing activity of many scholars, but it still survives (the words of Johnson 1992, xxiii, are still valid today). As a result of all this, we witness the paradoxical situation described above in the studies of dreams and their interpretation in ancient Egypt: the later period, for which we have more evidence, has received much less attention than the earlier one, for which the amount of evidence is less extensive.

With regard to the tradition of oneiromancy as witnessed in the demotic textual sources, an aspect of strong continuity with the earlier hieratic Pharaonic texts is evident, as will be shown in the next section. On account of this continuity, future studies on the topic of dreams in ancient Egypt should therefore take into consideration not only the evidence from either the earlier or the later period, but encompass them both as a *continuum*, albeit also accounting for their individual peculiarities.

Ancient Egyptian dream books: the published evidence

This section will offer a quick chronological overview of the known available evidence for *oneirocritica*, *i.e.* dream interpretation handbooks, which has been published at present, paving the way for a discussion of the most typical features of the demotic dream books and a comparison with their Pharaonic ancestors later on in this paper. For more thorough information about each text, the interested reader can see the discussion and the additional bibliographical references given in Prada (in press).

Hieratic dream books

The first *oneirocriticon* we encounter is the already mentioned pChester Beatty 3 r°, copied under the reign of Ramses II. The beginning and the end parts of the papyrus are lost, but a good number of columns of text survive. Apart from a section with an incantation to protect the dreamer (col. x+10/10–19) and a following one describing the characteristic of a category of men, certainly the *imy.w-ḫt Stẖ* 'followers of Seth' (col. x+11/1–18) whose dreams are treated later on, the rest of the papyrus contains a list of possible dream scenarios, each followed by their interpretation: the dreams starting with col. x+11/19 (only four of which survive before the papyrus breaks up) are said to pertain to the 'followers of Seth', whilst it is plausible that those discussed from col. x+1 to x+10/9 were those pertaining to another group of men, the 'followers of Horus'. A heading written vertically between the columns of text reads *ir m33 sw s m rsw.t* 'if a man sees himself in a dream', and has to be understood before each of the rows of the main text. These are divided into three elements: first, the description of the dream; then, its overall mantic significance, either auspicious or ominous, which is specified by the word *nfr* 'good' or *ḏw* 'bad'; and finally, its specific interpretation, that is, the prediction of what is bound to happen to the dreamer. All positive dreams are listed together, and are followed by the ominous ones (starting from col. x+7/1; one dream in this section, at x+7/5, is actually marked with *nfr*, but this has probably to be attributed to a scribal mistake). To give an example, in col. x+3/5 we read: *ḥr swri irp nfr ꜥnḫ pw m mꜣꜥ.t* 'drinking wine – good: it means living with equanimity'. What is surprising about this Ramesside dream book is that, while the layout of the text is extremely accurate and clearly aims at being user-friendly, with the vertically written protasis, and the tripartite structure of each line carefully aligned even in the writing (dream + 'good' / 'bad' + interpretation), the actual use of the text, if it needed to be consulted as a work of reference by someone interested in finding out the meaning of a specific dream, must not have been that easy, at all. Dreams are in fact listed without a thematic ordering criterion, so that, if one dreamt of, say, burying an old man, it must have taken him (or whoever else was consulting this papyrus) some time before finding the relevant entry in col. x+6/1, surrounded as it is by a dream about sawing wood and another about cultivating herbs.

As already mentioned above, we now know of two more hieratic *oneirocritica* from the Pharaonic period: of both of them only a few fragments survive, but these are yet of the utmost importance, as they provide us with evidence proving the survival of the tradition of dream books in the Late Period, before (and contemporary to) their earliest demotic counterparts. Both papyri are in Berlin and are published in Quack (2010). The first text is pBerlin P 29009, dated to the XXVI dynasty. Its layout is not as fancy as that of pChester Beatty 3 r°, so that there is no vertically written protasis, nor *nfr* or *dw* sign stating the value of the dream (elements which are absent also from all other *oneirocritica* that will be discussed later), but each line is introduced by a phrase of the type <u>s</u> *iw=f nw r=f* 'a man, who dreams of himself' (the underlined text is in red ink in the original; *cf. e.g.* frag. a, col. x+1/x+7), which is then followed by the dream's description, and finally by the prediction. Two points are of particular interest here, and concern the ordering of the text. In the first place, we notice that one of the criteria governing the Ramesside dream book, *i.e.* the main division between auspicious dreams and ominous dreams, is not found here anymore, as it will not be found in any of the later *oneirocritica*: here, good and bad dreams are mixed together, so that a prediction announcing a bad illness is followed by two favourable ones concerning joy and having a long lifetime, and, two lines later, another ominous prediction foretells instead the dreamer's death (frag. a, col. x+1/x+5–7, 9). Secondly, even if an ordering criterion concerning the overall mantic value of the dream is missing, a thematic structure seems instead to be appearing, at least *in nuce*: for instance, in frag. a, col. x+1/x+4–8, all dreams clearly concern being in or coming to a city or place. And a thematic structure, as will be seen, is what characterises all later dream books.

The other hieratic text is pBerlin P 23058, dated to the XXX dynasty (and possibly roughly contemporary to the earliest demotic dream book specimen, for which see below), which shows even clearer signs of a thematic ordering according to the subject of the dream. In the surviving lines of frag. a, col. x+2, Pharaoh plays an important role, so this may possibly have been a section describing dreams about the king. More importantly, in frag. b, l. x+4, a rubric survives from a heading, which probably started off a section about dreams concerning Nubians. Thematic headings are typical of the layout of demotic *oneirocritica*, and are thus here attested for the very first time. It has to be said that a heading introducing a list of dreams is also found once in pChester Beatty 3 r°, col. x+11/19, but this introduces the following list as that of the dreams of the 'followers of Seth', and is thus connected with the nature of the dreamers, and not of the dreams.

Demotic dream books

A quick overview of our sources for dream interpretation manuals in demotic will now show how dominating in quantity and variety the evidence in this phase and writing of the ancient Egyptian language is.

The earliest such text is pJena 1209, which dates to the IV–III century BC (original publication in Zauzich 1980, 96–98, pl. 8; correct re-dating in Quack 2006, 185 fn. 6), and of which additional fragments have been recently identified in the Jena collection, being currently prepared for publication by T. Sebastian Richter of Leipzig University and myself. At the beginning of pJena 1209, in l. 1, is a chapter's heading, *nꜣ ḥ.ṱw snqy* 'the manners of suckling', and all the following dreams concern suckling several creatures, including animals, people, and one's relatives. The structure of each dream-entry is similar to what we saw in the previous texts: first, at the beginning of the line, comes the protasis, the description of the specific dream (*i.e.* the mention of the recipient of the suckling, the action being here described by means of a circumstantial present clause), which is then followed by the apodosis, the prediction, in the third future. To give an example of this standard set up of the demotic dream books, l. 2 reads: *iw=f snqy n msḥ r rmṯ ꜥꜣ ḥry gr r ti n=f nkt* 'when he suckles a crocodile: a great man or a superior will give him property'. The additional fragments that are now being studied do not belong to this chapter about suckling, but to other sections of this manuscript.

All the other known demotic *oneirocritica* date to the Roman Period, and stem from the Fayum. Small fragments probably belonging to two different texts, although roughly contemporary and both from Tebtunis, are pTebt. Tait 16 and 17 (publication in Tait 1977, 56–61, pl. 4). Unfortunately, so little text survives with regard to the description of the dreams, that virtually nothing can be said about their topic and the structuring of these compositions.

On a similar note, further papyrus fragments, pCairo 50138–50141 (*cf.* Spiegelberg 1932, 98–103, pl. 59), belong to two or possibly three different original manuscripts, but their present condition is such that no single entire line of text survives in any of them, and, while it is certain that they all belong to the genre of divinatory writings, it is disputable whether or not they are specifically dream books. Only the final parts of the lines of some columns survive, which means that many predictions are preserved, but none of the entries which would allow us to say whether the *omina* described were dream-related or of another kind (dream books show in fact strong analogies and a phraseology very close to that of other divination texts, on which see for instance Quack 2006 and, with focus on astrological handbooks, Winkler 2009). Two of the fragments actually preserve traces from the beginning of some lines, but the surviving amount of text is not enough to solve the uncertainty about the specific texts' genre.

Much different is the situation with two manuscripts now in Copenhagen, pCarlsberg 13 and 14 v°, which, although also fragmentary, do bear a large amount of text, and have been, to the present day, the main and most extensive known specimens of demotic *oneirocritica* (edition in Volten 1942). Given their prominence within the other demotic evidence for dream interpretation, these papyri have often been mentioned in general studies on ancient Egyptian oneiromancy: yet, some misunderstandings have arisen concerning them, which have been repeated in several of these publications, first of all the idea that we here have an alleged 'Demotic Dream Manual' (see, most recently, Szpakowska 2011, 510–511, 515), which is not really the case. The two papyri belong in fact to two different manuscripts (besides the radical difference between the two scribal hands, pCarlsberg 13 is written on the papyrological *recto* of a papyrus whose back is blank, whilst pCarlsberg 14 v° is copied on the *verso* of a papyrus originally bearing a Greek text on the front; *cf.* Volten 1942, 3–4), and there is no reason to suggest that they might be two different copies of the same handbook. Other commonly repeated misunderstandings concern the topic of some of the manuals' sections, such as one about dreams where animals suckle the dreamer (in pCarlsberg 14 v° f), unlike the Jena text discussed above, where it was a person suckling animals (thus, the remarks in Szpakowska 2011, 511, need to be emended accordingly).

A detailed discussion concerning the topics of the thematic chapters found in pCarlsberg 13 and 14 v° is beyond the aims of the current paper: for this, I refer the reader to the original publication and to the discussion in Prada (in press, fn. 68 in particular). What has to be noted here is that the thematic ordering emerges perfectly clear throughout both Carlsberg texts. As for their layout, both manuscripts introduce new chapters with a heading, in the same way seen for pJena 1209. And the phrasing of the texts is also the same as for the Jena papyrus, showing a bipartite structure: first the dream, mainly described with a circumstantial present clause (the section on dreams about numbers, in pCarlsberg 13a, col. x+2, is exceptional, inasmuch as the numbers are listed by themselves, not within a circumstantial or any other type of clause), and then the prediction, in the third future. Particularly remarkable, from the point of view of the information we can extrapolate about the classification system followed by these texts in listing dreams, is the fact that in a few instances the Carlsberg fragments preserve parts of text before a new chapter heading is introduced. This is also true in the case of the newly discovered and still unpublished section of the Jena manuscript. As a result, in parts of these texts one can see what topic followed which one in the original sequence of the chapters.

One more fragment of a demotic *oneirocriticon* is published, pBerlin P 15683 (edition in Zauzich 1980, 92–96, pl. 7), but I will discuss this in the next section, as it belongs to a composition of which more unpublished fragments have been recently identified.

Finally, it is worth mentioning here that fragments of more *oneirocritica* of Roman date from Tebtunis (and additional fragments of pCarlsberg 13 and 14 v°) are about to be published by Joachim F. Quack and Kim Ryholt (see Quack 2010, 103 fn. 12, 108).

A new demotic dream book

Another text has to be added to the list of demotic dream manuals given above, and this is an *oneirocriticon*, for the most part unpublished, of which several fragments survive, and which I am reconstructing as part of my doctoral research, in view of its eventual publication. I have not yet completed my survey of the main European and American papyrus collections holding demotic literary items of Roman age from the Faiyum, and thus the following survey has to be considered a preliminary one, subject to change and additions in the near future. For reasons of space, this overview will be kept short (for more information, see Prada in press).

Most of the fragments of this text belong to one manuscript, although a couple of others come from different copies, thus proving the survival of multiple manuscripts (all Roman in date, and all stemming from the Faiyum) of this handbook. At this stage of my research, the copy for which the most fragments are attested includes items from the papyrus collections of Berlin and Vienna, which are: pBerlin P 8769, P 15796a+b, pVienna D 6104, D 6633+6634+6635+6636, D 6644, D 6668. None of these is published, although an image of pBerlin P 8769, accompanied by some observations on the text (whose exact nature as a dream book was not recognised), was printed in Spiegelberg (1902, 29, pl. 98). As for the Vienna items, most of them were simply listed in Reymond (1983, 53–54), and in one case, that of D 6668, not specifically as a specimen of a dream book, but more generally as a divinatory composition.

Another fragment of this text is pBerlin P 15683, which, as mentioned in the preceding section, is the only one to have been already published. The scribal hand of this text is extremely similar to that of the Berlin/Vienna manuscript presented above, yet some peculiarities in its orthography and differences in the writing of specific words (*cf.* Prada in press, fn. 72) suggest that this fragment was written by a different scribe from the one who wrote the other copy, although both must have been trained in the same scriptorium, given the overall resemblance of the two hands. Further, what I believe must be a case of pagination (*i.e.* column numbering) in pBerlin P 15683 should also prove that this papyrus belongs to a different copy, since no pagination is found in the Berlin/Vienna manuscript.

Finally, another copy is witnessed by pCtYBR 1154b, a fragment from Tebtunis in the collection of Yale University, which, by a random chance, preserves an exact textual parallel to part of the text of pBerlin P 15683 (from its line x+2/19). Also, this Yale papyrus belongs to a manuscript of which a few additional fragments are preserved in the Carlsberg collection, and which will soon be published (cf. the end of the preceding section).

Another item, pMichigan Dem. 516a (in the collection of the University of Michigan, Ann Arbor), is also a demotic Roman fragment of a divinatory text, quite likely of a dream book. It does not belong to any of the manuscripts described above, and there is no element to suggest whether or not it may be an additional textual witness of this new *oneirocriticon*. I include mention of it here for the sake of completeness: further study of this Michigan fragment will hopefully shed more light on it.

The number of fragments and the multiple copies of this new dream book listed above can already give an idea of the wealth of information that will come from this text once its complete publication is achieved, with the hundreds of lines of text it preserves. Before discussing its thematic chapters, the standard pattern of the text needs to be mentioned. As in the cases seen above, here too we have a bipartite structure for each entry, with the subject of the dream at the beginning of the line and then the prediction (again, mainly in the third future). What is unusual, however, is the way the dream is described: by far the most frequent pattern includes neither a circumstantial nor any other type of clause, but simply the mention of an entity (object, animated creature, *etc.*) which stands for the main subject of the dream. To give an example, in pBerlin P 8769, col. x+4/13, we read: [*n*]*ny n bny.t i*[*w*]=*f ir nb n mt*(.*t*) *nfr.t* 'Date palm [r]oot: he [w]ill be owner of goodness'. This feature, rarely attested in other *oneirocritica* (see *e.g.* the section on numbers of pCarlsberg 13 previously mentioned), makes the structure of this new dream book look distinctively 'encyclopaedic', with rows of text listing words one under the other, each followed by its prediction.

With regard to the way dreams and their topics are divided in this text, this too is reminiscent of an encyclopaedic approach to the world, and thus to the world as seen in one's dreams. In listing the main topics treated by this text, I will roughly follow the order of the list of fragments I have given above: this order does not claim to be the one in which the chapters followed one another in the original composition, since the papyrus fragments cannot generally be joined or repositioned with respect to one another, but are unfortunately 'floating'. Many entries are preserved from a large section (which covered at least three columns of one of the manuscripts) about stones, minerals, and metals one can dream of, and another contains trees, fruits, and other botanical entries. There is a chapter that lists birds, whilst another focuses on divinities that can be sighted in one's dream. Other fragments include: a section possibly on foodstuffs (only a few, damaged entries are still preserved for this group, which is the reason for my uncertainty), a long list of animals (including mammals, reptiles, insects), a section on herbs and plants (this is probably the case, although only one entry, the last one, survives for this section), and one on metal implements (not common tools, but items apparently pertaining to cult activities in temples, including incense-burners and sistra). Two headings introducing their respective chapters (the one about animals and the one about metal implements) also survive: one is in pVienna D 6644, col. x+2/6–7, and reads *n3 ḥ.wt* ... [*nt-iw*] *rmṯ nw r-r=f | iw=f fy n-im=w* 'the manners of ... [which] a man dreams of carrying out' (on the word following *ḥ.wt*, for which I can offer no reading, see Prada in press, fn. 81). The other is in pBerlin P 15683, col. x+2/2: <u>*k.t-ḥ*(.*t*) *stbḥ nt-iw rmṯ nw* [*r-r=w*] 'Another (chapter): (metal) implements</u> which a man dreams [of]'.

Demotic oneirocritica: *their taxonomical system in relation to the earlier tradition of dream books*

As seen above, what emerges from the demotic texts is a classification of the world, a taxonomy that encompasses not only the view of dreams that was held by the authors and the intended users of such texts, but also their view of the surrounding world. In the past as well as today, dreams could concern any aspects of life and human experience: hence, *oneirocritica* can be looked at as a sort of encyclopaedia, a most wealthy source of information on the reality of their time.

Now that the available evidence for demotic dream books has been presented, it is worthwhile to move back to the issue I touched upon earlier in this paper, that is, the relationship between the textual documentation for the dynastic period and that for the Graeco-Roman one, and in particular between pChester Beatty 3 r° and the demotic dream manuals (for the following discussion, see also Quack 2010, 108–110, and the references therein). Certainly, the tradition of demotic *oneirocritica* appears extremely compact, showing continuity in its structure and in the way dreams are listed for a time span of approximately half a millennium: from as early as the IV–III century BC, the date of pJena 1209, to the late II or even early III century AD, the time to which the manuscripts I am studying can be dated. For the similarities between these two texts, one can consider for instance the use of headings phrased in the same way in both, and following the pattern 'the manners of' + the action being carried out in the dream. Nor should this continuity be surprising: the dates given above are in fact those to which the papyri can be dated on palaeographical basis, but this does not mean that the texts themselves were composed at that time. We may well be dealing with manuals composed long before the earliest surviving manuscript copies. This would not be unusual, since, in the case of demotic literary compositions, we have direct evidence of instances of the same text having been copied for centuries, with surviving papyri of the same composition having very different dates (*cf. e.g.* Ryholt 1999, 88–91). The newly published hieratic dream books from Berlin also strengthen this picture of continuity, in particular pBerlin P 23058, with its partially preserved heading, and its date to the latest dynastic period, perhaps coinciding with that of pJena 1209. Also, this proves that what were thought to be peculiarities of the demotic dream books have little to do with their being in demotic, since they are also found in the hieratic counterparts of these texts.

When we look back at pChester Beatty 3 r°, the differences seem even more striking. But is it true that this Ramesside text follows no classifying criterion for the dreams it treats? As seen above, this papyrus does in fact have some form of ordering: but rather than a thematic one, based on the dreams' topic, it prefers two further-encompassing criteria. The first is the identity of the dreamer, 'followers of Seth' *vs.*, probably, 'followers of Horus'; and this identity-based criterion is not completely unknown even to the demotic dream books, as shown by sections from both pCarlsberg 13 and 14 v° where dreams (still ordered thematically as well) and predictions refer to women (*cf.* also Volten 1942, 8–9). The second criterion refers to the mantic quality of the dreams, *i.e.* whether they are good or bad ones: this functions as a second-level division within the identity-based one. In the first group of dreams (those of, probably, the 'followers of Horus'), the auspicious dreams precede the ominous ones, and so certainly happened in the section concerning the dreams of the 'followers of Seth', of which only a handful of lines survive, yet also starting with good dreams.

But there is perhaps even more to be observed about the Ramesside handbook, *i.e.* traces, here and there, of a thematic ordering as well: these have been already noted and listed by Volten

(1942, 14–15), and should be taken into serious consideration. The reason why pChester Beatty 3 r° shows such traces may be a sign of it being an excerpt from a wider, original composition which also included a thematic ordering, as already suggested by Volten (1942, 15–16). In the end, as already pointed out before, it is hard to imagine the utility of a dream book, a text meant to be used as a reference tool, if it lists the dreams without any thematic criterion. And it is plausible to suppose that pChester Beatty 3 r° may be an abridged copy drawn up for personal use also because of its provenance: it originally belonged to a scribe's personal library, that of Qenherkhopshef, whose collection of texts shows the interests not of a professional dream interpreter or expert of divination, but of a scribe of great culture and wide-ranging interests (on the owner of pChester Beatty 3, *cf.* Szpakowska 2011, 513–517).

Finally, to conclude this brief analysis of the taxonomy of demotic dream books, at least two more questions need to be asked. The first one concerns the internal ordering of each thematic chapter: is there any sub-ordering at this level, are there any sub-groups, or not? The answer is not straightforward. In most cases, it is impossible to see any order: in pVienna D 6633, for instance, the divinities are listed one after the other without any apparent sorting principle. Yet, there are cases were a system can be spotted: this is the case for pBerlin P 8769, where the section about stones, minerals, and metals tends to collect many of them in more or less coherent groups, or for pVienna D 6644, where the animals are listed according to size, from the larger to the smaller ones.

The second question is: can we discern any rational order in the way the thematic chapters follow one another? Unfortunately, this question is even harder to answer, and in fact cannot be answered for the time being. As pointed out before, in the description of pCarslberg 13 and 14 v°, we only have a few instances of fragments including consecutive parts of text from more than one chapter. Hopefully, further study and the discovery of additional fragments to the new dream book will shed more light on this issue. Also, the study of the Greek texts on the other side of a couple of dream books (namely, pCarslberg 14 v° and pCtYBR 1154b with its complementary fragments in Copenhagen) may perhaps provide further elements with which to reconstruct the original respective position of the fragments. Moreover, in the case of another papyrus, pBerlin P 15683, it is possible that the section on metal implements (and the preceding one on herbs) which it preserves stood originally very close to the beginning of the text: on the right of col. x+2/17, in the *intercolumnium*, is a sign which, although slightly damaged, seems to be quite clearly that for the number '2'. This can only be interpreted as a pagination number, indicating that this actually was the original second column in the papyrus roll. There are no known cases of pagination numbers written between columns of text, and it is commonly believed that pagination was written either in the top or in the bottom margin. However, in the papyrus collection of Vienna I had the chance to observe an unpublished, well preserved divination text, written in a hand very close to that of pBerlin P 15683, with a pagination number also included in the *intercolomnium*: this proves that, at least in the scribal milieu that produced these manuscripts, such a way of numbering columns was practiced.

Conclusion

The aim of this paper was to give an account of the wealth of evidence for the phenomenon of oneiromancy that is available in demotic and that in good part still lies unpublished, and to show how this is not unrelated from earlier such writings in hieratic. The ongoing studies on the topic and the gradual publication of more such texts are showing more and more clearly the strong link between the demotic and the earlier *oneirocritica*, and are making the study of either corpus in isolation and independent from one another unjustifiable from a scholarly perspective. No matter how late they might be, the demotic dream books appear to be rooted in a long-lived indigenous Egyptian tradition, with its own view of the world and of the world of dreams.

Acknowledgements

I should like to acknowledge here my debt of gratitude to a few individuals and institutions. First, to my supervisor, Prof. Mark Smith (Oxford), for continuous discussion and support throughout my MPhil and these first years of my DPhil. Then, to Prof. Joachim F. Quack (Heidelberg), who has always exchanged with me information about his research, and communicated to me the inventory numbers of some of the unpublished papyri discussed above and which he first identified. For similar generosity in sharing his research with me, I am also thankful to Prof. Kim Ryholt (Copenhagen). All my research has been made possible by the award of a DPhil scholarship from the AHRC in partnership with the Oxford University Scatcherd Scholarship programme. The Governing Body of The Queen's College has also awarded me continuous grants to facilitate my study visits abroad. My gratitude also goes to the curators and staff of the papyrus collections in which I have most often worked in the past couple of years, in particular to Prof. Bernhard Palme (Vienna), Dr. Verena Lepper (Berlin), and Prof. Arthur Verhoogt (Ann Arbor). Last but not least, thanks to Jenny Cromwell (Sydney) for proofreading this paper (and more).

Bibliography

Gardiner, A. H. (1935) *Hieratic Papyri in the British Museum: Third Series: Chester Beatty Gift I (Text)–II (Plates)*. London, British Museum.

Johnson, J. H. (1992) Preface. In J. H. Johnson (ed.), *Life in a Multi-cultural Society: Egypt from Cambyses to Constantine and Beyond*. Studies in Ancient Oriental Civilization 51, xxiii–xxv. Chicago, The Oriental Institute of the University of Chicago. Online version available at: <http://oi.uchicago.edu/research/pubs/catalog/saoc/saoc51.html>.

Perdu, O. (1985) Le monument de Samtoutefnakht à Naples [Première partie]. *Revue d'Égyptologie* 36, 89–113.

Prada, L. (in press) pBerlin P 8769: A New Look at the Text and the Reconstruction of a Lost Demotic Dream Book. In V. Lepper (ed.), *Forschung in der Papyrussammlung: Festschrift für das Neue Museum*.

Quack, J. F. (2006) A Black Cat from the Right, and a Scarab on Your Head: New Sources for Ancient Egyptian Divination. In K. Szpakowska (ed.), *Through a Glass Darkly: Magic, Dreams and Prophecy in Ancient Egypt*, 175–187. Swansea, The Classical Press of Wales.

Quack, J. F. (2010) Aus zwei spätzeitlichen Traumbüchern (Pap. Berlin P. 29009 und 23058). In H. Knuf, Ch. Leitz and D. von Recklinghausen (eds.), *Honi soit qui mal y pense: Studien zum pharaonischen, griechisch-römischen und spätantiken Ägypten zu Ehren von Heinz-Josef Thissen*. Orientalia Lovaniensia Analecta 194, 99–110, pls. 34–37. Leuven, Paris and Walpole, MA, Uitgeverij Peeters and Departement Oosterse Studies.

Renberg and Naether (2010) "I Celebrated a Fine Day". An Overlooked Egyptian Phrase in a Bilingual Letter Preserving a Dream Narrative. *Zeitschrift für Papyrologie und Epigraphik* 175, 49–71, pls. 1–2.

Reymond, E. A. E. (1983) Demotic Literary Works of Graeco-Roman Date in the Rainer Collection of Papyri in Vienna. In *Festschrift zum 100-jährigen Bestehen der Papyrussammlung der Österreichischen Nationalbibliothek: Papyrus Erzherzog Rainer (P. Rainer Cent.): Textband*, 42–60. Wien, Verlag Brüder Hollinek.

Ryholt, K. (1999) *The Story of Petese Son of Petetum and Seventy Other Good and Bad Stories (P. Petese)*. Carsten Niebuhr Institute Publications 23, The Carlsberg Papyri 4. Copenhagen, Museum Tusculanum Press.

Shushan, G. (2006) Greek and Egyptian Dreams in Two Ptolemaic Archives: Individual and Cultural Layers of Meaning. *Dreaming: Journal of the Association for the Study of Dreams* 16/2, 129–142.

Spiegelberg, W. (1902) *Demotische Papyrus aus den Königlichen Museen zu Berlin*. Leipzig and Berlin, Giesecke and Devrient.

Spiegelberg, W. (1932) *Die demotischen Denkmäler III: Demotische Inschriften und Papyri (Fortsetzung) 50023–50165*. Catalogue général des antiquités égyptiennes du Musée du Caire. Berlin, Reichsdruckerei.

Szpakowska, K. (2003) *Behind Closed Eyes: Dreams and Nightmares in Ancient Egypt*. Swansea, The Classical Press of Wales.

Szpakowska, K. (2011) Dream Interpretation in the Ramesside Age. In M. Collier and S. Snape (eds), *Ramesside Studies in Honour of K. A. Kitchen*, 509–517. Bolton, Rutherford Press Limited.

Tait, W. J. (1977) *Papyri from Tebtunis in Egyptian and in Greek (P. Tebt. Tait)*. Texts from Excavations 3. London, Egypt Exploration Society.

Volten, A. (1942) *Demotische Traumdeutung (Pap. Carlsberg XIII und XIV verso)*. Analecta Aegyptiaca 3. Kopenhagen, Einar Munksgaard.

Winkler, A. (2009) On the Astrological Papyri from the Tebtunis Temple Library. In Gh. Widmer and D. Devauchelle (eds.), *Actes du IXᵉ congrès international des études démotiques: Paris, 31 Août–3 Septembre 2005*. Bibliothèque d'étude 147, 361–375. Le Caire, Institut Français d'Archéologie Orientale.

Zauzich, K.-Th. (1980) Aus zwei demotischen Traumbüchern. *Archiv für Papyrusforschung und verwandte Gebiete* 27, 91–98, pls. 7–8.

Aspects of trading with New Kingdom Egypt

Birgit Schiller

Introduction

The trade connections of New Kingdom Egypt with the Eastern Mediterranean area are well established. Sources derive only from the 18th and 19th Dynasties. Merchants from Alashiya, a certain part of Cyprus (Goren *et al.* 2002), were mentioned in the Amarna letter EA 39:14 (Moran 1992, 112). Syrian merchants are shown in the tomb of Kenamun (Fig. 1) dating back to the 18th Dynasty. A letter of a King of Tyre to the King of Ugarit informs us about a group of Ugaritic ships that were sent to Egypt (Wachsmann 1998, 334, KTU 2.38). This dates to the 13th century BC and is thus contemporaneous with the later 19th Dynasty.

Sources are widely distributed chronologically, so changes can hardly be recognized. Although naturally merchants came from the south this article does concentrate on those coming by ship from Syria or Alashiya. The aim of this article is to follow the merchants possible path to Egypt and their trade in an Egyptian harbour as well as possible problems encountered.

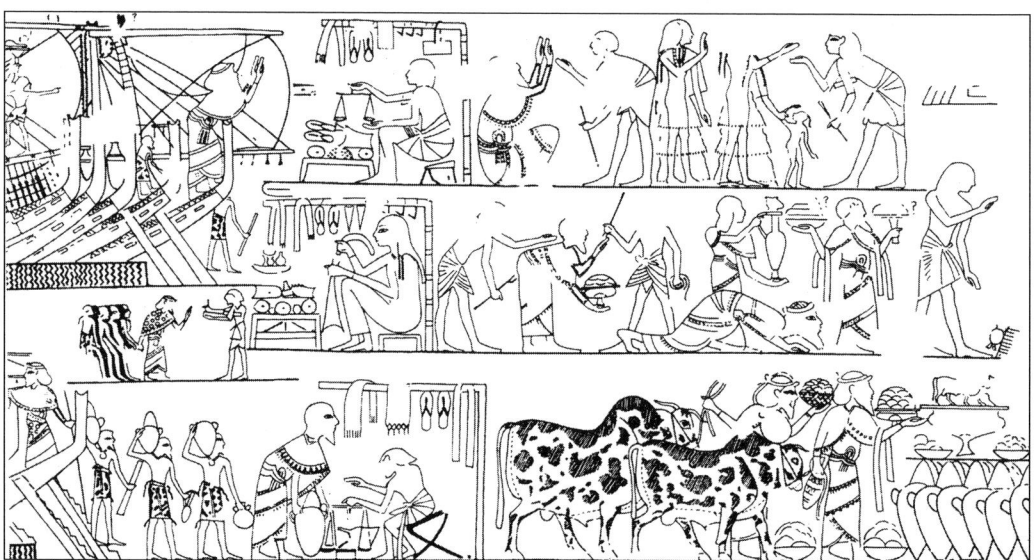

Figure 1. Scene from the tomb of Kenamun (TT 162) with harbour staff (from Wachsmann 1998, 314, fig. 14.6).

The way to the Egyptian harbour

At the sea

Both the letter of the King of Tyre and the depiction in the tomb of Kenamun suggest that there was not only one ship but a fleet sent out to Egypt. However, it is likewise possible that these might have been ships from different harbour towns of the Levantine coast – or (even) from Cyprus. Egyptians never developed a special iconography for Cypriotes. As they were Northerners it might well be that they were subsumed as 'Syrians'.

Piracy was mentioned repeatedly in the Amarna Letters. It always appears to happen in connection to wars, *e.g.* EA 113 or EA 114 (Moran 1992, 187–190).

Departing from Syria, the ships had to circle around Cyprus or at least go via Cyprus. Winds and currents on the Levantine coast make it impossible to sail along the coast from North to South (Höckmann 1987, 60).

Arriving in the Egyptian Delta

Delta fortresses

We may assume that system of lights was in place to guide the ships to the coast. Although there are no archaeologically recognizable traces we know from titles that there were military installations at the northern frontier. The title of an *jmj-rȝ ḥtm wr n wȝḏ-wr* 'Overseer of the great fortress at the 'Great Green'' (Jones 1988, 112, no. 7) can only generally be dated to the 18th Dynasty. Finally, from the end of the 19th Dynasty we have the title of an *jmj-rȝ pȝ ḥtm nb n pȝ wȝḏ-wr*, 'Overseer of every fortress at the 'Great Green'', on the Bilgai Stela (Gardiner 1912, l. 9 on the verso). These two titles prove the very existence of fortresses at the Delta frontier. Where did foreign ships enter the Delta? Whether they took the Pelusiac branch (see below) to get to the 'international harbour' as assumed or not, they have had to pass a fortress.

Thus, when they arrived at the Egyptian Delta, the foreign ships would most probably have had to make a stop at the fortress. It is highly likely that a scribe of the fortress recorded the arrival. Although the title of the scribe has not yet been attested, it can safely be assumed to have had existed as the fortress' organization would have been in need of such a person. The fortress might have been considered a safe anchorage as well. Ships approaching the coast may well have been targeted by pirates. Although Egyptian ships cast off at night as shown by the entry of pLeiden I 350 verso, IV 32 (Janssen 1961, 16) it appears – for safety reasons – doubtful that foreign ships sailed on the Nile at night.

Control and Customs Duty

We learn from the Amarna Letter EA 30 (Moran 1992, 100) that 'permits' were also written in Akkadian to be shown to a fortress commander. In this case a messenger would have received this permit to pass through. It is also thinkable that ships from abroad had a 'letter of recommendation' or a similar document to show to the fortress commander. Interestingly, a language other than Egyptian is used and must have been understood by some officials working at the frontier.

We have scarce information about a customs duty being demanded in the New Kingdom (Schiller 2010). If the commander of the fortress had the same function as some 600 years later in the Saite period and beyond, he would have collected the customs duty from the ships upon arrival. Unfortunately, there is no source from the New Kingdom itself. We do not know for sure if there was a ‚payment' of customs duty. But if so, ships certainly received a letter of acknowledgement to show that they entered correctly and did not smuggle their goods.

Sailing on the Nile
Security on the Nile

Apart from natural difficulties in sailing up the Nile (Graham 2005) there is also the aspect of security for foreign merchants. In the Amarna Letter EA 8 (Moran 1992, 16–17) Burnaburiash, king of Babylonia, complained that his merchants were murdered. He demanded a compensation for the loss of the goods they had with them. The raid took place in Canaan. Burnaburiash put the responsibility for the raid on his merchants to the Egyptian king as it happened in an Egyptian dominated area. Egypt appears to have been responsible for the security of foreign merchants and their ships for the length of their stay in Egyptian territory.

We learn from the Nauri Decree that a $šn^c$-police existed which patrolled the Nile. This kind of police might have been patrolling the Delta area as well. At the frontier there might have been military personnel patrolling on boats. In connection with this, we have the title of an jmj-$r\!\!\!/\,3$ $mš^c$ n $jtrw$ $jmnty$ 'Overseer of the $mš^c$-troop (= army) of the western river' (Jones 1988, 112, no. 6). Therefore the $šn^c$ or military personnel patrolling on the Nile might also have been responsible for their safety. The fleet may have been escorted to the final destination.

The 'international harbour' and its location

How much time would it have taken to sail along the Nile to the final destination? To answer this question we need to know where the harbour was and what the Delta looked like at the time of the New Kingdom. As it has changed over time (Sestini 1989) we are strongly reliant on geological analyses and reconstruction of ancient geography. A possible reconstruction of the Eastern Delta about 3500 BP (= 1550 BC) is given by Coutellier and Stanley (1987, fig. 271 C).

Whereas the 'international harbour' of the Ramesside period can be very likely assumed to be in Piramesse, the exact location of the 18th Dynasty harbour is a matter of debate. The above mentioned scene in the tomb of Kenamun who was jmj-$r\!\!\!/\,3$ pr wr m prw-nfr (Helck 1958, 366) might present this 'international harbour' of the 18th Dynasty, although it remains unclear whether the scene is in prw-nfr or somewhere else. Common opinion does localize it in Memphis on the basis of inscriptions from there mentioning prw-nfr and of a dedication to an 'Amun of prw-nfr' (Helck 1982b). Since the discovery of a dedication to this same god in Thebes, the last argument lost much of its power (Bietak 2009). As a harbour with fortifications dating to the time of Haremhab and to late 18th/early 19th Dynasties was discovered, both Habachi (2001, 106–107) and Bietak (2006, 126–130; 2009) localize prw-nfr in Tell el-Dab'a. Although doubts still remain on the equation of prw-nfr with a harbour in Tell el-Dab'a (Jeffreys 2006) Habachi's and Bietak's arguments are striking. If the harbour in Tell el-Dab'a – if it is prw-nfr or not – was used as a harbour for trade in the 18th to the beginning of the 19th Dynasties it would have been very close to the (as yet unlocated) harbour of Piramesse.

The Egyptian 'international harbour'

The harbour: organization, staff and local traders
Harbour organization and staff

As not many titles connected to a harbour are known it is difficult to reconstruct harbour administration. Some titles and functions have been taken for granted by analogy with other institutions.

Before dealing with the administration a discussion on *mry.t* and *mnjw.t* would appear to be necessary. The term *mry.t* has been translated as 'harbour' by Erman and Grapow (1928, 109–110) whereas Lesko (2002, 193) gives a different translation as 'bank, shore, quay, marketplace'. There are a few titles connected to *mry.t*. It is unlikely to have been an administrative organization other than a 'marketplace' or a 'quay'. Both seem to be very closely connected as the 'marketplace' can be situated on the quay. Beyond that, a quay is an installation to facilitate ships to land. What makes a 'harbour'? It is a place with built installations, an artificial basin that gives safe anchorage and a place where sailors were able to acquire provisions and have their ships repaired. It also includes an organization and is more than a mere 'landingplace' or 'marketplace'. Janssen (1961, 58) translated the term as a "river bank". As it is the *mry.t* of Memphis, it appears more likely to have been the 'harbour' of this town. Otherwise, at least two different 'harbours or landing places' in Memphis come to mind: a *mry.t* and a *mnjw.t* (see below) – which seems unlikely.

Other than that *mnjw.t* is also considered as a word for 'harbour' (Erman and Grapow 1928, 74) and also 'port', 'harbour' or 'landing place' by Lesko (2002, 186). The actual meaning of *mry.t* possibly depends on the context, whereas *mnjw.t* seems to have been a more specific word. Thus, both can be considered as synonyms.

ORGANIZATION

jmj-r3 mry.t : The title is attested in the New Kingdom by an *jmj-r3 mry.t n njw.t rsy* (Jones 1988, 118, no. 1). Therefore it might be safe to assume the 'Overseer of the harbour' to have been an *jmj-r3 mry.t*.

jdnw mry.t: There is no mentioning of this title. However, comparing the organization of other administrations in Egypt, it is highly likely to assume at least one deputy. As officials cumulated offices that may have been physically located very far from one another (Helck 1958) the *jdnw mry.t* might have been the official that kept the harbour administration running, only receiving a visit from the *jmj-r3 mry.t* at intervals.

jmj-r3 sš.w mry.t: This title is documented in *jmj-r3 sš.w mry.(t) n nb t3.wy* 'Overseer of the scribes of the harbour of the Lord of the Two Lands' (Kitchen 1980, 497:8).

sš mry.t: As an 'Overseer of scribes' is mentioned, it is only plausible to assume that he had several scribes to his assistance. Furthermore, scribes are depicted in harbour scenes at their work (Fig. 1). They recorded not only the arrival and departure of the ships but also the payment of the harbour staff and managed the correspondence of their chiefs.

ORGANIZATION: DOCKYARD

It is not unlikely that a ship was damaged during the journey and had to be repaired before starting the trip home. Therefore a type of dockyard must have been present in the harbour.

jmj-r3 wḫr.t: There is no mentioning of this title. It is likely to there would have been an 'Overseer of the dockyard'.

sš wḫr.t: The title of a *sš n t3 wḫr.t* is known from the time of Ramesses II (Jones 1988, 123, no. 21). Therefore the bearer of it might have been responsible for the recording of the materials needed as well as for recording the payment of the dockyard personnel.

ORGANIZATION: SECURITY PERSONNEL

jmj-r3 (?): We learn from pCairo 58056 that a *wʿw* was stationed in the harbour of Memphis (Wente 1990, no. 139). Unfortunately, the administrative structure of the security personnel of the harbour can be reconstructed with less certainty as the *wʿw* is too vague a title. However, there must have been guardians, not only for securing the goods in the warehouses and on board of the ships against theft.

sš (?): There was possibly a scribe belonging to the security personnel as scribes in military service are known.

ORGANIZATION: HARBOUR WORKERS (*šMḏ.t*)

sš smd.t: This title is known from Deir el-Medine (Helck 2002, 562). If a similar situation can be reconstructed the members of the *smd.t* would have received a monthly payment from the harbour.

STAFF: HARBOUR WORKERS

smd.t: This title in connection with a harbour occurs only once on the 'Turin tax list' dating to the Ramesside period where a *smd.t n t3 mnj[w.t]* of Memphis is mentioned (Helck 1992, col. III, 23). This term can be interpreted in two ways: (1) as a tax payment of every member of the *smd.t*-staff or (2) as the whole tax payment of members of different *smd.t*-groups. The latter interpretation appears to be a generic term of people working in the harbour. Unfortunately, the line is too badly damaged for which reason their labour is unknown. From other sources – mainly deriving from Deir el-Medina – it is clear that they could do various jobs (Bakir 1952, 34–35). In connection to a harbour it appears most likely that they would have helped loading and unloading ships or were working in storage houses. Obviously, this idea led Helck to add fragment no. 62 to this line, which depicts a ship. Warburton (1997, 161) rejected this from the entry and there is indeed no proof that Helck is correct.

ḳwr.w: Fabre (2004/2005, 137) considered these people as harbour workers who helped loading and unloading ships, referring to pLansing 12,6 (Gardiner 1937, 111). Fabre ignores Caminos (1954, 417) and Lesko (2004, 155) who consider these as a ship's crew. This latter interpretation seems more likely as the word is closely connected to the *ḳwr/ḳr*-ship (Erman and Grapow 1957, 21).

Local traders

As can be seen in the Kenamun scene, local traders are present at the harbour quay. Foreign ships' crews did not only require food and fresh drinking water as provisions for the trip home but also during their stay. These people would have supplied them and would have possibly had to pay a fee to the harbour administration.

Arrival of foreign ships

Upon arrival, it is highly likely that a scribe of the harbour recorded the day of arrival and how many ships anchored in the harbour. The ship's captain or captain of the fleet possibly had to prove that the ships entered legally and paid the customs duty – if this was demanded on entrance.

Bargaining

The 'merchant' at the Egyptian harbour

There is the *šwty* who is involved in trade in New Kingdom Egypt (Reineke 1979; Römer 1992; Allam 1998). From pBologna 1094, 5, 5 we know that he was also sent to Syria (Gardiner 1937, 5; Caminos 1954, 16). Thus, he might have also been involved in trade with foreigners in Egypt. It appears from the sources that the *šwty.w* were always acting on behalf of either an institution or a private person. In fact, no text exists that mentions a *šwty* in a harbour. At least, however, there is an ostracon that mentions a trade at the *mry.t* (see above) in Thebes (Allam 1998, 3–4). The person trading is not a *šwty* but acts in the same manner. Subsequently, people belonging to different professions could have gone to a harbour for trading on behalf of another private person.

For an 'international harbour' it seems more likely that professional trading agents would have been in place, who also had some knowledge of foreign languages (see below). Grain or gold seem to have only been available from the royal treasury or temples. At least the grain could have only been available from these institutions in considerable quantities. There might have been *šwty.w* of temples and – as no *šwty* is known to have been in service of a royal institution – officials working for the *pr-ḥd*.

Another term, *mkr*, is known from the 'Onomasticon of Amenope' dated by Gardiner (1947, 25) to the end of the 20th to the 21th Dynasties. The term in question was used in pGolénischeff 3, 12 (Gardiner 1947, 94–95) which lists various professions. As it is only mentioned once, one is left alone with speculation whether it describes an Egyptian merchant responsible for trading with Syrians/foreigners in Egypt or a Syrian merchant working at the Egyptian harbour to help facilitate trade of Syrians/foreigners in general in Egypt itself. Simultaneously, the date of its first occurrence and use in the New Kingdom (if at all) is unknown.

Language used

The actual language that was used has been recorded nowhere. It may well be that the foreign merchants had some basic knowledge of Egyptian as well as that the Egyptian could understand some foreign languages. Some of the *šwty.w* bear Syrian names (Römer 1992, 279, n. 95). Unfortunately, it is unknown whether these were actually Syrians or descendants of Syrians resident in Egypt. In both cases they could have been bilingual and therefore the best qualified.

The pTurin 2008+2016 rto., 2,14 mentions a *jrt šwj(.t).w m jrt rˁ n ḫ3rw* 'bargaining in the Mouth of Syria'. Janssen (1961, 73) proposed 'bargaining' as a transferred interpretation. On the contrary Monroe (2000, 287) interprets the meaning of this expression more literally. Whatever the exact meaning, this expression shows an influence of Syrian language in Egypt concerning trade.

Bargaining between local traders and foreigners implies a basic knowledge of Egyptian as well as of Akkadian, the then *lingua franca*.

Weight standard and measure of value

During the Late Bronze Age different weight standards were in use in the Eastern Mediterranean area (Alberti and Parise 2005). We learn from the Uluburun shipwreck that merchants had different sets of balances on board (Pulak 2000). The standard of Ugarit, the 'Ugaritic' Shekel, weighed about 9 g. This is nearly equivalent to the Egyptian *ḳd.t* of 9,1g. Interestingly, the Amarna Letter EA 369 (Moran 1992, 366) mentions objects and their value in Shekel as well as the equivalent value in the Egyptian *dbn*. From this it follows that 1 *dbn* is worth 10 Shekel (Ranke 1937) and that 1 Shekel is equivalent to 1 *ḳd.t*. This would have facilitate trade between Egypt and Ugarit greatly.

The Egyptian *dbn* is not only used to define the weight of a certain object but also to determine its value. Many prices were expressed in *dbn* of gold, silver or copper and its fractions, the *ḳd.t,* as well as in *snjw* (Janssen 1975, 101–108; Römer 1999). However, as Römer (1999, 127) rightly stated, the weight is not necessarily the price. Beyond that, we have no documented prices from international trade.

Cost of stay

During the stay the crew would have required daily provisions of food and drink. The expenses are dependent on the length of stay, the number of crew members and the kind of provisions. A list of a crew's provisions is preserved dating to the reign of Ramesses II. In pLeiden I 350 vs. III 34 (Janssen 1961, 14, fig. 6; 39) every man of the crew received one loaf of bread per day. Prices of bread do not exist in abundance and they are between 1/5 and 1/10 *dbn* of copper each (Janssen 1975, 346). This would have been quite cheap and provisions for a crew of 10 would have cost 1 *dbn* of copper per day at most. Bread is staple food. Therefore it is likely that they would have also had fish and vegetables. The higher ranks might have had some meat. While fish would have been very cheap (Janssen 1975, 348–350) meat would have been much more expensive, as the prices for animals such as cattle, pigs and fowl were higher (Janssen 1975, 172–179). It is probable that the crew acquired Egyptian beer which was worth between two and four *dbn* depending on the quantum (Janssen 1975, 346–348).

Repairs to the ship would have generated costs as well. Thus a mast of (imported) ꜥš-tree would have cost between three and four *dbn* of silver (Janssen 1975, 377–378) which are equivalent to 180 or 240 *dbn* of copper respectively. Beams were much cheaper and made of local woods. Prices do not exceed four *dbn* of copper (Janssen 1975, 372–374), although we do not know their measurements. Minor repairs seem to have been easily affordable.

Expenditure might have been the payment of harbour workers for helping to unload and load the ship.

Finally, a port due may have been demanded. If this was dependent on the length of stay, the ship's captain would – naturally – have tried to cut the stay short.

Corruption, bribery, smuggling and fraud

Corruption and bribery

Both corruption (Helck 1982a; Müller-Wollermann 2004, 129–149) and bribery (el-Saady 1998) is well attested in ancient Egypt. Unfortunately, there is no direct source for these in connection with trade. No letter exists complaining about a higher payment of customs duty than usual although there is no record preserved of what might have been a usual amount. Beyond that we do not know whether it was dependent on the value of the load or if was paid per ship.

On the other hand, it might have been that the customs stations' official (as 'tollkeeper') accepted a corrupting gift and gave the 'receipt' without receiving the correct payment.

Smuggling

There is strong evidence for smuggling in Old Assyrian trade (Veenhof 1972, 307–310) as well as in later Greek and Roman times (Kudlien 2000). Therefore we may well assume that the Egyptians also dealt with smuggling. Two methods of smuggling exist: 1) by bypassing customs stations or 2) by declaring a lower value of goods or hiding goods in order to lower the customs duty. To meet this problem, an effective method would be a kind of 'receipt' issued by the customs station (fortress?) permitting trading only on the 'international harbour'.

Fraud at market

It is also thinkable that some local traders tried to 'influence' the result of the weighing. From the reign of Ramesses II the title of an *jry mḫ3.t* 'Keeper of balances' Sethynakht (al-Ayedi 2006, 163, no. 560; Kitchen 1980, 149:9) is attested. Unfortunately, nothing else apart from this title is mentioned. We know from the Bronze Age shipwreck of Uluburun that the trading ships had their own balance weights with them (Pulak 2000) At least, these could exclude a swindle by means of manipulated balance weights. However, there is room for manipulation as regards to the scales themselves. Local tradesmen might have deliberately incorrect justified their scales. In the case of quarrel, it is most likely that the *jmj-r3 mry.t* or his deputy had to deal with this.

Departure

After having finished bargaining of goods, the ship would have been ready to depart. Both unloading and loading were probably done with the help of the harbour's *smd.t*. In addition, provisions for the journey home had to be taken on board. Also the port due might have been paid shortly before departure.

The ship's captain potentially received a letter of acknowledgement to prove the fortress' official to pass through. After having passed the fortress it was on its way home.

Acknowledgements

I wish to thank Anna Kathrin Hodgkinson MA for reading the article and for correcting my English. All mistakes are, of course, my own. I am grateful to Dr Angus Graham for drawing my attention to problems of sailing on the Nile and for discussing these problems with me as well as to Dr Shelley Wachsmann who gave me his kind permission to use the drawing from his publication.

Bibliography

Alberti, M. E. and Parise, N. (2005) Towards an Unification of Mass-Units between the Aegean and the Levant. In R. Laffineur (ed.) *Emporia I. Aegeans in the Central and Eastern Mediterranean. Proceedings of the 10th International Aegean Conference, Athens, Italian School of Archaeology, 14–18 April 2004. AEGAEUM 25,* 381–390. Liège, Université de Liège.

Allam, S. (1998) Vermittler im Handel zur Zeit des Neuen Reiches. *Studien zur altägyptischen Kultur* 26, 3–18.

Altman, A. (1988) Trade between the Aegean and the Levant in the Late Bronze Age: Some Neglected Questions. In M. Heltzer and E. Lipiński (eds.) *Society and Economy in the Eastern Mediterranean (c. 1500–1000 B.C.). Proceedings of the International Symposium held at the University of Haifa from the 28th of April to the 2nd of May 1985*, 229–237. Leuven, Peeters.

Ayedi, A. R. al- (2006) *Index of Egyptian Administrative, Religious and Military Titles of the New Kingdom.* Ismailia, Obelisk Publications.

Bakir, A. el-M. (1952) *Slavery in Pharaonic Egypt.* Cairo, Imprimerie de l'Institut Francais d'Archéologie Orientale.

Bickel, S. (1998) Commerçants et bateliers au Nouvel Empire. Mode de vie et statut d'un groupe social. In N. Grimal (ed.) *Le commerce en Égypte ancienne. Bibliothèque d'Études 121*, 157–172. Cairo, Institut Francais d'Archéologie Orientale.

Bietak, M. (2006) Nomads or mnmn.t-Shepherds in the Eastern Nile Delta in the New Kingdom. In A. M. Maeir and P. de Miroschedji (eds) *"I will speak the riddles of ancient times": archaeological and historical studies in honor of Amihai Mazar on the occasion of his sixtieth birthday*, 123–136. Winona Lake, Eisenbrauns.

Bietak, M. (2009) Perunefer: an update. *Egyptian Archaeology* 35, 16–17.

Caminos, R. A. (1954) *Late Egyptian Miscellanies.* London, Oxford University Press.

Coutellier, V. and Stanley, D. J. (1987) Late Quaternary Stratigraphy and Palaeogeography of the Eastern Nile Delta, Egypt. *Marine Geology* 77, 257–275.

Edel, E. (1975) Zur Deutung des Keilschriftvokabulars EA 368 mit ägyptischen Wörtern. *Göttinger Miszellen 15*, 11–16.

Erman, A. and Grapow, H. (1928) *Wörterbuch der aegyptischen Sprache II.* Leipzig, J. C. Hinrichs Verlag.

Erman, A. and Grapow, H. (1957) *Wörterbuch der aegyptischen Sprache V.* Berlin, Akademie Verlag.

Fabre, D. (2004/2005) *Seafaring in Ancient Egypt.* London, Periplus Publishing.

Faulkner, R. O. (1953) Egyptian Military Organization. *The Journal of Egyptian Archaeology* 39, 32–47.

Gardiner, A. H. (1912) The Stele of Bilgai. *Zeitschrift für ägyptische Sprache und Altertumskunde* 50, 49–57.

Gardiner, A. H. (1937) *Late Egyptian Miscellanies.* Brussels, Éd. de la Fondation égyptol. Reine Élisabeth.

Gardiner, A. H. (1947) *Ancient Egyptian Onomastica I.* Oxford, University Press.

de Garis Davies, N. and Faulkner, R. O. (1947) A Syrian trading venture to Egypt. *The Journal of Egyptian Archaeology* 33, 40–46.

Goren, Y. *et al.* (2002) Petrographic investigation of the Amarna Tablets. *Near Eastern Archaeology* 65, 196–205.

Graham, A. (2005) Plying the Nile: Not all plain sailing. In K. Piquette and S. Love (eds) *Current Research in Egyptology 2003. Proceedings of the Fourth Annual Symposium*, 41–56. Oxford, Oxbow Books.

Griffith, F. Ll. (1927) The Abydos Decree of Seti I at Nauri. *The Journal of Egyptian Archaeology* 13, 193–208.

Habachi, L. (2001) *Tell el-Dab'a I. Tell el-Dab'a and Qantir: The Site and its connection with Avaris and Piramesse.* Wien, Verlag der Österreichischen Akademie der Wissenschaften.

Helck, H.-W. (1939) *Der Einfluss der Militärführer in der 18. Ägyptischen Dynastie.* Leipzig, J. C. Hinrichs Verlag.

Helck, W. (1958) *Zur Verwaltung des mittleren und neuen Reiches.* Leiden, Brill.

Helck, W. (1975) *Wirtschaftsgeschichte des Alten Ägypten im 3. und 2. Jahrtausend vor Chr.* Leiden, Brill.

Helck, W. (1982a) "Korruption" im Alten Ägypten. In W. Schuller (ed.) *Korruption im Altertum. Konstanzer Symposium 1979*, 65–70. München, R. Oldenbourg Verlag GmbH.

Helck, W. (1982b) Perunefer. In *Lexikon der Ägyptologie IV*, 990. Wiesbaden, Otto Harrassowitz.

Helck, H. (1992) Anmerkungen zum Turiner Königspapyrus. *Studien zur altägyptischen Kultur* 19, 151–216.
Helck, H. (2002) *Die datierten und datierbaren Ostraka, Papyri und Graffiti von Deir el-Medineh.* Wiesbaden, Harrassowitz.
Höckmann, O. (1987) Frühbronzezeitliche Kulturbeziehungen im Mittelmeergebiet unter besonderer Berücksichtigung der Kykladen. In *Ägäische Bronzezeit*, 53–108. Darmstadt, Wissenschaftliche Buchgesellschaft.
Janssen, J. J. (1961) *Two Ancient Egyptian Ship's Logs.* Leiden, Brill.
Janssen, J. J. (1975) *Commodity prices from the Ramessid period: an economic study of the village of Necropolis workmen at Thebes.* Leiden, Brill.
Jeffreys, D. G. (2006) Perunefer: at Memphis or Avaris?. *Egyptian Archaeology* 28, 37–38.
Jones, D. (1988) *A glossary of ancient Egyptian nautical titles and terms.* London, Kegan Paul International.
Kitchen, K. A. (1980) *Ramesside Inscriptions III. Historical and Biographical.* Oxford, B. H. Blackwell.
Kudlien, F. (2000) Antike Bezeichnungen für Schmuggel. *Münstersche Beiträge zur antiken Handelsgeschichte* 19, 100–108.
Lesko, L. (1982) *A Dictionary of Late Egyptian I.* Berkeley, B. C. Scribe Publ.
Lesko, L. (2002) *A Dictionary of Late Egyptian I.* Fall River, Fall River Modern Printing Co.
Lesko, L. (2004) *A Dictionary of Late Egyptian II.* Fall River, Fall River Modern Printing Co.
Monroe, C. M. (2000) *Scales of Fate: Trade, Tradition and Transformation in the Eastern Mediterranean ca. 1350–1175 BCE.* Michigan, UMI.
Moran, W. (1992) *The Amarna Letters.* Baltimore, The Johns Hopkins University Press.
Müller-Wollermann, R. (2004) *Vergehen und Strafen. Zur Sanktionierung abweichenden Verhaltens im Alten Ägypten.* Leiden, Brill.
Pulak, C. (2000) The Balance Weights from the Late Bronze Age shipwreck at Uluburun. In C. F. E. Pare (ed.) *Metals Make the World Go Round*, 247–266. Oxford, Oxbow Books.
Ranke, H. (1937) Keilschriftliches. *Zeitschrift für ägyptische Sprache und Altertumskunde* 73, 90–93.
Reineke, W.-F. (1979) Waren die šwtjw wirklich Kaufleute? *Altorientalische Forschungen* 6, 5–14.
Römer, M. (1992) Der Handel und die Kaufleute im Alten Ägypten. *Studien zur altägyptischen Kultur* 19, 257–284.
Römer, M. (1999) Gold/ Silber/ Kupfer – Geld oder nicht? Die Bedeutung der drei Metalle als allgemeine Äquivalente im Neuen Reich mit einem Anhang zu den Geldtheorien der Volkswirtschaftslehre. *Studien zur altägyptischen Kultur* 26, 119–142.
Saady, H. M. el- (1998) Considerations on Bribery in Ancient Egypt. *Studien zur altägyptischen Kultur* 25, 295–304.
Schiller, B. (2010) Customs Duty in the New Kingdom. In A. Hudecz and M. Petrik (eds) *Commerce and Economy in Ancient Egypt. Proceedings of the Third International Congress for Young Egyptologists, 25–27 September 2009, Budapest*, 119–124. Oxford, Archaeopress.
Sestini, G. (1989) Nile Delta: a review of depositional environments and geological history. In M. K. Whateley (ed.) *Deltas: Sites and Traps for Fossil Fuels*, 99–127. London, Blackwell.
Uphill, E. P. (1968) Pithom and Raamses: Their Location and Significance. *Journal of Near Eastern Studies* 27, 291–316.
Veenhof, K. R. (1972) *Aspects of Old Assyrian Trade and its Terminology.* Leiden, Brill.
Wachsmann, S. (1987) *Aegeans in the Theban Tombs.* Leuven, Peeters.
Wachsmann, S. (1998) *Seagoing Ships and Seamanship in the Bronze Age Levant.* College Station, Texas A&M University Press.
Warburton, D. A. (1997) *State and Economy in Ancient Egypt. Fiscal vocabulary of the New Kingdom.* Fribourg, University Press.
Wente, F. (1990) *Letters from Ancient Egypt.* Atlanta, Scholars Press.

Yoffee, N. (1976) Review of Aspects of Old Assyrian Trade and its Terminology by K. R. Veenhof. *Journal of Near Eastern Studies* 35, 62–65.

Zingarelli, A. (2010) Trade and Money in Ramesside Egypt: the Use of General Equivalents in Economic Transactions. In A. Hudecz and M. Petrik (eds) *Commerce and Economy in Ancient Egypt. Proceedings of the Third International Congress for Young Egyptologists, 25–27 September 2009, Budapest*, 177–184. Oxford, Archaeopress.

On defining myth: comparisons of myth theory from an egyptological viewpoint

David Stewart

Introduction

Egyptian myth has long been regarded as the most problematic aspect of Egyptian religion and literature. The contrast between the appearance of a number of deities and the lack of any text that can be easily identified as myth has caused the situation where scholars have questioned the existence of myth during the Old Kingdom in Egypt (Baines 1991, 81). The likely date given for an emergence of what one might term myth has often been placed in the New Kingdom and, in this, scholars have tended to assert the primacy of narrative in their definitions, leading to the conclusion that in texts where no narrative is present it is assumed there can be no myth. The existence of the phenomena being discussed, thus rests on the definition of the terms used to describe it (Goebs 2002, 30). This could be avoided if that definition were clarified (Goebs 2002, 29). The task of defining myth however is a vastly complex one that is compounded by the legion of definitions and approaches that have been proposed since the study of myth became popular in the Nineteenth and early Twentieth centuries. While a strict definition can be helpful in gaining knowledge about a particular aspect of myth, it dismisses all other aspects in asserting primary importance to a singular meaning. Concurrently a definition that attempts to take into account all the varying features of myth can run the risk of being so inclusive and broad that anything can become myth. This paper seeks to frame the problem of myth in Ancient Egypt by surveying the definitions and approaches of more general myth studies. Mediation between the divergent opinions in Egyptology can then be sought.

Egyptological Studies

Early scholarship on Egyptian myth, most notably Brugsch (1891), assumed the existence of myths and used the fragmentary evidence to reconstruct cults and gather evidence for myth. Followed up by Kees (1941), this approach assumed that the extant evidence was only a small amount of what had existed and thus exploited the fragmentary nature of the texts to assemble scattered allusions and evocations as evidence for myth. While this approach is acceptable for periods after the New Kingdom due to the wealth of preserved information, for earlier times it involves assuming the existence of myth due to the fragmentary nature of the evidence. The euhemerism of scholars like Sethe (1930) who saw myth as able to be mapped accurately onto historical events is largely and rightly ignored today, with only some positive assessments of his work coming notably from Griffiths (1960) who followed Sethe's interpretation of myth when looking at the conflict of Horus and Seth.

In the post Kees era, Schott (1942) was the first to discuss the problem of Egyptian myth, choosing to focus on the Pyramid Texts containing within them allusions to the world of the gods. His basic conclusion was that Egypt had no true myth before Early Dynastic times, only folktales, and that traces could be found of them in the Pyramid Texts (Schott 1945, 88–90). Myth for Schott must have a narrative coherence as well as being set in the past (Schott 1945, 111–112). Since both these features are missing from the early attestations in the Pyramid Texts, it is assumed that myth could not have existed when they were written down. Schott argues that there were narrative myths which appear late, while ritual was performed separately from myth, having a self-contained meaning in itself without needing any reference to anything else (Schott 1945, 83–109; Otto 1958, 26–27). It is only when the effectiveness of the ritual had begun to wane that myths became associated with it, lending their inherent authority to the ritual. Myth, thus, re-sacralised ritual and made it effective once more but stood subordinate to it, being distorted or even created by it (Baines 1991, 83). While this approach was expanded upon by Rudnitzky (1956) and Otto (1958) it is difficult to uphold due to the distinction between myth and folktales. Zeidler (1993) has analysed a number a Pyramid Text utterances to establish if they were mythological based on a method developed for folktales meaning that under these definitions, myths would have been preceded by tales about the gods that are not distinguishable in form from myth (Willems 1996, 11).

The most extensive treatment of myth comes from Jan Assmann and it is worthwhile to give a fuller account of his approach as it is expressed in his more sharply stated article from 1977. Assmann understands a myth to be a tale about the divine world that has narrative qualities, a beginning, middle and an end (Assmann 1977, 20–21). By showing that mortuary literature from before the New Kingdom is non-narrative he argues that this corpus of texts cannot be used to substantiate the existence of myth in early periods. Events in the Pyramid Texts which mention the gods, while being interpreted in various ways, do not form narratives and thus do not qualify as myth. Likewise Assmann denies the status of myth to the Ramesseum Dramatic Papyrus (Assmann 1977, 15–21), as well as fragments of Middle Kingdom texts, the most notable of these being the Horus and Seth fragment from Illahun (Assmann 1977, 33). Due to the lack of mythical narrative in early times, Assmann posits his own formulation, the constellation (Assmann 1977, 14), or the icon (Assmann 1982, 40–41), groupings of deities and the relations between them that are not based on a mythical narrative that extends beyond the momentary grouping and is situated in the past. Fundamental to this conception is his view that, during periods before the New Kingdom, the divine and human or "real" worlds were so close as to prohibit the formation of myths (Assmann 1977, 14). The distinction between the divine and real worlds is problematic as it seems to suggest the unreality of the divine world which, it must be stressed, was real for the Egyptians. Also the reality of the gods and the predominance of the constellation in early times need not be connected, the same groupings occur at later stages when narrative myth is clearly attested (Baines 1991, 87). Assmann cites magical spells, calendars of lucky and unlucky days and literary stories such as the Late Egyptian Horus and Seth as having narrative elements about the gods, terming these "mythical statements" (Assmann 1977, 28–36). This term would seem to suggest that these are not simple narrative myths. He continues to present a model for the relationship between a myth and its mythical statement identifying three different possible relations: the operative or iterative, explanatory or etiological, and literary or entertaining (Assmann 1977, 37). The first corresponds to magical spells, the second to discursive texts such as the Memphite Theology (Junker 1941, pl 1; trans Lichtheim 1973, 51–55) and the third to purely literary texts such as Horus and Seth (Gardiner 1932, 37–60; trans

Lichtheim 1976, 214–23). Assmann would have these relations operate on myth and transform it into the mythical statement that is extant. This implies a process whereby the myth becomes a fixed, abstract entity unavailable for direct analysis (Geno-Text), while the mythical statement is variable, being created from the myth (Pheno-Text) (Assmann 1977, 38–39). However this means that in periods before the New Kingdom a lack of mythical statements says little about the existence of myth and certainly does not directly imply a lack of myth. Assmann instead argues that the existence of myth implies a distance between the divine and real worlds and that, the detaching of these worlds, creates disenchantment or scepticism and the creation of the temporal framework. Assmann dates both of these shifts to the First Intermediate Period implying that a search for myth before this time would be fruitless (Assmann 1977, 39–43). The connection between myth and the emergence of scepticism towards the reality of the world of the gods should be questioned, as it implies a simplistic world view that cannot deal with the realities of existence when this need not be the case for the Egyptians, who exhibit a complex worldview. At all times the gods were worshipped with cult statues in temple settings but they were not thought of as identical with those images (Baines 1991, 91), and it is possible that at no one point did scepticism set in making Assmann's model difficult to uphold.

Baines in his works has differed slightly in his interpretation of myth, defining it as a centrally sacred narrative (Baines 1991, 94). Here he dispenses with the Aristotelian view of narrative, that Assmann adheres to, instead arguing that narrative is simply transitive: the situation at the end differs from that at the beginning. Realisations of myth might appear as small transitive elements in a wider context such as a ritual or as a whole story with many parts (Baines 1991, 94). While admitting they could be mobilised in a non-narrative context, he adds that this would differ from a narrative realisation. Baines argues that there is little evidence for the existence of myth in the early written record. As a means of explaining this absence he questions the importance of myth for Egyptian religion asserting the primacy of ritual rather than narrative dogma (Baines 1991, 99–100). Mythic material in any ritual would not appear as narrative and so, according to the approach of Baines, can only produce limited evidence for myth. Three main reasons for the scarcity of myth thus arise. It was not important for the main types of texts, those texts did not have suitable forms for narrative and the discourse of the texts focused on other concerns (Baines 1991, 101). Rituals like those found in the Pyramid texts are vehicles for performance rather than knowledge and thus are not suitable to hold narrative, instead containing brief fragments about the gods. Baines cautions against the idea of assuming that oral tradition partook in transmitting myth and that it used narrative forms to do so (Baines 1991, 105). The idea that narrative did not hold a primary place in Egyptian religion is an important distinction to be made but it does not follow that myth by implication was also unimportant.

This survey of Egyptological thought, although not exhaustive, highlights a particular problem with the way in which myth is approached and defined in general, particularly with regards to early evidence. The idea that the primary attribute of a myth is that it is a narrative, permeates scholarship, leaving one to explain the appearance of the gods in early texts in other ways. The German school of thought has advocated for a down-dating of myth, locating its emergence in the New Kingdom when narrative appears. While Baines (1991, 99–105) gives valid reasons for this down-dating in stating a lack of narrative myth in early periods, his argument that myth itself was unimportant for the main types of texts is still predicated on the notion that a myth is inseparable from its narration. This seems to disregard early evidence for myth based solely on linguistic features. If scholarship is to up-date its thought on myth, then a different mode of interpretation should be sought.

General Approaches to Myth

It is with this in mind that this paper turns to more general theories more commonly associated with the study of myth, in order to give a fuller account of myth allowing a more inclusive definition and approach. General definitions and approaches to myth are legion and diverse and so here have been categorised according to their main focus. There are six main types of myth theory:

- That which treats myth as a universal same that can be analysed cross culturally and associated with the comparative school of thought.
- hat which sees myth as a form of symbolic statement where the expression itself is of prime importance reflecting the thought of the mythopoeic.
- Psychoanalytical theories that treat myth as an expression of the unconscious.
- The school of ritualism which stresses the link between the myth and its associated rite.
- Functionalism as a subset of the ritualistic school would see myth in terms of its function to legitimise social institutions and structures.
- Finally the structuralist school which seeks to determine the purpose of a myth by looking at its semantic structure.

Theories that see myth in terms of explanation have commonly been referred to as nineteenth century intellectualism. a form of armchair anthropology which attributes early man with a kind of intellectual curiosity which leads them to explain their world in terms of myth (Cohen 1969, 338). For Frazer (1919), myths are to be seen as literal, with the explanation of certain phenomena as their primary purpose. To take one example, the story of the Tower of Babel is simply about a way of explaining the variety of languages and cultures, given that man came from common descendants (Frazer 1919, 362–87). Frazer's master piece *The Golden Bough* sought to explain the curious ritual at Nemi which sees a candidate for priesthood murder his predecessor in order to take his place (Frazer 1959, 1–9). His explanation is based on a promiscuous comparative analysis that draws on a wide variety of evidence all tending in the same direction, with no regard for cultural context and based on the assumption that all societies are essentially the same and evolve in the same way. For Tylor, myths are also primarily explanatory, making use of metaphor to explain the forces of nature and by so doing control them (Tylor 1958, 368). While these theories recognise primitive man as having intellect, they are rooted in the Victorian milieu which sought to prove the superior intellect of western Europeans who had moved beyond an age of 'magic'. The theories lack any explanation of the social aspects or symbolic content of myth (Cohen 1969, 339).

Mythopoeic thought has, as its origins, the work of Max Müller whose primary aim was to show that myth was an attempt to explain solar phenomenon. Müller saw a contradiction in the myths of ancient Greece which he saw as absurd and irrational when compared to the Greeks themselves who were thoughtful and intellectual (Müller 1867, 11). He attempted to show that the origins lay in the Indo-European societies whom he describes as poets of language (Müller 1867, 127). But they were poets of necessity, using a linguistic tool that was in its infancy and lacked the complexity needed. Myth, for Müller, comes about when these observations still remain after the society has become linguistically sophisticated. At some point people no longer understand the expressions and create myths to explain them. This he terms the 'disease of language' which degrades the mythopoeic ideals of the Aryas and transforms them into myth (Müller 1867, x). Thus he sees the myth of Endymion as coming about from expressions to do with the setting sun and the rising of the moon (Müller 1867, 81–84). Likewise Cassirer grounds his theory in the mythopoeic, seeking to show that myth is a way of using language for expressive purposes and that the creation of myth is an end in itself. Myth comes about through the mind interpreting the world regardless of the real objects found within it, myth is fantasy and is thus opposed to science and philosophy (Cassirer 2000, 40) which see reality. However if mythopoeic thought can be inferred from myth it does not explain it (Cohen 1969, 340). When myth is reduced to an end in itself it loses any meaningful purpose. These theories do not recognise that mythical thought is a way of ordering the world and is connected to activities of the mind that project onto the world.

The works of Freud and Jung typify the attempt of scholars to define and explain myth in terms of the unconscious. For Freud, myths are like dreams in that they house within them the distorted vestiges of wish fantasies of whole nations (Freud 1906–8, 152). In this way they are aimed at the resolution of unacceptable behaviour like incest, infantile sexual curiosity, expulsion, exclusion, and rivalries between parent and child as well as siblings. Freud argued for universal content that could be found in dreams of more than one individual (Csapo 2005 94). Frazer had already shown that myths of early societies had a remarkable amount of similar content despite geographical separation (Frazer 1919). This allowed Freud to explain the universality of myths in the same way he explained the universality of dreams, as the products of psychic activities (Csapo 2005, 94). In contrast to the personal view of Freud, Jung posits the existence of the collective unconscious (Jung 1959a 88–110) that myths can inform on through the motifs they use. Myth reveals the collective unconscious and serves as the intermediary between it and the conscious (Segal 1998, 17–18). Positing the existence of universal symbols which he termed archetypes, mythology becomes the "textbook of the Archetypes" (Walker 2002, 17), the unconscious is not explained but represented by myth. Going beyond this, myth allows the experience of the unconscious (Segal 1998, 18). Through a retelling the unconscious processes are re-experienced allowing the link between conscious and unconscious to be re-established (Jung 1959b 280). Myth can thus reveal much about the collective unconsciousness' of mankind as a whole. These theories, while detailing a revealing aspect of myth, fail to justify the use of the method on all myth, some myths might be heavy with psychological material while others may contain comparatively few revelations.

Durkheim departed from the individualistic, economist and materialistic view of Victorian anthropology focusing on the sociological. For Durkheim myths are an essential part of religious life (Durkheim 1915, 100) and they express in word what ritual does through action. The contents of myth like ritual are symbolically significant, they provide a society with the means to categorise their world (Cohen 1969, 343–4). They reflect social values and structure and thus function to maintain the solidarity of a group of people termed a 'society' (Durkheim 1915, 465). Malinowski follows the functionalist view of myth developed by Durkheim but differs in substituting the symbolic focus of Durkheim for a more pragmatic view of myth. He asserts a connection with the word – which he calls the *mythos* or sacred tale of a tribe – and the ritual act, moral deeds, and even their practical activities (Malinowski 1954, 96). The function of myth becomes about strengthening tradition by tracing it back to a higher, more supernatural reality (Malinowski 1954, 146). It established social order and codified belief and morality. Myths, thus, justified and perpetuated the pattern of thought of a social group and served as a foundation and warrant for its customs and institutions (Csapo 2005, 142). Malinowski sees in the content of myth neither explanatory power nor symbolic representation but justification (Malinowski 1954, 107).

Arising concurrent to the functionalist theory, Harrison can be seen as the chief exponent of the ritualist school coming out of Cambridge. Although never expressly stating her position, for Harrison myths are explanations of ritual, they are etiological providing a reason for the performance of a rite (Harrison 1963). Harrison makes the distinction between the spoken word that is myth, and that which is acted out, which is ritual (Harrison 1963, 328). This distinction remained influential and brought to the fore an aspect of myth that had been under emphasised in the view of myth as primarily verbal or literary. Her scheme, assembled from her scattered remarks, lays out a complex system, whereby primitive man moves through stages of development often correlating to a move towards scientific thinking (Harrison 1963). Primitive man started with the need to express emotions physically, through mimetic dance (Harrison 1963, 45), and, through this development, attains an age where the ritual had become so abstract that it was no longer performed, and myth arose to provide a reason to perform the ritual. Her tendency to over emphasise ritual and explain every mythic theme as coming from ritual lets her scheme down as even the race of titans was thought to have been derived from the roles of primordial leaders (Doty 2000, 338). Lord Raglan defends the position of the ritual school, arguing that myth is needed to validate rite through the stating of the details of the rite suggesting that myths which seemingly have no connection to a rite, were once associated with one (Raglan 1958, 80–81). Graves argues that true myth may be defined as the reduction to narrative shorthand of ritual (Graves 1955, 10), while Leach says that myth and ritual are both different methods of communicating the same message, they are symbolic statements about social structure (Leach 1954, 13–14). Ultimately however the ritualist school of thought does not provide a reason for the social function of myth to be performed by myth and not some other phenomena.

Finally the structuralist theory has attended more closely to the semantics contained within a myth rather than the anthropology behind it. For Lévi-Strauss the main function of myth is to mediate between oppositions and contradictions that men experience (Lévi-Strauss 1955, 56). The significance of a myth is thus not in the narrative itself but in the structure that first poses a contradiction and then mediates it (Munz 1973, 5). His most notable example is his analysis of the Oedipus myth which he breaks down into four main aspects: Oedipus marries his mother, kills his father, kills the sphinx, and becomes swollen footed. The first signifies an over-rating of blood relations, the second, an under-rating. His killing the sphinx denies the autochthonous nature of man, while his being swollen footed is symbolic of being born from the earth and so affirms the autochthonous nature of man. Thus the structure of the myth is that the over-rating of kinship is to under-rating as non-autochthony is to autochthony. The myth thus has to do with the inability of a society which holds the belief that man is born from one, to find a transition to the knowledge that people are born from the union of a man and woman (Lévi-Strauss 1955, 55). It provides a logical tool which relates the original problem (which is unsolvable) to the derivative problem (born from different or same) (Lévi-Strauss 1955, 56). While this method can have significant analytical outcomes its reduction of thought to binary contradictions is not necessarily the case all the time. It is not the case that all myth is oriented towards the mediation of contradictions.

Two Problems of Defining Myth

Returning to the original issue of this paper concerning the problem of the early evidence for myth in Egypt, contrary to clearing the situation up this survey confirms the problem and compounds it. There seems to be a reciprocal relationship between the definition of myth and the approach taken under that definition. Definition quite naturally defines approach but the approach also affects the definition, leading to a self confirming argument that ignores all others. Naturally a definition that a myth explains ritual (to take one example from above) is going to lead to an approach that analyses myth this way. But conversely an approach that emphasises the importance of ritual to myth will cause a circumscriptive definition that highlights that approach. Each aspect confirms the other in an almost cyclic pattern. The same can be said of the other schools discussed above that claim precedence over all other theories by stating that "myth is…". This highlights the first of two problems that a restrictive definition leads to a restrictive view of myth. Myth is not just explanation, psychology, sociology or semantics; it has autonomy of its own that needs to be understood in isolation as well as in conjunction with other modes of interpretation. Myth can also perform different functions simultaneously under a principal of functional economy, this being the tendency of early societies to fill an institution with multiple levels of meaning and interpretation which lend credence to the others (Cohen 1969, 351). Little is gained when just one aspect of myth is studied, for it cannot answer the question of why myth is made or why it is significant. Cohen (1969, 351) advocates that the answers to the questions of myth can be found in the linked functions that myth exhibits. This multi-functional approach provides a greater understanding of myth although he does not make an attempt to formally define myth except to say that narrative is of prime importance (Cohen 1969, 349).

This leads to the second problem of myth, the idea of narrative. As has already been seen, with Egyptological approaches narrative holds prime position as the defining factor of myth which leads to the notion of a lack of myth where this is not present. The same can be said of the general theories surveyed here which are all predicated on the idea that a myth is inseparable from its narration. Myth analysed as narrative only works when narrative is present and so, when this is lacking, the interpretation breaks down. This may not be an issue for the majority of civilisations but in Egypt the movement towards a canonisation of myth into narrative occurs fairly late, suggesting a formative process that, while being non-narrative, still could be considered myth. Honko (1984, 49) suggests that non-narrative allusions to myth can only be understood if a narrative is known to give a background, but this need not be the case. Narrative can serve the function of crystallising events and establishing a moment of creation. In essence it anchors the present in the past and provides a timeline back with a point of reference that need not be past beyond (Cohen 1969, 349–50). Given this moment of canonisation, a mode of interpretation and analysis for time periods before this occurs would still prove useful in identifying how myth functions outside of any narrative constraints. This would allow a much more comprehensive view of myth particularly in the field of Egyptology where narrative is lacking for the early periods.

Polyfunctionality and Myth

Advocating a more expansive and inclusive approach to myth, Doty (2000) lays out a complex definition that proves very useful to the study of early myth in Egypt. Doty's definition runs thus:

> "A mythological corpus consists of a usually complex network of myths that are culturally important, imaginal stories, conveying by means of metaphoric and symbolic diction, graphic imagery, and emotional conviction and participation, the primal, foundational accounts of aspects of the real, experienced world and humankind's roles and relative statuses within it. Mythologies may convey

the political and moral values of a culture and provide systems of interpreting individual experience within a universal perspective which may include the intervention of suprahuman entities as well as aspects of the natural and cultural orders. Myths may be enacted or reflected in rituals, ceremonies and dramas, and they may provide materials for secondary elaboration, the constituent mythemes (mythic units) having become merely images or reference points for a subsequent story, such as a folktale, historical legend, novella or prophecy" (Doty 2000, 33–34).

This sort of definition lacks the usual brevity of other approaches but in its complexity it allows for a more comprehensive and polyfunctional view of myth. A few notes on the ideas expressed by this definition help to highlight its usefulness in forming a mode of interpretation that can be applied to many different realisations of myth. A complex network of myths implies the interrelation of items in a mythological corpus (Doty 2000, 34). It is seldom the case that one myth can constitute a canon, so to speak, that actualises a world view of the culture. Myth can be the simple linking of categories (Scheid and Svenbro 1996, 3) that together make up the canon rather than just a sample of the corpus. Myth may undergo a multitude of transformations throughout its transmission, which means that it can fit several different classifications at one point depending on the function of the myth within the society or the external framework imposed upon it by the analyst (Doty 2000, 37). This alone would suggest a need to move away from the monomythic definitions that emphasise one aspect of myth, as the above definition allows for a diverse range of elements and functions while realising that each feature or function may be actualised completely in one context. The definition includes the troublesome (and ambiguous) term 'story', asserting that a narrative story is implied no matter the outward appearance of the material (Doty 2000, 42). However, in a revision, Doty (2000, 49) includes his reservations at the continued use of narrativity, given the importance of texts like genealogies which were, for the Greeks, mythological. Instead he advocates a move towards looking at mythicity, a term used by Gould (1981, 3) to define the nature of myth as opposed to just certain myths. This move is aimed at a generalised orientation to the experienced world based upon a myth or series of myths which could prove useful in studying non-narrative myths. Distinction is made between the degrees of elaboration that can occur with a myth, ranging from the most important, where a myth is given a direct cognitive status, to the least important, where a myth has become an empty image. This range is referred to as 'functional vitality' (Doty 2000, 79), where a myth can have differing levels of vitality at different times or as experienced by different members of society.

Doty (2000, 137–140) distinguishes between three phases of vitality: primary myth, implicit myth and rationalised myth. In the first, the myth addresses itself to the needs of a society to answer significant problems and questions regarding human existence. There are no mythic narratives at this stage as it is formative, where inconsistencies and timelines have yet to be established (Doty 2000, 138). The second phase of implicit myth sees the central mythic story become widespread and accepted, as contradictions are solved and orthodoxy established. The myth is so much a part of culture that it is accepted as the only natural way of seeing the world (Doty 2000, 139). Finally the third phase comes about when the myth is no longer accepted wholly as new myths might come into existence to challenge the world view (Doty 2000, 139). The concern of myth, here, is to preserve the original by rationalising it and incorporating it into a newer understanding. Moore (1972, 37) remarks that when people say "what the myth really means is…" they are well into the third phase of rationalising a myth. It must be kept in mind that an over broad definition can run the risk of straying to the opposite extreme of the monomythic, in skating over the significant differences between myths (Scarborough 1994,

29) and that, by their very nature, definitions are restrictive in being external to the phenomena they seek to explain (Hatab 1990, 17). Nevertheless this above approach to myth can highlight its multiplicity of uses and functions and allow for a better understanding of myth in contexts where no narrative is present.

Conclusion

Some positive and negative conclusions can come from this paper regarding the lack of treatment, in Egyptological thought, of early myth. Any attempt to define myth formally is going to be problematic; mythic language, by its very nature, is prone to a plurality of meanings that are however not all present in all examples of myths. There are as many definitions of myth as there are students and to reach a consensus is likely a flight of fancy. However, in trying to include different types of mythological tradition and expression that are not just valid for one culture but applicable to many differing cultures and time periods, Doty has made a remarkable contribution to the study of myth, allowing leaps forward in the way that myth is approached in Egyptology. The inseparability of a myth and its narrative has caused the tendency to down-date the appearance of myth in Egypt to later periods where narrative is present. Far from helping the issue, modern theories of myth compound the problem, but in this they confirm the need for a wider more inclusive definition of myth that can be applied in a wider variety of contexts. The poly-functional approach of Doty, combined with his notion of operational vitality, allows one to analyse non-narrative myth without the need to dispense with the notion of narrative that is a key aspect of the later stages of myth formation. This could have wide reaching potential in Egyptology, allowing one to up-date the appearance of myth to an earlier time and giving a more comprehensive understanding on the way myth was used in the early texts. What remains is an in depth study of the early texts, such as the Pyramid Texts, in order to gauge the type of mythic information contained in them and the way in which it operates and its importance for society.

Bibliography

Assmann, J. (1977) Die Verborgenheit des Mythos in Agypten. *Göttinger Miszellen* 25, 7–43
Assmann, J. (1982) Die Zeugung des Sohnes: Bild, Spiel, Erzahlung and das Problem des agyptischen Mythos. In J. Assmann *et al.*, *Funktionen und Leistungen des Mythos: Drei altorientalische Beispiele*, Orbis Biblicus et Orientalis 48 (Freiburg, Switzerland and Göttingen, 1982) 13–61.
Baines, J. (1991) Egyptian Myth and Discourse: Myth, Gods and the Early Iconographic Record. *Journal of Near Eastern Studies*, Vol. 50, No. 2, 81–105.
Brugsch, H. (1891) *Religion und Mythologie der alten Aegypter.* Leipzig.
Cassirer, E. (2000) *The Logic of the Cultural Sciences: Five Studies.* Trans. S. G. Lofts. New Haven, Yale University Press.
Cohen, P. (1969) Theories of Myth. *Man, New Series,* Vol. 2, No 3, 337–353.
Csapo, E. (2005) *Theories of Mytholog.* Oxford, Blackwell.
Doty, W. G. (2000) *Mythography: The Study of Myths and Rituals* 2nd Edition. Tuscaloosa, University of Alabama Press.
Durkhem, E. (1915) *The Elementary Forms of Religious Life.* Trans. J. W. Swain. New York, Free Press.

Frazer, J. G. (1919) *Folklore in the Old Testament: Studies in ComparativeReligion Legend and Law.* Vol. 1. London, Macmillan.
Frazer, J. G. (1959) *The Golden Bough: A Study in Magic and Religion* Abridged ed. London, Macmillan.
Freud, S. (1906–8) *The Standard Edition of the Complete Psychological Works of Sigmund Freud.* Trans. J. Strachey ed, 24 Vols. London, Hogarth Press.
Gardiner, A. H. (1932) *Late-Egyptian Stories,* Bibliotheca Aegyptiaca 1. Brussels.
Goebs, K. (2002) A Functional Approach to Egyptian Myth and Mythemes, *Journal of Near Eastern Religions,* Vol. 2, 27–59.
Gould, E. (1981) *Mythical Intentions in Modern Literature.* New Jersey, Princeton University Press.
Graves, R. (1955) *The Greek Myths.* Vol. 1. Harmondsworth, Penguin.
Griffiths, J. G. (1960) *The Conflict of Horus and Seth from Egyptian and Classical Sources: A Study in Ancient Mythology.* Liverpool, University Press.
Hatab, L. J. (1990) Myth and Philosophy: A Contest of Truths. La Salle III, Open Court.
Harrison, J. (1963) *Themis: A Study of the Social Origins of Greek Religion.* New York, World Publishing.
Honko, L. (1984) The Problem of Defining Myth. In A. Dundes (ed.) *Sacred Narrative: Readings in the Theory of Myth,* 41–52. Berkely, University of California Press.
Jung, C. G. (1959a) The Archetypes and the Collective Unconscious, trans R. F. C Hull. In *The Collected Works of C. G. Jung,* Ed. H. Read, M. Fordham and G. Adler, Vol. 9 pt 1. London, Routledge and Kegan Paul.
Jung, C. G. (1959b) Aion: Researches into the Phenomenology of the Self, trans R. F. C Hull, in *The Collected works of C. G. Jung,* Ed. H. Read, M. Fordham and G. Adler, Vol. 9 pt 2. London, Routledge and Kegan Paul.
Junker, H. (1941) *Die politische Lehre von Memphis,* Abhandlungen der Preussischen Akademie der Wissenschaften, Phil.-hist. Kl. No. 6. Berlin.
Kees, H. (1941) Der Gotterglaube im alten Agypten. *Mitteilungen der Vorderasiatisch-Ägyptischen Gesellschaft* 45.
Lévi-Strauss, C. (1963) Structural Anthropology 1, trans. C. Jacobson and B. G. Schoepf. NY.
Lichtheim, M. (1973) *Ancient Egyptian Literature: A Book of Readings,* Vol. 1. Berkeley, University of California Press.
Lichtheim, M. (1976) *Ancient Egyptian Literature: A Book of Readings,* Vol. 2. Berkeley, University of California Press.
Malinowski, B. (1954) *Magic, Science and Religion and Other Essays.* New York, Anchor Books.
Moore, R. E. (1972) Myth America 2001. Philadelphia, Westminster.
Müller, F. M. (1867) *Chios from a German Workshop.* Vols. 1–2. London, Longmans, Green.
Munz, P. (1973) *When the Golden Bough Breaks: Structuralism or Typology?* London, Routledge.
Otto, E. (1958) *Das Verhaltnis von Rite und Mythus im Ägyptischen, Sitzungsberichte der Heidelberger Akademie der Wissenschaften.* Heidelberg.
Raglan, L. (1958) Myth and Ritual. In *Myth: A Symposium.* Ed. T. A. Sebeok, 76–83. Bloomington, Indiana University Press.
Rudnitzky, G. (1956) *Die Aussage iiber "das Auge des Horus": Eine altdgyptische Art geistiger Ausserung nach dem Zeugnis des Alten Reiches.* Analecta Aegyptiaca 5. Copenhagen.
Segal, R. (1998) *Jung on Mythology.* London, Routledge.
Scheid, J. and Svenbro, J. (1996) The Craft of Zeus: Myths of Weaving and Fabric. Trans. C. Volk. Cambridge, Mass and Harvard, University Press.
Schott, S. (1942) Spuren der Mythenbildung. *Zeitschrift für Ägyptische Sprache and Altertumskunde* 78, 1–27.
Schott, S. (1945) *Mythe und Mythenbildung im alten Agypten.* Untersuchungen zur Geschichte und Altertumskunde Ägytens 14. Leipzig.

Sethe, K. (1930) *Urgeschichte und älteste Religion der Ägypter.* Leipzig, DMG.
Walker, S. (2002) *Jung and the Jungians on Myth: An Introduction.* New York and London, Routledge.
Willems, H. (1996) *The Coffin of Heqata: A Case Study of Egyptian Funerary Culture of the Early Middle Kingdom.* Leuven, Uitgeverij Peeters en Departement Oriëntalistiek.
Zeidler, J. (1993) Zur Frage der Spätentstehung des Mythos in Ägytpen. *Göttinger Miszellen* 132, 85–109.

Manipulated corpses in Predynastic Egyptian tombs: deviant or normative practices?

Veronica Tamorri

Our modern western views of the world lead us to put boundaries between what is 'normal' and what is 'abnormal', with the latter always embodying a negative meaning. Ancient societies are generally interpreted through such lenses, although it is unlikely that past people would read their world and the events of life with our same 'sensibility'. In this respect, it would not be surprising if Predynastic Egyptians did not perceive as aberrant both the funerary practices that we would label as 'deviant' (*e.g.* manipulation of corpses), and the individuals who underwent such treatments. Preliminary analysis of the evidence carried out for my doctoral research, and deriving from Predynastic Egyptian cemeteries such as Adaïma, Gerzah, el Amrah and Naqada, suggests that a considerable number of tombs, dating between *c*. 4000 and 3000 BC, exhibits unusual funerary body treatments. These practices range from incisions of bones, full or partial disarticulation of bodies and displacement of parts of the skeleton as well as their substitution with objects. Such treatments have frequently been attributed a negative connotation and have been associated with deviant practices such as cannibalism, human sacrifice, punishment for incorrect behaviours (*e.g.* Petrie 1896; Crubézy *et al.* 2000) or, more simply, with the result of tomb looting. These interpretations are not entirely convincing for two reasons: first, they assume that bodily manipulation embodied a negative meaning for the people who practiced them and expressed marginal identities; second, my preliminary analysis of the funerary context does not support any of the explanations proposed so far. Although the use of violent practices to punish or make the deceased innocuous might, in some cases, be a plausible hypothesis (*e.g.* Dougherty and Friedman 2008), the frequency and variety of forms of body treatments, identified in Predynastic cemeteries, requires a more articulated explanation. The preliminary results of my research reveal that funerary body manipulations were an integral component of mortuary rituals and do not seem to have embodied a deviant connotation. The presence of a manipulated body in a grave is, in fact, not sufficient *per se* to indicate that a tomb was anomalous. This hypothesis needs to be supported by contextual elements such as the atypical location of the tomb, the presence of unusual grave goods or the evidence of non-conventional rituals. In the funerary context examined here, such elements are not present, hinting at the normative nature of practices of body manipulation.

Results of preliminary statistical analysis carried out on a sample of approximately 1000 Predynastic tombs, and the presentation of specific case studies selected from the sites of Adaïma, el Amrah, Naqada (Upper Egypt) and Gerzah (Lower Egypt), will show that manipulated tombs were an integral part of the Predynastic mortuary landscape. The analysis of the material culture and funerary rituals associated with individuals selected for practices of body manipulation will indicate that those who underwent such treatments were likely to have been considered valued members of the community in the same way as those who were buried intact. Practices of body manipulation were not sporadic and atypical events, necessarily reserved to those at the margin of society (*e.g.* criminals), but in fact cross-cut the sample considered here, and must have been legitimate practices coexisting with the rest of the rites. The location of manipulated burials in the formal cemetery, as well as the fact that they do not display anomalous patterns in the composition of the grave assemblages in respect to non-manipulated graves, will further support my argument.

Normative versus deviant funerary ritual: a short history of study

In order to provide the reader with some fundamental notions which will allow a thorough understanding of the argument presented here, the following section of the paper will present a theoretical and historical background to the use of the term 'deviant' in funerary archaeology.

The concept of 'deviant' was first adopted during the 1930s to draw a distinction between normative and anomalous mortuary practices (Aspöck 2008, 19). Since then, 'deviant' has become synonym with rare, idiosyncratic or abnormal mortuary behaviours falling outside the standard funerary ritual of a given culture. On the other hand, the concept of 'normative' has embodied the more positive meaning of standard, common and typical funerary customs, representing the rules set by a group or society to dispose of their dead. Deviant and normative have also often been put in contrast with each other (*e.g.* Korpisaari 2006, 189), in order to emphasize the abnormality and negative value archaeologists tend to attribute to some funerary behaviours. Forms of deviancy can concern every aspect of the funeral: the tomb can be located in an unusual place or outside the cemetery or it can be provided with uncommon grave goods. Unusual treatments of the corpses, especially those involving the destruction of the body of the deceased, are most commonly interpreted as 'deviant' by researchers (*e.g.* Chapman 2010), probably due to their rare use (in respect to normative ones) and to the sometimes macabre outcome of some of such practices.

A deviant burial has been associated to the deposition of 'deviant social persona' by Saxe (1970). This latter concept was created to indicate individuals whose social identity was considered exceptional, either in a positive or negative sense (*e.g.* 'hero' as well as 'criminal'). Saxe believed that the extraordinary conditions of life and/or death of 'deviant social personae' could result in either a particularly lavish funeral, or in the loss of their rights to be buried according to the rules of the group they belong to. Saxe's model was further developed by Shay (1985), who elaborated three hypotheses to identify forms of deviancy. First, she noted that each society has its own criteria to define what is deviant (Shay 1985, 223). Second, the social persona represented in a deviant burial may not correspond to the identity the deceased embodied in his/her life, but to the altered identity they acquired by breaching the social norm. Anomalous identities positively evaluated by the group would result in 'complex social personae', and in the deposition of wealthy or prestigious 'funerary components' in the tomb (Shay 1985, 226). If, instead, the deviancy were negatively valued by the community it would originate 'shallow social personae', characterised by poor grave assemblages (Shay 1985, 226). Third, simple societies are not able to distinguish between volitional and non-volitional forms of deviant behaviour (*e.g.* suicidal *vs.* death in childbirth). Therefore, both behaviours are likely to result in the same kind of either complex or shallow social persona, and to receive similar funerals, very difficult to distinguish in the archaeological record (Shay 1985, 228).

More recently, in his study on the funerary practices of Postclassical Maya, Duncan (2005) has discussed the implications of the concepts of veneration and violation of the deceased. By adopting ritual practices of veneration, the community attempts to grant both a safe journey to the soul of the dead and the preservation of his/her memory. Violation, instead, aims at destroying the soul and memory of the deceased (2005, 207). Indeed, the social identities of the individuals who undergo funerary practices of either veneration or violation are perceived very differently by the group, as very different is the treatment of their remains. For example kings, saints, or prominent members of the community, destined to become ancestors, will be venerated by means of the appropriate rituals and practices in use in that specific cultural context. On the other hand, people who committed suicide, sick individuals, or murderers are likely to become the victims of acts of violation, because they are perceived as a danger for the community. Despite of these marked differences in purpose, Duncan (2005, 208) argues that the remains deriving from processes of violation and veneration may be very similar – as in the Postclassical Maya context – given that even practices not intended to mistreat the deceased might imply the adoption of forms of ritual violence. According to Duncan, the use of destructive funerary practices to express veneration is better explained by Bloch's (1992) model of ritual violence (Duncan 2005, 209). In all the three stages of Bloch's model (Separation, Liminal Phase, Incorporation), violent acts are essential to the correct performance of the ritual and are not intended to express deviancy or abnormality (Duncan 2005, 209).

Methodological considerations

The theoretical approaches described above provide interesting hints which can help build an *ad hoc* methodology to study practices of body manipulation in Predynastic Egypt.

The most appropriate starting point for the analysis of either processes of veneration/violation or of normative/deviant behaviours is to establish what constitutes the normative mortuary ritual of the context under investigation, as this will make deviancy relatively easier to identify. Statistical analysis has been adopted to investigate Predynastic funerary practices and some preliminary results will be presented later in the paper. It is also worth noting that, when verifying what is normative as opposed to what is deviant in a given culture, some general rules should be kept in mind. Firstly, to attribute an *a priori* meaning – either normative or deviant – to some practices, only based on our modern western perception, is misleading. The value of any practice is not intrinsic, but given by the context in which it is performed and varies significantly according to place and time. Secondly, it is possible that, due to a lack of information on aspects of the ritual which rarely leave material remains, the resulting interpretation of the archaeological record might be biased. Finally, the representation of the deceased provided by the mourners may not reflect his/her real identity in life, and consequently it might compromise the interpretation of the evidence.

In order to be considered normative, a tomb needs to be consistent with the rest of the graves in the cemetery or, in other words, it needs to represent the standardised set of rules that a culture, group, or community adopts to deal with death. A normative burial might be located inside the formal cemetery, namely the area chosen by the community to dispose of their dead. It is worth noting, however, that, in the past, graveyards were not necessarily sacred delimited areas as today; the dead could be buried under the house, burnt and the ashes dispersed, or just abandoned at the mercy of nature. These practices, despite their anomalous character for our modern perception, might have been considered normative for the culture that produced them. Moreover, if the funerary ritual of a given culture prescribes the use of grave goods, normative burial will be provided with them, or *vice versa*. Finally, in normative tombs the corpse(s) are treated as required by the protocol of such culture.

On the other hand, a deviant burial is usually very different from the average tomb of the culture under study. Such diversity can be represented by an unusual or different location in respect to the other burials – *i.e.* outside, at the margins, or in a particular area of the cemetery. Furthermore, if the normative funerary ritual prescribes the use of grave goods, abnormal burials will contain no items at all (and *vice versa*), or will enclose non-standard objects (namely items which are usually not employed as funerary implements and seem to be aimed to emphasise the non-normative nature of the deposition). Finally, the body treatments reserved to anomalous burials tend to be inconsistent with the rest of the cemetery.

Predynastic normative funerary ritual

During the Predynastic or Naqada period (*c.* 4000–3000 BC) a set of mortuary practices, by and large common to all the communities of the Nile valley, can be considered the normative funerary ritual of the time. Inhumation is the only type of burial known in Predynastic Egypt, and tombs are almost always located into cemeteries nearby the settlements (although some rare cases of infants buried under the floor of the houses have been reported; see Crubézy *et al.* 2000). More in detail, tombs dating to Naqada I (*c.* 4000–3500 BC) are roughly circular or oval shallow pits directly dug in the soil without any kind of lining. Covered by a layer of sand (more or less thick), Naqada I tombs were provided with few grave goods such as pottery, jewellery and cosmetic palettes. During Naqada II (*c.* 3500–3200 BC) tombs are mostly still circular or oval, but rectangular shaped pits become quite common. The use of mud mixed with sand, wood and mud to line the internal walls of tombs increases. The range of items accompanying the dead is similar to that of Naqada I, although changes in the manufacturing techniques of the objects may reflect the growth of a more specialised craftsmanship. This is particularly evident for objects such as decorated pots, animal-shaped cosmetic palettes and flint blades. During Naqada III (*c.* 3200–3000 BC), the architecture of tombs becomes far more elaborate, with multiple storage rooms equipped with hundreds of grave goods and protected by more sophisticated superstructures, usually in mud-brick. During the Naqada period bodies were disposed of in foetal or crouched position, laying on one side (more commonly the left), with the hands in front of the face or the chest, the head pointing towards south and the face directed to west. The habit to cover the bodies with mats of reed, linen or animal skins starts from Naqada I. Practices such as the wrapping of the head and hands of the deceased into linen bands, soaked in resin, as well as the appearance of wooden and mud coffins, are documented from Naqada II (Stevenson 2009, 4).

Some examples of Predynastic normative burials will further clarify what said thus far. Located within the formal burial ground at the site of el Amrah (Upper Egypt), non-manipulated Tomb A91 belonged to an adult male. The man was laying on his right side in an oval pit, simply dug in the sand and without any elaborate architectural feature. A number of grave goods such as two limestone pegs, a turtle-shaped cosmetic palette, an alabaster vase and a couple of tusks were all near or in contact with the body of the deceased. The 12 to 18 year-old individual buried in Tomb 216 at Adaïma (Upper Egypt) did not show any sign of body manipulation. The corpse was laying on the left side with the hands before the face and was oriented south-east to north-west. The grave goods placed in this tomb were three ceramic vessels and a nodule of ochre. Also in this case the grave was inside the cemetery and consisted of a simple pit dug in the sand. Tomb 133 from Gerzah (Lower Egypt) contained the remains of an adult disposed of in a foetal position on the left side, covered with dried mud and accompanied by a large amount of grave goods. Over 600 beads of various materials adorned the head of the deceased; an ivory spoon, a palette, some stone and pottery vessels were also arranged in the tomb.

Variability in Predynastic funerary record

What has been described so far accounts for the arrangement of the majority of Predynastic tombs. However, it would not be entirely correct to picture Predynastic burial costumes as homogeneous or standardised. The archaeological record illustrates a far more complicated situation in respect to that usually pictured by scholars. Predynastic funerary ritual was all but static or confined in pre-determined rules. Variability seems to have pertained to a large portion of graves in each cemetery, hinting at the presence of marked local traits (Stevenson 2009, 129–130). It encompassed all aspects of the ritual, ranging from the architecture of the tomb, to the grave goods as well as the body treatments. Each Predynastic cemetery analysed in my research presents peculiar features often unique to one site. A detailed account of this phenomenon cannot be given here for reasons of space; however, a short summary will suffice for the purpose of the paper. The first index of diversity is that existing between the north and south of the country. In the Delta and Lower Egypt tombs of the Maadi culture (Midant-Reynes 2003, 53–56) remained poor (from a quantitative point of view) at least till the end of Naqada II and the beginning of Naqada III (*c.* 3500–3100 BC) (Seeher 1992, 231), when Upper Egyptian culture seems to have spread to the north (Stevenson 2009, 2; Bard 2003, 58). In Upper Egypt a more marked and increasing social differentiation has been considered at the origin of the changes in funerary customs (Midant-Reynes 2000, 188). Furthermore, between Naqada I and Naqada II the preferred tomb shape changes from circular to rectangular, although the former was never entirely replaced by the latter. Consequently, great variability in the form of tombs, also among contemporaneous graves in the same cemetery (*e.g.* Petrie *et al.* 1912; Crubézy *et al.* 2000), is not rare. This is also the case for the habit to dispose of the body into leather bags or reed mat as opposed to leaving it unwrapped (Crubézy *et al.* 2000). The more emblematic element of variability is, however, represented by the orientation of tombs (Petrie *et al.* 1912, 5; Castillo 1982). This aspect of the funeral can significantly vary even within the same cemetery, with even neighbour tombs often oriented differently.

Up to a certain point, variability can be considered physiological of every culture; however, it is likely that the crucial transformations which were affecting the political and cultural asset of Egypt during the 4th millennium (see *e.g.* Wengrow 2006, 33–38) increased the phenomenon to a great extent, as my sample is starting to underscore. This variability, which can pertain to all aspects of the funeral, cannot be labelled as deviant *per se*. Rather, the phenomena illustrated until now indicate that variability, accompanied by the basic normative practices described in the previous section, was the characterising feature of Predynastic funerary rituals. As discussed below, therefore, the manipulation of bodies can represent just one of the ritual options adopted by Predynastic communities to deal with their dead.

Manipulated human remains

As mentioned above, in Predynastic funerary archaeology the discovery of uncommon body treatments has frequently been associated with cannibalism (Petrie 1896), human sacrifice (*e.g.* Crubézy *et al.* 2000), and punishment for deviant behaviours (Dougherty and Friedman 2008).

The frequency of practices of funerary body manipulation is not too high in the sample considered in this paper, representing only 16.2% of the specimens. However, other elements of the ritual pertaining to manipulated individuals suggest that they were valued members of the group and that, therefore, such treatments of the corpses were not necessarily aimed to mistreat them.

Of the overall sample considered here, 38.1% of the individuals whose body was manipulated were males, 39.4% were females and 22.5% were undetermined (most of the latter aged between birth and adolescence). This shows a homogeneous distribution of the practices across the two sexes, with a slight predominance of women. The results concerning the age distribution of practices of body manipulation are more heterogeneous. Young adults (20–35 years) seem to be the preferred subjects of the rituals, as they represent 37.3% of the sample, followed by middle adults (35–50 years), representing 26.2% of the dataset, and adolescents (12–20 years), that represent 16.1% of the sample. The elderly (50+ years), infants (b–3 years) and children (3–12 years) also underwent some form of manipulation (9.4%, 5.1% and 4.2% of the sample, respectively). Given the uneven distribution of the age groups across the sample (*e.g.* scarcity of children at certain sites), additional analysis will be carried out in future publications to ascertain whether the percentages delineated above represent real trends in practices of manipulation in relation to the age of the deceased.

All burials with manipulated individuals were located within formal cemeteries. In some instances they occupied prominent locations, such as the highest area of the site, or were the oldest tombs within the site (*e.g.* Tomb 55 at Adaïma). Tomb architecture was, in most of the cases, very simple with the bodies just arranged into a pit and covered with mats of reed. The occurrence of mud coffins and mud-brick lining is rare but worth mentioning. Tomb structures of this kind are also attested for non-manipulated individuals. Grave goods were granted to 22.5% of the manipulated individuals, a figure in line with the non-manipulated sample. None of the individuals who underwent funerary body manipulation seem to have suffered from diseases or malformations which could single them out in the community, making them perfect candidates of funerary deviant practices. According to the preliminary results of my research, the most common forms of manipulation were disarticulation, bone removal and incision as well as de-fleshment.

Case studies

The following paragraphs will illustrate selected cases of bodily manipulation at the Predynastic sites of el Amrah, Adaïma, Naqada, (Upper Egypt) and Gerzah (Lower Egypt).

In Cemetery A at el-Amrah, at least two tombs seem to have contained manipulated human remains (Randall-MacIver and Mace 1902). Tomb A96 (Randall-MacIver and Mace 1902, 19) was a single burial in which the body had been disarticulated and then disposed of in the tomb (Randall-MacIver and Mace 1902, 19). The leg bones were separated from the trunk and arranged parallel to several flint blades. The rest of the body was not in anatomical connection, but the bones were orderly grouped in the centre of the tomb, facing a quite rich array of objects. These included two cosmetic palettes, two mace-heads and some pins. All around the disarticulated human remains several pottery vessels were also arranged. At a closer look it would seem that human remains and grave goods had been purposely intermingled to convey a certain message. In this case, it is likely that the aim of bone disarticulation was to render the human remains more easily combinable with the many grave goods displayed in the pit, and not to show disrespect towards the dead. Moreover, Tomb A96 was in the cemetery and its architectural features were in all similar to the rest of the graves of the cemetery.

At the site of Naqada, Cemetery T offers several interesting examples of manipulated human remains (Petrie 1896). Intact Tomb T 5 is indubitably one of the most representative cases of body manipulation of the entire Predynastic period. The structure of the tomb suggests a quite accurate work, since the walls had been cut to give a quadrangular shape to the grave. The presence of six skulls would indicate that at least six individuals were buried there. Five out of the six skulls were lined up in the middle of the tomb, whereas the sixth was placed on top of a brick near the southern wall. The centre of the grave was occupied by a heap of completely disarticulated bones – presumably belonging to the six individuals. Most of the bones were broken at their ends and 'the cellular structure had been scooped out forcibly', suggesting to Petrie the possibility of cannibalism (1896, 32). A number of grave goods were recorded by the excavator (Petrie 1896, 19–20). Beneath and between the skulls beads, stone vases, malachite and a schist palette had been arranged. All around the walls of the grave pottery, probably containing food offerings and ashes, had also been placed. Intact Tombs T 19 and T 42 were single inhumations containing manipulated human remains (Petrie 1896, 20). The legs and twelve vertebrae of the individual buried in T 19 were in the centre of the tomb, apparently in anatomical position. The rest of the bones had been disarticulated and dispersed, with the arms placed parallel near the southern wall of the grave (Petrie 1896, 20). The funerary equipment of T 19 was quite large with several jars containing ashes and fat, placed along the north and west walls of the tomb. The individual in Tomb T 42 had the legs scattered on the north-western corner of the grave, whereas some vertebrae and rib bones were on the opposite side, and the arms in the centre of the pit (Petrie 1896, 20). This tomb was provided with one jar.

The site of Adaïma (Upper Egypt) consists of two cemeteries (east and west) and a settlement area (Midant-Reynes 2002, 5–7). Cases of missing heads, fragmented and disarticulated bodies, secondary burials as well as incision of bones are well documented in both cemeteries. Two cases of bone incision have been identified in the west cemetery, respectively in Tombs 26 and 28. The first case consists of a disturbed triple burial. Several parallel incisions are clearly visible on the third cervical vertebra of a female aged between 25 and 35 years, while the other individuals are untouched (Midant-Reynes 2000, 84). Tomb 28 was also disturbed and contained the mingled bones of two individuals, an adult female and a child. The fourth cervical vertebra of the female presents cut marks (Crubézy *et al.* 2000, 86). The bodies found in the two graves were probably put into a leather bag, as it was common at Adaïma also for non-manipulated remains (Crubézy *et al.* 2000, 86–87). No grave goods seem to have accompanied the deceased; however, occurrences of non-manipulated corpses given no funerary provision are also attested.

Bodies found without head are also common at Adaïma. Tomb 2 was the single inhumation of a female aged 40–60 years, arranged in foetal position on the right side and disposed of into a leather bag (Midant-Reynes 2000, 23). The head of the deceased had been pulled out of the sand, without reopening the grave. This was possible because some time after the interment the tissues had decomposed and the procedure was easy to carry out even without reopening the grave (Midant-Reynes 2000, 24). Also in the case of Tomb 135 it is likely that the officiants performed the ritual in the same way. The deceased was a 20–30 year old woman laying on her right side and disposed of in a leather bag and on a mat (Midant-Reynes 2000, 296). Except for the skull and the first cervical vertebrae, the rest of the bones were present and in anatomical position (Midant-Reynes 2000, 296). These two simple pits were located in the formal cemetery, but not provided with grave goods.

The Lower Egyptian cemetery of Gerzah offers some examples of funerary body manipulations too. Petrie *et al.* (1912, 8) identified at least twelve graves containing manipulated remains. Tomb

67 was an oval pit hosting a young adult laying on the left side. The skull had been removed from the body and was *in situ*, standing on its base. A neck vertebra, also disarticulated and displaced, had been found near the shoulders. Interestingly, Tomb 67 was provided with quite a rich array of objects such as a mudstone palette, a golden necklace, a macehead, pots and several beads. The body found in Tomb 142 was that of an adult, laying on the left side in a rectangular pit and entirely coated with a thick layer of mud. The body was apparently intact, but researchers (Petrie *et al.* 1912) found that the feet had been removed before covering the body with mud. The grave goods displayed in the tomb were quite numerous. Among them there were stone vessels, 73 beads, a granite disk, a mudstone cosmetic palette and several pots.

Discussion

According to the theoretical and methodological frameworks as well as the case studies presented here, clear occurrences of deviant burials have not been identified so far in the Predynastic mortuary ritual. To provide a comparison with an evident case of deviancy, an example will be borrowed from another cultural context. In Oppeano, an Iron Age site in Veneto (north east of Italy), the deposition of a 35 to 40 year-old man dating to the 6th century BC was uncovered (Perego pers. comm.; Saracino 2009; Zanoni 2009/2010). Interestingly, the man was inhumed and not cremated as it was more frequent in the Venetic funerary ritual; indeed, cremation was the only burial rite for the elite. Very peculiar is the prone posture in which the corpse laid, as in late prehistoric Veneto prone burial was an anomalous funerary treatment and a possible marker of stigma and marginality (Perego pers. comm.). Furthermore, the man had been disposed of outside the formal burial ground, in a large pit initially used for the extraction of sand, and then turned into a rubbish damp filled with food remains and ceramic debris. The body of the deceased was incomplete, but articulated and showed evidence of abuse datable to six to eight months before death. In contrast with the wealthy and finely arranged tumuli of Venetic cemeteries, this discard pit indubitably stands out for its abnormal nature. Possible explanations to such treatment could be identified in the physical deformity of the man, a hunchback also affected by other pathologies, who was probably perceived as too different and, thus, dangerous by the members of his group.

It is worth noting that, in respect to the Venetic case, the Predynastic non-manipulated and manipulated examples presented above are different. Indeed, it is clear that the aim of the deposit at Oppeano was to mistreat and exclude that specific individual from the formal funeral reserved to the other members of his community; on the other hand, in the Predynastic cases of manipulated human remains a formal ritual was performed and the deceased were placed within the cemetery and disposed of as all the others.

Conclusion

The evidence presented in this paper illustrates a quite complex and variegated funerary ritual in which variability plays a significant role. As discussed earlier, clear occurrences of deviant burials seem absent from the Predynastic Egyptian funerary landscape. Therefore, funerary body manipulations are more likely to represent one of the several forms of mortuary ritual adopted by the communities of Nile valley, rather than the symbol of social exclusion, marginalisation, disrespect and fear of the dead. This is demonstrated by the presence of grave goods, the architectural features recurring also in cases of non-manipulated burials, the location of the tombs within the formal cemetery as well as the care towards the dead. Furthermore, the fact that the use of such treatments was reserved to all segments of society and not aimed at mistreating abnormal individuals would suggest that rituals of manipulation were integral to Predynastic normative funerary practices.

Indeed, practices of funerary body manipulation require further research (carried out for my doctoral thesis) and to be analysed and interpreted without preconceptions deriving from the researchers' modern view of the world. The attribution of a deviant or negative nature to practices of funerary body manipulation in Predynastic Egypt is most likely a modern construct, which does not seem to correspond to the perception of Ancient Egyptians. As suggested by the examples provided, other than the treatment of the corpses, manipulated burials do not show any other obvious difference in respect to non-manipulated ones such as the man in the Venetic case. The not yet standardised funerary ritual which leads to a high degree of variability in the archaeological record also suggests cautious in the attribution of a negative value to some practices only on the base of their rarity. During funerary rituals, the performance of violent acts on human remains does not necessarily mirror the will of making the dead innocuous by destroying their body and soul, as pointed out by Duncan (2005). Although the results of my research are still preliminary, they suggest that body manipulations in Predynastic Egypt were legitimate practices coexisting with the rest of the rites, in an ever-changing funerary landscape.

Bibliography

Aspöck, E. (2008) What really is a deviant burial? Comparing German-language and Anglophone research on 'Deviant Burial'. In E. Murphy (ed.) *Deviant burial in the archaeological record.* Oxford, Oxbow Books.

Bard, K. (2003) The emergence of the Egyptian state (3200–2686 BC). In I. Shaw (ed.) *The Oxford history of Ancient Egypt.* Oxford, Oxford University Press, 56–83.

Bloch, M. (1992) *Prey into hunter: the politics of religious experience.* Cambridge, Cambridge University Press.

Castillos, J. J. (1982) *A reappraisal of the published evidence on Egyptian predynastic and early dynastic cemeteries.* Toronto, Benben Publications.

Crubézy, E., Janin, T, and Mydant-Reynes, B. (2002) *Adaima. 2. La nécropole prédynastique.* Cairo, Institut français d'archéologie orientale.

Duncan, W. (2005) Understanding veneration and violation in the archaeological record. In G. F. M. Rakita *et al.* (eds) *Perspectives on mortuary archaeology for the new millennium.* Florida, University of Florida Press.

Dougherty, S. P. and Friedman, R. (2008) Sacred and Mundane: scalping and decapitation at Predynastic Hierakonpolis. In, B. Midant-Reynes and J. Tristan (eds) *Egypt at its origins 2. Proceedings of the International Conference "Origin of the State. Predynastic and Early Dynastic Egypt".* Toulouse, Orientalia Lovaniensia Analecta, 138. Peeters Publishers.

Korpisaari, A. (2006) *Death in the Bolivian High Plateau: Burials and Tiwanaku society.* BAR S1536. Oxford, Archaeopress.

Midant-Reynes, B. (2000) Les sacrifices humaines a l'époque predynastique: L'apport de la necropole de Adaïma. *Archeo-Nil* 10, 21–39.

Midant-Reynes, B. (2002) Adaïma 1997–2002. *Archéo-Nil* 12.

Midant-Reynes, B. (2003) The Naqada period (4000–3200 BC). In I. Shaw (ed.) *The Oxford history of Ancient Egypt.* Oxford, Oxford University Press, 41–57.

Petrie, W. M. F. and Quibell, J. E. (1896) *Naqada and Ballas*. London, British School of Archaeology in Egypt.

Petrie, W. M. F., Wainwright, G. A. and MacKay, E. (1912) *The Labyrinth, Gerzeh and Mazghunah*. London, British School of Archaeology in Egypt and Bernard Qauritch.

Randall-MacIver, D. and Mace, A. C. (1902) *El-Amrah and Abydos 1899–1901*. London, Egypt Exploration Society.

Saracino, M. (2009) Sepolture atipiche durante il Bronzo finale e la seconda eta' del ferro in Veneto. *Padusa 45*, 65–71.

Saxe, A. A. (1970) *Social dimension of mortuary practices*. Unpublished Ph.D. thesis, University of Michigan.

Seeher, J. (1992) Burial costumes in Predynastic Egypt: a view from the Delta. In E. Van Der Brink (ed) *The Nile Delta in transition; 4th–3rd millennium BC* Tell Aviv, Pinkers.

Shay, T. (1985) Differentiated Treatment of Deviancy at Death as Revealed in Anthropological and Archeological Material. *Journal of Anthropological Archaeology* 4, 221–241.

Stevenson, A. (2009) *The Predynastic Egyptian cemetery of el-Gerzeh. Social identities and mortuary practices*. Orientalia Lovaniensia Analecta 186. Paris, Peeters Publishers.

Wengrow, D. (2006) *The archaeology of early Egypt: social transformations in North-East Africa, 10,000 to 2650 BC*. Cambridge, Cambridge University Press.

Zanoni, V. (2009/2010) *Reperti scheletrici in contest inn necropolici. L'Italia settentrionale nel I millennio a.C.* Unpublished PhD thesis. Universita' degli Studi di Pavia.

Hippo goddesses
of the Egyptian pantheon

Aroa Velasco Pírez

The hippopotamus is a very large, heavily built amphibious mammal with short, stout legs, four toes, and a short tail. The brownish-gray skin is nearly naked except for bristles on the muzzle and tail. The male is larger than the female and has more massive forequarters and jowl (Osborn and Osbornová 1998, 144–146).

The hippo, like numerous other animals, was considered an ambivalent creature in Ancient Egypt. Because of the hippo's destructive habits, eating and trampling crops, it became symbolic of the king's enemies; therefore, by killing it, the king conquered all the evil powers that were against him. Throughout the Dynastic Period, the male hippo was hunted by noblemen, and peasants killed it to protect their crops as well as to obtain its various products: skin, flesh, fat for hair-growing remedies and ivory for carving. In the Late Period, the hippo became assimilated to Seth and its hunting, according to Plutarch (6, 19), supposedly evoked the memory of the struggle between this one and Horus. Therefore, while the males were regarded as dangerous and destructive, evoking Seth, and were hence persecuted as a symbol of evil, the females, despite having the same power and destructive potential, were usually seen as benign animals with a protective force, which led them to have maternal symbology. The two aspects, the good and the evil, appear consistently distinct throughout the whole body of evidence presented here and they are, with very few exceptions, always attached to the two sexes, a fact which is of no small interest from a phenomenological point of view.

This paper will deal with the female specimens, whose form was adopted by certain goddesses. The Egyptian pantheon includes goddesses with hippopotamus form; however, their exact names are unknown; on the other hand, one goddess can have two names; in view of this, we can ask ourselves, how many hippo goddesses did the Egyptian pantheon have, or how many goddesses in the pantheon adopted the hippo form?

I will examine the various goddesses and their different names and functions within Egyptian religion. This study merely presents a starting point for further investigation. My initial goal is to clarify the different spheres within Egyptian life in which the hippo goddesses featured during the Dynastic period; we can differentiate, in general terms, three areas: domestic, funerary, and astronomic.

Iconography. Presentation of the goddesses

I described the hippo in its natural animal form above, but the hippo goddesses are in fact hybrids. These goddesses generally share one common form: a female hippopotamus with the hands and feet of a lioness, pendulous breasts, an enlarged belly and a crocodile tail (or a complete crocodile on her back, in particular contexts). This female is usually depicted with big, expressive eyes and her mouth ajar, showing her large and threatening teeth and/or her tongue. This may remind one of the bizarre pantheistic deities of the late first millennium BC, but, in fact, Taweret-one of the goddesses to be examined – has a composite form, which already occurs in amulets as far back as the end of the third millennium BC (Pinch 1994, 39).

Sometimes, her leonine hands carry or rest on the *sȝ* symbol – which means "protection" – as a "powerful apotropaic mechanism" (Wilkinson 2004, 209), particularly when she appears on magical wands and rods; alternatively, she may hold an *ʿnḫ*, the sign of life. In other depictions she is often shown carrying a knife, a flaming torch – emphasizing her protective function – or even a vertical crocodile (though this only occurs in the astronomical ceilings). On her head she wears the tripartite wig; moreover, she can also be portrayed wearing a rather abbreviated *modius* crown with an *ureaus* at the front; usually this crown is topped with the solar disc and feathers of the Hathoric headdress; lastly, a lunar disc resting on a crescent moon above the *modius* crown, identifies the goddess as Ipet, as shown in the bronze statuette from Walters Art Gallery 542067.

Domestic sphere

The hippo goddess Taweret played an important role within the household. She was a domestic and a mother goddess, whose name means "The Great One" in ancient Egyptian. She was a protective deity revered by people of all social classes. Her cult is materialized in the domestic sphere, especially the female sphere. It appears in the Predynastic Period (Seligmann 1916, 59, cited by Vandier 1962, 197, note 1), but from the Middle Kingdom her protective and magic function is consolidated. Finally, in the New Kingdom her cult takes on more importance, especially for the lower classes of the Ramesside Period.

Her composite appearance (especially her face) seems to have served an apotropaic function, frightening off evil spirits (Fig. 1). Taweret was invoked, often along with the deities, Hathor and Bes, to protect women during pregnancy and childbirth and to safeguard the health of children. Similarly, these three gods presided over various rites of passage, such as the maturity rituals for adolescents or the rebirth of a deceased person into the afterlife. In short, Taweret was known for her facet as protector of the weak (children and pregnant women); consequently, she was connected with the protection of both mother and newborn during childbirth.

Figure 1. Red breccia statue of Taweret. Late Period. British Museum 35700. Courtesy of British Museum.

Moreover, Taweret was the ideal mother for children; through her amulet and statuettes the children were ensured perfect protection and help. In particular, *sw3dt* amulets carried by infants were quite popular at Deir el-Medina (Sadek 1987, 125).

Her connection with childbirth is expressed through two epithets: "she who removes the water..." (Wb IV, 65:11) and "Taweret of water" (Bruyère 1934–35, 334–5, fig. 206), which suggest that she was attributed an original and particular gynaecological function, that of assisting with labour. The implications of this are that Taweret was not only considered the mistress of "pure water" – referring to the water of the Nile – but also that she was responsible for successful childbirth. In effect, the first epithet refers to the waters of the pregnant woman during labour, which Taweret removes prior to assisting with delivering the baby. This is portrayed in a stela from Deir el-Medina (Tosi and Roccati 1972, 93, stele 50057):

> "Amon-Re, lord of the heaven. Taweret, mistress of heaven, she who removes the water..."

This presents a good example of a plea expressed in words; however, a monument itself may serve as a plea. In this stela, where Taweret is entitled "she who removes the water", a whole family appears before Amon-Re and Taweret with two hippopotami. This family probably had problems with a difficult childbirth and this stela was their plea for Taweret's help. The head of the family and all its members invoke the deities by their names and titles only because of the delicate nature of their request, a plea for help in a special case of delivery (Sadek 1987, 126–127); however, in the case of Taweret, they add beside her title another epithet more specific to her function: one referring to the removal of the water of the placenta which enveloped the baby in his mother's womb.

Taweret's relation with childbirth is confirmed by a decorated birth-brick from South Abydos, where a hippo goddess is depicted (Wegner 2009, 450, fig. 2). Specifically, the hippopotamus deity is depicted on side B, although only feet and tail are preserved. The apotropaic imagery that decorates the edges of the brick is of the same typeused on the magical wands, which according to Altenmüller's analysis (1965, 178–185), evokes the notion of protection of the young sun god from the enemies of chaos. Moreover, the raised bed featured in the houses at Deir el-Medina, which could at least in some cases be decorated with images of Bes and Taweret, suggests the possibility that birthing procedures might also have occurred within the household (Lesko 1994, 97–111).

On the other hand, Taweret is also the protectress of the weak as mentioned, and as such, she provides an early example of the practice of combining all the fierce and protective powers of a deity in one image (all mother goddesses have, within their mythical discourse, negative aspects of her personality, according to Spieser 2009, 5–19). Due to her hostile aspect, she has the power to scare off evil spirits who could harm children or pregnant women, especially in their dreams. She has a bellicose nature, and she does not hesitate to use her force to destroy her potential enemies.

In one statuette from the Louvre Museum (Louvre Statue E 25479; Vandier 1962, 199), we can read about her protective function on her dorsal pillar. Although the statuette has the form of the hippo goddess, she is referred to by three different names (the third one will be dealt with later as part of the astronomical ceilings). The first one is Taweret:

> "I am Taweret of the power, who fights for what belongs and who reject those who do violence on their child, Horus"

The second name is Reret (the sow) and she:

"Is someone who fights with her voice, who can devour whatever it approaches; strong voice and great cry (scolding), which protects whoever leaves her body"

As mentioned before, she often holds a knife and a hieroglyphic sign meaning "protection", particularly when she appears on magical wands and rods. When she carries that sign, her iconic quality increases, for the sign acts as a cane to the goddess. Normally, this element is attributed exclusively to male figures, such as gods, kings or high dignitaries, representing authority, power and violence (Spieser 2009, 9–10). However, Taweret carries it in this context, suggesting masculinity. As well as this, these objects are an example of her protective function.

These wands (especially those from the Middle Kingdom) are flat, curved objects usually made of hippopotamus ivory (coincidence?), and they are decorated with some of the earliest representations of a whole range of supernatural beings and divine manifestations like Taweret (Fig. 2). Another term that has been used to describe these objects is "apotropaic wand", meaning something that turns away evil, particularly evil spirits. Their decoration includes lions, panthers, cats, baboons, turtles, snakes, the griffin, a panther depicted as a beast with an elongated neck, Bes, and, of course, Taweret.

These items would have been used in ritual and were probably laid either on the stomach of a pregnant woman or on the body of the baby, according to Altenmüller (1965, 149), while reciting the appropriate spells; they could also have been used to draw a protective circle around the mother and the practitioners, as perhaps indicated by patterns of wear along their edges (Roberson 2009, 427–445). In addition to their use in daily life, the wands were also deposited in tombs for the purpose of achieving divine rebirth in the afterlife, and they were especially made to protect the recently deceased.

In certain instances of inscribed wands, the mother and child are identified with the divine mother and the infant sun-god. The mechanism by which these magical acts were made effective was the identification of the child (and, by extension, the deceased) with the newly

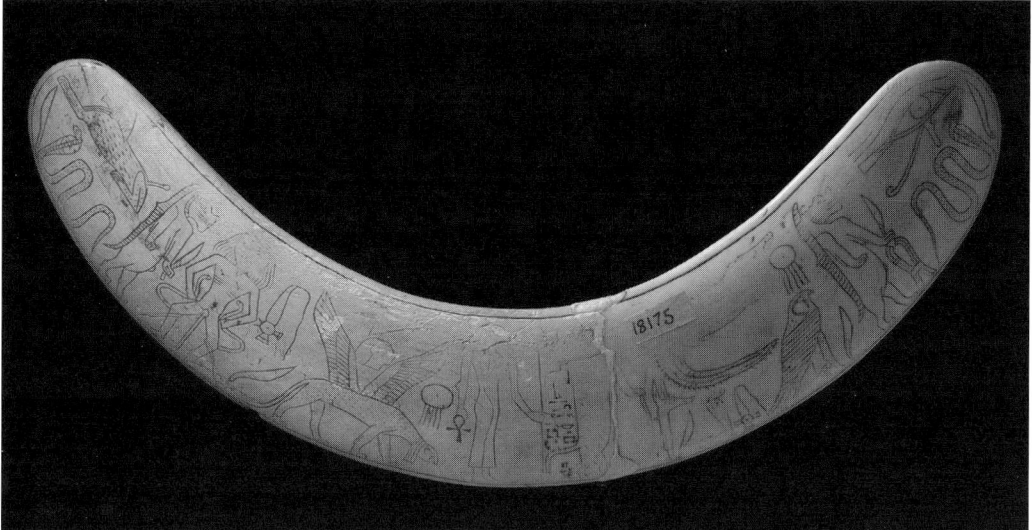

Figure 2. Magic wand with hippopotamus goddess, XII Dynasty. British Museum 18175. Courtesy of British Museum.

born sun god – who was also threatened in his youth by such monsters – in order to harness the protective power of his entourage. Others would have been used in fertility magic (Pinch 1994, 131), as can be observed in an interesting headless wooden "paddle doll" – a type of fertility figurine – where the protective figure of a hippo goddess – presumably Taweret – was painted in the place where the genitals would have normally been shown (EA 23071).

Another example of the domestic and protective nature of the hippo goddess is a votive stela from Deir el Medina (XVIII Dynasty, The Metropolitan Museum of Art, 47.105.4.) where the goddess, identified in the text as Taweret, is portrayed with Mut, represented by the likeness of her head atop an altar. Taweret holds a stalk of papyrus and the stem of a lotus flower over the libation vase on an offering stand; both goddesses wear a flat *modius* crown topped by the horned solar disc. On this occasion, the hippo goddess is standing beside an acacia tree, clearly identifiable from the pods hanging from the branches. The physicians of Ancient Egypt recognized the beneficial qualities of the acacia tree, and medical texts contain examples of recipes that include acacia for uterine complaints (Ebbell 1937, 111–112). The presence of the acacia tree on this stele suggests that the hippo goddess should be identified as Taweret, due to the protective nature of both herself and the acacia tree.

Lastly, it is worth mentioning the amulets. Taweret amulets occur as early as the late Old Kingdom and were manufactured throughout the duration of the Dynastic Period. Blue- or green-glazed faience composition modelled in the round or moulded with a flat back is by far the most common material, but glazed steatite, lapis-lazuli, jasper, breccias, serpentine, rock crystal, granite, amethyst, cornelian, glass and bronze also occur (Andrews 1994, 40–41). Jewellery could also be used as amulets, as exemplified by a gold necklace found in the burial of the wives of king Tutmosis III, perhaps to protect one of the king's wives during childbirth (Fig. 3).

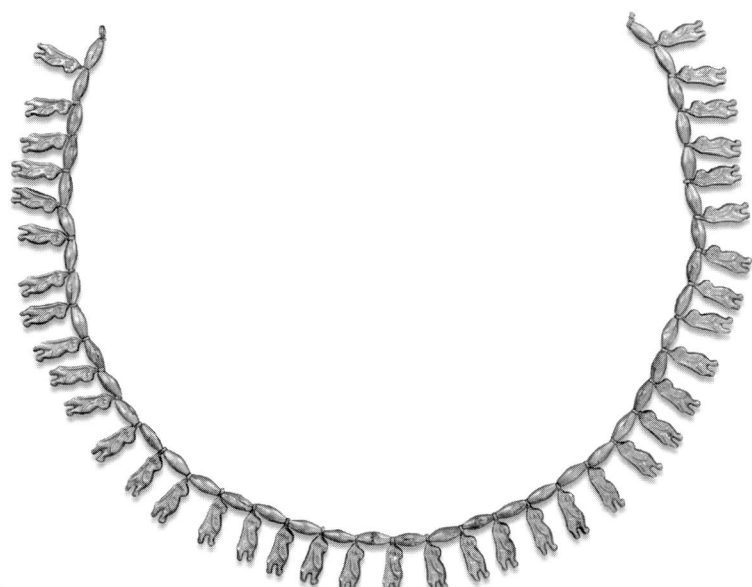

Figure 3. Gold Taweret necklace, XVIII Dynasty. British Museum 59418. Courtesy of British Museum.

Funerary sphere. Texts

Another hippopotamus goddess who appears in the oldest Egyptian funerary texts – the Pyramid Texts – is Ipy.

She is the "Divine Mother" who gives birth to the deceased in the afterlife. Her name means "harem" or "favourite place". In mythology she was the mother of the king, whom she nourished with her milk, as described in this fragment from the Pyramid Texts of Unas, V Dynasty (Faulkner 1969, 78. PT § 381–382):

> 381: O my mother Ipy, give this breast of yours
> that I may apply it to my mouth
> and suck this your white, gleaming, sweet milk.
>
> 382: As for yonder land, in which I walk,
> I will never neither thirst nor hunger in it for ever.

The hippo goddess adopts here a cosmic character, since she suckles the king with her divine milk when he travels to the stars so that he never again feels thirsty or hungry. Like water, milk was a feminine substance that also symbolised life, which is evidenced by the fact that many goddesses were wet-nurses. The milk is inexorably linked to the special relationship between mother and child. We can hardly comprehend this Egyptian goddess without taking into account the warmth and nurturing quality of maternal breast milk, the security of mother's breast and the protective embrace. The actions of embracing, surrounding, enclosing, containing, or encircling belong to one of the most important schemata of the Ancient Egyptian mind (Hassan 2004, 790–791).

Some hippopotamus figures also feature in the Book of the Dead. The first one appears in Spell 137B, a spell for 'kindling a torch for N' (Faulkner 1985, 132):

> "The bright Eye of Horus comes, the glorious Eye of Horus comes; welcome, O you who shine like Re in the horizon. It drives off the powers of Seth from upon the feet of Him who brings it. It is Seth who would take possession of it, but its heat is against him; the torch comes. When will it arrive? It comes now, traversing the sky behind Re on the hands of your two sisters. O Re. Live, live, O Eye of Horus within the Great Hall! Live, live, O Eye of Horus, for he is the Pillar-of-his-Mother priest".

In addition, in the Papyrus of Nebseny (BM 9900) the hippopotamus goddess, Ipet, Mistress of Protection, sets fire to incense placed in a bowl on top of a tall stand. She has the same iconography described above (female hippopotamus with the hands and feet of a lioness, pendulous breasts, an enlarged belly, big expressive eyes and her mouth ajar), and holds a torch with her hand (Fig. 4).

On the other hand, in spell 186 of the Book of the Dead there appears another goddess with hippopotamus form. In the Papyrus of Ani (BM10470) a hippopotamus goddess who wears in her head the solar disk with horns is depicted behind Osiris; in her right hand she carries a torch – a promise of light and life in the afterlife – and in her left hand the sign of life, ʿnḫ. In the background, there is the divine cow, Meh-urit, who looks from the funerary mountain while wearing the *menat*. She carries a torch with which she refuses the evil spirits at the entrance of the Occident Mountain.

According to Spieser (2009, 12–13) this is a representation of the goddess Ipet, a hippopotamus goddess of the funerary sphere who is the guardian of the Occident and who is part of the cohort of guardians on the way to the afterlife, and who therefore has the mission of protecting the deceased.

In the statuette from Louvre analysed before (Louvre Statue E 25479; Vandier 1969, 199), Ipet is the third name of the statuette, and appears as a protective goddess, like Taweret or Reret:

> "I am Ipet, who lives in the Horizon and who protects the knife and the Universal master, the mistress who fears, one whose appearance is adorned and decapitate those rebelled against him"

Lastly, according to the Lexikon der Ägyptischen Götter und Götterbezeichnungen (vol. 1, 218), both Ipet and Ipy are the same goddess. Both Ipet and Ipy have a protective and motherly function and can therefore be compared to Taweret.

In conclusion, Ipet is a mother and funerary goddess and her task is to protect the weak, embodied here – in the Book of the Dead, according to Spieser – in the deceased, through his journey to the afterlife. This can be seen in direct relation to the goddess Taweret and her protection of the weak, such as the baby (during childbirth), children and pregnant women. And if we bear in mind that the deceased, when reborn, is considered a newborn, we can see a connection between the functions of the hippo goddess (Taweret and Ipet) in these two spheres: to look after and to protect the newborn. Consequently, it seems that these goddesses are different portrayals of a unique hippo goddess.

Astronomical ceilings

The astronomical ceilings are those that represent the circumpolar constellations, the Planets and the Decans. These are found in the New Kingdom; although there are astronomical depictions in the sarcophagi of the First Intermediate Period, they are very different from the ceilings. In the astronomical ceilings, there appears a hippopotamus figure with the morphology that has previously been described. This hippo figure is a constellation which forms part of the northern constellations.

This figure is a standing female hippopotamus, who may or may not be depicted with a crocodile on her back, and whose front feet usually rest on a mooring post, or one on a mooring post and the other on a small, vertical crocodile. At times, cords or chains run from the mooring post to *Mes* (the Big Dipper). On the Middle Kingdom coffins, *Mes* is always depicted as a bull's foreleg and it is also shown in this form on certain later monuments; however, from the New Kingdom onwards, *Mes* – in the astronomical ceilings – is variously shown as a bull with an oval-shaped body and tiny legs, as a striding bull on some kind of support or as a bull-headed foreleg, always facing away from the hippopotamus figure (Neugerbaur and Parker 1969, vol. 3, 183); both are essential figures in the depiction of the constellations and are never absent from the astronomical ceilings.

Figure 4. The hippopotamus goddess Ipet, Nebseny Papyrus, XVIII Dynasty. British Museum 9900. Courtesy of British Museum.

The astronomical ceiling from the tomb of Senmut (the oldest of its kind, dating from the XVIII Dynasty) depicts the hippo constellation with the legend (Fig. 5):

3st- ḏ3mt ḥb pt

Also, in hall K of Seti I's ceiling we have the inscription *s3 mwt*, although Neugebauer and Parker read *ḥs3- mwt* (therefore translating this inscription as "The mother is fierce", which combined references to the hippopotamus in the form of Taweret, the goddess of childbirth, and her fear-inspiring aspect (Neugebauer and Parker 1969, vol. 3, 190)).

The different hypotheses concerning the reasons for the presence of these depictions in an astronomical context are beyond the scope of this paper (for more information see Lull 2004, 223–225) and here I will only deal with the description of the figure itself. Several texts are relevant for this purpose, and some of the texts collected by Neugebauer and Parker will help us understand her function in the astronomical ceilings. The first one is the Book of the Night (Neugebauer and Parker 1969, vol. 3, 190), found in the tomb of Ramesses VI, which reads:

> "As to this Foreleg of Seth, it is in the northern sky, tied to two mooring posts of flint by a chain of gold. It is entrusted to Isis as a hippopotamus *(rrt)* guarding it".

According to some documents from the Ptolemaic Period, after defeating and dismembering Seth in the form of a red dog, Horus put Seth's leg in the northern sky, giving the great hippopotamus responsibility for ensuring that the leg always be tied to this part of the sky (Lull 2004, 226). To this end, she has the leg tied with a chain of gold to two mooring posts (Lull 2004, 225).

Therefore, *Mes* is identified with Seth's leg, while the hippopotamus in charge of guarding the leg is another form of Isis.

Figure 5. astronomical ceiling of Senmut, XVIII Dynasty. After Lull 2005, 206.

In various texts, we can identify the hippopotamus figure with *rrt* (the sow), and with Isis, who also has responsibility for guarding the leg. In the Jumilhac Papyrus (Lull 2005, 226), from the Ptolemaic Period, we have an example:

> "After he (Horus)cut off his leg (of Seth), he raised it to the middle of the sky, deities being there to guard it, the Foreleg *(msht)* of the northern sky, and the great hippopotamus (*rrt-wrt*) holds it so that it cannot travel among the gods".

A text from the Roman temple of Esna gives a slightly different role to Isis with regards the Foreleg:

> "It is Isis as a hippopotamus (*rrt*) who tethers the Foreleg (*msht*) in the northern sky, not letting it go upside down into the Duat. It shall be with her, being (the goddess) Ipy, in the sky and she shall not release it forever and ever"

Isis is, of course, the link between the hippopotamus and Sothis, since she is identified with both; but the fact that the latter is far away in the southern sky among the Decans clearly underlines the difficulties inherent in the use of mythological texts to identify constellations.

An image of a hippopotamus goddess holding the Eye may relate to the heliacal rising of Sothis heralding the Inundation. (Darnell 1997, 47). The connection between Isis and Sothis is also mentioned by Plutarch (6, 21) who states that Sothis was the *ba* of Isis. Moreover, Taweret is often considered the divine mother as well as being symbolic of the fresh water of the New Year (Desroches-Noblecourt and Kuentz 1968, 112–113). This shows a fusion of ideas surrounding Isis-Sothis-Taweret and the Inundation (in fact, the crocodile on the back of the hippo is another god of the Inundation (PT §507–510; Faulkner 1969, 99)).

However, it would not be accurate to use these facts to assert that Isis can always be identified with the hippopotamus (although we also have Isis the Saviour, with hippopotamus form, in a cippus of the British Museum EA 36250), because the Egyptian myths are sometimes contradictory, and this one is not an exception. For example, on a bull sarcophagus lid from Kom Abu Yasin, of Nectanebo II's period (middle IV century BC), there is a depiction of the Great Hippopotamus; however, on this occasion, she is not identified with Isis:

> "They (the stars) are in the following of the Great Hippopotamus (rrt-wrt) of the northern sky as your Foreleg, when it goes to the southern sky near the souls of the gods who are in Orion…"

Here, the hippopotamus is called *rrt-wrt* (the Great Hippopotamus). This name never appears in any of the versions of constellations on the astronomic ceilings, but it does appear among the constellations that served to indicate the hours in Ramesside star clocks.

It is worth considering that the second most frequently mentioned constellation in the tables of Ramesside star clocks is *rrt* "the sow" (or hippopotamus) with eight stars:

The determinatives of the pig and hippopotamus can sometimes be mistaken. In any case, the hippopotamus of the Jumilhac Papyrus and other texts is known as *rrt*, as is the pig (or hippopotamus) constellation. Moreover, the fact that the hours marked by the Ramesside star clocks follow the hours marked by the hippopotamus, in the same way that, in the zodiac of Denderah, the norays precede the boreal hippopotamus, could point to a possible equivalence between the *3st-dꜤmt*, from the astronomical ceilings of the New Kingdom and later documents, (explained above) and *rrt*, in the Ramesside star clocks and texts from the Ptolemaic Period (Lull 2004, 227–228. Neugebauer and Parker disagree, 1969, vol. 3, 161). Consequently, *rrt-wrt* and Isis in her hippo form are the same goddess, and have the same function in the northern sky.

Negative aspects of the hippopotamus goddesses

Lastly, I would like to mention the negative aspects that are also attributed to female figures.

Roeder (1915, cited in Säve-Söderberg 1953, 46), who collected most of the evidence regarding the hippopotamus goddesses, mentioned one instance where a female hippopotamus appears as an evil divinity. This is in the magical Papyrus Harris (Lange 1927, 93), where "the living Taweret (*ꜢꜢ-wrt Ꜥnḫ[t]*)", as well as "the beautiful (*nfrt*) Sakhmet", are mentioned amongst the animals and "all human beings of evil face" to be kept away from the field by the god Urun. The agricultural reference in these instances is obvious; it would appear to be rather natural for a peasant to pray for protection against hippopotami because of the immense destruction these animals could inflict on the crop.

Another similar exception appears in the Pyramid texts (Faulkner 1969, 103 PT §522), this time featuring a female hippopotamus (*dbt*) who is an evil demon, purveyor of illness.

Finally, Plutarch, in *de Iside* (6, 19) tells us that Taweret was the mistress of Seth-Typhon, but, in their final struggle, she sided with Horus. According to Säve-Söderbergh, (1953, 55), Plutarch's tale is connected with the pacification theme and may be nothing more than an aetiological myth designed to explain the differing natures in theology of the male and the female hippopotamus.

Final conclusions

This study was only intended as a first approach to the knowledge of the Egyptian hippopotamus goddesses and as a starting point for future investigations. I have outlined the different facets attributed to such goddesses and included a brief analysis of each of them here, but much work remains to be done.

The initial aim of this study was to elucidate whether the representations were portraying only one goddess with different facets, or different goddesses with the same physical form. In the funeral and domestic spheres, this question remains unanswered, due to the inconvenience of finding two distinct depictions, but only one name. However, it is clear that, within these two spheres, the importance of the goddess resides in her connection to changes of state, birth and death, and in her protective function, as shown in the astronomical ceilings, where the hippo takes the form of Isis.

Bibliography

Altenmüller, H. (1965) *Die Apotropaia und die Götter Mittelägyptens: eine typologische und religionsgeschichtliche Untersuchung der sogenannten "Zaubermesser" des Mittleren Reichs*. Munich.

Andrews, C. (1994) *Amulets of Ancient Egypt*. London, British Museum Press.

Bruyère, B. (1934–35) *Rapports sur les Fouilles de Deir el Médineh*. Cairo, Institute Français d'archéologie orientale.
Capel, A. K. and Markoe, G. E. (1996) *Mistress of the house, mistress of heaven. Women in Ancient Egypt.* New York, Hudson Hill Press.
Darnell, J. C. (1997) The Apotropaic Goddess in the Eye. In *Studien zur Altägyptischen Kultur* 24, 35–48.
Desroches-Noblecourt, C. and Kuentz, C. (1968) *Le petit temple d'Abou Simbel*. Cairo, Centre de documentation et d'étude sur l'ancienne Égypte.
Ebbell, B. (1937) *The papyrus Ebers. The greatest Egyptian Medical document*. Copenhagen, Levin and Munksgaard.
Faulkner, R. O. (1962) *A concise dictionary of Middle Egyptian*. Oxford, Griffith Institute.
Faulkner, R. O. (1969) *The Ancient Egyptian Pyramid Texts.* Oxford, Oxford University Press.
Faulkner, R. O. (1985) *The Ancient Egyptian Book of the Dead.* London, British Museum Press.
Gundlach, R. (1985) Thoeris. In *Lexikon der Ägyptologie*, 6, 494–497.
Hasan, F. A. (2004) Between man and goddess: the fear of nothingness & dismemberment. In S. Hendrickx, R. F. Friedman, K. M. Cialowicz, M. Chlodnicki (eds) *Egypt at its origins. Studies in memory of Barbara Adams.* 779–799. Leuve-Paris-Dudley, Orientalia Lovaniensia Analecta 138.
Lange, H. O. (1927) *Der magische Papyrus Harris*. Copenhagen, A. F. Høst & søn.
Lesko, L. H. (1994) *Pharaoh's workers villagers of Deir el Medina*. New York, Cornell University Press.
Lull, J. (2005) *La astronomía en el Antiguo Egipto*. Valencia, Universitat de València.
Neugebauer, O. and Parker, R. A. (1969) *Egyptian astronomical texts* (3 vols.). London, Brown University Press.
Osborn, D. J. and Osbornová, J. (1998) *The mammals of Ancient Egypt*. Warminster, Aris & Phillips.
Pinch, G. (1994) *Magic in Ancient Egypt.* London, British Museum Press.
Plutarco, (1995) *Moralia, vol. 6: Isis y Osiris*. Madrid, Editorial Gredos.
Roberson, J. (2009) The early history of "New Kingdom" netherworld iconography: a late Middle Kingdom apotropaic wand reconsidered. In D. P. Silverman, W. K. Simpson, J. Wegner (eds) *Archaism and innovation. Studies in the culture of Middle Kingdom Egypt*, 427–445. New Haven and Philadelphia, Yale University and University of Pensylvania.
Sadek, A. I. (1987) *Popular religion in Egypt during the New Kingdom*. Hildesheim, Gesternberg.
Säve-Söderbergh, P. (1953) *On Egyptian representations of hippopotamus hunting as a religious motive*. Uppsala, Horae Soederblomianae.
Spieser, C. (2009) Avaleuses et dévoreuses: des déesses aux démones en Égypte ancienne. In *Chronique d'Égypte* LXXXIV, 5–19.
Tosi, M. and Roccati, A. (1972) *Stele e altre epigrafi di Deir el Medina*. Torino, Ediziones d'arte Fratelli Pozzo.
Vandier, J. (1962) Une statuette de Touéris. *Revue du Louvre* 12, 197–204.
Wegner, J. (2009) A decorated birth-brick from South Abydos: new evidence on childbirth and birth magic in the Middle Kingdom. In D. P. Silverman, W. K. Simpson, J. Wegner (eds) *Archaism and innovation. Studies in the culture of Middle Kingdom Egypt*, 447–495. New Haven and Philadelphia, Yale University and University of Pensylvania.
Wilkinson, R. H. (2004) *Cómo leer el arte egipcio. Guía de jeroglíficos del Antiguo Egipto*. Barcelona, Crítica.